ADVANCE PRAISE FOR *Luck by Design*

"*Luck by Design* provides solid guidance to help you *wonder about* your life instead of merely *wandering through* it. Goldman shares a lot of practical insights from his successful business career. These can make a difference in yours."

—ROGER VON OECH, AUTHOR,
A WHACK ON THE SIDE OF THE HEAD

"In today's world, college students and recent grads face new challenges, every day. *Luck by Design* shows that attaining success is a choice that you have, every day, in school and in the world. And the sooner you get started, the sooner you move in that direction, the better."

—RICHARD L. MCCORMICK, PRESIDENT,
RUTGERS UNIVERSITY, NEW BRUNSWICK, NJ

"Unlike many other successful entrepreneurs, Goldman didn't stop pushing himself after making a lot of money. Instead, he grappled with some of life's Big Questions in pursuit of meaning. His story and insights are inspiring: it *is* possible to win big in business with heart as well as mind."

—BEN CASNOCHA, AUTHOR,
*MY START-UP LIFE: WHAT A (VERY) YOUNG CEO LEARNED
ON HIS JOURNEY THROUGH SILICON VALLEY*

"In *Luck by Design*, Richie Goldman, a successful, self-made entrepreneur, makes a convincing and engaging argument for his deeply-held belief that life's solutions are in your hands. No matter where you are now, the potential for change, growth and learning is yours."

—JANET L. HOLMGREN, PRESIDENT,
MILLS COLLEGE, OAKLAND, CA

"There are two kinds of luck: the luck that we go out and find, and the luck that we hope finds us. We can trust the first with our lives; the second will always let us down. Richie Goldman's heartfelt book tells us exactly how to create the first, enriching our personal, business, and inner lives every step of the way. For anyone about to embark on the adventure of life, *Luck by Design* will be a warm and supportive friend."

—DAN ROAM, AUTHOR,
*THE BACK OF THE NAPKIN: SOLVING PROBLEMS
AND SELLING IDEAS WITH PICTURES*

"This is a great time to be young or climbing a career ladder –if you listen to Richie Goldman. He challenges us to go beyond job titles to craft a life that anticipates an uncertain economic future. Combining practical advice with hard-won wisdom from the world of corporate America, Goldman will convince you to create your own *Luck by Design* by embarking on a difficult, courageous and ultimately rewarding journey."

—BRUCE R. MAGID, DEAN,
BRANDEIS INTERNATIONAL BUSINESS SCHOOL, WALTHAM, MA

"Richie Goldman speaks the truth about how to find the kind of success we are all seeking. He speaks with authority and authenticity. Take it from him; he knows what he is talking about!"

—RABBI SHERRE HIRSCH, AUTHOR,
*WE PLAN, GOD LAUGHS: TEN STEPS TO FINDING YOUR DIVINE PATH
WHEN LIFE IS NOT TURNING OUT LIKE YOU WANTED*

Luck by Design

Certain Success in an Uncertain World

RICHARD E. GOLDMAN

MORGAN JAMES PUBLISHING • NEW YORK

Published by:
Morgan James Publishing, LLC
1225 Franklin Ave Ste 32
Garden City, NY 11530-1693
Toll Free 800-485-4943

ISBN: 978-1-60037-433-3 (Paperback)
        978-1-60037-432-6 (Hardcover)

Library of Congress Control Number: 2008936943

Dedicated

with love

to

the Goldman girls

Ava and Zaia

and

the Goldman women

Beeb, Ethel, Weez, Traci, and Emily

He's not really a fighter. He's an adventurer. There's a difference. He doesn't attack, he engages; he doesn't defend, he expands; he doesn't destroy, he transforms; he doesn't reject, he explores...

TOM ROBBINS, *HALF ASLEEP IN FROG PAJAMAS*

Contents

RICHARD E. GOLDMAN

To the Children of the Baby Boom Generation:

On behalf of my entire generation, I apologize. We — the great Baby Boom generation, we who were going to change the world — certainly have. Except we haven't exactly changed it for the better. We missed a few steps along the way. If you feel disenfranchised or alienated, you are not alone. Despite our good intentions, the Baby Boomers have compromised your future.

A few examples:

- We have altered the notion of "family" by divorcing in more than one of every two marriages, often leaving you on unmanageable and unstable ground.

- We have run up tremendous personal debt, living a lifestyle generally beyond our means, forcing you to run up your own debt just trying to go to college and to live day to day.

- Our federal government, which helped *our* parents buy homes, build cities, and educate their children is now swimming in debt.

- We have found no solution to our nearly cracking Social Security system.

- We have made incremental progress, but not solved the problems of world hunger, poverty, HIV, AIDS, or any of a multitude of other diseases.

- We have continued to pollute the environment, to the point that before long there might not be an environment as we now know it. This alone may render meaningless all of our other mistakes.

- We, who were dealt perhaps the best hand ever and who have been witness to many of the most powerful and inspiring people in history, can only hope that great people remain for you to emulate.

- We have tarnished the global image of our country in ways that might prove difficult to correct.

- And finally… we've left you with one nation — undereducated.

Our bad.

But there *are* solutions, all of which require hard work, careful thought, consistent effort — and the luck that *you* can create to help in all you do, every day.

Richie

Preface

You might have heard that now is a terrible time to be young. Certainly the Open Letter you've just read would make it seem so. But guess what? If it is *now* and if you are *young*, you have no choice. You didn't choose this time to be young; it chose you. This is a terrific example of one of the primary tenets of life: you choose some things, and some things choose you. It's what *you* choose and the process that *you* use in making those choices that determine the course and character of your life. *Luck by Design* will help you to make better, more informed, and wiser decisions about the things that you choose. It will help you to be better at handling, acknowledging, and embracing those things that choose you. It will help you know, understand, and deal with the facts and challenges that you will face. It will also help you to live a happy, prosperous, and fulfilling life— however many years of it you have ahead of you. No doubt about it: that's a lot to ask of one book.

Chances are you've read a self-help book or two. In most of them, the author makes a basic assumption—you are broken. Therefore, all you need to do is read the book, follow the steps, and you will be fixed. This book challenges that assumption with the following simple truth: your life is not a problem to be solved. Instead, it is a miracle of an opportunity to experience all the unexplored aspects of your being. This book will show you that the solutions are in your hands and they are in your hands *now*. And more: the solutions have been in your hands since you became a conscious being. *Luck by Design* will help you to access your own capabilities and competency, not by rote "how-tos" but by digging in to find your authentic self. What it requires of you is deep and personal honesty, courage, commitment, and fortitude. Easier said than done? Yes and no. Yes, because if you could do it, you already would be. And no, because the focus and control over your life is not something to be found on the outside; it's all on the inside. Like anything else you'll encounter in your life, the potential for change, growth, and learning is in your hands—and another choice that *you have*. If you don't like what's happening in your outer life experience, then *now* is the time to review, revise, and reclaim your right heading.

Who Should Read This Book?

In my work at Men's Wearhouse over three decades, in my family life, and in my volunteer activities, I have seen that the children of Baby Boomers have a perspective and world experience that is vastly different than that of their parents. In writing this book, I have had the children of Boomers in mind as the primary audience. So if you are starting college, in college, beginning your working life, or climbing up the ladder of your career, as you read *Luck by Design*, you will find practical solutions to everyday situations and problems.

You'll find advice that comes from my experiences managing people in your parents' generation of workers and in your own. You'll find work advice and life advice that will help to draw luck toward you. It's not an Easy button, but a way of life that can be ever improving.

Who Am I, and Why Did I Write This?

My formative years were about as far removed from today's digital age as could be while still living in the United States. I grew up in a middle-class Jewish family in Hazleton, Pennsylvania, a small coal-mining town in decline as the coal industry was sliding out of favor nationally. My father owned and ran a local retail store, Boston Hardware, as had his father before him. It was a family enterprise, and all of us, including my siblings and our mother and aunt, helped out.

I was not a great student. In fact, I was a rather poor student at the private high school I attended in Freeland, an even smaller coal-mining town ten miles from Hazleton. A wealthy coal-mining family had founded the school, Mining and Mechanical Institute (MMI), to educate the miners and their sons. MMI's motto was, "Making men individuals." It was certainly the case for me, although I doubt that I was the kind of "individual" that MMI had in mind. At MMI, I discovered that I had an eye for the arts but was overwhelmed by a math- and science-dominated environment in which, no matter how hard I tried, I failed (or came very close to it). I had an ear for dissent, which I was always ready, willing, and able to try. I also had a mouth for trouble, which I was constantly in. My behavior was a simple response to the complicated issue of barely surviving academically and feeling like I was not living up to the expectations of others (the school and members of my extended family), despite my best efforts.

Thankfully, survival turned into success. In September 1968, I enrolled at Rutgers University in New Brunswick, New Jersey—my father's alma mater. It was the beginning of an experience as completely positive as high school had been utterly negative. It was both the time (1968–72) and the place (a very liberal university) that piqued my interest, enthusiasm, and creativity. My formal education and the many things I learned outside the classroom opened up avenues for exploration that I continued to follow for the rest of my life. Rutgers helped to show me my potential, instead of belaboring my weaknesses. Positive as the experience was, I didn't acquire any academic honors, other than a BA in English and a great interest in (and little practical knowledge of) advertising.

My degree in hand, I returned to Hazleton to work at my father's store. It had never been explicitly stated, but for some time I had thought that it was going to be my destiny to take over the store one day. After about a year, however, I realized that this was *not* what I wanted to do for the rest of my life. Although my father was a patient and understanding teacher, I was a restless kid who just couldn't adjust to small-town life after my college experience. I had an incredible urge to go out into the world and make my own mark. Buoyed with my BA in English and an independent study paper written while at Rutgers, titled "The Psychology of Television Advertising," I was confident that Houston advertising agencies would be clamoring for my talents. So in 1973, I moved from Hazleton to Houston, Texas, with all of my worldly possessions in the trunk of my car and about $300 in my pocket. It was a bold and impetuous move, which somehow I did with a lot of confidence.

At age twenty-two, I had decided that I was willing and able to live my dream—or at least what I *thought* at the time was my dream. I struggled a bit, made a few false starts, and soon found a closely related dream that set me on a career path for the next twenty-nine years of my life. It was a path that enabled me to retire long before standard retirement age—and without any financial worries. By moving to Houston when I did, I put myself in the right place at the right time. My decision to move and then *acting* on that decision came from a place of deep personal trust. Although I could then barely fathom this place, and certainly could not verbalize it, what I did was act upon that trust rather than think about it, procrastinate, or second-guess myself. I was in touch with my higher self, mostly because I was very young and very open.

Did I realize all of this at the time? Of course not—and that's not the point. The point is that I knew that *something* was going on, and my inner voice told me to pay attention. And most important, I listened. Doing that allowed me to rewrite the rules that had been placed on me by others up until then. I allowed myself to be open to what I wanted, and I began to write my own rules. These rules and some of the stories of my life are laced throughout the book, told not for the sake of my story but to help *you* develop your own.

I've often been told how "lucky" I have been in my career. For a long time I questioned the idea myself. However, one day I finally realized that it wasn't luck at all. I made one thing happen (moving to Houston), which, after a few more steps, landed me at the door of Men's Wearhouse back when it was just one store with a hand-lettered sign. I was with Men's Wearhouse as it rose from obscurity to a nationally known business. Dumb luck? More like some luck! Or, as the innovative Major League Baseball executive Branch Rickey once said, "Luck is the residue of design."

In this book, I share with you some of my own design in hopes of helping you create your own luck. You want to win the lottery? Go ahead, buy your tickets. It's a great fantasy—but little more than that. *Luck by Design* puts wheels under your wagon and enables you to be off to your destined adventure. This book is all about helping you learn how to create your own luck, by design.

What's Here, and How Can You Use It?

Now that you've got some background on the purpose of the book and on me, how can you use it? First is the obvious: read. As the American writer Samuel Clemens (better known by his pseudonym, Mark Twain) has been quoted, "The man who does not read . . . has no advantage over the man who cannot read." Understand that holding the book in your hands will not increase your luck. Flipping the pages will not increase your luck. It's reading the book and putting it to use that will help you design luck for your life. Many of the ideas here I've run past a wide-ranging group of people I like to call my advisory board. These are people whose ages range from seventeen to forty, with circumstances and questions that may be very similar to yours. Over the course of the book, you'll learn more about how they enlightened me.

Now that you've nearly read the preface, ahead are nine chapters, a postscript, and a reference list. But first, here are a handful of tips before you read on:

1. Take your time. Reading the book is not a race. Reading it and using it well is a process.

2. As you read, you'll find a number of places in which you're told to **stop!** This is not a test; there's no one standing nearby to demand that you shut the book. It's just that you'll get more from your reading if you actually take the time to stop and actively consider the questions raised.

3. Each chapter has at least a reminder or two in the margins. These exist to reinforce important points, in case you miss the overarching one, which is to be present while you read and to attend to what you read as you read it—just as you attend to your life as it unfolds.

4. I've had successes and made my share of mistakes over the years. Some of these are encapsulated in the "Lesson Learned" sections that conclude each of the chapters, starting with chapter 2. Reading them may just keep you from repeating some of my mistakes.

5. I'll also be supplementing *Luck by Design* through my website, www.richiegoldman.com, which will include a Q&A section, a reading list with books that should be useful to you on your journey, and further tips. There you

will also have the opportunity to share your design with me and with the other readers of this book.

How you use the lessons in *Luck by Design* is up to you. My advice? Keep an open heart and an open mind. Read on. Enjoy the process.

1

It's In Your Hands

YES, YOU HAVE INHERITED the "perfect storm" of problems at the national and global levels. Much of it may be on my shoulders, together with those of the other Baby Boomers, but the reality is that many of the solutions are in your hands. And you have the time ahead of you that Boomers do not. Along with this responsibility, you have your personal life challenges. You might view the world with great pessimism. You have been told that you are the first generation to predict that your life prospects will be less than those of your parents in terms of opportunities for advancement and financial rewards. You live in a world where change occurs in seconds, not days or weeks. Your competition in the job world is not simply local or national, but global. It might seem like everywhere you look there are threats—to your economic future, to your political freedoms, to the environment, and to your own safety.

And everywhere you look, there are great opportunities as well. Is it possible that your life will be far *more* productive, fulfilling, and engaged than the lives of those in your parents' generation? Is it possible that rapid change is an asset, not a liability? And is it possible that although the competition is global, the opportunities are global as well? And is it possible that the threats can be windows of opportunity for social and global change? The answer to all of the above is an emphatic *yes*!

The Basics

As a foundation for moving forward, think of the following as "givens," even though for now you might not believe or fully understand them. More information will come later, in this book and in your life, to help explain. In the meantime, know this:

- Life is not hard. It is complex, and it is unpredictable, but it's not hard. You want to know hard? How about a world without antibiotics or polio vaccinations? How about the homeless in our country, or the starving people in Somalia? How about the Great Depression?

- Life is a series of illusions and disillusions. You move from the comfort of the womb and the comfort of the breast to the harsh reality that we're all flawed human beings and that somehow, despite our flaws, all of our lives are enhanced when we work together.

- You are not broken. You are a piece of unformed clay, and you are the artist whose duty is to create the magnificent being that you truly can be.

- The more gracefully you can accept how things are at the moment—not how your desires and preferences want them to be—the more energy and joy you will experience.

- Whatever you really want, you already have all the inner resources you need to make it happen. You need to learn to trust that you are in the right place at the right time to allow yourself to learn and to make something happen for yourself.

- Everything in your external world comes to you as a lesson; if you pay attention and stay awake, you will learn quickly. Every lesson—good or bad—is a great gift. Take it as such. You can figure it all out *for* yourself, and you don't have to figure it all out *by* yourself.

- You are powerful. Surprised? Even if you haven't thought of yourself as powerful, you've been so since you were about two years old. Why do you think they call it the "terrible twos"? Because it was all about your unstructured yet powerful realization that there was power in the word *no* and that by using no (albeit over and over again), you could get attention. Your power is still there; it's just been diminished a bit by time and your own life experiences.

- Learn it now, or learn it later: there are certain immutable laws. Among them are that you are going to have the following in your lifetime: pain, loss, suffering, gain, and success. How you respond to these is what defines who you are and the course of your life. (Hint: you respond to all of them in the same way ... with equanimity, grace,

3

humility, reverence, and thanks.) This book will help you access your own ability to handle whatever life hands you and to grow a big enough personal container so that none of what life doles out will knock you off balance.

- You have a place on this earth, and you have a reason for being. Your job, obligation, and sacred contract is to figure it out. At the most global level, you are here to leave the world a better place than it was when you got here.

- Heroes are a dime a dozen. *Real* heroes are few and far between. This book will help you emulate the real heroes of the world. It will help you to become that which you emulate in others. You can be the real hero of your own life and the lives of others.

- Life is a process, not a destination. Everyone starts out at the beginning, bagging groceries, as it were. From this point forward, instead of looking at the end result—the success of a person, the success of a team, a beautiful painting—think about the time, effort, and love that went into making it happen. Learn to accept life on its own terms. Take the journey. It's called a *process*.

- You will hear *no* far more often than you will hear *yes*. Accept this and move on. Use no as a test of your inner desire to get something accomplished. Understand that *no* is an outer reflection, usually from someone else; your own heart and your own gut are the inner reflection.

- Life is not going to hand you what you want; you're going to have to create it. Life *will* give you the chance to "get it." Use this book as part of the toolkit for your creation.

The Journey Ahead

This can be the beginning of a life-changing journey for you. It can be a journey of self-discovery and a journey that opens your eyes to your own possibilities. It can also be the journey that sets you on the path of finding your place in this world and your true calling. Or it can be a waste of your time. The book is in your hands, and the work is up to *you*. Will you choose to do the work? You're going on the journey anyway; consider the upside of doing the work.

How Can My Journey Help You on Yours?

Sandwiched between my older sister, a whiz-bang student and ace Girl Scout, and my precocious younger brother, who was the talk of the town, or at least the talk of the neighborhood, I was neither a great student nor particularly outspoken. It was only natural, then, that I was constantly being compared to both my sister and brother. And it was likewise natural for me, the quiet one, to take this comparison very personally. While I am no therapist, I do know (now) that this truth was a gift that opened up countless paths in a life of self-reflection.

If you've read the preface, you know already that I was never the perfect student. While my grades were As and Bs in grade school and middle school, my teachers constantly told me that I could do better and asked why I didn't perform as well as my siblings. I didn't know what doing "better" meant, especially in light of my grades, and I couldn't comprehend the comparisons. With no understanding of how to process the criticism, I began to believe it, to take it to heart, and to doubt my own abilities and question my self-worth. By the eighth grade, even though I was still in search of "better," I began to flounder. By my senior year of high school, I had all but given up. Still, I slogged along, requesting a transfer into the section that was not "advanced" but "less than advanced." My grades were awful, my attitude worse. Graduation was a relief, and to this day, I'm proud to say that I graduated eighteenth in my class. And unless I revealed it, who would guess that the class consisted of only twenty-six students?

The leap from a small school in a coal-mining community to Rutgers University in New Brunswick, New Jersey, was a big one. Although the prospect of being a classic small-town boy thrown into the big-school environment was terrifying, I realized that this was a chance to reinvent myself, to respond creatively and with a renewed sense of enthusiasm for dealing with life's challenges. I thrived at Rutgers and succeeded in reinventing myself, so it should not have been a surprise that I didn't last in Hazleton long after graduation. Thanks to my college experiences, I once again trusted life at this point. My decisions were part of my own master plan.

> *Trust life.*
> *Make decisions as*
> *part of your own*
> *master plan.*

After arriving in Houston, I went out to get the advertising job of my dreams. My first agency interview was most promising. I had found Marcom-Day Advertising in the Yellow Pages. It was a meager shop, just down the street from my more meager apartment. It had five employees and a handful of clients.

6

How did I get the interview? In retrospect, it must have been because Bob Day, the owner, couldn't believe my chutzpah. Who was this kid who just walked in the door late on a Friday afternoon and asked for an interview, with nothing: no appointment, no resume, and no portfolio—nada. What I lacked in brains and experience, I made up for in guts and enthusiasm. I wanted to work at an advertising agency; of that, I was certain. When Bob resisted hiring me by telling me that there wasn't enough business at the agency to warrant another salary, I countered by telling him I'd bring business to the agency. No doubt startled at the thought, if not intrigued by the prospect, Bob told me that if I could bring enough business to the agency, the next time they needed to hire someone, it would be me. Bob and I shook hands on the deal, and I was out of there. I didn't have a job, but that didn't faze me; I had a *prospective* job. I went home and spent the weekend mentally turning down fantastic offers from countless other advertising agencies.

But it wasn't that simple. Unfortunately, my interview with Bob was not only the first, but it was also the best. Other agencies that I approached were clearly not interested in my talents and I was turned down coldly, most often rudely. On the few occasions when I did get past the receptionist, my obvious lack of experience was soon unearthed, and my plea for a job was turned down. Yet I didn't let it demoralize me and I kept on plowing ahead. I knew, deep down inside, that everything was going to work out.

After three stinging weeks of rejection and of sweltering as I drove around in my un-air-conditioned car in the ninety-degree Houston heat, I ran out of money, ran out of guts, and had to look for a real job. Although I believed that advertising was still my calling, Bob Day was not calling. I needed a job—any job. The calling would have to wait.

I found a job selling display-advertising space in an all-advertising, free weekly circular called the *Greensheet*. The paper consisted mostly of classified ads—people selling everything from new kittens to used cars. The rest of the paper was display advertising, placed mostly by retail stores. I had the perfect setup. I spent mornings on the phone, making calls to current customers; in the afternoons, I scoured the streets looking for new *Greensheet* customers—as well as looking for clients for Marcom-Day. I figured that any company that was inexperienced enough to buy an ad in the *Greensheet* would also need the expertise of an advertising agency like Marcom-Day.

A few weeks later, as I was driving around town making cold calls for the *Greensheet*, I drove by a shopping center consisting of a handful of retail stores and a dilapidated, yet well-known, steak house. In the middle of the shopping center sat a store with a crude, hand-painted, black-and-white wooden sign precariously attached to the roof of the building. The sign read, "The Men's Wearhouse." To me, it looked like an interesting prospect. I walked in, discussed the *Greensheet* with Harry Levy, one of George Zimmer's original partners, and sold him a quarter-page ad. A few days later, I returned with a sample of the ad and met George.

At that moment, did I know that Men's Wearhouse would eventually become a household name and a billion-dollar company with stores throughout the country? Did I know that I would play a big part in all of that? Did I know that I'd be inspired by and grow with my many co-workers? No, no, and no. But, even at that very young age, I did have a certain sense of where and how things should be for my life. By rewriting the rules for how my life should have been, I allowed myself to be open to what I *wanted.* And I had the sense to follow my intuition and see where my instincts and business sense would take me. But the happily-ever-after story most assuredly does *not* begin here. I took a few detours and stubbed my toes along the way.

I continued to sell ads for the *Greensheet,* while trying to lure customers to Marcom-Day Advertising and dreaming of working there.

> *Allow yourself to be open to what you want.*

And I stopped in at Men's Wearhouse every so often, because I had developed a friendship with both Harry and George. Despite having grown a clientele of small retailers who actually had wonderful success with their advertising (Men's Wearhouse was not one of them), I was becoming bored working at the *Greensheet.* At the same time, Men's Wearhouse had learned that advertising, including the *Greensheet* and most of their other advertising efforts, was not panning out. At my recommendation (and for a finder's fee of $600), Men's Wearhouse hired Marcom-Day Advertising. Marcom-Day immediately directed the media efforts for Men's Wearhouse to radio and newspaper only, eliminating everything else. That also meant they dropped the *Greensheet.* It was a small price for me to pay. And it also gave me a reason to occasionally go to Marcom-Day, to keep an eye on "my" account—Men's Wearhouse.

One day, while hanging out at Marcom-Day, I overheard a phone conversation between George and Drew Cherner, Marcom-Day's account executive for Men's Wearhouse. George was in search of a new employee and was offering $1,000 a month. As I sat there thinking about my current income of $800 a month, it dawned on me that *I* was the ideal candidate. I had retail experience from my father's store, and I had clothing experience from my days at Rutgers, where I sold shirts out of my fraternity house, and working one summer at Brotherhood, a retail-clothing store in State College, Pennsylvania. I expressed my interest to Drew, who suggested that I speak to George. I did, and the next thing I knew, I was in the retail business once again, working on the sales floor of Men's Wearhouse. It was October of 1973.

Marcom-Day's advertising efforts had begun to pay off, and Men's Wearhouse experienced a temporary lift in sales for the holiday season, but business slowed after the first of the year. I became bored again and anxious to get that advertising job. By comparison, standing on the floor of a retail store that wasn't doing a lot of business was backbreaking and mind numbing. By May of 1974, I knew I couldn't stay at Men's Wearhouse. It was then that I finally received the call I had been waiting for from Bob Day; he was ready to hire me. At that moment, there wasn't much to consider in making my decision to leave. My inner voice still wanted fame and fortune in the advertising business, and even though George and I had become good friends, I had this underlying advertising dream.

Before I left Men's Wearhouse to work at Marcom-Day, George made me an offer that he thought I couldn't refuse. He wanted me to buy stock in the company and be more than just a person on the sales floor—he wanted me to become his partner in the company. To his surprise, I turned him down. Again, I had this underlying advertising dream.

On my first day at Marcom-Day Advertising—in the very first minute that I sat in my new office—I knew I had made a giant mistake. My inner voice was screaming at me, but I didn't listen, believing that there was no way I could have made such a huge mistake. The screaming voice got hoarse, but that nagging feeling never left. Fortunately for me, six months later, George once more asked me to be his business partner, again offering stock, this time as an incentive to return. By this time, Men's Wearhouse had opened two more stores in Houston, so there was a lot more to do than be on the sales floor. Having by then realized that it was not so much a career in advertising that I wanted as a career advertising for Men's Wearhouse, I accepted his offer and returned to Men's Wearhouse for good in January of 1975.

George had originally hired me to work on the sales floor of the first (and only, at the time) Men's Wearhouse. I was not the executive vice president, and in fact, I was not any vice president at all. I was not the manager, or the assistant manager. I was a salesperson—a grocery bagger, if you will. I started at the very bottom. Upon my return to Men's Wearhouse, I took over responsibility for all aspects of advertising and began my work overseeing the merchandising for the company. My energy level ratcheted up a notch, and my new intent drew more opportunities to me. In retrospect, it was an example of intent magnetizing opportunities (the law of attraction at work). I bought the stock that

> *Intent magnetizes opportunities.*

George offered me, based on a decision I made and against outside advice, as you'll see in chapter 3. Twenty-nine years after I was first hired, I retired. Of course, a lot happened in those intervening years, much of which I've mined in writing this book.

11

Looking back, I realize that I expended very little energy worrying about my future as I was growing up. Others may have worried about me, but I recall thinking that I could do anything. The hitch was that I had no idea what "anything" was going to be. Well, here's a newsflash: I'm not that unique. You, too, can do anything. Your challenge, just as mine was, is to find out what that "anything" is; what's right for you. Much of this book is dedicated to helping you find the way to your own anything and helping you learn to paint the canvas of your own life. The big picture is this: somehow, some way, you need to find the ability to bridge your heart with your mind. To do so, you need to first *open* your heart and your mind.

In this book, I share with you many of the important lessons I learned while helping to create a company that went from obscurity to being a part of the national consciousness, at least in terms of men's apparel. I will share with you some of the great successes that the company had and that I had as well. And I'll share some of the failures. Failures? Why bother with failures? I look at failures because they are the ultimate opportunities in life. Failures are the benchmarks by which we can really define our souls and ourselves. They're often not pretty, but they're always important, and they're always defining—but only if you're paying attention and learning quickly.

Who Are You, and What About Your Journey?

What about your journey? Your journey is all about finding your sacred contract and your unique purpose in life. (There will be much more on that throughout the book.) You've made a good decision in buying *Luck by Design*. Doing so demonstrates a curiosity about looking into the unknown and expanding your own awareness. This book will help you to find your authentic self—someone who may not be the person you currently *think* you are. This person is the one who lies deep in your heart and your soul. It is the person who you *feel* you are and can be, and who is ready to come forward.

This book will help you to design your own empowerment—to learn and to understand that the life you've been given is one that you have great control over. This book is merely your toolbox for making all of this happen. The work is all up to you.

As you move on, ask yourself the following questions:

1. Do you have the courage to create your own destiny?
2. What would you choose to do in life, if whatever you chose as your goal were unequivocally guaranteed?
3. Can you build a big enough personal vessel to learn how to accept yourself for all of the good and all of the warts?
4. Can you learn how to accept and embrace change and realize that fluidity is part of a conscious and expanding mind?

Can you be an element of change? You can, and you *have to be*. As Gandhi said, "You must be the change you want to see in the world." In other words, you have to believe it and practice it before you can see it. Understand that your life is your message, and you write the rules.

Will you be able to turn around all of the woes that have been placed at your feet? Not by yourself. But one by one, you, along with the others who might read this book and the others with whom you interact, can begin to manifest change.

All of the problems mentioned in the Open Letter didn't happen overnight, nor did they happen as the result of the actions of one person. Many people were part of that process, and it is a process that can be changed and improved. It *has* to be. Once again, it's up to you.

You are about to find out what you can do, to find the width and depth of what you are capable of doing with your life. Love your life and use it well.

2

Life Is Misadvertised

LIFE AS IT APPEARS TO you from the media is not life as it really is. For example, consider advertising: the goal of any advertisement is to sell that particular product. Along with it, there's always another message. It's often disguised, but it's a message about you (as a member of the market the advertisers are attempting to reach). In the process of trying to sell toothpaste or deodorant, for example, advertisers also tell you the way that you "should" be.

And that's where the misadvertisement sneaks in. Over time, sometimes subtly, sometimes not, as we're constantly bombarded by ads depicting perfect people in perfect settings, we're led to believe that our lives are lacking. By comparison to the perfect people in the ads, we're not only lacking the product being advertised, but the benefit of the product as well; hence, we're lacking in general.

The same holds true for the other messages we get through media—the nonadvertising messages in the form of "news." Yet the media depicts only certain parts of life, and it is very selective in doing so. Media paints a certain "there" that exists in the world. It

15

creates the same landscape for millions of people who are nowhere near the same. But when you as an individual look at the media and then look at your own life, you find that they're very different—the "there" that is portrayed in the media is not the "here" that is you. Therefore, life is misadvertised.

So, it's misadvertised. What do I think accurate advertising for life would be? Would that opinion be relevant to you and to your life? Could there be accurate advertising for life? To know that, one would have to know the secrets to life, and there would have to be such a thing as completely accurate advertising—advertising that tells the whole truth and more and that doesn't play into contrived or real weaknesses. We know what life is not. Despite what the old song said, life is not a bowl of cherries. Nor is life like a box of chocolates, as Forrest Gump's mother advised him. Advertising is all about a vision for the future. And our view of life is wrapped up in our vision of the world and our place in it. What is the source of that vision? These are heady questions. But first we need to back up a bit.

Consider Your Vision

This chapter centers on the concept of vision, so a good place to start is to check out its definition. *Random House Webster's College Dictionary* defines vision as:

1. the act or power of sensing with the eyes; sight. 2. the act or power of anticipating that which will or may come to be; foresight: *entrepreneurial vision.*

"Sensing with the eyes" implies sensing with your own eyes, just as "foresight" implies your own foresight. "Vision" is clearly meant to be your own thing. Now think about this: what is your vision of the world? What is your vision of your place in the world? What is your vision of happiness? *Stop!* Close your eyes and think about any of these questions for a moment.

Chances are, the picture that you created in your mind's eye is not strictly your own vision. It's a vision based on information that you have gotten from the media. Whether through "unbiased" yet biased news stories, the subtle yet not-so-subtle advertising messages, or even that mass of information known as the Internet, what we learn from the outside world is all a vision—and all too often it's someone else's vision. Consequently, our behaviors, many of our opinions and values and what we each might see as our place in the world are also visions—again, quite possibly someone else's. As well, what we come to expect from the outside world is also a vision.

The influence of the media is all around, all the time; it influences all of us. But it is possible to become more savvy about the part that the media plays in your life and in the formulation of your opinions. The faulty assumptions you may make as a result of being influenced by media help to keep you from truly understanding your own self and your place in the world. By accepting the underlying reality of the title of this chapter, "Life Is Misadvertised," you can put yourself on the path of being a more critical thinker.

Saying that life is misadvertised assumes certain expectations. My expectations of life were very clearly formed by growing up in a particular time (the 50s and 60s) and place (Hazleton, Pennsylvania). It was an environment that influenced my personal sense of self and my sense of the rest of the world. Life for me in Hazleton was about as different as life can be imagined for a child growing up today, or for that matter, a child growing up ten or twenty years ago. Hazleton was a rural coal-mining town, secluded at the southern end of the Pocono Mountains. The nearest big cities were Philadelphia and New York City, more than one hundred miles away. Given the cars and roads of the day, that hundred-mile drive was vastly different than it is today.

The thirty thousand or so residents of Hazleton were an uncomfortable blend of Irish, Polish, Italian, and Jewish. For the most part, each group lived in their own section of town and generally had a mutual disdain for one another. There were no African Americans, no Hispanics, and no Asians. My "worldview" was about as far as I could see—pretty much to the end of my almost-all-Jewish block. Although we often went to New York City as children, the Big Apple was "there" as far as I was concerned. The world we saw there, while staying in Greenwich Village and going to Broadway shows, was only a small part of the big city, but it was enough to tell me that it was an entirely different world than ours.

My world—my "here"—was Hazleton. Any other "there," whether it was across the state, across the country, or across the world, was something I read about in books. My world was very insular, very controlled, and very safe. While the Cold War, Sputnik, and the Berlin Wall were all big world events, Hazleton seemed very far away from it all, and my place as a little boy in Hazleton made for an even deeper sense of remoteness. We played ball in the street, went in and out of each other's unlocked homes, and generally worried more about the Yankees than anything else.

With the exception of the Mickey Mouse Club, there was practically nothing on television that had any appeal to me or to my friends. Books were my main source of media entertainment. I went to the Hazleton Public Library weekly, borrowing the maximum four books at a time. The books I chose were always the same genre: two sports books, where the underdog somehow becomes the hero, and two books of history or biography about the early days of the United States.

Imagine it—limited television, no Internet, no voicemail, no email, no instant messaging, no Federal Express, no fax machines, no photocopiers, no computers, no calculators, and no Sesame Street. For that matter, no national fast food chains, like McDonalds, Pizza Hut, or KFC, and certainly no Starbucks. Compared to the early twenty-first century, I could have been living on a different planet. Come to think of it, in many ways, I was.

But even with my limited view of the world, my foundations and my visions of who I was and what my place was were formed from the outside, not the inside. At a very young age, I never imagined myself living anywhere else but Hazleton; I never imagined working anywhere but my father's store. My foundation came from what I knew. Beyond my forays to the library, what I knew of the world came mostly through the insular view of what came into Hazleton directly. Generations that followed built on a very different foundation.

What Is Your Source of Self?

Along with many of the Baby Boomers, I grew up as television was spreading geographically and its offerings and place in society were being forged. There were high hopes for what it would bring to all of us: education, community, and access to information. TV was a brand new and exciting medium—much as today's Internet in recent years. Before TV, newspapers and radio had been the primary source of information about the outside world. Television changed all of that, and for the first time in history, people across the United States became "connected" in a visual sense and almost in real time. It was revolutionary. Radio news broadcasts had been revolutionary in their time; TV expanded upon that revolution by adding film footage and the possibility of seeing events in real time, long distance. It was a far cry from news via radio, Teletype, or the pony express.

Technology has certainly advanced, and our sources for information have gone from the few to the infinite. In the process of writing this chapter, I've thought long and hard about the role of the Internet in everyday life. Certainly, everywhere you go, it's hard *not* to find someone using the Internet; there are few things more pervasive. It's a great place for information, but it has its drawbacks, as I'll articulate.

Years ago, an elderly Stanley Marcus (as in Neiman-Marcus) told me that the effect of the Internet on society was going to be equal to the invention of the wheel in its time. He was very right—but there is a big difference. I suppose that once everyone got the *idea* of the wheel, everyone could use it to their heart's content. There was little "controversy" as to its place in society, and there wasn't a lot of room for mistaking the wheel for something that it wasn't. That's not the case with the Internet.

The Internet is enabling us to be more aware and is giving us more opinions, but its vastness often creates more confusion than coherency. Even with the Internet, given today's supercharged political atmosphere and the global questions and problems that we face, there is little chance to get unbiased information. While the Internet might be boundless, it's also loaded with hyperbole masquerading as fact. If the lack of regulation on the Internet is its strongest asset, it is also its biggest weakness, as every day, tens of thousands of bogus news events are disseminated worldwide. Being "connected" also means that fact or fiction can make its way across the planet in a matter of minutes or hours, with not nearly enough fact checking to back it up. Long before the Internet, a popular saying had it that, "A lie can travel halfway around the world while the truth is putting on its shoes." Now, it could be that a lie can "travel *around* the world *twice* while the truth is *looking for* its shoes." Everything has sped up, even the speed with which news (whether truth, lies, or something in between) travels.

My bottom line about the Internet is the following: its role in being a major media player is indisputable, but it's still a work in progress and a work that will likely be dramatically changed in the next few decades. And anyone who tells you what the future of the Internet will be is a fool.

One doesn't have to go far to find advocates of the Internet in general, as well as the new and innovative changes that are taking place. Challenges are few and far between. But as you'll see throughout this book, I encourage you to challenge convention. I've done so myself and found a terrific, albeit controversial, book focused on the Internet and its potential downside: *The Cult of the Amateur: How*

Today's Internet Is Killing Our Culture by Andrew Keen. In perhaps the most compelling paragraph of the book, Keen argues:

> We—those of us who want to know more about the world, those of us who are the consumers of mainstream culture—are being seduced by the empty promise of the "democratized" media. For the real consequence . . . is less culture, less reliable news, and a chaos of useless information. One chilling reality in this brave new digital epoch is the blurring, obfuscation, and even disappearance of truth. (page 16)

More traditional media, such as television, has its own shortcomings when it comes to news. Too often television "news" is little more than a video tabloid: lots of hype, lots of sordid detail, and little substance. One need look no further than O.J. Simpson's Bronco escapade several years ago, or Dan Rather's fall from grace to confirm this. One missing girl in Aruba gains national attention, while daily our soldiers are killed and wounded in Iraq. Good news doesn't draw audiences to TV stations; celebrity scandal, falls from grace, and sensationalism do. Who created this environment? Who knows? But it's an awful statement on our society.

As you will soon see, most of the "information" that you have acquired has come from the mass media in one way or another. It has been the "vision" for you, a vision that has come from the outside, not the inside. One of the first steps in creating your own luck is to start drawing the design for your life and to begin to create your *own* visions and your *own* rules. These will be visions and rules that come from *inside* of you, not from the outside. You'll need to think about a few questions for yourself, distinguish your responses from outside influences, and be certain you're answering the questions from the inside:

1. Where did your foundation come from? What does your foundation tell you about your place in the world?

2. What have you learned about relationships? And how has that formed your relationships?

3. How do you get your news and information—and then form your opinions, both as a citizen and a consumer?

The sections that follow will provide some help along the way.

KNOW YOUR FOUNDATION

What are the foundations of your life? They are the ideas of where and how you are to be in the world. They are the things that you know—or at least think you know—about the outside world. They encompass your values, customs, habits, and beliefs.

Where did your foundations come from? The foundations of life are not the things you learned in school. Assuming you were paying attention back then, what you got in school was content—how to add and subtract, the capitals of the states, the basics of research, and all that. Did you get the foundations of your life from your parents? To a certain extent, probably. But given the nature of the dynamics between kids and parents and given the fact that your parents were most likely spending so much time out of the house trying to make a living, it's likely there are gaps. Like your parents, you probably built a portion of your foundations of life from the available media. It's the *percentage* of the foundation that may have come from media that has changed over time. In addition—and unlike your parents—the available media in *your* life has been dramatically different, creating more of a worldview for you. Witness the earlier comparison between my upbringing in the far outskirts of the Poconos, isolated from the rest of the world, and yours, hooked in via the Internet and other media.

When you think about your foundations, have you considered what part advertising has played? Advertising wants to sell you a solution to a problem you didn't think you had. It is not by chance that advertising plays on people's insecurities.

Advertising is also about the intersection of what is being sold with the little voice in your head, the acquisitive, baby voice that says, "I want, I want, I want." This is not your inner voice of wisdom. When the product being advertised (or the way it's advertised) and that voice are in alignment, you're much more apt to buy the product. Consider the tagline in the many advertisements and commercials for prescription drugs: "Ask your doctor about …" More and more patients are showing up in doctors' offices with problems that they may not have known they had. Now, thanks in large measure to advertising, people think they have the advertised ailments and that they can be cured—with the advertised drug. And for the record, all of this cynicism about advertising is coming from someone who made his career out of convincing the public (through advertising) that Men's Wearhouse was the absolute best place to shop for men's clothing. (It is, by the way.)

When you think about your foundations, what parts have television programs, movies, the Internet, and other technologies played? To begin with, television shows, from cartoons to comedy to drama, have taught you that messing up all of the time is okay (think *Friends* and *Seinfeld*). You've learned (if you hadn't already learned this from your parents, or their siblings, or your siblings) that relationships are disposable. Over half of marriages in the real world end in "bail," and any number of TV *comedies* (!) have divorce as their premise, perhaps reflecting just how thoroughly the notion of "work or bail" has been baked into the national psyche. How's that for a not particularly great message for you and the rest of the TV audience?

You've learned that violence is endemic, acceptable, and an answer that many people choose. One need look no further than the entire *CSI* series of shows to see widespread violence and the high-tech ways the "good guys" find the bad guys.

What is the message in *The Simpsons, Family Guy,* or *South Park?* One message is that if you dress the players up as cartoon characters, there is no limit to what they can say, do, or think. There is no limit to tasteless, unsophisticated, ignorant, coarse, unrefined, demeaning, or simply vulgar (take your pick) characterizations of sex, religious beliefs, or ethnic backgrounds. Lest you think that I'm an old curmudgeon, I watch these shows myself; my point here is what the *message* of these shows is. Just because it's accepted on TV doesn't mean that it has to be accepted in your personal life. At some point, you have to take responsibility for your actions. So if you're going to embody the value system of another person, maybe that person ought to be someone other than Homer Simpson.

What have you learned from the "reality" programs? How real are they, *really?* How often are you in contact with the kinds of people you see on *Survivor* or *The Jerry Springer Show?* What is the message and redeeming social value in *American Idol* and similar programs? The real message is how we as a people can fall head over heels dreaming someone else's dream.

Now is a good time to take a step back from the Internet, technology soup, and the television and challenge yourself. Begin to change how you look at your foundation. Ask yourself the following questions:

1. When I think about who I am, is that thought, that vision, something that I have created or is it something that has been created for me? (It doesn't matter who created it; what matters is that *you* know who did.)

2. When I daydream about my life, both now and in the future, what does that look like? And how close is that to my reality?

By asking these questions and developing your answers, you're working on the design of your life and moving yourself steps closer to luck by design. Since chances are good that in your daydreams you are not alone, either in your personal life or your home life, the next questions have to do with relationships.

What about Relationships?

Most human beings need to feel they are part of something. This basic need for love and guidance begins in infancy, through instinct. It soon becomes a genuine want, as we try to create our space in the world and feel like we're part of something bigger than ourselves. At first, we're part of a nuclear family. We all came from some sort of family, and no matter how functional or dysfunctional it was, this family has been a driving force in our lives. It has molded us in many ways, made us who we are, and helped to create our worldview. This foundation is what we bring into every other relationship in our lives, whether the relationship is a friendship, an intimate relationship, or a working relationship.

What Does Advertising Have to Do with Relationships? Like it or not, mass media has played a role and may have helped to distort your vision of relationships. When you think about relationships, what part does advertising play? To begin with, it has influenced how we look at ourselves and others in a purely superficial way. We're constantly bombarded with advertising messages suggesting that we'll look better if we wear this, smell like that, whiten our teeth, color our hair, and lose weight—in short, if we use the advertisers' products. We're being told that—no matter how we look—we either don't measure up, or that we could always look better. When was the last time you saw a clothing model who wasn't svelte and beautiful or handsome and buff? So we find ourselves constantly trying to look like the picture of the stars and the models the advertisers make look most appealing, instead of simply looking like ourselves.

As a result, we walk *into* potential relationships, whether intimate or social, with an unbalanced and unrealistic sense of how we really want and need to look at *ourselves*. A fundamental insecurity is almost inherent. Is it any wonder that relationships fail?

What Role Has Technology Played in Your Vision of Relationships? Stop and think about these two words: *relationship, communication*. Really. **Stop!** Think about the words. What comes to mind? Think of three or four people in your life with whom you would describe

27

yourself as having a relationship. How do you communicate with them? What does that communication look like? If the answer to the latter is all about emails and text messaging, here's a challenge for you: begin to evaluate your current notion of relationships. Relationships and communication are about human interaction—look, feel, and emotion—real senses, in real time. Relationships are also about human beings *relating* to other human beings—looking them in the eye, watching their reaction, and listening to their inflections in sentences. It is through this direct communication that we find the soul qualities in ourselves and in others.

Mankind is pre-wired for relationships, and it's how we have evolved over millions of years. Those who are *not* pre-wired to communicate (people with disorders in the autism spectrum) are the exceptions; their difficulties reading social signals underscore the comparative ease with which most of us navigate social situations. For the most part, nature has seen to it that we learn more about life and more about ourselves when we are *in* relationships, and no amount of technology is ever going to replace that.

How often have you had to backtrack on an email or text message because the recipient totally missed what you were trying to say? Compare that to how often that has happened in face-to-face conversations. There is more to relationships and communication than IMs and text messaging. And, truth be told, there's not a lot of emotion in an emoticon. In fact, it's the contrary: emails and the like cannot take the place of communication, real emotion, real confluence, real contact, and perhaps even real confrontation. Every now and then it's good to get out from behind—from behind the cell phone, the Internet, the video games, and the TV. Get into the street—the living, the feeling, the touching, the smells, and the sounds of the real world. You don't have to abandon technology and virtual reality; just learn to understand and experience the tangible aspects of reality, and know that they count for something.

What Is Your Vision of Relationships? In my research and in my interaction with seventeen- to forty-year-olds, I have sensed a genuine sense of isolation—an isolation that many of them cannot voice. This isolation might have come from the fact that both parents were working and that often they (and any siblings) came home to an empty house. Perhaps the isolation came from the amount of time spent in front of a TV, a video game, or at a computer as a child. This was an amount of time enormously larger than any time their parents might have spent in front of a TV or (less likely) a computer. The sense of isolation tags along every day with the anonymity of Internet sites such as MySpace and Facebook. It has all become part of the current generation.

MySpace, Facebook, and similar sites—what are they about? I've been told that they're about people reaching out for "genuine" interaction. Really? How genuine is it if you're throwing it all out there for everyone, anyone, or no one to see? How genuine is it if instead of creating the persona you are, you can—and might—create an entirely different person? When you meet someone face to face, there is no chance to hide the physical flaws. When you speak to someone face to face, there isn't much of a chance that you're going to hide internal flaws, either. Flaws are more an internal creation, and you're never really going to be able to hide them for long. Flaws are part of the human condition. You've been trained by the media not to accept them, but to cover them up, or disguise them. The media is not helping you. Instead, evaluate for yourself, accept what you want, and choose to change what you want. It's *your* life—take control over it.

If you frequent these sites, take a moment to *stop!* Think about the following: how do you feel when you're "interacting" online versus interacting face-to-face with one of your friends? Is it the same connection? One of the most important lessons to learn is this: you're *not* in this life by yourself—you are alone only if you choose to be. And for the record, you'll be much better off if you choose to be with others, in person, and choose not to be alone and physically isolated. You will learn most things about life and, more importantly, about yourself when you're in relationship. Mankind has evolved and survived for millions of years based on the same premise.

Several years ago, everyone was touting the "new economy" and that in this new economy, there would be little or no paper, everyone would be working from home, and the Internet would make shopping malls obsolete. Look around: I'll bet you have more paper than ever. Certainly no less. Are you working full time from home yet? Unlikely. The malls? Still there. Why? Because no matter what, there is one thing that technology can't overcome: the need for fundamental interconnectedness among people. We want tangible realities, not the ethereal. Whether it's in the form of paper, or a co-worker, or the social experience of shopping together, we want *tangible* experiences.

And whether it's in the workplace or at home, we all need *someone.* We all want to be connected to another person and another thing—

someone and something more and bigger than just ourselves. This is true in our personal lives and in our work lives.

I discovered a chilling exception to this back in 2006, when I attended an event and sat next to the founder and chairman of a very high-profile and successful Internet business. This company has one of the largest and most well-known sites, one that touts "connectivity" and "relationship." I casually mentioned that I was writing a book and said that I thought that it would be helpful for me if I could talk to the employees of the company, figuring that many of them would be in their twenties and thirties. I asked questions to try to find out more about them—where they lived, their age, experience, interests, and more. The CEO then proceeded to inform me (and proudly, I must add) that he had absolutely no idea about any aspect of his employees; he hadn't met 99 percent of them. Further, he told me that he felt no need to or interest in doing so. I was stunned and continue to be. The attitude may work for this particular person— for now—but I wonder how well it works for the employees of the company. What I can tell you is that this is *not* the way to run a business, and it's not a way to run your life.

Do you want to find out who you really are or how you're doing in the world? Look around. See who you're hanging out with. Talk one-on-one, in person, with another human being. There are reasons people—or most people—are hard-wired for personal interaction, and one of them is this: the way we get to know ourselves and draw out soul qualities is through relationships. In short, there are times for the Internet and times to interact directly, in person.

> *The way we get to know ourselves and draw out soul qualities is through relationships.*

The World Out There

While it has yet to reach expectations of many, the Internet has changed the world, in ways large and small. It's part of our world—and I encourage you to reconsider how you use it. Use it as *a* source for your news of the world—just not *the* source. Use it to help you research. With the Internet, you can easily check out the differences between the same news story as reported by several different media sources. That can help you tease out the bias and help you develop a reasoned point of view. And keep doing it. Don't make the mistake some do by reading only the sources that you agree with. Get to know what the "other side" is thinking and saying. Make doing so a practice. The more you know about the "other side," the better. Keep learning so you can see the same issue from your side, the "other side," and even the additional sides you might not have known were out there.

Coming a little closer than your view of the world and international events, consider how you make decisions as a consumer. What is your source of information when it comes to you, as a person making purchases? What does this outside world tell you? Regardless of what medium you access, every day you are subjected to hundreds of advertising messages, many of which are so subtle that they don't register on a conscious level. In fact, even if you don't actively access *any* medium, there are still advertising messages all around you in the form of billboards, bus boards, and advertising that is on all packaging. The messages implore you to buy, buy, and buy. And, in one way or another, the messages all promise the same thing: to make your life better than it currently is.

While it may be obvious on the surface that your life isn't going to change at all by buying *anything*, you'd be surprised at how the subtle messages of advertising can get to you. Consider the following choices that you're likely to have faced in your life: what soft drink you might drink, what beer you might drink, where you get your fast food. Did you make those decisions based upon your own personal taste experiences or by the advertising message that you might have seen? Or even because the products showed up in the background on your favorite show (whether you noticed or not)? Product placement advertising is everywhere. More likely than not, your choice had little to do with the end product and a lot to do with the image of the accumulated advertising on your brain.

The reality is that in today's world, we are all victims of the hype that we see every day through every single means of advertising. And, except for those few who are unplugged and avoid the media, we are bombarded with sounds and images that influence our perspective on the world. How do you build a foundation that will work for you and how do you move forward in the world? What does your source of information need to be?

You need to take in a lot of information—as much available information as you can handle—and then you need to find a way to balance the sources and find what is true—for you. This requires you to trust yourself and to trust your abilities. That might seem challenging at the moment, but stay tuned: there's help in the following chapters. In the end, the true source of your information needs to be yourself. Once you have the tools, you'll discover that the solutions and the "truth" are not outside—they are inside.

Get Out of Your Own Way

You are the architect of your destiny, but in order to craft that plan, you also have to understand that you may also be your own worst enemy, armed with the little stories that you tell yourself. These stories have been ingrained in your psyche, some by the mass media and some by the otherwise well-meaning people around you. These stories get in your way more often than you can notice, and they hinder development, limit personal growth, and keep you from being the person you can truly be. You need to develop the technique to learn how to get out of your own way.

One of the best books that I've ever read on the subject is *A Whack on the Side of the Head,* by Roger von Oech. In this book, von Oech talks about the ways we put limits on ourselves, and therefore limits on our creativity. The essence of the book is the "mental locks" that we have arbitrarily made up. These "locks" are the negative, doubting little voices in our heads that prevent us from not only being more creative, but also from finding our true selves. If you can look beyond these locks, you can refine your personal and professional skills by hearing your true voice, overcoming fear, and discovering your areas of expertise and passion.

The "Mental Locks" are as follows:

1. The Right Answer.
2. That's Not Logical.
3. Follow the Rules.
4. Be Practical.
5. Play Is Frivolous.

6. That's Not My Area.

7. Avoid Ambiguities.

8. Don't Be Foolish.

9. To Err Is Wrong.

10. I'm Not Creative. (page 23)

The "whack on the side of your head" that von Oech suggests is to begin to break away from the locks by little steps, by changing, in ever-so-subtle ways, how you conduct your everyday life. The "Right Answer" lock says a lot about von Oech's wisdom. With numerous examples, he illustrates how people tend to look for one right answer, discarding or ignoring others in their quest for *the* answer. But those who look beyond the obvious find more. He reminds us that Gutenberg used a wine press for an entirely different purpose, and that Picasso turned a bicycle seat into art.

Similarly, many of us go through life thinking that eventually the "right" or "perfect" opportunity will come along to rescue us and miraculously change everything for the better. But what if there are plenty of opportunities and we've just plodded right past them because we weren't paying attention? There are opportunities—every day—and only rarely are they accidental. Instead, it's up to each of us to create and recognize our own opportunities by paying attention to our inner voice and to the outer world. That's what designing your own luck is all about.

The most pervasive dis-ease on the planet is the doubt of who we really are and the doubt of our power and potential. Learn how to trust that your knowledge is a valuable resource, and be comfortable in the reality that your knowledge is often grossly underestimated—mostly by you. No one has lived a life quite like yours. As a result, you have acquired experiences, knowledge, insight, and creativity that can be evolved, developed, and improved. Your unique insights far outweigh the degrees and honors listed on your resume. In every situation, professional and personal, you bring *something* to the scenario that varies from the next person. Stop selling yourself short. Be bold, be confident, even when you're not—for that matter, *especially* when you're not.

I learned this lesson very early, and in a somewhat amusing way, thanks to my Aunt Ethel.

Lesson Learned: Yes, You Can

Aunt Ethel was my father's sister, and an interior decorator who ran a very successful business on the second floor of Boston Hardware. She was tough but kind; worldly, yet a homebody. She approached life with a level of gusto and zeal that was unheard of for a woman in those days. When she wasn't working as a decorator, Ethel was also a painter. Her paintings often were the object of conversation for the rest of the family; I always found them to be colorful, if not interesting. At that point, I had never heard of Monet or Chagall, but the idea of creating something on canvas with paints and brushes intrigued me. Ethel would spend summer weekends camped out in her backyard with paints, brushes, and canvasses—classical music blaring from the record player—loving every minute of it.

One Sunday, when I was about nine years old, I went to spend the day at her house, something I liked to do. There was always an adventure to be had. That day, next to her easel, she had set up another easel with brushes, paint, and a chair—for me.

"Sit down. Paint," she intoned.

"I can't. I don't know how to paint," was my knee-jerk response.

"What do you mean?" she replied. "You have arms, you have hands, and you have eyes. What else do you need?"

So I sat down with Aunt Ethel, and we painted. And while my project looked like a bunch of squiggles and lines, I was just as proud as any "artist" could be. And when Aunt Ethel reminded me to sign my work, I truly felt like I had accomplished something.

Although I couldn't appreciate its importance at the time, Ethel's attitude—her absolute refusal to accept "I can't" as an answer—made its mark. I might have said, "I can't" after that experience, but if so, it wasn't without at least *thinking* about Aunt Ethel and her lesson to me.

It seemed a small moment at the time, but often the biggest impacts come from smallest moments. Then, I had no idea how the simple command to paint could be a first shot in immunizing me against potential mental blocks in my future.

Certainly, overcoming blocks is not a one-shot deal; it takes constant consciousness and work. It's a life-long process—and everything counts.

3

Everything Counts

THIS CHAPTER, PERHAPS MORE THAN any other, is the basis for how you can learn to deal with the experiences and people in your life. It is the basis for how you can identify your authentic self—that person who resides deep down inside of you. That person who, for whatever reason, you may not yet have tapped into. If you get nothing else out of this book, get this chapter.

You weren't born with a personal map of how to traverse through your life; you have to rely on your own resources. You have to rely on your intuition, your trust, your hope, and your ability to deal with the unexpected. There are life lessons in every interaction and in everything you do. And while it's impossible to have your radar turned on and focused at all times, too often, your radar isn't on at all. You must learn to stay awake, to find the meaning, and to learn quickly.

Also—like it or not—you're going to have to create your own solutions. That may sound hard, nearly insurmountable at times, but there are answers. Some, you will learn by paying attention, and by using your radar to learn from each situation and each person. Know that inherent in every problem there resides a ready-made solution. It is your willingness and ability to get quiet and tune into your own self that will help you to find these ready-made solutions. And in the end, because they will be *your own* solutions, they will be worthwhile and enduring life lessons.

How do you tune into your own life and what goes on around you? How do you begin to *wonder* through your life instead of *wandering* through it? How do you begin the path necessary to make your own solutions? How do you establish your own "self"—a self that you can be comfortable with and be proud of? That's the whole point of this chapter, to provide guidance in four main areas, to help you:

1. Be present.
2. Learn to trust yourself and your instincts.
3. Learn how to listen—without your ego.
4. Develop your integrity.

This isn't a shopping list of things "to do"—this is your life list of ways "to be." Work on these areas is continuous. These are not tasks you can complete once and be done with. But by practicing the skills you develop, and using them in your life, you'll be designing your life and creating more positive opportunities; together, these are the foundations to creating your own "luck."

Being Present

The idea of being present exists on a number of levels. The most literal, of course, is to be where you need to be physically at the right time. But being present is far more than this—it's not merely about punching a time clock or raising your hand to let the teacher know you're in attendance. It's truly attending—attending to every moment—at work, in class, with your family, or in your community. Being present is about showing up—with all of your faculties.

Every day, you have a choice—to be actively part of what you're doing or not. You are no longer a child: your mother is not going to push you out the door to go to class. Your own life—every day of it, everything single thing you do—has meaning. Even though up until now you might have approached a new day with the same rote behavior, now would be a good time to stop. Now would be a good time, upon waking up, to really have an awakening—to say to yourself, "*This* is the day."

What is presence? Presence is the ability to sit serenely and in silence and to be aware, alive, and in touch with what is going on *in the moment*, whatever that moment is. It's the ability to quiet the competing voices that are inside your head and outside your body. Presence is learning how to focus on the *one thing* that's in front of you, to get yourself quiet and to quiet the world around you.

Getting quiet with everything that is in you begins by learning how to quiet your own mind—that part of you that is the constant chatter in your life. The chatter is often your personal experience—that endless library of what "was." Instead of opening that library, try to approach every encounter and experience in your life as if it were new. Because guess what? It is. That chatter can also be the source of biases—ones that you are very aware of, and those that you might not even be aware of on a conscious level.

41

What you're faced with in a particular moment might *seem* similar to a previous encounter or experience, but it's not the same. Every day and every situation you encounter is different. You are unique, every person is unique, and every situation is unique. Every situation and every person with whom you interact has to be dealt with *in the moment,* with a sense of attention and detail that is consistent and appropriate *for that moment.* And while it might be nice (not to mention convenient) to deal with every situation and every person the same way, it's just not feasible or wise to do so.

> *You are unique, every person is unique, and every situation is unique.*

The past is clear, but it is nothing more than the journal of where you have been and something that you can't change. The future is some point down a road that you have no way of knowing or controlling. The present is the only thing that you have any control or any power over, and the way to *deal* with the present is by *being* present. By being present, you can learn to quiet the people in your life, many of whom may be trying to help. This doesn't mean to literally shush them, but to recognize their voices and advice when they appear in your head and to balance those voices with your own inner voice. Since no one but you has lived your life, no one but you can be the best judge of what is right for you, what to do, and who to be.

Here's another way to explore the idea of presence. You're no doubt familiar with the kiosks in shopping malls that show the layout of the stores. In order to help you determine where you are relative to the stores, the signs typically have a brightly colored X, labeled, "You are here." And yes, you are. Think of your life as a series of Xs—and all you ever are is just "here." As you're reading this, you are "here" too. And you'll still be "here" for the next thing that you do. And if you keep repeating to yourself, "I am here," you'll be that much closer to practicing presence.

Take a moment to try a little experiment. ***Stop!*** Do you remember what you read three pages ago? Think about it for a moment and then go back and check it out. If you couldn't remember, then you weren't practicing presence; instead, you were reading words while your mind was engaged in something else. Make it a habit to stop periodically and ask yourself if you've just paid attention to the last thirty minutes of your life. If you had to, could you relate to someone else what you had done for those last thirty minutes? If it all just "slipped by," then you're not practicing presence.

Can you be "present" all of the time? Of course not—that's why it's called "practicing" presence. To help you practice, try every now and then to look inside yourself in a physical, not mental, way. Stop and notice how you are breathing: are you taking short, quick breaths, or is your breathing long and deliberate? What is your posture like? Do you have to do something different in order to be present? Are you doing more than one thing at a time?

When you notice that you're *not* present, here's a quick way to bring yourself back to the now:

Open your hands and spread your fingers, palms facing each other. Touch opposite fingertips together, all at the same time. Repeat a few times. Sometimes the simple act of feeling your own skin can reconnect you to yourself and to the present moment.

If all of this seems like I'm trying to sneak in a little meditation and yoga, you're absolutely right. Both are excellent practices to help mind and body—and will be covered in more detail later in the book. For now, I'll rely on a little teaser from *Yoga Mind, Body & Spirit* by Donna Farhi: "Yoga is a technology for arriving in this present moment. It is a means of waking up from our spiritual amnesia, so that we can remember all that we already know" (page 5).

I can't overstate the importance of being present. Once you are able to be fully present and to access your inner wisdom, your life will change and take on new depth. Being present enables you to see and to really understand that for every action there is a reaction. You see that when you treat someone with respect, that person— whether it's someone you know or someone you encounter on the street—reciprocates with respect. It becomes clear that in order to get respect, you have to give respect. Plus, it's the right thing to do. And you just never know: the people you pass on the way up might be the same ones you see on the way down. What goes around comes around. Sounds like a cliché, you might be thinking. Well, it might be, and it's the truth. Treat everyone with respect; you'll not regret it. In a similar fashion, you see that in order to be trusted, you have trust yourself and be trustworthy.

Trusting Yourself and Your Intuition

Before you can *trust* your intuition, you have to *discover* your intuition. How do you go about it? Step one is to recognize that intuition isn't a thing. It's something that is in your heart and your soul, not in your head. *It's a voice. Things* are easy to find—car keys, the laundry, or a golf ball. *Voices* are much more difficult to isolate. But when you're paying attention—when you are present—the voices are more obvious than any golf ball. The voices can range from the ones that are encouraging you to the ones that are second-guessing you. Sometimes the voices are those of chaos, crisis, and confusion. Sometimes they can be the voices of truth and trust.

The voices of chaos, crisis, and confusion are generally a lot louder. They come from your mind as it is constantly reviewing information and passing judgment based on "experience." This feedback from your brain is part of human nature, but these voices are rarely helpful. *Now* is the time to learn how to change that part of your humanness. The voices of truth and trust are much softer because they are much closer to your heart and have nothing to do with your mind. Learning how to tune out the multitude of voices and finding and listening to the *one* that's worthwhile can be a daunting task, but by getting quiet and being present, it becomes a lot easier.

Unlike instincts, which are innate, intuition can be thought of as both innate and learned. The innate portion of your intuition is an internal gift from a much more evolved part of you that's plugged into your own "grand design." You might not be always aware of it on a completely conscious level, but on some level, you do know it is there. Tuning in to your intuition involves tuning out the unhelpful voices and practicing presence.

Step two of discovering and trusting your intuition is to learn about trust. And what about trust? Trust is the number one ingredient in every single relationship in your life—especially your relationship with yourself. Before you can even begin to *think* about trusting others, you're going to have to trust yourself. Learning to have trust in yourself is a matter of trial and error and discovering how to learn from past mistakes. The key is to *remember* the past mistakes and the lessons they taught you. Here's an example that you might have experienced as a child, or if not, you can certainly imagine it. Pointing your finger or wielding a stick or pencil, you were drawn toward an electrical socket, as if you were on a mission. Observant child that you were, you'd seen other people put things into similar sockets with seemingly positive results. Your curiosity said, "Me too!" Well, unless someone older and wiser swooped in to intercede, sparks flew—and you probably weren't going to try *that* again.

Now think of the last time you made a mistake—choose a really big one. What do you remember about it? Was there a chance that before you made the mistake, there was a little voice that was telling you to do something other than what you ended up doing? Did you ignore that voice? No problem; it happens. However, in thinking about that mistake, what did you learn from it? Did you take the time then to stop and ask yourself what you had learned? The most important thing you can do after making a mistake is to stop, look, and learn. What went wrong? How did it go wrong? And what can you do to prevent that from happening again? These are good questions and questions for which only *you* have the answer.

So, put it together—intuition and trust—how do you develop the wherewithal to trust your intuition? There is only one way: through trial and error, experimentation and learning by making mistakes, and by reflecting upon the successes and knowing *why* you succeeded.

Yes, the younger we are, the more we rely without reservation on our instincts and trust. However, innocence does not equal ignorance. Quite the contrary—our youthful innocence allows us to be much more free in our experimentation. In retrospect, I see that I had a very powerful lesson about intuition and trust when I was just barely a teenager.

Be Quiet, Don't Worry

I was a very quiet child. *Very* quiet. It wasn't because I didn't have anything to say. I just couldn't really find my platform, and the constant comparisons to my siblings further complicated my search to find my place. It wasn't until the night of my bar mitzvah—December 6, 1963—that I had an opportunity to find that platform. For nearly a year, I'd prepared for the event with diligence, yet with a certain rote sameness that neither intrigued nor intimidated me. I was thirteen years old. At that age, everyone I knew had a bar mitzvah. It was the standard coming of age celebration within the Jewish community. In my world, it was no big deal.

Two weeks prior to my big event, President John F. Kennedy had been assassinated in Dallas. Everyone I knew and everyone I looked at was in a state of complete shock: this was a surreal experience in universal grief that I had never before witnessed. The heartbeat of the world had stopped, and the shine of America seemed to dull. It was also the first time in history that a national tragedy was played out on the new medium of television. Kennedy's assassination—its very occurrence, its visibility, and the fact that anyone within range of a television knew of the events practically as they played out—changed the sense of isolation. And of innocence. As best as a thirteen-year-old could, I tried to separate this universal grief from my own sense of joy and excitement. I knew that the crowd at temple two weeks later would be gathered there because it was *my* bar mitzvah. I hoped they would focus on my every word in rapt attention. On this one night, *my night*, there would be no comparison with my sister or brother. I was sure of that.

As my parents, rabbi, and I sat behind the pulpit waiting for services to begin, there was an air of tension that was clear, but not spoken. A few minutes before we were to sit in front of the congregation, my mother turned to me and asked where my notes were. I had kept a package of papers that included the translations, the Hebrew, and my speech. It had been part of my daily routine for several months; however, bringing all of that with me on that night had not even occurred to me. "What for?" I thought. "I know all of this stuff." I turned to my mother and told her that the notes were at home. The fright visible in her face was perfectly counterbalanced by the calmness in mine. "I don't need them," I replied. "I know what I'm doing." Moments later, as I stood in front of the congregation—noteless and calm—I experienced an unfamiliar surge of adrenaline pulsing through me. At the time, I couldn't label the feeling. I didn't understand it, but I knew that it was *something*. It was confidence—*inner confidence*.

Somewhere deep inside, in a place I could barely fathom, let alone trust, I had great instincts and an inner confidence. Of course, as a child, I had no concept of this. And if I'd had a clue, I doubt that I would have understood, appreciated, or trusted any of it. Generally, I was unable to balance the sibling comparisons with my sense of self, and I believed what I had been told up until then: *I just didn't match up.*

But when push came to shove, and all was calm, I was able to employ what would later become an important business and life practice—I got quiet, trusted myself, and allowed my inner confidence to speak. My intuition, which I was beginning to sense, told me where to join and where to flee. My quiet confidence made me the attractive leader of most organizations I joined, yet I rarely knew why at the time. Often, others could see this clearly, while I wondered why. I constantly struggled with leadership qualities that I barely understood and my own inner confidence, which I understood even less. Yet somehow I knew that "quiet" was a good thing for me.

As we get older, we don't necessarily lose our intuition; we lose our *ability* and *willingness* to trust it. Of course, not all experiences are as eye opening as the shocking socket or the affirming bar mitzvah. But every decision you make, every opportunity you have to rely on your instincts and your intuition, is based on your own experience. While experience is an important factor in approaching something new, intuition is the more important factor.

How do you know you're on the right track to something? How do you know when your intuition is serving you well? Watch the flow of your thoughts, feelings, and senses. When they feel like they are all flowing smoothly, you're on track. If you're pushing yourself to get through it, then you're on the wrong track. Your gut tells the truth; your mind, which is not particularly helpful, rationalizes and justifies. Stay close to your gut.

Fortunately, I did so naturally when I went away to college. Unlike many of my friends, I had no earthly idea what I was going to major in or what I was going to *be* when I graduated. At Rutgers, I decided to study what interested me—books. So my answer was to become an English major. While my friends were killing themselves studying organic chemistry, biology, accounting, and American history, I was reading. Reading Hemingway, Fitzgerald, and Faulkner. Mailer, Bellow, and Vonnegut. The reading lists, all of them, were an absolute treat for my brain. As my fraternity brothers were cramming for finals, I was writing papers and expanding my creativity. While I still had no vocational "goal," I just wasn't worried, and I didn't let the concerns of those around me affect me. Somehow, some way, I knew that I'd be fine. Once again, quiet confidence let me be in a comfortable place, despite being surrounded by peers who knew what they were going to be (and were, perhaps, a bit frantic about it).

I recognized college as more than a means to the end of getting a degree: I recognized it as a time to experiment, to explore, and to have an all-around good time. When academic life became less than a challenge, I found a way to earn money in my spare time—and without a boss. Who would have known that selling sweaters out of my fraternity room was a beginning step to my career?

Sweater City: An Adventure in Trust

In my sophomore year of college, I spent my bar mitzvah money to buy a '69 Volvo. Between the car upkeep, occasional trips to New York, and my phone bills, I soon needed to make some extra cash.

The father of a friend of mine from high school owned a men's shirt and sweater factory back in Hazleton. The factory had an outlet store as well, selling overruns and irregulars. When I was at home for spring break, I went to the outlet store to buy a few shirts for myself. While shopping, it dawned on me that if I could get a slight price break on the shirts and sweaters in the outlet store, I might be able to resell them at school. On the spot, I negotiated a price for the purchase of as many shirts and sweaters as could fit in my Volvo, and I was in business. With more confidence than money, I wrote a check, knowing full well that it wouldn't clear. But I also knew that as soon as I got back to New Brunswick, I'd be able to sell enough shirts to at least cover it. This marked the beginning of my first solo retail venture, and my first venture in the clothing business.

The message? Blind faith trumps that doubting voice that says, "No way." I didn't think twice about writing that check. I never worried about the consequences of what might happen if it bounced. My motivation was partly experimentation and partly fear—fear of not having enough money for all that I wanted to do. I trusted my instincts over the reality of my meager checking account balance. I realized who I was and what I could do. And I was right. There were lessons for me here that I carried with me long past my college days.

Learning to Listen—Without Your Ego

A terrific quality to develop and a most underused skill in everyday life or at work is a fundamental understanding of human nature. That understanding begins by listening. From a place of listening, you can build rapport and be able to respond to the people around you in a meaningful way—with integrity and with a sense of trustworthiness. You can't account for the place that someone else is coming from; you can only account for your own place. When you listen with your heart and acknowledge your intuitive power, you gain confidence, direction, and courage. And by listening with your heart, you do a tremendous service to the person who is talking to you.

Perhaps you're murmuring to yourself, "I hear what other people have to say all of the time." But think about that for a second. There's a *big* difference between hearing and listening. Hearing is a sense that most of us are born with. The frequency, intensity, and duration of a sound travel through auditory nerve fibers to the brain, allowing our body to process and interpret these signals. That's all very nice but very mechanical. Listening, on the other hand, is not a sense, and it's not mechanical; it is a trait that you have to develop. Here's a practical approach to listening. You know that you want to be heard. If you want to be heard, learn how to listen. Although this sounds simple, it's far from it. Listening requires practice, and it requires presence. Learning how to listen is an art, not a science—you aren't going to learn how to do it unless you *practice* listening.

That said, I'll offer some information and practical reminders that should help. No doubt you're well aware that we all spend a great deal of the day communicating in one form or another. But how much of that communicating involves listening? Unfortunately, not nearly enough. To help yourself get quiet and learn how to listen, make it a practice to assume that there is more information in front of you than inside you. You already know what you already know. What you *don't know* is what the other person knows. If you can learn to control your mouth and keep your mind from wandering, you'll be able to learn much more by *just listening.*

ALL KNOWLEDGE IS NEW

You're not born with knowledge; it's something you attain throughout life. And we all attain different facts at different times in our lives. Be patient with others in their goals to attain new knowledge. That's a lesson I learned by example—a very unpleasant one.

Many years ago, I was thrust into a situation in which I instantly became the dress shirt buyer for Men's Wearhouse. I was young and unprepared, and my first buying trip to New York was the day after I became the shirt buyer. I knew absolutely nothing about dress shirts other than the fact that I wore one every now and then. I met with a vendor who had been selling shirts to Men's Wearhouse for a few years, but of course he hadn't been selling shirts to *me.* He was showing me patterned dress shirts and said something about "woven" and "print" shirts. I had no idea what the difference was, and in the moment, without regard to the consequence of my question, I asked what the difference was. In *his* moment, he was stunned at my ignorance and gave me a several-minute lecture about how stupid I was that I didn't know the difference. (And yes, he did use the word "stupid.") As I sat there being berated by this person, it dawned on me that at some point in *his* life, *he* hadn't known the difference between a print and a woven shirt, either. I knew for sure that neither one of us had been born with this information, and the only difference between us was

53

when we acquired it. I refused to let him make me feel "less than," thanked him for the clarity and the lesson, and moved on.

To listen effectively, you must be *actively* involved in the communication process. It's so simple, yet for so many, so elusive. If you take the lessons you've already learned about practicing presence and apply them to the tips below, you'll become an able listener, a better friend and colleague to those who are talking to you, and best of all, you'll open your mind to those things you might not have thought about or even truly heard before.

TIPS FOR BETTER LISTENING

As Samuel Clemens (that's Mark Twain, again) said: "If we were supposed to talk more than we listen, we would have two mouths and one ear." Unfortunately, most of us conduct our lives as if we *do* have two mouths and one ear. The most natural thing for most of us is to *not* listen. Our world is filled with information, and we move very quickly—most of the time too quickly to stop and just listen. But it doesn't make it right. As you read the tips that follow, spend time thinking about each one. They may well be new ideas to you and might force you to rethink what you've thought until now. They'll also make you a better listener and better friend to those to whom you're listening.

Use the Five-Minute Rule. Whether it's in business or in your personal life, how many times has someone come to you with an idea that, at first blush, you rejected? How many times, during that mental rejection and while the other person was still talking, did you begin to formulate your reasons for thinking that the idea wasn't a good one and completely ignored what the other person was saying?

The next time, try this: for at least five minutes, approach every outside idea as a good one—as a great one—and think of ways that you can build on, rather than destroy, that idea. There's always a time and a place for rejection. The seeds of a good idea are best cultivated when the idea is still new and fresh, when there is still excitement in the heart and voice of the creator. Albert Einstein, certainly an advocate of new ideas, said, "For an idea that does not first seem insane, there is no hope." So, no matter how wild the idea, don't bash it; embrace it. You'd want the same thing if it were *your* idea.

Be Calm and Receptive. Always assume that you're getting information that is new to you. Don't let your mind start rummaging through the old files in your memory bank to find what may be familiar about the information that you're hearing. It may be *familiar,* but it's not the *same.* Your mind and your ego might also be telling you that what you are hearing is "incorrect" in an effort to protect any hidden prejudices and closed-minded opinions. But it's only your mind playing the "same old, same old" game with you, a game that prevents you from hearing what is said. So be present and let everything you hear be new. Use that five-minute rule and let it seem correct for at least those few minutes.

Be Quiet and Don't Interrupt. From a place of quietness, you can tap into your soul and expand your mind. In order to be quiet, you have to be calm. (In order to be calm, see above.) Your desire to put your own information out there should be tempered by your desire to listen and wait your turn. Let the other person have his say. Hopefully, he'll be able to watch you and your listening style, appreciate it, and do so the same when it's his turn to listen. Pay special attention if something pops up to you as the "dumbest" or the "most outrageous" thing—the thing that you *least* agree with. Guess what? There is someone on the other side with as much positive passion about their belief and point of view as you.

Pay Attention. It's natural to be working on your response at the same time as you are listening. Stop doing this! If you're "listening" and simultaneously formulating your response, you're violating all of the above rules. How? Listening to someone else and talking to yourself at the same time is chaotic, which is the opposite of calm. And if you're talking to yourself while listening to someone else, you're interrupting, in a way. Granted, you're not making audible sounds, but there is plenty of noise—in your head. You're talking, just not out loud. Clearly, you're a far more effective listener when you're not talking. It's not the worst thing to first listen and then have an actual pause in the conversation before you respond.

Leash Your Ego. Here's what is, for many, the most difficult tip. Put your ego away. Think of it as the accumulation of all of the mental garbage that you have collected over the course of your lifetime. Lock it in a drawer. At least keep it leashed. Why? We can only *really* hear others to the degree we can hold, contain, acknowledge, and validate ourselves. Personal validation begins with winning the battle with the ego and becoming comfortable in your own skin.

Imagine if I had taken seriously what that dress shirt vendor said to me about my brainpower. Instead of listening to what he told me about shirts (after having berated me), I'd have been defensive and tending to my battered ego. Chances are I couldn't have absorbed all the information and would have had a hard time continuing the task at hand, which was buying shirts. The lesson? If you are unsure about yourself, or unsure about a specific belief that you might have, it's going to be very hard for you to hear that belief challenged, to ask questions, or to gain new information. If you are unsure, *ask questions.*

Need a little more reason to leash your ego? Think about ego and realize that it has more than one gear. It can be in neutral, moving forward, or going in reverse. When you remove your ego from a situation, you are admitting that someone else has something to say and has a point of view. (That's your ego in neutral.) Sometimes that new point of view doesn't agree with yours. (Reverse.) But what someone else has to say *counts!* It's a point of view, albeit sometimes not *your* point of view. If you are truly in a relationship, there's plenty of time to promote your own point of view. (Forward.) As you probably were told in kindergarten, *wait your turn.* Keep your ego in neutral (leashed). When you have your ego in neutral, treating others with respect comes more naturally.

LIFE IS OFTEN LIKE A POKER GAME

Life is not like one of those poker games on the Internet, but the kind where real human beings sit down at a real table and play with real money. True, there are gambles involved in both, and human interaction, but why talk about poker when the topic is learning how to listen? Poker is not entirely about gambling on the cards—it's about observing physical actions and listening to what's going on at the table with the other players. If you try to watch it all, you will almost certainly become frustrated, fail, and observe nothing, not to mention not winning anything. The trick is to balance a variety of information, and to focus on *one thing* at a time. It is not enough to just "see" the betting patterns. You have to constantly recognize the behavior of your opponents, know intuitively when they are bluffing or have a good hand, and truly capitalize on that information. Of course, watching your own hand and having a basic understanding of your own odds in a given situation is important, but what distinguishes the great poker players from the not-so-great and the difference between poker on the Internet and "live" poker is the human connection.

My poker-playing days at Rutgers taught me that you could learn just as much from watching the players as you can from the cards. And those lessons were very worthwhile: my frequent winnings helped pay my way through college. I was able to become keenly aware of the motivation and body language of the people I played with, and was thereby able to move the odds slightly in my favor. Paying attention also enabled me to not make the same mistakes twice—something I noticed the others at the table doing constantly. It's not that I got better cards or started out with better skills. But I stayed with the game and focused primarily on playing poker. And when their attention drifted to drinking and joking around, my fellow card players made enough mistakes that my odds increased still more. We all had a good time, but by focusing on the one thing that counted, I controlled my game and increased my chances.

Essentially, good poker playing is more about discovering how to learn by observing habits. Poker is not just a skill. It's an art in learning how to turn up your listening and intuitive skills, and reading between the lines. If you can quiet your ego, pre-conceived judgments, and feelings of self-doubt, you'll be surprised by what you see and hear in poker and—more importantly—in life.

Establishing Integrity in Your Life

Integrity is the powerful force behind what you say and what you do. It's the most vital piece of who you are and who you will ever become. Integrity is the intersection of your systems of beliefs and your value systems. Having integrity means living your life with honesty, honoring your word and beliefs, and taking responsibility for your actions. It is the result of thinking, making decisions, and opting for the right motives. It's about vision and judgment of the person who practices it. It's about doing good for the sake of doing good—when no one is watching—and without expecting recognition. You do it because the behavior outwardly reflects your beliefs and is woven into the fabric of your being, beliefs, and values and frames the way you consciously want to lead your life. It's the person who distributes two hundred homemade lunches every month to the homeless at the train station on his lunch hour. It's the person who pays a debt that may have been long forgotten by someone else. Or the person who shovels her elderly neighbors' walkways so they can get out and about safely. It's conducting yourself a certain way, not because your mother told you so, or to earn a pat on the back.

Like learning to listen or trusting your instincts, establishing your integrity requires risks, uncertainty, practice, and continual mental effort. The risk and uncertainty come from the fact that establishing and sustaining your integrity might mean that you're going to be at odds with someone else. You might have to call people on their behavior or ethics; you might have to go as far as to sever a friendship or a business relationship because you're at a fundamental crossroads. The practice and mental effort might be a chore at first, but with time, they'll come naturally. It's an effort that's worthwhile and essential, no matter what the cost.

Any time you compromise your integrity, you've essentially lost the most important character trait you have. Any time you fail to do what you *know* in your heart or in your soul is right, deep down inside you lessen your self-worth, impede your outlook on the world, and damage your ability to live a happy life. Your goals can become harder to reach, you attract people who make you feel bad, and you lose your trust in yourself.

Instead, be honest. Know that everything you do and everything you say sculpts your character. There is no such thing as a "little" lie—any non-truth gets embedded in your psyche.

Lie detectors are great at monitoring what happens to your inner body when you tell a lie. Absent the lie detector, try an experiment of your own. Watch what happens to your outer body the next time you try one of those "little lies." Your breathing might change and become more shallow. Or if you're talking to another person, you might stop making eye contact. You might even have trouble just sitting or standing without being fidgety. The honest soul in each of us refuses to allow a lie to go unnoticed. But over time, that soul does have the flexibility to allow us to learn to lie. If you get comfortable with the "little" lie, you'll be that much less uncomfortable with the slightly larger lie. The more lies, the easier the next one becomes; and then the next may be slightly larger, larger, and larger still. This is clearly not the kind of flexibility that one can be proud of.

Studies have shown that our brains register and remember everything we do. Our ability to *recall* any one thing in the moment is the difference between good and poor memory. It's not too much of a leap, therefore, to assume that the same holds true for little lies versus any other kind of lie. Little untruths leave an imprint on the soul, just as the larger ones do. The bottom line? Learn to tell the truth: be honest. It's the right thing to do—for your soul and for your physical well being.

There is no denying it: your life is the sum and substance of what you put into it. No one deserves the credit for the things you've done well other than you. By the same token, no one else deserves the blame. While it is often convenient and ego soothing to assign blame when something goes wrong, often there is no blame, and there are no victims.

Similarly, there are no shortcuts or easy ways, and you rarely "get away" with anything. You are going to have to work to get the things you want. That work might be long and laborious, but when you do the work, you'll feel much better at the end of the process, knowing that you didn't take the easy way out. If you take what appears to be a shortcut, you might *think* you've gotten away with something, but you haven't. Sooner or later, everything catches up with you. Whether it's something as simple as wasting your time on the supposed shortcut or as complicated as making a large mistake that you're going to have to unravel at a later date, what you do will reflect on you. Thanks to the Internet, even your online posts and YouTube videos can follow you into the future. Be aware of what you're projecting into the world, both in what you do and don't do. Shun the shortcut. Behave as you wish to be known, and not just for today.

Work, don't bail. When a problem arises, your initial instinct might be to bail—to abandon—whether it's in a relationship or some other issue that needs to be solved. Decide now to *work*. Bailing without working is the easy way out, and like lying, it can become habitual if you don't watch it. There is nothing to be gained from walking away from a problem. If the problem becomes a failure, *that's* where the gain comes—in learning from the failure. (For more on that subject, see chapter 5.)

At a dinner that I hosted with about twenty members of my advisory board, we discussed the notion of bailing. About half of those present felt they had been well trained on the notion of bailing, by parents whose relationship didn't work out and ended in divorce. It was hard for me to argue that specific case of bailing, having been guilty myself, but I tried.

I certainly know that there were times that I could have walked away from Men's Wearhouse. We went through some very trying years when all of our hard work amounted to little more than financial loss, and the easy way out might have been to sell off the company to another one in better financial shape. But rather than bail, George and I and the rest of the management team decided to redouble our efforts. Why? We had two big reasons. One, we believed in ourselves and in what we were doing and knew that with time, we'd be able to improve the company. Two, we realized that we had our hopes and dreams and those of hundreds of employees at stake as well. There were a lot of people counting on us. Bailing (as in selling the company) might have been easier, but it wasn't the right thing to do. For us, the decision became more like the notion of bailing a cherished boat that had taken on water. We knew that the store and the employees were worth the effort, and we weren't about to let them sink or drift away.

It was the Buddha who once said, "How you do anything is how you do everything." And indeed, that's the consistent thread that runs through these recommendations to be honest, be accountable, shun the shortcut, and work rather than bail. It comes down to this: Be aware of your actions. Be aware that how you do anything *is* how you do everything. Think about it also as you watch others. If you can lie about a small thing, you can lie about a bigger thing. Similarly, if you know a friend or associate has issues with the truth, know that you need to be cautious extending your trust. You are accountable, so *be* accountable. Skip the shortcut; don't bail. Value your integrity.

STINKY SUITS: IN SEARCH OF INTEGRITY

In my entire career at Men's Wearhouse, the single most egregious act committed against the company took on its own aroma and became a lesson for many. Beyond this, it bears mentioning as a failure of accountability and integrity that forever changed my view of a particular vendor. It had to do with what came to be known as "stinky suits."

By way of background, you'll need a crash course in the manufacturing of men's suits, so here goes. Before a suit is actually sewn together, the fabric has to be woven, generally at another factory, also known as a piece-goods mill. After the fabric is woven, it is then "sponged." Sponging does what the name implies—a light coat of water mixed with chemicals is applied to the fabric, allowing it to shrink so that shrinkage doesn't occur later on. Enough with the lesson.

One day, I went into our warehouse to look at a delivery of suits from a certain supplier. As I walked around, I noticed an awful smell, like a skunk. Assuming it *was* a skunk, I spoke to the warehouse manager, who mentioned that he also had smelled something, but he couldn't pinpoint the location. We hunted around for a skunk, didn't find one, and we both let it go.

Several weeks later, at a meeting, a few managers commented that they had smelled something odd in their stores. When I asked them what it smelled like, they unanimously responded, "A skunk." So the original "skunk in the warehouse" theory was gone. The question now became this: where was the smell coming from? Again, for lack of any definitive cause, we all had to let it go. A few days later, I received a letter from an irate customer, who explained that he had bought a suit at Men's Wearhouse for a job interview and that en route to the interview, he got caught in a light drizzle. Of course, his suit got wet, but that wasn't his issue. His issue was that by the time the suit dried, it smelled terrible—like a skunk. But he had to go to the interview. And, of course, he didn't get the job.

I quickly found out exactly what suit the man had bought and started to put the pieces together. Not only had he bought a suit from that certain unnamed manufacturer, but he had also bought one of the suits that was in the warehouse on the day that I initially smelled the skunk-like odor. I immediately called the manufacturer, who let me know that I was the first to call with such a problem. Unsure whether to ask for a reward or something, I asked if this crazy notion seemed even plausible. "Of course not," I was told. Two days later, a call came in from another customer with a similar story. Two days after that, three calls came in from three different Men's Wearhouse stores complaining about a foul, overwhelming smell. I made another call to the manufacturer. Once again, the answer was basically, "Not my problem." Except it now *was* a problem, and I was getting very nervous. I immediately called all of the stores and told them to return the suspect suits to our warehouse ASAP. I told the vendor that I was doing so as well. More stonewalling ensued, and I was accused of overreacting.

Fortunately, the manufacturer's sales rep was more cooperative. He flew to our Fremont, California, warehouse, and he and I walked through it, examining and smelling the suits. We pulled a few out, sprayed them lightly with water, and the smell got worse. He then called the manufacturer, and *he* got the run around.

That was the last straw for me. There was no question that the suits were going to be returned. What I wanted to know was is why I got stonewalled, and what exactly had happened. The sales rep agreed and obliged, and through his contacts in the factory, he discovered something astounding. When the piece goods had originally been delivered to the factory, the smell was so overpowering that they had to close down the facility for part of the day. Whether the cause had been the chemical mix or how it had been applied didn't matter; what mattered was that rather than resolve the problem, the manufacturer had ignored it and proceeded to make the suits.

In a roundabout way, and after weeks of no cooperation, the manufacturer recognized that there had been *some* sort of problem. Their quick solution? They wanted to lower the price of the suits to us, so we could lower the price to our customers. Of course, this was no solution. Instead, it just underscored the manufacturer's lack of integrity and accountability.

Bottom line? We didn't pass the suits onto customers— they went right back to the manufacturer. And we learned some valuable lessons:

- How a person or a company responds to adversity is a window on their character and soul. The decision to go ahead and make the suits was made by a middle-level manager. But the ethos of looking the other way was not his—he was no doubt repeating something he had seen at another time, further up the corporate ladder.

- There are people in the world who put their integrity before everything else. The manufacturer's sales rep who worked to get to the cause of the problem did what he believed was right. By choosing not to stonewall or deny, he didn't do the "corporate" thing but went up against his company. And, as a postscript, he didn't last much longer in that company. He did, however, maintain his integrity.

We're all tested at many points in our work and personal lives. Sometimes exercising your integrity can make you unpopular or even cause tangible damage, such as losing your job or losing a friendship. Know that you *can* do good and do business. Integrity in relationships involves responding to and communicating with others—whether it's a co-worker or a close friend—with complete openness and honesty. When truthfulness is paired with integrity, you can make promises that will be respected and have meaning. Personal integrity counts. Similarly, despite corporate scandals that have undermined the public's faith in business, most companies *are* honest, and many do lots of great things.

Time Examining Your Motives Is Time Well Spent

Any time you interact with another person, examine your heart and examine your motives. When you treat people with respect and compassion, you're on stable ground. Remember the Golden Rule: Do unto others as you would have them do unto you. Are you not listening to someone who is talking with you? Have you treated them with contempt? Indifference? Dispassion? It's not only *that* you might be treating them this way; the question is *why*.

You want to really start to change your life? Sit down quietly for a bit and examine your motives. Start with honest self-observation. To transform yourself, start from the inside—the same inside where (once again) all of the answers reside. If you don't, you'll make things more difficult for yourself than they need to be. After trial and error, you'll find that the really hard things in life are resistance and lack of forgiveness and that the really easy things are acceptance, compassion, and kindness. The idea might seem backwards. After all, sticking to your guns no matter what the cost or holding a grudge appears to be easy and require little self-awareness and contemplation. But when you start down the path of practicing acceptance, compassion, and kindness, through self-awareness and contemplation, you'll find yourself moving through life with a little less resistance—from the inside and from the outside.

Here's another way to think about it, and a great piece of advice (even if I do say so). If you're one who highlights and dog ears book pages, do so to this page. The advice is: *Pick up after yourself.* Yep, just like your mother used to say. Except that what I'm really referring to is to pick up the pieces of your life. Remember: you need to be accountable. Accountability is a component of integrity, and it's part of the package of living an authentic existence.

> *You want to really start to change your life? ... Pick up after yourself.*

An awful lot has been covered in this chapter, and if you've gotten this far and are a bit dizzy, be patient. The material you've just read is really the foundation for the rest of the book. But at a very basic level, what it all comes down to is two words: "Trust yourself." When you learn to trust yourself, the rest of the pieces of your life begin to fall into place more easily.

Lesson Learned: Trust Yourself

It doesn't matter how or why or when you begin to trust yourself. What's important is that you learn to do so at some point. I'm fortunate to be one of those people who did so at a very young age. Why? I suspect that having had exposure to personal failure at an early age, I was forced to turn inside to the one person I could trust—myself.

As it happened, my early years in Houston were rife with smart decisions based on little more than self-trust. When I returned to Men's Wearhouse from Marcom-Day, George wanted me to stay for good, so he offered to sell me stock in the company. His proposal was to sell me one third of the company for $3,000. While today that amount of money might seem trivial, at the time, and to me, it was not at all trivial. I simply didn't *have* $3,000 to invest, and had few personal assets to use as collateral. I sought the advice of my father, who, working from his own paradigms, tried to talk me out of investing. First, he pointed out that Men's Wearhouse had a negative net worth. I would therefore be investing in a company that was worthless, which it was at the time. So he warned that my investment looked shaky, at best. Second, he believed that not owning 51 percent of something was the same as owning none of it. No more, no less.

Fortunately, I wasn't asking for the favor of borrowing money. I was seeking advice, which I listened to, and then decided to ignore. I knew it was wise to ask for advice—and to make an independent decision. I knew that, in this instance, I had to effectively say, "That's nice, thanks. Now get out of my way." I relied on my instincts and intuition and made a decision contrary to the opinion of a man—

my father—whom I trusted and respected. I had a good feeling in general about the future of Men's Wearhouse, and George Zimmer in particular; that feeling was strong enough to override the advice. In retrospect, this decision, based on strong self-trust, was my smartest business decision—ever.

Ask for advice—and make an independent decision ... Know when to say, "That's nice, thanks. Now get out of my way."

I went to a Houston bank and using my car as collateral, secured a one-year $3,000 loan to become a Men's Wearhouse stockholder. It all felt right. And I certainly had done my homework; I knew the business, having been associated with it in one way or another practically since its inception. Beyond that, what I trusted then was my intuition—not my intellect, my heart, my head, or any outside advisor. I also trusted my own abilities to work hard and make things happen for myself and for what now represented my single largest asset.

For the record, my dad has a great sense of humor in remembering this story and often retells it to friends as well as to me with a big smile on his face. One of the wonders of time is that it changes everything. At the time, my decision to buy Men's Wearhouse stock seemed like a risky one. Over time, the decision was obviously less and less risky.

Time is an important element in our lives, and it's a commodity that has an unknown duration. An integral part to creating your own luck has to do with the way in which you use time, a topic examined in detail in the next chapter.

4

We're All Playing for the Same Thing: Time

TIME AND OUR PHYSICAL HEALTH are the most precious and the most personal assets we have in our lives. While we may have some control over our health, we have no control over our time. We each have a finite amount of it: twenty-four hours each day, 365 days each year. Our total allotment of years might be known—but not to us. It's one of the great mysteries of life. So really, we're all playing for the same thing: time. As it turns out, the bumper stickers are correct: Life is not a dress rehearsal.

Because we're all playing for the same thing, it creates an even playing field. There are no advantages to any one person. And although you have no control over the total amount of time you have in your life, you can exert control over the time that you *do* have control over—the present time. In this chapter, I set forth a number of strategies to help you learn how to make time work for you, instead of the other way around. But first, take a few moments to think about the relativity of time.

Time Is Relative

Do you remember when you were a kid and you were looking forward to your birthday? I certainly do, because I was born in December, and in that month our family also celebrated Christmas and Hanukah. The closer that December got, the slower time seemed to pass; in fact, I was sure that there was some time demon out there deliberately slowing things down for me. Conversely, in the summer, when we had three months of no school, time sped by; that same demon was probably messing with me again.

In other words, as children, the notion of time was relative to the events taking place in our lives: some time went quickly and some, slowly. I also remember as a child thinking that time was something that almost stood still. I had little sense of what "time moving on" meant. At four, I thought I was always four and would always be four. Someone who was forty—as my parents were—had always been a parent. (And by the way, forty was really old.)

The older we get, the faster time passes, and there is very little "relativity"—it all seems to fly by with a blur. It's the adults who say, "I can't believe it's Halloween already." The kids feel they've been waiting an eternity to dress up and get armloads of candy. Why? One reason is that, depending upon our focus, our goals, and what else is happening simultaneously, equal amounts of time—as measured by a stopwatch, a clock, or a calendar—can seem to pass very differently. When we're utterly focused on one thing (as a child often is), time can seem to expand. If you've been in an accident, an earthquake, or put on the spot in a classroom discussion or an interview, you know that just a few seconds can seem to stretch out for long moments.

If Time Is Relative, How Do You Measure It?

It wasn't as dramatic as an accident, an earthquake, or an interview but a slow-moving incident at the Men's Wearhouse that provided me with a new perspective on time. We were making a commercial and trying to fill the time between active work on the shots so that we wouldn't be frustrated by the amount of down time. It was a particularly long, monotonous, and grisly day that drove us to invent a game. By way of background, you should know that for many years, the "team" that made Men's Wearhouse commercials was George, as the owner-spokesman; Jordan, the president of our advertising agency, the producer; and Ivan, the director. I was the referee.

During one of the many breaks in the action, Jordan was bemoaning the lack of "effective" copy in the spot we were shooting. Jordan said: "Ahhh … We never get to really say what we should in a commercial. We shoulda added a lot of things to this spot we're doing, like …" Whereupon, Jordan went on to name a few more selling points that weren't already in the spot.

Ivan took issue, saying: "Wait a minute; this spot is already stuffed like a sausage. You have no idea about the concept of time."

So, more as a way to pass the time than anything else, Ivan came up with a contest to prove his theory about the differing senses of time. He explained the rules, saying, "Okay, while we're sitting here doing nothing else but waiting, I'll start three stopwatches at the same time and say 'go'! We'll each have a chance to shout out when we think thirty seconds are over."

This game sounded interesting, and lacking anything better to do at the moment, I decided we should all play.

With three stopwatches in his hands, Ivan began, "Here goes: ready, set, go … but we have to continue talking now. Jordan, tell us about yourself. Just remember: We're each going to shout out when we think thirty seconds is over."

Ivan asked Jordan a question, then asked one of me; we went back and forth. The questions weren't related to making commercials. They were just general kinds of things. After some time, as Jordan was answering a question, I said "Now." Jordan continued.

After some more time, Ivan said, "Now." Jordan continued … and then he finally said, "Now."

We looked at the stopwatches for the results. I had said, "Now," after seventeen seconds. Only seventeen seconds. I was probably thinking about how much all of the "down time" was costing, and how little we get to say in the short span of thirty seconds. Ivan said, "Now" in exactly thirty seconds, because it was just time, and he had spent a lot of his life timing things like thirty-second increments. Jordan said, "Now," after forty-five seconds, because that's the amount of copy that he *wanted* to put into the thirty-second spot.

It was all about thirty seconds—a sacrosanct number in the advertising business. And there we were, three people—to whom thirty seconds meant a whole lot—with totally different ideas on what thirty seconds actually *was*. None of it was a lot of time, but our sense of it was very different.

For a holiday gift that year, I bought Jordan a stopwatch.

TIME MOVES ON

One final point about time: the older you get, the more you realize how precious time is and how invincible you're not. If you're between twenty and thirty, you're probably rolling your eyes hearing this—yet again—from some old guy. But it's very true and if by noting it here I can help just one person "get it," then it's worth it.

Time in the Balance

Given that time is what you've got, it makes sense to learn how to use it, how to use it well, and how to balance different aspects of your life in relation to it. The following strategies—don't follow the crowd, do one thing at a time (at least sometimes), slow down, meditate, respect timing, and rethink how you spend your time—are designed to help you to get time to work more for you. They're not hard and fast—maybe more like soft and slow. They're easy to do and designed to help you be more efficient with your time—and to not waste it. And, as you'll see, they are all interrelated.

DON'T FOLLOW THE CROWD

Just because "everyone is doing it" doesn't mean that "it" is the right thing for you. As a teenager, you probably heard something along these lines from a parent or other authority figure who might have also said, "If everyone went out and jumped off a bridge, does that mean you would, as well?" Learn how to find your own path, to find the way that works best for you. It's not the easiest thing to do, and there are risks, but in the end, being the author of your own playbook and rulebook will be the way to go. How do you do this? By learning how to trust yourself, your instincts, your intuition, and your judgment. And how do you learn to do that? By trial and error (again) and with a little assistance from this book.

Here's a very practical example of what I'm talking about. Let's say you're in an airport and see several lines that proceed through the security checkpoint. Or you're at the supermarket and have to choose which of the checkout lines to queue up in. You're in just about any situation where you have to choose which line to enter. Do you go left or do you go right? The answer is, go left. Why? Most people are right-handed, and their entire world is governed by going right. You want to beat the crowd instead of following it? Do what they *aren't* doing. Go left. I wish I could tell you that I had this amazing vision when I figured this out. I didn't. I'm left-handed, and after years of going left, missing the lines, and wondering why, it dawned on me that the reason I missed the lines was because I went left.

The crowd is just that—a crowd. There is no wisdom in numbers— in fact, a crowd's mentality can be downright unwise or even dreadful. Establish your own rules, your own roles, and your own path. If, after doing that, your decision is consistent with the crowd, then so be it.

Do One Thing at a Time (at Least Sometimes)

Remember the five-minute rule? Well, here's a great place to invoke it, because I know that many of you cannot begin to imagine what I now suggest: forget multitasking and learn to do things one at a time. Use the rule and read on—please.

In a phone conversation with my daughter Emily (age thirty-one), I mentioned that one of the points I was going to make in this book was that multitasking isn't a good thing, and that people need to stop doing it. Her response was immediate and unequivocal: "Are you kidding? That's *all* that we do. In fact, while I'm talking to you, I'm also emailing a friend of mine, checking out something online, and listening to music on my computer."

My argument was: Try to learn to pay attention to *one thing*. Computers are meant to multitask, *people aren't*. While it might seem like you're getting more done by doing several things at the same time, most of the time you end up paying much less attention to any *one* of those several things. The effort that you have to exert to re-do something that you weren't paying full attention to the first time around is totally wasted, unproductive, and probably less "in the moment" than it was when it first came up. If you are present—focused on one thing, and then present and focused on the next thing, and then the next thing—you're going to be far more productive than you would have been had you been doing them all at the same time. So do one thing well. Then go out and do the next one thing well. And so on, and so on. It may seem like a risk (that you're losing time, not doing what everyone else is), but try it.

My argument was a retelling of something I felt rather strongly about. Emily's argument was a succinct reminder of the need to keep an open mind and "know that I don't know." In the survey I sent out to the advisory board, 44 percent of the respondents considered themselves "very much" multitaskers, and 31 percent considered themselves "extreme" multitaskers. So I was not surprised that, at a dinner with part of the advisory board, the "need for speed" (not the video game, but the general pace and attitude) kept popping up. As I thought about it, it dawned on me that this was almost part of the DNA of the group. One participant mentioned that theirs was an era of the microwave. There was no need to wait for everyone to have dinner together, because not only was everyone not coming home at the same time, but the defrosting, lengthy roasting, and elaborate cooking were no longer necessary because of the microwave. The microwave could be the symbol of getting things done in the fastest way possible. The discussion of what has been lost in this generational change is for another time, but simply put, it's connectedness.

Some participants at dinner mentioned that one of the advantages of IMs and text messaging is that they get the chance to cut out the BS and get to the point. They said that they rarely leave a voicemail message other than to say, "Call me" and that when hearing a voicemail, if it's more than a sentence, they tune out. Some said that they don't even listen to voicemails, just scan the numbers of missed calls. What can I say? Once again, just because "everyone" is doing it doesn't mean it's a particularly good idea. True, it suits life in a rush, but is it a good use of time? We've all found ourselves in games of telephone tag. And with voicemail and text messaging available, why not give at least the pith of the topic? Assuming your friends and colleagues aren't long-winded, why not listen to the message? If someone took the time to leave it, could be you'll learn something by listening to it—in terms of time, we're only talking about a few seconds.

In fact, we've always multitasked to some degree in our lives (and long before cell phones and other gadgets) but the multitasking usually involved only one piece of technology. (Talking on the phone and washing the dishes, for example.) Technology has allowed us to take it to another level. Since it's now possible to have several technology-based events happen simultaneously, the next logical step might be to *do* them at the same time. Taken separately, these new technologies have produced on the promise of improving the productivity in our lives. The problem is that for some reason, we have decided to use all of these wonderful devices at the same time—whether we're exercising, having coffee (at home or at the local beanery), en route to a meeting, in a meeting, or even on vacation. Fast-moving video games, television programs with multi-visual messages happening at the same time, the ever-present crawl at the bottom of the screen, PDAs, emails, and instant messaging have all created a situation where one rarely has the *chance* to do one thing at a time. But that doesn't negate the benefits of at least *trying* to do one thing at a time.

I've moved away from my former stance on multitasking, which was to offer three words—stop doing it—and then an explanation. Instead, I offer a compromise: Let's not look at this as an "always or never" situation; let's think of it as one of those "in the moment" things. And again, just because "everyone" is doing it doesn't make it right.

Here's one example. How often have you witnessed a driver totally run a red light while talking on the cell phone? That potential consequence is possibly fatal and the message should be clear: using the cell phone while driving has potential for serious trouble; therefore, in *that* moment, it's better to choose one over the other, or at least use your headset or speakerphone and keep both hands on the wheel.

Here's another, more subtle example. Let's say a friend wants to share some good news with you, face to face. As a way to show your support for your friend, it might be a good idea for you to turn off your cell phone (or at least turn it to vibrate) and not multitask for that time. Think about the shoe being on the other foot, in different circumstances. This time it's your news, and it's bad news, not good. You have something that's personally really disturbing that you want to share with your friend. You sit down, face-to-face, and begin to talk. Suddenly, his phone rings, and he answers it. Not only does he answer, but as he speaks, you realize that the call is pretty inconsequential. How would you feel?

And here's something in between for you to try as an experiment. The next time you begin a routine task—something you have to do often, like paying bills—try to *not* multitask while doing it. Notice the result. Did you do it faster? With less effort? Did it take less time? The important thing for you to do is to just *try* it—then be the judge.

Maybe children raised today amid technology's latest wonders will become more used to multitasking, but will they be more efficient? Time will tell. In the interim, I can be quite certain that for me, being in the moment and doing one thing at a time will often yield more productive results than doing several things at the same time. Whether it will for you is something for you to determine. Just try the experiment of doing one thing—*any* one thing—without doing something else. Make a concerted effort to stop and decide when multitasking is appropriate and when it isn't. If the supposed point of multitasking is to get more done in less time, the next tip may surprise you even more.

SLOW DOWN

This section is all about getting less done in less time, by learning how to slow down. It's not a typo, and you didn't read it incorrectly; it really is "less done in less time." Moving at a measured pace is one of those things that comes naturally to our bodies. Speeding things up is one of those things we impose on ourselves in an effort to "get more stuff done." Slowing down gives you the chance to notice and appreciate the subtleties in life, to give your senses a chance to do what they're supposed to do—help you become more aware. Slowing down can also help you to find what's meaningful in your life and to help you to find more meaning in those things. The idea of slowing down is really no more than a call to do what comes naturally to your system.

In his novel, *Slowness,* Milan Kundera writes about how we slow down and speed up as relates to our memory. Kundera argues that when a person wants to remember something, he purposely slows down everything else around him in order to concentrate on what he is trying to remember. Conversely, when a person is trying to *forget* something, he speeds up time around himself in order to create distance.

I couldn't help but think back to some of the conversations at the dinner with part of the advisory board. I was still trying to digest the concept of not taking the time to listen to phone messages, of wanting to "cut to the chase and get stuff done." What I thought of as the "need for speed" may as well be part of the air in which many people find themselves today. In fact, much as the idea of speed kept popping up in conversation, many of the twenty- and thirty-year-olds indicated they hadn't been asked to think about speed before—and why should they? They don't see that contemplating the questions and attempting to answer them gets them anywhere. People seem to be in a rush—even if they don't know what they're rushing for or toward. It's "hurry up and get there" and without the "there" being defined. Or, as Yogi Berra said, "If you don't know where you're going, you might not get there." True enough. But when you take a little time to slow down, you'll see more and develop a better sense of your ultimate destination—finding the "there" there.

A good place to begin to slow down is to ask yourself the following question: "What is urgent and what isn't?" This question is "in the moment," meaning that you can answer it only by being calm and being present. It's another example of how the "answers" that you might seek in life are sitting there right inside of you.

Another good question to ask yourself is, "What's the rush to get through something?" Anything that's worth doing is worth doing well or at least with a modicum of intention and attention. Rushing leads to exhaustion, exhaustion leads to carelessness, and carelessness means having to take extra time to correct mistakes or to complete the overlooked details—both resulting in a waste of (you guessed it) *time*.

Finally, be conscious of getting trapped in someone else's speed and pace. It's possible to enter a situation with your own sense of calmness and order and get caught up with external energy and find yourself moving at the speed of the person around you. This can happen without your awareness at a conscious level. What are some clues to tell you that this is happening? Your breathing is the best clue. Are you breathing more rapidly? Is your breathing shallow? Is your pulse rate faster than it normally is? They're all related, and a dramatic change in any one of them is a sign that you're "out of body" at the moment. Again, figuring it out takes awareness, presence, and practice.

Here's a great exercise in slowing down and what can happen when you do. Give yourself time for a long meal by yourself. Make sure it's a meal that doesn't include any caffeinated beverage (coffee, tea, or soda) and that you don't have to rush or watch the clock. Sit down for the meal with no other distractions. Turn off the cell phone, TV, and iPod; put away all reading materials. This is going to be all about you and the food. Sit at the table and eat your meal one bite at a time. After every forkful of food, put your fork down and sit and chew—perhaps even count the chews to yourself—no fewer than twenty times before you swallow. Then pick up your fork again, with another forkful. Try to concentrate on the flavors and smells of the food and the noises that you make while chewing and swallowing.

It may be very difficult to rein in all the little voices, but by focusing on the process of eating, you'll end up slowing down. And if my experience is any indication, you'll find that you eat far less than you normally would. Plus, you'll walk away from the table more relaxed and with a lowered pulse rate. Think about the last meal that you ate. Can you even remember it? What else were you doing when you were eating? Were you just filling up the tank, or were you trying to be a conscious eater? I know that it's not possible to eat consciously all of the time, but doing it every now and then will help you to slow down and also help you to appreciate food.

A terrific resource for the idea of slowing down is *Stopping*, by Dr. David Kundtz. Dr. Kundtz actually differentiates between slowing down and stopping and believes that slowing down doesn't work, per se. I won't split hairs and will agree with Dr. Kundtz that stopping (in my case slowing down) should "precede everything we do as well as assume a position of priority in our lives" (page 31).

MEDITATE

There isn't any way to slow down the passage of time, but there is a way that you can make the minutes and the days *count* more and perhaps be more meaningful. That way is through meditation.

Once again, I'm asking that you employ the five-minute rule. I'm not trying to win you over to an obscure religion or some wacko thought process. I'm trying to get you to think a bit out of the box. Meditation can help you slow down, help create an internal sense of calmness, and help you make better and more informed decisions. While the word *meditation* might conjure up images of incense, beads, or exotic music, try to take a step back and realize that it's just your judgmental voice taking over.

So many people spend so much time trying to get high—I suggest meditation to get low, to get quiet, and to get peaceful. Training your mind to tune out the noises of everything from outside traffic to inside voices is a challenge, but a very worthwhile one.

The cornerstone to meditation is breathing—learning how to control your inhalations and exhalations. Why pay attention to breathing? Think of it like this: what is the *first* thing you do as a being outside of the womb? Breathe. What is the *last* thing that you do as a being outside of the womb? Breathe. It's all the breaths in between (about a billion or so by age fifty) that determine how you are to be in the world. Think about it—if someone told you that you were going to do *one thing* a *billion times* in only part of your life, do you think you would want to pay some attention to it?

There are lots of books and helpful practitioners out there. Two that I recommend are *Wherever You Go, There You Are* by Jon Kabat-Zinn and *The Wooden Bowl* by Clark Strand. And you can try it on your own—now. To begin with, all you need is a floor, a couple of pillows and/or a wall (the pillows and wall are optional and might add to your comfort), and a little patience. Put it together and just sit. Sit and see what happens. Try to sit and be still without attaching any judgment.

Meditation in Ten Easy Steps

1. Find a quiet space.
2. Sit down.
3. Stop thinking.
4. Close your eyes.
5. Stop thinking.
6. Support your back by sitting against a wall, if you need to.
7. Stop thinking.
8. Begin to take slow, deep breaths—inhaling through your nose, then exhaling through your nose. Try to focus all of your attention on just this.
9. Stop thinking.
10. Every time you notice that you are thinking, relax and say, "Just thinking" to yourself.

Those are the basics, but truth be told, it's a little more involved. The hardest thing to do is to quiet all of the little voices that are in your head while you're trying to sit and breathe. While most of the time we don't even realize that the voices are present, they are generally what guide us (for better or for worse) day in and day out. They become especially present and loud when the rest of our being is quiet. Once again, it all takes practice, and once again, it's an example of finding the answers inside of you.

Mediation gives you the ability to be "in the moment"—to see with

> *It all takes practice. The answers are inside of you.*

greater clarity and focus. When you can do this, you can have increased control over situations, can see and implement solutions, and generally approach the world with a greater sense of equanimity. Mediation can also help you to get "out" of the moment, if need be. You might find yourself in a situation that is either tense or uncomfortable—something you have no control over—like a traffic jam. A practice of mediation can give you the ability to not become the traffic and the associated stress, but to simply keep breathing and remain calm. A practice of meditation helps you to focus on the "now" without getting too wrapped up in it. And you need no cool shoes, no colorful bodysuits, and no fancy corkscrews. Yes, it takes time to meditate, but the time you spend in mediation will provide rewards that make it worthwhile, including spending *less* time worrying about things that aren't worth stressing about.

And one final point about mediation. Like any other practice, there might be long stretches of time where you just don't do it—for whatever reason. If my experience is any example, after several days, even weeks of not meditating, getting back into it is quite easy. In fact, the first few times that you do it after a hiatus, you might find your "sit" to be especially meaningful.

RESPECT TIMING

There are three aspects to timing: your internal timing, your external timing, and the external timing of others.

Internal Timing (Yours). Your internal body works with its own sense of rhythm and timing. It's a very subtle and real process, so subtle that you are rarely aware of it. But through the process of slowing down, trusting yourself, getting quiet, and trusting your intuition, you can allow your inner body to do what's right for itself in the moment.

I have recently experienced a great example of the importance of knowing my internal timing. While I was working on this part of the book, I underwent some involved knee surgery (a partial knee replacement and ACL reconstruction). I understood that I was going to be out of it mentally for a few days and then spend several days alert, but not getting around much physically. I was looking forward to this time as a chance to get some quality writing done. I was wrong on all fronts. While the good news was that I was awake and alert hours after surgery, it was not the only news. The bad news was that I was mentally out of it for several hours a day for many days after the surgery, thanks to the pain medication that I badly needed. I realized that if I was going to get any serious work done, I'd have to find that short window every day in which I was alert, yet pain free. The process made me much more aware, almost on an hourly basis, of my mental state. The recuperative experience wasn't what I had planned, but by paying attention to my internal timing, I was able to focus when I needed to.

External Timing (Yours). Ego and its function in your life came up in the previous chapter. Here's another way of looking at ego: its goal is to remain on your personal payroll—job assurance, if you will. Procrastinating helps keep your ego working—by encouraging you to resist at all levels. It encourages you to resist change, effort, and anything that might upset your status quo. Think about the things that you procrastinate about. Chances are that many of them have to do with things on your to-do list. Maybe procrastinating about doing your laundry or washing the car comes to mind. They're good small examples, but what about the big ones? Take a look at the larger examples, maybe "holding off" on doing a paper for school or "waiting until later on" to lose weight and get into shape. Bigger yet: not being proactive about changing jobs, if you're not liking your current job.

Procrastinating doesn't get you where you want to be, and it's an enormous waste of time. The amount of energy that you can expend in *not* doing something is often greater than the energy that is needed to do the task to begin with. The psychic energy that you waste in worrying, thinking about the consequences, and second-guessing yourself isn't worth the effort. Put your ego to rest and call up your trust to allow you to move on and stop stalling.

External Timing (with Others). This is simply a fancy way of saying that you should be on time. Be considerate of others' time. If you make a plan to have dinner with a friend at seven, be there at seven.

Being chronically late is not something you inherit; you do have control over it. Try it. Likely you'll find that being considerate of others' time, aside from being the right thing to do (remember: we each have the same number of hours in a day) does actually help you both in the long run.

Rethink How You Spend Your Time

Whether you're a student, employed in the workforce, work out of your home, unemployed, or on vacation, how you spend your time is key and something over which you have more control than you might think. Depending upon your circumstances, some of these tips apply now; some may be useful to you at another time.

Evaluate Your Working Hours. Sure, we've made progress with advances in technology and the advent of telecommuting, but the unfortunate reality is that cell phones, email, and IMs have only made it easier for *more* work. What used to be 9 to 5 has become 24/7. Sit down and create work boundaries. They don't have to be hard and fast—leave room for flexibility and the occasional "emergency" at work. But if a co-worker is calling you at eleven at night to shoot the breeze about office politics or something along those lines, it's a good idea to articulate boundaries with that person. If it's your boss, of course, you may have to handle it differently.

Learn How To Say *No*. One of the greatest time savers in the English language is the little word *no*. The inability to use this word (or fear of using it) leads to overextending oneself, procrastinating on tough projects, and failure to focus on priority tasks. Resist the pressure to perform when you don't think you can do the job right. If you are honest with your employer, chances are you can arrive upon an alternative that makes you both happy.

Look at Your Workspace. If you arrange your work environment in a haphazard and cluttered way, chances are the work that comes out of it is going to be haphazard and cluttered. (Kind of "garbage in, garbage out.") While there is no need to be a neat freak, you can be more productive and waste less time if you are organized.

You can also alter the dynamics of your workspace by doing some simple maneuvering. If you have your own desk in an office, consider *where* your desk is. Can it be moved elsewhere? Sometimes a change of scenery in the room can be energizing. Sometimes, it can also make you more efficient. Move the things on your desk to a different place, to clear the desk and make for a clear surface. Is your phone on the right or the left? Consider this relative to whether you're right-handed or left-handed. It makes a difference when you need to talk and write. Reduce clutter. Is there any reason for piles of papers when those same documents are stored on your computer?

Consider changing the writing materials you work with often. Try something new—new legal pads (they come in different shades), new ink colors, new fonts on your PC—it'll change your whole perspective.

In the overall scheme of things, these are small time savers that can be used to make you more efficient and even more settled in your space. But everything contributes to the whole. On a much larger scale, consider your work in and of itself. If you're working at a job that you don't like, no amount of organizational schemes or furniture rearranging is going to change it. If you're working at a job that you don't like, there is little else that can measure up in terms of wasting your time. Further analysis of the workplace and your place in it is coming in the next chapter. Stay tuned.

What about Free Time? To begin with, forget about the notion of free time. There is no such thing. It's all time, and it all counts. And, as already established, you don't know how much of it you have. Think of free time more like "down" time, which is a necessary part of life. The question is: how much down time do you really need?

Anything you do in your down time is fine. Where many people go astray is how much time they're spending on any one thing. Think of video games. While they're good for hand-eye coordination, fun to play, and a great way to let off steam, playing several hours at a sitting can waste a lot of time. How often do you sit down to do work using the Internet and find yourself aimlessly surfing from one unrelated site to another? It's very easy to get lost, and the next thing you know, your work time has become a lot of down time.

Consider Facebook (and similar social-networking sites) and how much time you spend on it. In an article in the *Washington Post* on December 2, 2007, "Getting to Not Know You," Felipe Schrieberg, a student at the University of St. Andrews in Scotland, explained how he found himself logging in five times a day, reuniting with childhood friends as well as friends of friends of friends—out to people he would neither recognize nor converse with in the real world. Then, finally, during a summer internship, Schrieberg's boss (having viewed *his* profile) unnerved him when he commented on Schrieberg's personal status and movie preferences. Schrieberg reassessed how much information he'd provide on Facebook, stopped updating it and checking it incessantly, and discovered he had a lot more time—time he's since used to meet people face-to-face.

You'll have to self-monitor how you spend your time. A good place to start is to designate the time and the duration of down time and stick to those limits. It's called practicing discipline. Remember that all we have is time—and, it seems, there's not enough of it. So use it well.

Here's one final idea about remembering to have time work for you. The next time someone asks you what time it is, try saying (probably to yourself), "It's now."

When Time Is Up

One day, your time will be over. You're not immortal. You don't have all the time in the world. What do you want to leave behind? Have you thought about your legacy? Have you thought about what endures? What is your passion? Have you thought about what exactly you are going to give back? These are all good questions to consider *now,* because you can start doing something about your legacy *today.* A meaningful, lasting legacy may take many forms—children, grandchildren, a business, an idea, a book, a home … some piece of yourself. It doesn't have to be money or even require money. It can be your time, your experience, or your knowledge. At its core, a real legacy is that piece of yourself that makes

> *You're not immortal. You don't have all the time in the world.*

a difference in the big puzzle of the universe. We all have a piece to contribute. It's up to us to fashion it and put it into place. In order to have the legacy, you have to be conscious of your behavior, your time, and your goals. Now is the time to think about your legacy. It may be a big piece or a small piece—and each piece matters.

Lesson Learned: Legacies

My Aunt Ethel left me a number of legacies. It turns out that in addition to teaching me to try, not to succumb to mental blocks, and assume that I couldn't do something (the story of getting me to paint, as mentioned in chapter 2, is just one example), my Aunt Ethel also taught me about the value of time—my time and other people's. And in the process, she also taught me about confidence and not selling yourself short.

When I graduated from college, I had no idea what I wanted to do, so I moved home to sort out my possibilities. I went to work at Boston Hardware, the family's store. The second floor of the store was mostly my domain—the carpet department. Customers would choose what they wanted from the large rolls of discontinued or irregular carpets, we'd cut the appropriate amount off of the roll, and that was it. But the real money maker for the second floor—and for the entire store—was my Aunt Ethel's interior design business. In her small second-floor studio, she generated nearly half the store's income and considerably more than half of the profits.

Ethel was bright, brash, and afraid of nothing. She was talented and not at all shy about it. She decorated the finest homes in the area and beyond—including homes in New Jersey and Manhattan. Her clients would schlep for hours to come to Hazleton for her advice and expertise. Often, Ethel would confer with me for carpeting questions and advice, more for show for her customers than to acquire any real knowledge. When she did, she introduced me as her resident "expert" in floor covering.

One day she came to me to inquire about a particular roll of carpeting that was in stock and selling for $9.95/yard. (Keep in mind that this was 1973.) She needed carpeting for the playroom of one of her customers, and she wanted to know if there was enough on the roll for her use. There was, and she asked me to set it aside and write up a bill of sale for her client—at $15/yard. It was a huge markup. I was appalled. "How can you sell this to your client for that price, knowing that they could walk back here by themselves and buy it for less?" I asked.

Her answer was short and to the point. "Because they are buying it from *me*, not you," she answered. She went on to explain that the store was entitled to the extra income because of her expertise (and of course implying that in buying it from me, they *weren't* getting the same expertise). Part of what her customers were buying was her vast knowledge and experience, and their time savings. "Your knowledge is worth something. Never sell yourself short," she said. Her voice, and her advice, have stayed with me ever since.

There's also an important legacy that my father, Aaron Goldman, provided to me. He was from a generation of men who naturally picked up where *their* fathers had left off. His father, my grandfather,

Sam Goldman, had opened the first Boston Hardware store in West Hazleton, Pennsylvania, in 1912, and his second store in Hazleton a few years later. (It would seem that the multi-store gene is in my DNA.)

The stock market crashed in 1929, followed by the Great Depression. Consumer demand from 1929 to 1941 was low, and factories making consumer goods scaled back on their capacities, creating short supplies of practically everything. In 1939, a year after he graduated from Rutgers, my dad returned to Hazleton to help out at Boston Hardware, which was struggling to stay afloat. By all accounts, the best plan then would have been to declare bankruptcy, but my dad wouldn't allow it. Instead, he worked with the suppliers of the store to continue to ship merchandise, but by 1941, that struggle became almost secondary as the U.S. entered World War II, placing even *more* demand on supplies of practically all consumer goods and the materials needed to make them. The resulting pressure on retail stores, such as Boston Hardware, was crushing.

In 1942, my dad enlisted in the Army and made an unheard of deal with all of the suppliers (somewhere between forty and fifty companies). He devised a fifty-month deferred payment plan— paying everyone 2 percent each month of the balance owed them. The transaction was accomplished with no attorneys, just with a lot of promises. My dad ended up "minding the store" while he was off in Europe, fighting the war. His choices in all of this mess? Just this: he chose to enlist (the alternative was being drafted), and he chose to pay the suppliers. He had his own dream, which was not Boston Hardware, but continued the family business through difficult times, war, and military service. It could not have been easy for Dad, but it was a given.

Having not had—or not felt he had—a choice, my father's legacy to me was choice. While there was certainly a lot to be said about the family business and the legacy that I might have inherited, the real legacy for me was not the business per se; it was the clear message that my father constantly gave me about choices. The message was that I had a choice—I could choose the business, or I could choose anything and everything else. How did I know this? He simply stated this option repeatedly. Dad had no choice, and he made sure that all three of his children knew that they did. And while none of us chose to remain in Hazleton and take over the store, there is no way that any of us could have (or would have) even attempted to live our dreams if it weren't for this precious legacy that he gave us: choice and thus the time to pursue our own dreams. And, having been raised in business, we all knew there was work ahead, whatever our dreams entailed.

5

You Are Going
to Have to Work

OVER THE COURSE OF YOUR life, the one thing that you're going to do that will take up most of your time and much of your energy and that, in the long run, will be what ultimately defines who you are is the work that you do. It is also a large part of the meaning of your life. It is the way in which you can draw out and exercise your unique qualities in order to expand your consciousness and in order to leave your mark on the world. Whether you work for yourself or are part of a company with thousands of workers, work is the portal to the rest of your life.

And while it is often not referred to as work, parenting definitely falls in this category. It is, without a doubt, the most difficult work that there is. It is a "job" that requires extraordinarily long hours, pays no money (in fact, requires your money, constantly), grabs at your soul like nothing else you'll ever experience, and that, in the long run, will be the most rewarding job you ever have.

If you have chosen to be a stay-at-home parent and can make this happen in your life, I applaud you. There is nothing—nothing—that will ever come close to the meaning, importance, and satisfaction you will get out of being a parent. Unfortunately, because of a bit of misadvertising and a bit of misogyny, in many circles, "just" being a parent does not carry a lot of status. How often do you meet someone and one of the first questions you or they ask is, "What do you do?" If the response is, "I'm a stay at home parent," or something along those lines, too often the reaction is often a murmured, "Oh" followed by the next question, "What did you do before you were a parent?" as if the *now* of being a parent is meaningless. Far from it.

If being a stay-at-home parent is what you have chosen to do, wear that decision with pride. Your child has no idea how lucky (and I *do* mean lucky) he or she is. And the next time you're asked what you do, answer that question with pride, as well. If you get a dismissive, "Oh" in response, remember that the answer is more a reflection of the other person than a statement about you. And if you're so inclined, you might want to mention that if you do what you are doing effectively, you'll change a generation. The rest of this chapter might not appear to apply directly to you as a stay-at-home parent, but there are important lessons for you nonetheless. And one day, once your child is either in school or in some way less needful of you, there will be the rest of the working world waiting out there for you, whether you join in as a paid employee or in some volunteer capacity. This chapter will help you along those lines as well.

For now, whatever your role today, take a few moments to consider a Zen story that has taken many forms and been retold through the years; this version is drawn from *Soul Prints: Your Path to Fulfillment*, by Marc Gafni:

> A Zen master enters a village and sees people scurrying about. "Where are you running?" he asks. "To make a living," they respond. "Why are you so sure that your living is in front of you?" he probes. "Maybe it's behind you and can't catch up. Do not run to make a living, be still and live." (page 35)

Living and Working with Purpose

Everything that arises in your life is there for one purpose only—to teach you to exercise an underutilized aspect of your life. Because work involves contact with other people, the underutilized aspects of your life can become more apparent as you compare and contrast yourself with others. Of course, this can only happen when you're present. Sometimes this can be particularly painful; it's a natural reaction to resist and avoid those aspects of ourselves that are weak. But sometimes the most painful lessons are the ones that have the most benefit in the long run.

First, there has to be a you, and then there is your job. Similarly, as a parent, although you are responsible for the development of your child, you are still you. The previous chapters have helped you look at that being who is you; this chapter takes it one step further in helping bring that inner self to the workplace. The most important aspect in doing that is congruency—striving to match your inner self with your outer self and creating harmony between your heart and your head. When we look at the outer world, we don't see the world as it is; we see it only as we are at that moment. Yes, you're going to have to work, but if you can see that when you change your beliefs, you change the world around you, the chances of your creating congruency increase exponentially.

Here's a simple way to think about changing your beliefs and how doing so changes the world around you. Have you ever bought a car and then suddenly noticed how many cars the same as the model you bought are on the road? It's a pretty common reaction. But there aren't really any more of those cars on the road (except yours): what has changed is your awareness of that particular make and model of car. By purchasing the car that you did, you changed your vested interest in the car, and you brought a new level of attention to it, thereby changing your view and belief about that car.

The discussion of work in this chapter is divided into seven sections:

1. Why work?
2. What are you "supposed" to do?
3. What are you doing?
4. You are going to have to struggle.
5. You are going to have to develop discipline.
6. Success isn't easy or self-sustainable.
7. Are you going to be the CEO?

These sections cover work from the inside (how do *you* approach work) to the outside (what does your *work* have to do with you).

Why Work?

When you sit down and think about your life, think about this: the question is not what or why, but *how* are you going to live? Work is an integral part of how you're going to live and how you are going to be in the world. A fulfilling life is passion driven and a big part of that life derives from the work that you do. It doesn't matter *what* the work is. What matters is the passion that you have behind it and that you put into it. The same applies for the rest of your life.

Each one of us has a reason for being and a contribution to make; why not strive to make these more than financial survival? Yes, finances are important, but if you work at a job that just pays the bills without providing an outlet for your passion, then the ultimate cost to you is far more than the bills that might be due. The cost is compromising and stifling your creative intellect and wasting your time—a whole lot of it. Know that you can be in control, at the helm of your own destiny, by the decisions you make in all aspects of your life—especially regarding the work that you choose to do and how you choose to do it. Remember that everything counts: you will be at your happiest when you are expressing your essential nature and creating your mark on the world through the work that you do.

Do you always seem to have a "bad boss" or "never get a break" at work? It may have something to do with what *you* are presenting to the world. Your outer working life has to reflect your inner organization. Make sure that you have your personal values and ethos in order, and then take them to the workplace. The reality is that there are no bad bosses, and there are no bad breaks. And there are no victims—unless you choose to become one. **Stop!** Take a moment to re-read this paragraph. It's easy enough to read, but really understanding the content can take a

> *There are no bad bosses, and there are no bad breaks.*

lifetime. Give yourself an advantage and contemplate it now: what you bring to your work makes all the difference.

What Are You Supposed to Do?

Each of us has our own specific "true calling"—an answer to the question, "What am I supposed to do?" At the most fundamental level, we each need to feel like we are doing something worthwhile and that we are making a positive contribution to the planet. We need to be able to leave work at the end of the day, feeling tired yet energized because we've done something that matters and that our work outside the home has meaning.

How do you figure out who you are, what your place in the world is, and what you're "supposed" to do? If you grew up in a supportive family, you were told that you could be anything you set your mind to. That's a lovely message, but it's pretty nonspecific. If you grew up in a household with less support, non-specificity is the least of your problems.

Figuring out what you're supposed to do is actually simpler than you think: *do what brings you joy.* **Stop!** Think about that right now. If there were no negative consequences—financial or otherwise—what do you see yourself doing for work that would bring you joy? Is it possible for you to be doing that "thing" at this moment in your life? Perhaps not, but you've taken one important step in getting to that "thing" by identifying it to begin with. You can begin the process of getting there *right now.*

Is it easier said than done? Sure, but if you pay attention, your intuition will guide you. Sometimes it's tricky to differentiate between the voice of your ego and the voice of your soul. The voice of your ego is the one that tells you what you "should" be doing, based mostly on voices and opinions that you have heard and continue to hear from the outside world. This is *not* a helpful voice. The voice of the soul is the one that will keep gently drawing you to the things you love. When you follow your heart's desire and listen to your intuition, work turns into pleasure. Will it always be this way? Probably not, which is why paying attention—being present, quiet, and calm—is also imperative in your work life. What you're sure you should be doing at this stage of your life might end up being what you need to be getting away from five years from now. Times change, and people change. Getting quiet not only helps you find your *self,* it also helps you find your right *place for the right time,* by trusting your own inner voice.

What Are You Doing?

As you're contemplating what you're supposed to be doing, also ask yourself this question: "What am I doing with my life now?" It is certainly a pretty big question, and it's one that you have to pause and ask yourself often. Time, that old enemy, is moving on, and if you don't stop and ask the really tough questions, you'll find yourself very old and very upset that you've spent your time doing "work" that you didn't want to do.

When was the last time you woke up in the morning and were really *excited* about the work that you're about to do? Take a moment to really think about that question. Was it this morning? Yesterday morning? Maybe it wasn't even last week or last month. If it was last year, then it's past time to take a hard look at what you're doing. And read on.

If the work that you do is diminishing your ability to live an abundant life rather than adding to it, it is time to make a change. By identifying your unique skills and talents, you can discover the true meaning in your life and live more authentically. You won't be able to do this if your work is taking from, rather than adding to, your life.

If you're currently employed and wondering about why you're there, ask yourself the following questions:

- Is the work inspirational as well as perspirational?
- Are you inspiring others?
- Are you leaving others in a better condition than you found them?
- Are there people in the company that you admire?
- Do you admire the company?
- If you weren't working there and it was possible to avail yourself of your company's product or service, would you?
- Is the work complementary to the rest of your life?
- Is it using your abilities to develop greater capacities?
- Is there a place for your beliefs and values?
- Are your little idiosyncrasies welcomed, tolerated, or outright shunned?
- Does it just plain feel right?

If your answer to most of these questions is no, then you need to take a long, hard look at what you're doing. First, make your best effort to change your own position, and even take a stab at improving the culture around you. If you feel that you've done this to no avail, you need to develop your exit plan. I'm not advocating that you turn in your resignation tomorrow—there are bills to be paid and responsibilities to be met—but for your own well-being, you need to begin to work in the direction of leaving your current work and finding something else that has more meaning for you.

If you are a student in college or graduate school and you feel that you're in a rut or have answered *no* to many of the above questions, then you need to reevaluate your situation. Again, start from a place of changing the current situation—don't let "bail" be the default answer. Maybe the *no* answers have to do with what you're doing when you're not in class, or not studying. You're the best judge.

A degree is important, but if it comes at the cost of boredom, then it's an expensive lesson, both financially and spiritually. Perhaps you've chosen the wrong major; know that it's never too late to right that wrong. Perhaps you're trying too hard to graduate in X number of years and have overloaded yourself with courses; that decision is another wrong that can be righted. Maybe you're just burned out with school. Most colleges make it pretty easy for you to either take a leave of absence or to cut back on your course load. Take advantage of that flexibility in any way you can.

If you're a parent who feels like you have stayed at home too long, you have choices as well. How old are your children? Do they need you 24/7 or is there a way that you can get out of the house during part of the day to do something that challenges your intellect a little more? For that matter, given the wide range of possibilities on the Internet, you can take a course, start a business, or be involved in something greater than yourself from your home at any hour of the day—even at sporadic naptimes. You just have to make the commitment to do it.

The question, "What am I doing?" is not a question that you can ask yourself once in life and then be done. It is a question that you should ask yourself often—maybe daily. It's far too easy to get stuck in a situation where you are comfortable, where asking *any* question, especially, "What am I doing?" involves way too much risk. Well, know this: the risk, the penalty, for *not* asking the question often enough is far greater than the reward for ignoring the question. If work is indeed the portal to the rest of your life, and the way you can bring out your unique qualities, then you need to ask the questions to ensure that you are being and doing the best that you can. If a path feels like a struggle, is part of the struggle because it's not the right path for you? This is not to say that the path will be easy, but if the obstacles come from within, they may be telling you something you need to pay attention to.

And finally, one of the ways to find out what you "should" be doing is to discover what you *shouldn't* be doing. I suppose this is code for *get a job*! One way to find out what you like is to discover what you don't like, so don't be dismissive of jobs that you don't *think* you're going to like. And be careful of becoming a "professional student." Several members of my advisory board indicated that they were going to school because they hadn't figured out what they wanted to do with their lives. An undergraduate degree is important, but unless you know what you want to do with a degree beyond that, be careful. School is very expensive and very time-consuming; some breathing room and exposure to the working world after so many years in school is probably a good thing.

You Are Going to Have to Struggle

Somewhere along the line, whether you're taking required college courses, applying for a job, looking for a raise, or contemplating leaving a job, you're going to have to struggle with some issues and strive for your goals. No matter what the job, no matter what the circumstance, *you* are going to have to be your biggest advocate. The reason is simple: no one knows you better, and no one is going to look after your own interests better than you. The struggle doesn't have to mean anger, hostility, or fisticuffs. It can mean taking your stand, making your argument, and then listening to the other side. One way or another, these will be defining moments because they will make you look to your values to decide what's worth the struggle, if it's a battle for you, and how to live with the resolution.

Is the Issue Worth the Struggle?

Choose your moment, and choose your fight. There is never any shortage of issues that arise. You have to decide what is worth fighting for and when. How do you do that? To begin with, you decide by being calm and not overreacting to a stressful situation. Your lessons in practicing presence will help. You will also have to develop a sense for looking at the other side. In order to conduct a reasonable fight, you have to be able to get out of your own shoes and get out of your own way and understand what the other side is thinking. Your new habit of reading conflicting points of view (recommended back in chapter 2) will help. Remember that no matter how passionate you are about your side and your beliefs, there are others out there who are equally passionate about *their* beliefs. Understanding this will not only make you better at arguing your point of view, but it will also make you better at being compassionate, as opposed to merely passionate.

Is It Your Battle?

The comments about integrity in chapter 3, "Everything Counts," also apply to fighting. No fight is worth compromising your integrity, and no fight is worth risking the chance of permanent scars, either literal or figurative. You can always agree to disagree agreeably. Doing so requires discipline and a sense of maturity on both sides. You have control over your part. You might have to model some different behavior to make your point to the person on the other side. Keep in mind, though, that you don't have to win all of the battles, and some you should and can sit out entirely.

Can You Live with the Resolution?

At some point, there will be some sort of resolution. Can you be flexible? Sure, you can see your side, but how well have you seen the other side? Are you willing to compromise? Are you willing to move on, regardless of the outcome, and without holding a grudge? Holding your ground means sticking to what you believe in; and this shouldn't preclude new learning. Be willing to change your mind as circumstances and the world around you change. The ground moves sometimes; so should you. These are all situations for which only you have the answer, and that answer can only be dealt with in the moment—in that time that you're in conflict with someone else.

When resolving an issue, trace the history of the dispute and put yourself in the other person's shoes. Resolution is not about settling the score or getting even. Instead, resolution is about doing what's right and comfortable—and forget about getting even.

You Are Going to Have to Develop Discipline

Not doing something may very often seem to be the easiest way. You get a phone call from someone and you either don't know the person or you know it's someone don't want to talk to. What's easy way out? Ignore the call. You get a document or proposal to review, but you just don't have the energy to review it. So you approve it with nothing more than a cursory glance. You wake up in the morning and just don't feel like going to work. You go, but without first making the effort to get in the proper frame of mind. As a consequence, you are so unproductive that your co-workers might have been better off without you that day.

The hard work is always in the present. The day you think the hard work is in the past is the day there is no future. You have to develop the discipline to work and to work hard, no matter what the circumstances. And you're going to have to develop the discipline inside what you're doing to stay focused and not let yourself be swayed by the "shiny object" or get lost on meaningless work. This personal discipline has to then be directed toward your career, to keep you focused on what it is that you want to accomplish and what you're willing to sacrifice in order to make that happen.

Success Isn't Easy, and It's Not Self-Sustainable

Decide right now that you're going to be successful, and decide right now that you're going to be able to handle that success when the time comes. "Ha!" you might say—"I should be so lucky! I'll cross that bridge when I get to it." If you want to design your own luck and put yourself on the path to success, start planning for it now. The graveyard of successful people who didn't know how to handle their success is full. There's no need for you to join them.

What really is success? Maybe a good place to start is to articulate what success *isn't*. It's not a big house, a fancy car, or a bunch of bling. It's not the American Express platinum card or the limousine. Success isn't easy, and once you have it, there is no guarantee that you'll keep it. So prepare for success by accepting that success does not equal significance or security. Success is, quite simply, peace. Peace of mind that you've done the best that you can. Peace of heart that you are part of something—perhaps a family—whose members support you, love you, and will always be there for you.

Success does not equal significance or security.

What might success look like? Is it giving your all? Is it doing your best? Is it getting the job done? Again, it's none of the above. Success is much more about the journey than the end of the road. It's about the experience of your passion. It's the satisfaction you can get from planning and then doing, and then watching the seeds of your planning and doing take root and create something that wasn't there before. Real success is the ability to embrace the discoveries and enlightenment you encounter along the journey in whatever it is that you do. Crossing the finish line is inconsequential. Or, as late singer Harry Chapin once wrote, "It's got to be the going, not the getting there that's good." You will never arrive; you're always, and only, just "here."

Who defines success? We all measure success differently. The best measure and the only one that really counts is how *you* define it. Before beginning a project, decide what *you* think a successful outcome might look like. Use that as your barometer—nothing else.

Then, what are you going to do once you're successful? Once you've done *well*, redouble your efforts to do *good*. Once you've become successful, you might have the money to give some back. You'll certainly have the expertise, so part of what you can give back is the knowledge that you've gained on the way to being successful.

At any point on the trail to success, and at many points after, there is always the temptation to take the easy way out. If you've achieved some success, chances are you already know that there aren't any shortcuts. But once you've achieved this success, you have to remind yourself of how you got there in the first place; surely it wasn't a single-handed effort. Remember to thank, appreciate, and reward the people who have helped you along the way. Have the self-discipline to do the right thing, rather than the easy thing, and hopefully integrity will intersect the two.

With success comes privilege. While I would love to contest that, it's a reality that is far bigger than I am. It's important to keep in mind that the greater our privilege, the greater our obligation to avoid acting special—more importantly, to avoid even *feeling* special.

If you're successful, then good for you! But just let it end at that. And move on. Nobody's *that* special.

Sometimes the road up the corporate ladder can be so consuming that you miss your original goal. You push and push to get that next raise, that next promotion, and one day you turn around and you've lost touch with yourself—and in many cases, you've lost touch with your family. You don't *always* need the next toy, that bigger house, or that office with the big window and great view. None of it is worth it if in the process you lose sight of who you are or lose your connection with the people most important to you. All of that is a danger if you subscribe to the theory that success equals money.

Are You Going to Be the CEO?

Just as money doesn't buy happiness, if you think being the CEO will bring you happiness, there's another bubble to burst. If you've envisioned yourself as the Big Kahuna, don't bet the farm. So many people want (or at least *think* that they want) to lead. But the numbers are against them. By definition, there is only one captain, one quarterback, or one CEO and a limited number of teams and companies. Given that, what do you do? Realize that there are leaders and there are followers. For the vast majority, the question is, how can you be a good follower and still have that role be consistent with the rest of your life? How can it be consistent with your values and your dreams? A great way to start is to attach significance before you attach meaning: be absolutely clear about what your objective is when you're getting into a job. If your values and your dreams are more important to you than a title, then it should be pretty easy to accept that you're not going to be the CEO.

It also helps to know a little about group dynamics. Whether it's a class, a fraternity, a club, a company, or a nonprofit, whenever you get a group of people organized under one name or entity, group dynamics are critical. In any group, the work that you do is an exchange between you and the group. It is an exchange of ideas, values, time, effort, energy, and sometimes money. The difference between successful and unsuccessful groups is the ability to keep that exchange open and productive. If people are free to ask questions and know what they can expect from each other, they are more inclined to be productive and content in their roles, to trust one another, and to want to share in a commitment to a common vision.

In any group, people will sift out to a leader, an additional person or two who lead in certain areas, some willing followers, and some followers who are less than willing, to say the least. If most people become followers, how do you become a great follower? To begin with, you have to learn to shelve your ego. There will always be times that you think you know more or can do more than the leader. What do you do then? You learn to make your point, state your opinion, and *move on.*

Some other tips on not only living with but also *being* a great follower:

- Recognize that being a follower is not a failure—it's a function. It's a necessary function, just as any and every other part of a team.
- One day, you are going to be *a* leader, just not *the* leader. (See chapter 6.)

- Within any organization, opportunities exist for any one person, regardless of rank, status, or title, to shine.
- Oftentimes being a follower means acting like you're the leader when faced with any and everything that you do. If it's your project, then you're the leader.
- You can be a follower without abdicating your self. In fact, being a follower can help you in defining your self—it's a terrific lesson in learning how to put your ego in neutral.

In thinking about being a follower or a leader, consider that it may be a matter of perspective. Are you looking up the ladder to see who's above, are you looking at the rung you're on to see who else is there, or are you looking at the rung below? Instead of worrying where everyone else is, try to reconcile yourself with the possibility that you are in the right place, making the absolute best of the resources you have available to you *on that day*.

Lesson Learned: Work, not *Rachmunus*

For several years, I was the person who planned out the buy for suits, sport coats, and slacks; went out and bought them; scheduled the deliveries; decided what merchandise was going to what stores; and finally, presented the buys to our employees in the stores. Needless to say, it was an intense job, but it kept me close to the merchandise and close to the stores. I always believed that figuring out why something was selling was easy; the hard part was trying to figure out why something was *not* selling. To know why products weren't selling, I needed to stay close to the stores, and talk to the people who were dealing with customers on a daily basis.

There was a particular manufacturer (not the Stinky Suits vendor) from whom we bought many suits. This vendor's suits were some of those that just didn't sell well—year after year. After speaking to the employees, I found out that the biggest problem was the inconsistency in the manufacturing of the product: sometimes the suits fit well, and other times, they fit poorly. Sometimes the fabrics were great, other times, poor. The sales force had basically lost confidence in the product, thus not showing it to customers, resulting, of course, in poor sales. I had told the president of the company on several occasions that the suits were not selling well. He was a good friend, with whom I often shared more than business reflections, so when I had to inform him that we weren't going to buy any more suits from his company, he wasn't entirely surprised.

That night over dinner, he acknowledged that he was also concerned about the problems that I had discussed, and he told me that he was considering leaving the company because of his frustration and because he felt like he wasn't being heard. He had an offer from another company and wanted to know my opinion about leaving. The owner of the company he was working for was a very tough man, and I could only imagine his frustration in working for him. I thought the job change was a good idea and told him as much.

A few months later, my friend became president of the other company. He called and asked me to see him on my next trip to New York. I did and looked at his clothing and found that it wasn't really a good fit for Men's Wearhouse. Why? I had an issue with

115

the quality and the price. He countered by suggesting that I buy something as a good-will gesture to him—the Yiddish word he used was "rachmunus."

I told him that our friendship was one thing and that our business relationship was another. I went on to explain that when I bought suits for Men's Wearhouse, I was putting my reputation and the reputation of the company on the line. My reputation was at stake because I knew that I had to "sell" the suits to the store managers in order to get them behind the product. The reputation of the company was at stake because the managers and the sales people had to sell the suits to actual customers. I went on to explain that when a Men's Wearhouse store manager wanted to know why we were now carrying that particular suit, I didn't think "rachmunus" was going to be an acceptable explanation for the manager *or* the customer.

What happened to our relationship? There is bad news and good news. The bad news is that we didn't speak to each other much for a few years, and when we did, the communication was tense and short. The good news is that time—as is so often the case—heals all wounds. After a few years, and after the suits by his new company had greatly improved in quality, we became friends once again, and Men's Wearhouse began to sell the suits. And after a drink or two at an apparel show, my friend looked at me, winked, and said, "You were right. Thanks." I wasn't sure what I was "right" about, but having my friend back meant more to me than knowing that particular answer.

It's clear that the work part of your life is going to take center stage. And once that you've entered that arena, the next hurdle is management—both management of yourself and yourself as a manager. After all, one day, somehow, some way, you will be called upon to manage. There is no time like the present to start preparing, as you'll see in the next chapter.

6

Manage Yourself First; Then Manage Others

THIS CHAPTER IS ABOUT MANAGEMENT: first, learning how to manage yourself, and then managing others. Self-management begins by knowing yourself from the inside out—an idea broached in the first few chapters of this book. And there's more. Self-management is about self-discipline—learning to know the difference between impulse and desire. It's also about establishing priorities—and having the discipline to stick with those priorities.

This chapter is also about taking control of your work life, whether it's while you're in school or once you enter the workplace. Yes, as I pointed out in the last chapter, you're probably not going to be the CEO—few people are. However, you are already *a* CEO—of yourself. So first, make sure you manage yourself well, and then look to managing (otherwise known as leading) others.

Managing Yourself First

To help you learn to manage yourself, I offer a set of don'ts: habits and traits to watch. If you find them in yourself, learn to take control of them, and make sure that you manage to best advantage. Conquer these don'ts with the recommendations given here and you'll be a better person, a better manager, and a better leader.

Don't Wait for Someone Else to Teach You

Practically whatever the task, if you teach it to yourself, you'll learn it better. The easy way out is to have someone sit down and parse information to you, kind of how toddlers are fed before they learn to manage using spoons on their own. The harder way is to go out and figure it out by yourself. This might require a bit of research on your part; you may need to end up asking a bunch of questions. It may be time consuming—and it's the right way to go. Just keep in mind that the only "stupid" question is the one that you don't ask.

When you're done asking and researching and when you've figured out something new, whatever it is, the next thing that you have to do is to share the knowledge—pass it along. Learn to be a mentor and to be helpful in having the next person gain the knowledge.

Don't Wait for Someone Else to Give You a Choice; Choose for Yourself

If you have to wait for someone else to make choices for you, in all likelihood, you'll have poor ones to choose from. If you're unsure about your choices, make the best possible choice given the information you have in front of you. Whether the decision is right or wrong, making your own decision will still be better than letting someone else make the decision for you. It's part of the process of learning.

Don't Settle For Less; Follow Your Dreams

Every dreamer pays a price, but so does everyone who fears to dream. The price for not dreaming or ignoring dreams is much higher. Every now and then, sit down and let yourself imagine. Let your mind go, and let all of the inner voices have a rest. Think about what the world might look like if your contribution to it was unfettered, if it was pure and simple and unbiased. Daydreaming is an important part of your creative process; allow yourself to do it often. It is the way to open your heart and to shut down your head. There is nothing to lose and everything to gain. Your head has all the "what ifs"— the obstacles, the speed bumps, and the warning signs. And yes, it's important to be conscious and present, with your eyes open and in protective mode most of the time. But it's equally important to do the exact opposite: to let go and put no limits on yourself. After all, it's only a daydream.

Here's a good way to encourage yourself to daydream: every day, spend at least five minutes looking at something that's several miles away, or even better, looking into infinity. Most of our day is spent looking at objects that are merely a few feet in front of us—like computer screens and cell phones. For many of us, the farthest that we might be looking over the course of the day is the distance that we look while we're driving. You don't have to live in the mountains or on the beach in order to look out at nothing—sit back and look at the sky. Let your eyes focus on nothing; it will help open your mind to doing the same. After your mind has done this, daydreaming becomes much easier.

Don't Sell Yourself Short—Ever

Don't doubt your abilities, and don't doubt your talents. Forget about what you've been led to believe by the media or people in your life. That's a journey that's not productive. As the American psychologist Abraham Maslow once said, "Learn to become independent of the good opinion of other people." Recognize your strengths, and listen to your inner voice; believe your inner voice over the voice of advertising or of others. Eliminate "I can't" from your personal lexicon.

Don't Accept or Expect Mediocrity

Expect excellence of yourself to begin with; then, with others. The minute you expect less of yourself is the same minute that your inner self will get the compromised message and start delivering less. Push yourself—always.

Push others, as well, in a gentle, affirming way. Push yourself as a consumer out in the marketplace. Let's say you walk into a fast-food restaurant. You're probably hungry and not expecting a lot. Does that mean you have to put up with something less than courteous service, a clean environment, and a warm meal? Absolutely not. As a consumer, you are entitled to great service wherever you go, and when you don't get it, speak up! The people running any business you frequent can't be at every location every day, and they can't always see what's going on, so they really want and need constructive feedback.

Don't Worry about Being the Best

Believe it or not, you just have to be better than the people around you. Do you think that Men's Wearhouse assembled the smartest and the best retailers on the planet? Not quite. The company *did* assemble the people who demonstrated the want and the desire to succeed. And the company did everything *just a little better* than the competition. There's a wonderful joke that relates to this:

Two men were walking through the forest when in the distance they saw a bear approaching them. The first man started to run away. The second man stopped and put on his running shoes. In disbelief, the first man called, "What are you doing? The bear is running after us!" The second man answered calmly, "I don't have to outrun the bear; I only need to outrun you."

Just learn to outrun everyone else. Instead of trying to be the absolute best, strive to be the best that you can be at that particular function on that particular day. It's the experience of trying that really counts.

Worrying about being the best can also prevent you from even *trying* new things or taking on new responsibilities. Let new things just be that—new—with no personal judgment attached and no preconceived notions of how they're going to proceed or work out and with no worries about how you might look.

Don't Ask for a Favor; Bring an Opportunity

A long time ago, my gut told me not to accept Bob Day's opinion that I wasn't ready to be hired by his advertising agency. In a nanosecond after hearing him say, "No," I was able to come up with a "yes" scenario and an opportunity that cost him nothing and ultimately helped both of us. The next time that a problem comes up, stop and look at it and let yourself contemplate the first solution that comes to mind—no matter how crazy. The worst thing that's going to happen is that you'll ultimately decide against it. Learn to look at problems as opportunities for learning and for expanding your universe.

Don't Hide Your Strengths; Develop Them and Use Them Well

You undoubtedly have some aptitudes you were born with and more that you've developed. Use them all. Develop your confidence in them and in yourself. Know your weaknesses, and use your strengths to overcome them.

Why do many of the most successful people succeed? Confidence. Learn how to *act* confident, even when you might not *feel* confident. Confidence is the result of the most important relationship you will ever have: the relationship with yourself. Like all relationships, it begins with trust. The ability to trust yourself draws out of you an emotional power that reflects outward as self-assurance. Being confident is reflected in the expression of your creative abilities and is demonstrated in your power to create. Confident people are in control of themselves, exude composure, and are emotionally secure relative to trusting their own ideas. One of the many tests of true confidence is the ability to stand in your truth against all odds. When you know something is right while everyone else is saying "No! No! No!"—that's confidence. Your self assurance, coming from the trusted place within you—deep down inside—is your truth. You will be tested many times.

> *Know that your confidence will illuminate the path to the next step.*

Remember: if you know *why* you feel very confident about your idea, decision, or direction, even if the solution is not *yet* visible, know that your confidence will illuminate the path to the next step.

DON'T BE AFRAID OF YOUR OWN POWER AND OF USING POWER

Power is one of the most misunderstood ideas. Many of us have had the experience of power, both personally and through the observations of others and dramatization through the media, and have been led to believe that power is a bad word. The *misuse* of power—the use of power over someone or something else—deserves a bad rap. The power that I refer to here is the power that is inside of you: your ability to use your energy to influence outcomes. Find your power and use it wisely. When you find your power, it's ... powerful. Honor your own gift. Don't run away from it just because it's outside your comfort zone. Enduring power—power from the inside out—sustains and maintains. After you have found and honored your power, you then have to find the fine line between power and humility. The question is—can you be both powerful and humble? The answer is—you have to be. The alternative—being powerful with no humility—easily slides into arrogance.

Don't Be Afraid to Share the Credit; Get a Partner

Don't buy into the ideas behind the old expression, "Lead, follow, or get out of the way." There are always many more options than those three, and decisions are not black or white, do or die. You'll learn a lot when working as a team. Or as Grover from *Sesame Street* said, "We'll have fun and get things done when we cooperate." The bottom line is that the sum of the parts *is* greater than the whole when there is teamwork. Successful players on a team are eager to ask questions and will get help from others around them in order to improve the team. Team players seek to motivate and inspire, and they put the needs of the group before their individual well-being. Your ability to ask for help, and other people's willingness to help you will affect your success more than you can alone.

Be part of a new paradigm of cooperation. Winning is something that you can do with a team. With a team, each member has a piece of the puzzle that can fit perfectly into what is needed. And the team doesn't have to be big. To make the most of your talents and time, recognize that you can't know everything, and take on a partner or build a team that's strong in the areas that you don't know. With a bit of synergy, you'll be able to create and accomplish more, and you'll find that the rocks in their heads fit the holes in yours.

Don't Just Succeed; Succeed by Helping Others Succeed

Success is not a one-person venture. Real success is inclusive of other people and also means helping other people succeed. Be sure to let other people shine. Successful leaders know how and when to delegate, as well. Successful delegation is about surrounding yourself with great people, knowing what their special skills are, and making best use of those skills.

It's quite a list. Certainly it's one I wish I'd had (and paid attention to) much earlier in life. As one example, time management somehow seemed unimportant and without consequences or penalties before my working life. So I have another recommendation to add to the list: Don't wait for any further explanation of these don'ts. Instead, make a point of practicing these ideas now, before more time passes. That's what it takes, as I learned early, and on the job at Men's Wearhouse.

Learning on the Run

Self-management was critical in the early days of Men's Wearhouse. There was always more to do than time to do it, so discipline in establishing priorities became key. By about 1976, the company had three, and then four stores; it was still in its infancy and growing. We had no "grand plan" other than opening more stores in Houston. We also didn't have the benefit of any of the fine management books that were written subsequently. We used what we thought was common sense and fairness in managing the company.

Back then, we did a little bit of everything. One moment we might have been discussing marketing and the next moment unpacking boxes and ticketing merchandise. If the manager of the store was out for lunch, one of us would come out of the office and work on the sales floor. While there were still only four stores, most days were similar. George and I would meet at the office in the back of store number one, make phone calls, sort through mail, and then head out to the other stores. We'd load up the car (or van, depending on which had more gas) with new merchandise and inter-store transfers, jump in, and go. We'd stop at each store, drop off the merchandise, and pick up paperwork. And we'd walk around: we'd talk to the employees, we'd talk to the customers, we'd look at the store, and we'd look through the merchandise.

This was guerilla research at its best, and a classic example of "Management by Walking Around" (MBWA)—the clever management technique described by Tom Peters and Robert Waterman, authors of *In Search of Excellence: Lessons from America's Best Run Companies*, in the 1980s. Cell phones were not ubiquitous, so while driving between stores, the two of us would talk about business—literally setting up the foundation for what was to come years later. We didn't put in sixteen-hour days, but we worked most every day, and even when we were not physically in the office, we were hanging out somewhere talking about the company. While we might have thought we were simply managing a small chain of men's clothing stores, what we were really doing was beginning to build something much larger and greater than either one us could probably have imagined at the time. It was, and is, an important lesson in management: we were managing each other, managing our company, managing our time, managing our expectations, and trying to manage the part of our lives that wasn't Men's Wearhouse. We had control over most, if not all, of it.

Managing Inside and Out

The lessons that I learned about self-management in those early days were important for me throughout my career at Men's Wearhouse, first on the floor as a worker and then, as the company and my responsibilities grew, as a manager and leader.

Know that one day, somehow, some way, you are going to be a leader—you will be called upon to lead *something*. You are going to be responsible for managing other people, whether at work, in a nonwork organization, or at home. Every day is an apprenticeship for that day that you become a leader. How are you going to lead? Start now. Learn now so that you will be prepared when the time comes. In the meantime, you *can* distinguish yourself so that you will be called upon to lead or manage. But before you lead, you're going to be *asked* to lead. How do you distinguish yourself so that you will be called upon?

Act like a leader by taking the initiative on new projects. Act like a leader by developing positive relationships with as many of your co-workers as you can. Act like a leader by working hard and not taking the easy way out. And finally, act like a leader by *acting like a leader*: by being the kind of person *you* would like to see in a leader.

Browse through the business section of any bookstore, and you'll find no shortage of books on leadership. Helpful as they are, these books are not going to teach you exactly how to lead. Leadership is not "one size fits all," and it's certainly not "one size fits all circumstances." But leadership does have a particular style. For some, it's an art; for others, it's war. Clearly, it's a challenge. And how you meet that challenge is the first step in what kind of leader you will ultimately become.

I prefer to think of leadership as an art, a war, and a style—all at the same time. Leadership is *in the moment*. There is no "right" style of leadership, because there is no "right" leader or person—employee or employer. There is *always* the right moment—it's *now*. The particular style is in the hands of the particular leader. What leadership really demands is presence, listening, and flexibility. I'll cover some personal leadership experiences and lessons and trust that they will be helpful in developing your *own* leadership style.

How Do You Become a Great Leader?

The Chinese Zen states that there are three essentials of leadership: humanity, clarity, and courage. I learned of these essentials through a book by Thomas Cleary called *Zen Lessons: The Art of Leadership* (at page 8). Yes, you'll find it grouped with today's leadership books. And its reliance on Zen serves as a reminder that leadership and leadership questions long predate the many current books on the market. Of the three essentials, clarity and courage can be taught, although not easily. It's the humanity part that has to be developed—with effort and over time, a long time.

To be a great leader, think of the most basic and cherished human values, values that start early in life. What do children crave? Love, attention, and recognition. Few of us get enough, and we bring into adulthood a sense of loss and sadness from this reality. For some people, this sense is overt; for others, it's covert. In either case, the sadness can be a drain and a strain on people's ability to grow. As adults, these childhood needs might be rephrased: people want to feel that they are respected, visible, and acknowledged, that they are held and heard. These needs come right back to love, attention, and recognition—all of which can be found and shared, especially if you're going to lead.

How can you do this? Again, there is no one size fits all. But understand that to become a great leader, you will need to be flexible, surround yourself with great people, learn from others, let others shine, delegate responsibility, nourish creativity, and reach out to the disaffected.

BE FLEXIBLE

Being a great leader means that you have to be a child, a student, a warrior, a teacher, and a parent—all at once. It's about being present enough to know what hat you're going to have to put on, depending on the circumstance.

- Be a child. You have to have a child's innate curiosity, the willingness to experiment, to not let the "past" be your guide. And you have to be willing to take risks.
- Be a student. Be open, be interested, and be always willing to listen. If you are, you'll see that there are lessons all around—especially from your co-workers.

- Be a warrior. Sometimes you have to go it alone—fighting for your idea, for your company, or for yourself.
- Be a teacher. You have to teach every day. This teaching can be literal: by explaining what you're doing. This teaching can be by example: letting others see how you manage and how you lead.
- Be a parent. The people who report to you often end up looking to you for more than leadership. At times you represent the authority that they might have missed in their lives. Keep their needs for love, attention, and recognition in mind and help to fulfill those needs in ways appropriate to the business setting.

In all of these, you need to mentally adapt to each situation as a new experience and remain flexible when reasoning and problem solving.

SURROUND YOURSELF WITH GREAT PEOPLE

Everyone has their own special skill. Think of that as good news and know that you aren't going to be—and needn't be—the best at every aspect of the organization. Find the best people that you can at every level of the organization, and reward them. Don't allow yourself to be threatened by someone, but rather be heartened by their existence. Leadership is about only one ability—being a leader. It's not about being the best, the smartest, the most clever, or getting things done single-handedly. By finding the best and the brightest, you can develop synergy at all levels. People look to the leader for how to lead themselves. When they witness synergistic leadership, they pass on synergistic leadership, thus strengthening the entire organization.

LEARN FROM OTHERS

You've got great people around you. Learn from them. Successful leaders learn from everyone, and they put personal power second to the overall well-being of the company. They know that management is not control—it's collaboration. Great leaders focus on the team instead of being inaccessible figures perched high on a pedestal. Leaders learn along the way and know they can never stop learning. Their information can come from many sources: formal education, business experiences, employees—and keeping their eyes and ears open all of the time.

Every once in a while, even if you don't need to, ask someone else, "What do *you* think?" Sure, you might have already made up your mind or have a strong feeling about the subject, but if you remember that there's always more information in front of you than in you, there's a chance that you'll hear something new. Besides, it's an opportunity to solicit another person to engage in conversation.

Learn to embrace feedback wholeheartedly. Be open to the idea that someone else has an idea that might be better than yours. Learn to learn.

LET OTHER PEOPLE SHINE

Lao Tzu, the Chinese Taoist philosopher, once remarked, "Of the best leaders, when their task is accomplished, the people all remark,

'We have done it ourselves.'" When I first read that many years ago, I wrote it down and taped it to my phone at the office, so that I'd never forget it. It is what leadership is all about: letting other people shine. It's about training people to one day come in and take over *your* job, so that you can move on to bigger things. If you're already a leader, how much more do you need to shine? Is your need to shine more valuable than the importance of reaching out and helping someone else? If it is, then whoever you are and however you became a leader, you need to step back and reevaluate.

I learned at least part of this lesson back in my junior year of high school when I was president of the Hazleton Temple youth group. It was a small group, and we were good—so good that we were voted the best youth group in our region (Northeastern Pennsylvania). This feather in my cap was supposed to lead me onto bigger and better things—like being the president of the Northeastern Region of Temple youth groups in my senior year. However, I wasn't nominated. I was shocked. I had been *sure* that I would be. I had a proven track record of leadership and success, and so as far as I was concerned, all of the parts added up. When I found out who *was* nominated, I was furious—until I spent a bit of time thinking about the whole situation, especially the person who was nominated.

He was a friend of mine, someone I had met a year earlier and shared not only good times but also good conversation with. He was bright, energetic, and had many qualities that I greatly admired. Even though other people encouraged me to run against him, I decided against it. Why? Because I thought he'd do a better job than I would have, and I told him so. Not only did he run, and I didn't, but I supported him in the election, and he won. It was a defining moment in both of our lives. And although we now live on opposite coasts, we remain friends and in contact with each other more than forty years later.

Long after this experience, I learned that sharing love, attention, and recognition is part of "team building" and part of creating the "family" at work. One of the most important (and, quite frankly, fun) aspects to team building and leadership is learning how to create that space that lets other people shine. It's that space that lets others wake up, realize, and appreciate their own special gifts and their own contributions. Let the people who report to you reach for their own stars. And be sure that they get the credit when they do. Don't worry about yourself. In the end, if all things are fair and even, their successes will reflect well on you.

If you can do good deeds for others from a genuine place of kindness and without expectations, it inspires others to do the same and makes the work environment a kinder place. Your selfless giving and credit to others are seeds that your teammates will return to you as blossoms. Make an effort to regularly thank and praise your co-workers, for the little things and the big things. The same applies for your partner and your children. The sentiments take only seconds to express, but will be long remembered and appreciated—when they're genuine.

In addition to letting other people shine, you also have to let them slip. They have to find their own space, make their own mistakes, and then learn from those mistakes. Sometimes when you do this, you create a situation where a decision is not the best decision in the short term for the company. Then what? My experience is that generally, if it doesn't appear as if it's going to hurt the company in the long run, it's okay, because what's equally important is the growth of the individual. As a manager and a leader, this is a decision you have to make—most often, in the moment.

DELEGATE RESPONSIBILITY

You *may* be able to do everything, but you don't *have* to. If you trust other people to help you out, you'll contribute to the overall morale and growth of the team. Even though you might not be sure that a specific person you're delegating to can handle the task, delegate it anyway. Doing so can be a great experience in stretching someone else's capabilities, and the task can be a great learning experience as well.

NURTURE CREATIVITY

In his delightful and informative book, called *Orbiting the Giant Hairball,* Gordon MacKenzie argues that, like a cat accumulates a hairball, an organization accumulates all its collective thoughts, rules, and regulations. This ungainly hairball becomes part of the corporate structure. Unfortunately, over time, any organization can get completely caught up in itself, like a hairball. MacKenzie worked at Hallmark cards for thirty years, so he can speak from experience about the hairball. However, he wasn't the CEO—he was a great follower and evidently a great manager.

The idea of orbiting means that at all times, you have to pay attention and make sure that you're not getting all caught up in the company "hairball" at the expense of your own creativity and the creativity of others. Orbiting means extricating yourself from the hairball and allowing yourself to follow your dreams and even your whims. A whim comes from the most creative part of your being that has an enormous amount of energy and force. You can always reject a whim later, but it's easier to change lanes once you're moving than from a dead stop.

REACH OUT TO THE DISAFFECTED

Learn how to love your enemies. Why? No one else is going to tell you the truth. It doesn't get much simpler than that. You are going to learn more, if you really listen, from the people who oppose you than from the people who support you. The key is listening. ***Stop!*** Think about it. Think of the people on your team. It probably seems to them as though it's in their best interest, and perhaps yours, to support you and your ideas. Where the window opens—if you let it—is when you can learn from the people who are opposed to your idea. True, sometimes others are opposed to your ideas because they are opposed to you in general, but most of the time, people are opposed to your ideas because they have ideas of their own. Those ideas are valid—just as valid as yours.

> *Learn from the people who are opposed to your idea.*

The disaffected—those people who continue to oppose you, especially those who do so vocally—are the ones with the potential create havoc. You have to learn to reach out to them. Doing so is the ultimate test of your management skills. The vast majority of these people are bright and decent, but somewhere along the line, they got lost in frustration, anger, or confusion. It's not an easy task, but if you can focus on finding the good in these people, you have a chance at educating and inspiring them. When you're successful at this, you will have really helped to create something great. You'll know it at the time and perhaps soon find that those "disaffected" are now the most energetic and eager members of your team. This is something I found out, in a big way, back in college, as the next story explains.

Lesson Learned: Turning Confrontation into Cooperation

In my junior year at Rutgers, I was president of my fraternity, Zeta Beta Tau (ZBT). I did it for three reasons. Ever looking for a way to make a buck, and ever conscious of the fact that I didn't want to saddle all of my college expenses on my parents, I knew that being president meant free room, board, and fraternity dues. But more than that, I had so enjoyed my sophomore year living in the house that I wanted to spread the word, not only to attract new brothers to ZBT, but also to polish up the reputation for all fraternities on campus. Perhaps, though, the most compelling reason I became president was that no one else wanted to. It was a thankless job that had only one reward: the free ride.

In the process of going over the finances shortly after I became president, I discovered a massive scam involving money, food, and kickbacks in the kitchen, which was the single largest source of income and expense for the fraternity. I was faced with not only confronting the suspected brothers, but also having to raise dues and board to cover the missing funds. I called an emergency meeting of the house to try to articulate the dire situation. But concern quickly turned to chaos, and I became the focus of several of my fraternity brothers' wrath. They were not at all pleased with the increased fees. At one especially heated point in the meeting, a fellow brother stood up and haughtily asked, "Is this a fraternity or is it a business?" I looked him straight in the eye and said, "For *you*, it's whatever you want. But you have elected me as your president and for *me,* it's a fraternity *and* a business." Dues had to be raised, and I had to deal with the fraternity brothers who had taken the money *and* with the many disenchanted fraternity brothers, who were seriously considering quitting.

As I began to feel the "brotherhood" unraveling, I decided to take a gamble and try to entice some particularly disaffected brothers into the fold. I had read about the success another ZBT chapter had with an ingenious idea for fund-raising—a dance marathon. I approached my fraternity brothers and convinced them that this was something that ZBT could do to become a better part of the overall Rutgers community. I convinced them that it was something much more than a weekend party, or any of the other aspects of fraternity life that some of these brothers so abhorred. I suggested that they work as a team, put together a plan, and see what developed. Although hesitant at first, the more the group talked and worked on the project, the more they liked it. The more they liked it, the harder they worked at it. The harder they worked, the easier it all came together.

The rules for the marathon were pretty simple: organizations on campus would sponsor a couple and raise money for that couple.

The winning couple was the one whose backing organization raised the most money. Both the winning organization and the winning couple would receive prizes, but the money they raised would go to the American Cancer Society. The marathon itself was made very easy for the couples to live through. The point wasn't to get them to fall over; the point was to have their organizations go out and raise the money on their behalf.

Everything for the event—the prizes for the couples, advertising, food, and entertainment—had to be donated. The members of ZBT solicited it all. We convinced Rutgers to loan us the gym for the weekend at no charge, but they insisted on a security deposit of $5,000—no small sum in 1971. This deposit became a bit of a sticking point. The American Cancer Society couldn't put the deposit up; doing so was against *their* charter. ZBT couldn't put up the deposit; doing so was against *our* charter. But, as President, I looked the other way and wrote out a check, with the assurance from Rutgers that it would be cashed only if there was damage done to the gym—and that, in any case, it wouldn't be cashed before the weekend ended.

My most vivid recollection of the weekend was a moment about thirty minutes before the marathon began. We had just finished preparing the fifty or so couples as to what was going to occur and sent them off to another room to rest up. Like dutiful soldiers, the fraternity committee members were busy with last-minute details, leaving me alone in the empty gym. As I sat on the stage of the darkened room gazing at the reflection of the lights shining on a mirrored ball suspended from the ceiling, I sighed, smiled, and shook my head, knowing that this event was either going to be a roaring success or a colossal flop. I knew that I had done the best *I* could. I knew that my fraternity brothers had done the best that *they* could. All we could do was sit back and wait. It was a scary, yet tremendously enervating moment.

My fear of failure caused me to blank out on the next two hours. The next recollection I have of that evening was being in a room adjacent to the gym that was set up as the central site for collecting the money. A knock on the door brought with it a demand from campus patrol wanting to know who was in charge. All eyes and heads turned to me as I sheepishly answered, "I guess I am." "We have a problem," I was informed. Dozens of potential problems raced through my mind, but not this one—crowd control. There were *so many* people in the gym watching the event that campus patrol had to start turning them away at the door. In fact, there were so many people in the gym that we couldn't get out of the room to see them. The gym was a madhouse, and the street in front of the gym was an even greater madhouse.

One of the other "problems" that we hadn't anticipated was what to do with the money that was being raised. Much of it was cash, and much of the cash was change. Several hours later, and long past midnight, four of us, with Campus Patrol in tow, rolled a footlocker loaded with money (mostly change) down College Avenue in New Brunswick. We knew that the event had been a smashing success. I, for one, had a new appreciation for the word "brotherhood." We were all tired and spent, but we knew we had been part of something really great.

From this experience, I learned a few things about leadership, lessons that have stayed with me ever since:

- **Reaching out to the disaffected brings everyone closer.** The brothers who organized the marathon could just as easily have left the fraternity. They barely liked the idea of fraternity, and they were the most vocal about the dues increase. By including them in a new project, I was able to re-energize their spirits as individuals and get them to reach out to other brothers for help and cooperation.

- **Synergy.** The entire event was organized by a handful of people. They worked hard, and they worked well—together. They had a common goal, didn't let their egos get involved, and accomplished far more by working harmoniously than I could ever have hoped for. Their efforts became contagious, so much so that the weekend of the event, nearly every one of the one hundred-plus members of the fraternity were present and working. It was a proud moment for all of us.

- **You can make your point, but you don't have to MAKE YOUR POINT.** The brothers who stole the money knew that they had been caught red-handed. They offered up no excuses or explanations, nor did they offer to pay the money back. I decided that the best thing to do was to let them quietly remove themselves from the fraternity. While the fraternity had every right to press charges, I didn't think it was right to jeopardize their futures. They knew they had done something wrong, and, as far as I was concerned, that was enough.

One of the other important aspects to leadership is creating something that is lasting. By taking positive action in the face of a crisis, we established the dance marathon as a fundraiser, one that, more than thirty-five years later, is still an annual event at Rutgers.

Yet another part of leadership includes effective problem-solving and creating an environment that encourages it. The starting point for problem solving is the realization that all outer problems have inner solutions, as you'll see in the next chapter.

7

All Outer Problems Have Inner Solutions

MANY OF US ARE GUILTY of falling into the trap of assuming that the problems in our own lives emanate from the outside. It's a natural inclination, but that perception is backwards; instead, life—*your* life—is an inside job. Everything about your life begins from the inside—inside of you—including any outer problems. And the solution to all of your outer problems also rests inside of one place—you.

Everyone encounters problems in life, but it doesn't mean that life itself is a problem. Quite the contrary—life is an experience to be lived. The necessary bumps along the way, and your ability to counter, recover, and learn from them are all part of that experience. ***Stop!*** Think for a moment about your own problems. Isolate the biggest one of them at this moment and ask yourself the following questions:

- How did it become a problem?
- Who are the contributors to the problem?

- Do you continue to do things to contribute to the problem?
- Who is going to solve it?
- How is it going to be solved?

Obviously, these are questions for which only you have the answer, but at a more global and simplistic level, there is one answer—you. You are the source of any problems that you have, you maintain these problems, and you're the one who is going to have to solve them. This is a "learn it now or learn it later" lesson—and you'll do yourself a great service by learning it now. This chapter will help you redirect your effort to approach and solve problems from your inside, using many of the tools articulated earlier in this book.

But first, a little side trip. In chapter 4, I talked about meditation and hinted at what was to come as relates to yoga. Well, here it comes. Once again, invoke the five-minute rule. That should give you enough time to read about what has become an important part of my life, and a way to solve mental as well as physical problems. Who knows? It might become an important part of your life as well.

An Inner Journey

We all have personal horror stories—things that have happened in our lives that, upon looking back years later, we said, "How did I get through that?" One of mine follows. As for the situation that caused the horror story, in retrospect I can now also say, "What was I thinking?"

January 4, 1998. There aren't a lot of times in my life in which I've asked the universe for a specific favor—one just for me. On this day,

I did. I asked for help to not to feel what I was feeling so that I could safely drive from San Diego, the place I had called home for two short years, to San Francisco, the place that had been my occasional home for the same two years. I needed help to literally keep me on the road for the long drive that marked the end of a relationship. It didn't matter that many years later I would realize the relationship had been ill-fated and misguided. In that moment, it felt like my dreams and hopes were over. I was left with failure and fear—failure based on the past, and fear of the future. The present was a long drive ahead of me to San Francisco, to begin to pick up the pieces of my life.

January 14, 1998. There is a belief in yoga that the teacher arrives when the student is ready. On this day, I was ready. Just ten days after returning to San Francisco, my misery and I headed over to the club where I worked out. I had tried to make it a habit to exercise late in the day, in an effort to exhaust myself enough so that I could sleep and again to not feel. On this night, after finishing my workout, and on the way out of the gym, I peered into the yoga studio and noticed several men and women on their mats, preparing for a class. "Why not?" the little voice in my head urged, and fortunately, I ignored the opposing voices.

And on this night, my teacher presented herself to me. Since then, I've practiced yoga and meditation with Kristen—learning a new way to breathe, learning a new way to feel, and learning a new way to approach the world. The pain that I felt on the night that I met Kristen didn't miraculously disappear, but my way of *dealing* with the pain began to. I had found an inspirational teacher who helped open the inner solution to what at the time felt like a monumental outer problem.

I can't promise any such wonder for you if you begin a yoga practice, but I can promise you this: *something* will happen. I don't profess to be a master or a guru—I am merely a student, who continues to practice. I'm one of the many people whose lives have changed because of the practice of yoga. As I began to integrate the practice of yoga with who and what I was, I began to find more peace and equanimity in my life. Yoga has also made me a better partner, a better parent, and a better businessman.

Yoga literally means union—union with yourself. Yoga is a five-thousand-year-old technique for spiritual development. It isn't a religion or a stylish exercise regimen; it's a way of living, by integrating three key elements—posture, breathing, and mindfulness. Yoga can help you find that place between your external physical self (your body) and your inner self (your emotions, your mindset, and even your soul) where you can develop discipline and find peace, serenity, and happiness. Yoga is one of the ways of unlocking the answers that you already have.

You don't need to be in shape to begin a practice of yoga—in fact, the most important thing you need is an open mind. Interestingly enough, through a practice of yoga, you will be able to develop a *more* open mind.

> *Through a practice of yoga, you will be able to develop a more open mind.*

To my mind, there are six basic aspects of yoga that make it a very attractive practice and spill over nicely to how you might consider *handling* your life; these are:

1. There's no competition, either with others or with yourself. The best you can do on any one day is simply that—the

best that you can do. It has nothing to do with what you might have done on another day and nothing to do with what anyone else in a class might be doing. You learn by listening, watching yourself, and being patient and kind with yourself.

2. Yoga forces you to stay within yourself, and it teaches you boundaries about yourself. It teaches you to find your greatness, one day at a time.

3. There is no judgment in yoga; you learn how to just "be."

4. The practice of yoga helps you to develop self-reliance, to harness all parts of your being, and to give you the capacity to take care of yourself, especially in times of crisis.

5. Yoga is about achieving subtle results, both physically and mentally. If you lift weights or do any muscle-building work, you can see the results in the literal increase and tone of your muscles. In yoga, the results are less obvious, but over time, you'll acquire a more toned body. Beyond the physical, there are the mental benefits. Find out for yourself—just once, go to a yoga class. You'll walk out of your first class feeling calm, rested, and with a much different perspective on the world than you had going in.

6. Yoga is called a practice. You will never see an Olympic yoga event, you'll never get a trophy for "Most Improved Yogi." All you will ever do is practice. It's all about being present. It's a great lesson that's fantastic to implement with the rest of your life.

Since yoga is a discipline of the body and the mind, its benefits naturally translate into your relationships—both personal and professional. Because, after all, what your life is about is discovery and re-discovery, and if these tools can help take you to the place that once was safe, then it's worth the trip.

In a certain way, yoga is a wonderful metaphor for a lot of what I've been trying to speak to in this book: not only are the answers inside of you, but they're also connected to a part of you that you may have abandoned long ago—your childhood. It is in childhood that you were most free, light, and perfectly flexible (mentally and physically). It is in childhood that you may have been fearless (or nearly), because you then had no frame of reference from which fear or inflexibility could manifest. Yoga, if not this book, can help you to rediscover that freedom and the light that you had as a child.

A Journey through Life

In your inner journey and your journey in life, you will encounter problems and find solutions. In order to be more proficient at working out those solutions, you need to first understand the nature of problems.

Encountering Problems

Among the many choices you have in your life, when it comes to problems, the choice comes down to this: How are you going to live? Are you going to live with problems and drama, or are you going to live in peace? Here's a little help with that conundrum—choose peace. Start from a place of peace within yourself and try to create peaceful coexistences. You've already been given the tools and two great practices—meditation and yoga. When you start from a place of peace, you set the stage for problem *solving* rather than problem creating. Not only that, but you also create an environment around you that is less problem-filled to begin with—one where you *attract* fewer problems.

Problems encourage us to invent solutions and draw out of us inspired thoughts and insights, but only if we are present and willing to open our minds to creative thought. Part of the nature of problems is to show us the parts of ourselves that are yet to be mastered. We all mature and grow at different speeds and what might be a problem for one person is something easily solved by another. Think of a problem as a "pop quiz"—it's going to generally come when you least expect it and when you are least prepared. Despite how it may feel at the time, problems do have a purpose. You're not better off if you avoid them; you are better off if you don't look for blame and if you don't label others.

Problems Have Purpose. There is a purpose to problems: they are a blessing on many levels. They are there for your benefit, to help you create, to bring out your creative genius, and to help you to grow. They exist as a way for you to constantly check in with yourself; to make sure that you are grounded, present, aware, and in touch with all that is around you. They require you to use your imagination and tap into a sense of yourself that you might not often rely on. You are always in a state of "becoming"; there is no endpoint. Can you be comfortable with being uncomfortable? You have no choice; like the rest of the plant and animal world, you're either growing or you're dying. Choose to grow. Problems are part of that growth.

Avoidance Won't Work. When you avoid problems, you are setting yourself up for receiving them back again one day, this time with penalties and interest. All too often, when ignored, problems tend to magnify and get exponentially worse. *Stop!* Think about some old problem that you ignored. Did it get better on its own or worse? Probably, it got worse. When a problem arises, attack it—with every bit of your being. You'll find a great lesson, if you pay attention.

This Is a Test. You are always going to be tested in life, even long after you're out of school. The tests may come from the least expected places; they also come from the places where you need the most amount of work, those places that are least developed in your consciousness. Have you noticed that the same problems keep arising in your life, only from different sources? Maybe it's relationships—you've been in and out of several but just can't seem to get it "right." That's the universe's way of testing you and bringing you back to square one—and you'll be tested until you get it right. Everything that you do, every thought that you have, and every outward expression that you make counts as a building block, preparing you for the tests. Hold onto your truth, hold onto your integrity, and hold onto your heart, and you will be guided in the right direction. Pay attention. Be present.

Here's a way to deal with a problem and begin to solve it while being "in the moment." I call it, "The mantra of the air raid alert." Radio and television stations occasionally run signals as tests in case of an emergency. At the conclusion of the test, the announcer declares, "This has been a test of the emergency broadcast system. In the event of a real emergency ..." Think of any problem as a test—only a test—of your own emergency broadcast system, of your ability to come up with a creative solution. Dealing with problems as they come up—not avoiding them—is your assurance of keeping the "real emergency" at bay.

Blaming Doesn't Help. What is the first thing you do when you spot a problem or when you see something gone wrong? If you're like most of us, your first move is to think, "Whose fault is it?" This question is usually followed by blame. And the blame is not usually directed toward yourself. Blame has a misdirected and tragic underpinning—it assumes that you sit in a position to dole out judgment. This self-appointed position gives you the power (as in negative power) to be ultimate arbiter of the behavior of other people. It's a terrible throne to sit on, because there is nowhere to go from there. Attributing blame is a no-win situation that leaves everyone involved depleted and reactive. Rather than start from a place of *blame*, start from a place of *solution*. Blame may get you temporary freedom, but eventually, you're going to have to confront the problem, deal with it in a reasonable manner, come up with a solution, and then move on. Skipping blame allows you to get to the solution faster and to learn the lesson in a peaceful way.

Don't Label Others. Chances are you label others without realizing it. Just as often as we needlessly label ourselves, we also place unnecessary labels on the people around us. How many times have you ignored someone because you've already labeled him as a "nuisance" (or worse)? Here's a novel thought: we're *all* a "nuisance"—sometimes. Think about this: "sometimes" is the same as "existential"—how we are in any one moment. "Always" is how we essentially are. Few people are nuisances all of the time. When you automatically apply "always" to people, you avoid getting to really know them, and instead, you make judgments about them from a distance. Learn how to *really* see people so we can better get along and work in harmony with them. Pay attention to the person you consider a nuisance. Wonder about the possibility that he might be your polar opposite and that there may be great synergy in that. Remember that the rest of the world and that nuisance are pretty much like you: we all want to be loved, desire freedom, want happiness, want to be visible, and desire peace. Be a generator of all of these, and your actions will come back to you with interest. Be a labeler and that will also come back to you—with penalties that can cost you.

People label others in interpersonal dealings, at work with co-workers, and at work with customers. In the retail business, labeling a customer is about the biggest error that can be committed on the sales floor. Every person who walks in the door of any store is a potential lifetime customer.

I once had the opportunity to explain this to the senior management of Bergdorf Goodman, a division of Neiman Marcus. The then-president of Bergdorf's men's store had asked that I speak about customer service to the group. In retrospect, he deserves a lot of credit for asking me to speak. It was an admission on his part that the esteemed store he was running didn't have one very important aspect well done. The president didn't know me personally, but he knew the reputation of Men's Wearhouse. I felt that my speaking didn't exactly amount to divulging any top-secret information, especially since Men's Wearhouse had no stores in the New York area at the time and our customer base was rather different. For my part, I was honored that Men's Wearhouse was so well thought of.

Two days before I spoke, I decided to go to the store and experience it as a customer. I went there with a seven-year-old boy who was the son of a friend of mine and who *really* had to go to the bathroom. The sales force in the store avoided me like the plague and were only too happy to usher us to the bathroom and then out the front door. The next day I walked into the store by myself, wearing a suit—a Men's Wearhouse suit, naturally. Strangely enough, I was treated the same way. The sales force apparently didn't think I looked like I had what it took to be a Bergdorf customer. And I doubt that it was just about the suit; it could have been that I just didn't appear to be hip enough.

The day after that was the day that I spoke to the senior management. Again, I wore a Men's Wearhouse suit and before I started my presentation, I asked the group a question: "If I came into your store today looking like I do, would you wait on me?" The answers around the room were, "Of course, yes!" My next questions were: "Why didn't you yesterday? Why didn't you the day before?" These were rhetorical questions, but I think I had made my point. It was then very easy for me to convey a basic rule in retail and in life: don't judge a book by its cover. A retail business is not the place to be judging people. It is about treating them all the same way—with respect, regardless of what you might think about their appearance or demeanor. In business, as in life, what you see on the surface is not necessarily what is really there.

The best that could be said about Bergdorf's service at that time was that it was consistent—consistently bad. As I looked out at the people in the room that day, I noticed that they all appeared to be wearing clothing from Bergdorf—and they all looked much hipper than I did. But once I had their attention I broached the thought that the hip factor might have been at the root of their judgment. My talk seemed to go well, but I had little feedback. I left the meeting wondering what they were going to do and knowing that only time would tell.

Several months later, I walked into the store as a "customer," and this time I was treated very well. Ditto for the next few trips to the store. Honestly, I don't know what Bergdorf did specifically to improve their service, but I know that they listened. Whatever they did, they did it very well and very consistently. I can only hope that my hour or so talk made a difference. Either way, I was just a catalyst. Someone got the message and made sure that the quality of help at Bergdorf Goodman was the same as the quality of their merchandise. With the problem in sight, someone (more likely many someones) solved it. Similarly, now that you have a sense of the nature and challenge of problems, you're ready to tackle solutions.

UNCOVERING SOLUTIONS

Embedded in every problem is the solution, and generally, it's a solution that you already know. What do you need to find the solution? Patience, your own knowledge, and sometimes a little help from the outside. And more. Before you can even begin to solve a problem, you have to recognize that there is one to begin with. This is easier said than done, especially if it's a personal problem (such as addiction). Recognizing that there even *is* a problem often requires you to be open, honest, and present with yourself.

Shed the Past. Once you've established that there is a problem, don't dwell on it. Instead, use that energy to begin to create a solution. If you're in a group situation, don't let the "collective wisdom of negatives" take over. This dangerous group dynamic dwells on the problem and not the solution, often making matters far worse.

When thinking about a solution, a great way to begin is to eliminate two words: *always* and *never*. What does *always* get you? "Why, we *always* do it this way. Every time we do *this...* we *always* get *that* as a result." Always is the lazy way out, the path of least resistance, the universal cure-all for unimaginative thinking, and the absolute guarantee of mediocrity. Allow yourself to thrive on change and invention, and it will make for a more organic way to solve a problem. And quite frankly, it'll be more *fun*. If there has to be an always, let it be always challenging the status quo—yours and others.

What does the word *never* get you? "We *never* do ..." Never is the guarantee that all conversation will come to a standstill. Like

> *Allow yourself to thrive on change and invention.*

the word *always*, *never* traps you in the box of no creative thought or expression. Worse, since with the word *never* comes the implied threat of reprisal if you actually *do* break a rule.

If you want to create new paradigms for your life, one of the best ways to do so is to break free of the past. The only way to change the future is to not bring the past into the present. The very concepts of always and never are rooted in the past. Learn to invent present solutions to create a better future.

Calm, Quiet Confidence for the Future. Sometimes the solution to a problem arrives with quiet and inner confidence. Every now and then you don't have to bowl people over with your knowledge or your thoughts; sometimes just being yourself is more than enough. While I didn't fully realize it at the time, I saw the value in this a very long time ago.

When I arrived at Rutgers for my first day, I realized one thing that would have been obvious, had I thought it out beforehand: I knew absolutely no one on campus. Most of the other guys in my dorm section knew several other people on campus. In fact, many of them had gone to high school together and had chosen each other as roommates. I knew no one—not a soul in my dorm or in the entire university system. I knew no one in the state of New Jersey, for that matter. I felt lost, adrift, and downright scared. It was a problem that only I was going to solve, and I had no choice but to move on. Shaken though I was, I realized that I could solve another problem simultaneously by reinventing myself. It was a chance to leave all of the labels I had grown up with back in Hazleton and start with a clean slate in New Brunswick. Even so, settling into my dorm room and meeting my roommate and everyone else in the dorm was overwhelming. As a classic small-town boy thrown into the big school environment, I was dazed but determined to gut my way through it.

The first night, everyone in the dorm gathered for a meeting, outlining the do's and don'ts of dorm living. Later, each floor of the dorm got together for a smaller meeting. We went around the room and introduced ourselves, delivering a statement of who we were and what brought us to Rutgers. We then had to elect a floor representative, someone who would serve on the board of the dorm, organizing events, creating policy, etc. There I sat, knowing no more than the name of anyone other than my roommate. Next thing I know, *I* was elected the floor representative. Four months later, I was elected president of my fraternity pledge class under very similar circumstances. Once again, when it came time to select a leader, the thirty or so guys all turned to me. In both cases, I asked myself, "Why me?" The answer didn't come until many years later when I realized it had been more than naïveté that was emanating from me; it was honesty and quiet leadership. By then I'd learned that leading with quietness and solving problems by just being me was all that I needed.

Stay Calm; Work in Harmony. When you're calm, you are most receptive to new thoughts and ideas. It's a great start to solving problems while working with others. Solving problems requires your internal harmony, and it requires you to be in harmony with the people you are working with on the solution. You don't have to be in the problem by yourself. And you shouldn't assume you know where others are in their lives or their problems. Instead, ask questions, and understand where people are coming from before you begin to go about problem-solving with them. If you don't get caught up in the problem, if you seek out help and guidance from others, often you'll see that the solution is a lot easier to find.

Give It Time. Today's huge problem might be something you end up laughing at tomorrow. Or, as my grandfather, Sam Goldman, used to say: "Today is the tomorrow you were worried about yesterday." Sometimes the best solution to a problem is to let it marinate for a bit—to look at it later on when you might have a fresher perspective—to make sure that you're acting, not reacting to the situation.

Moving Past the Solution

When a problem is solved and the crisis is over, there are two more processes to go through to ensure that you learn the most you can from the problem and move forward.

Practice Failing, Forgiving, and Forgetting: 3 Fs. You might have made a mistake that caused the problem. Deal with it, be strong enough to admit your mistake, and move on. We all make mistakes—some are more magnificent than others.

If the mistake was yours, forgive yourself—you're only human. If others were clearly part of it, forgive them as well. They too are only human. If you really want personal freedom, then forgiveness is the path to it. We are all perfectly imperfect. Forgiveness releases you from the demons of guilt, shame, and remorse. If you don't forgive, these demons will eat away at you. They will steal the sacred commodities that you have: time, peace, and freedom.

Being freed from the past gives you the ability to forget. Being freed from the past gives you the power to be in the now—to be present. Don't hold a grudge—either against yourself or someone else. Despite your best efforts, you will make many more mistakes and if you let yourself get too tied up in any one mistake, you won't recover well enough to tackle the next problem.

Learn the Lesson. Take a step back and appreciate what you've done in solving the problem and realize the lessons you've learned, so that you don't repeat the problem. Certainly we had plenty of opportunities for lessons at Men's Wearhouse, as the next section highlights.

Lesson Learned: Stay Calm and Stick to Your Knitting

When I was the general merchandise manager at Men's Wearhouse, I tried to stay focused—and to keep employees focused—on what customers wanted and expected to find in the stores. Questions over the merchandise selection constantly underscored the importance of patience—especially mine. Well-meaning employees would often suggest that we sell everything from life insurance to surf gear. My answer was most often "No," and I had to politely explain that while we *could* sell anything in the stores, the real question was always *should* we be selling it. Then I proceeded to talk about snow tires, explaining that I believed that if we had snow tires in our stores, we'd sell them— but not enough of them to pay the rent and other expenses, and that snow tires weren't what the company did *best,* and that selling them wouldn't be enhancing the Men's Wearhouse brand.

The company was clearly successful at capturing the wallet of Baby Boomer men when it came to dress apparel. Many years ago, we thought: we're good at men's clothes; why not women's? Since we already had women shopping in our stores, either with or for a man in their lives, we thought it would be a natural. We very quickly discovered that selling women's clothing was *much* easier said than done. It was a disaster. We lacked the merchandising talent and had no understanding of how women shopped for clothing. We did nothing right other than have the good sense to stop and cut our losses.

A more recent foray into something new, however, turned out differently and was a great example of "sticking to our knitting." One of the things that I used to lose sleep over was how the company was going to attract the *next* generation entering the workplace. Several years ago, the man who was then the District Manager in Seattle came up with the idea of renting tuxedos in Men's Wearhouse stores. He had done some research and thought the idea made sense—or at least enough sense to warrant giving it a try. "Go ahead, give it a whirl," we told him. We created a small infrastructure to make it happen, and we began renting tuxedos in the Seattle stores.

At first, the employees in the stores resisted because we were also *selling* tuxedos. Furthermore, renting tuxedos was a paperwork headache for the sales force and a merchandising challenge for the company. It was one thing to sell inventory that was housed in a store; it was quite a different thing to rent inventory that was stored in a warehouse hundreds, if not thousands, of miles away. Both were examples of potential impediments to success—they weren't reasons for not trying to make an apparently good idea succeed. For a few years, the company stumbled as it got used to a whole new way of doing business. Soon enough, something magical happened: the concept began to work, the impediments decreased, in large part thanks to technology, and—as we had expected—the rental customer who came into the stores was a *different* person than the customer who bought a tuxedo and a person who otherwise might never have stepped into a Men's Wearhouse store. The rental program turned out to be a giant success, and Men's Wearhouse capitalized on what it was already proficient in—customer service, advertising, sourcing of merchandise, and distribution. The stores got to benefit from the tuxedo rental, additional traffic in the form of high school students renting for proms, and younger men renting for weddings.

By 2007, tuxedo rentals had become a business with revenues in excess of $100 million for Men's Wearhouse. And in early 2007, the company completed a transaction of a chain of tuxedo rental stores, making Men's Wearhouse the largest renter of tuxedos in the country. This was a great example of taking an external problem (whether the company was going to outlive its customer base) and creating an internal solution (expanding the brand through a logical merchandise extension). It was also a great example of overcoming resistance through tenacity and hard work and an example of patience overcoming force. It was a case of successful experimentation in something new that was well worth the effort, risk, and expense.

The lesson? Sometimes it helps to "go with the flow" and to appreciate that you control your own destiny. It's a lot easier when you have a little wind in your sails. That wind can be in the form of practicing presence, listening, yoga, or meditation. These are also tools that will help you implement the rest of the ideas in this book.

8

Life Is a Continuum of Beginnings, Middles, and Ends

Throughout our lives, in various ways, we are told to, "Stay calm and stick to your knitting." The previous chapter showed the importance of this advice at Men's Wearhouse: playing to our strengths was the difference between the failure in selling women's clothing and the runaway success of tuxedo rentals. But there is such a thing as too calm and too much sameness. Experimentation and every once in awhile reaching just outside the comfort zone are also important.

How, then, do you stay calm, stick to your knitting, and also experiment? The key is to understand that life is a continuum of beginnings, middles, and ends. The definition of continuum speaks to the thought that there is a link and a seamless transition between events. Nothing stays the same. You can calmly experiment. You can stick to your knitting while at the same time pushing yourself to explore the unknown. Nothing is static—and certainly this includes your own life.

In order to understand and appreciate that life is a continuum, take the long view and get some perspective. Think way back to what seemed like a very big problem in your life—maybe you were in the sixth grade and were worried that Sally or Sam didn't like you. In time, you managed to get through the crisis, and Sally/Sam is just a memory (pleasant or not). Think back to a more recent problem, one that in retrospect made the Sally/Sam issue insignificant. Perhaps it was choosing courses in college, or choosing your first job. Again, at the time it might have seemed monumental, but with the benefit of perspective, it's no longer that big of a deal. These examples are all part of your own continuum, just like any other learning experience that has occurred in your life.

The way our school systems are structured, we get trained to believe that life is linear. Things happen in a set order, starting at a very early age. You go to school and proceed from first through twelfth grade. After that, you might go to college or you might get a job. Either way, the next linear step is to find work, and perhaps find a partner. While that part of your life might in fact roll out that way, it's probably the last time that your life will be truly linear. The rest of life is far from it, but your mind and nervous systems have been trained otherwise—since the first grade.

Soon after you enter the workplace, your world becomes clearly separated. You have a work life, a home life, and a life that can best be described as your inner world—the part that deals with your personal development, if you so choose. It is then that you can better witness the continuum of your own life. Your nature wants you to treat all three of these the same—moving in the same linear fashion. But it's at this point that you have to extricate yourself from your linear existence and experience. If you don't, there is less potential for change, for growth, for effective problem-solving, and for rational decision making. This chapter will help sort out the continuum and give you the tools to deal with change and to solve problems.

A New Beginning: From One Continuum to Another

Perhaps the idea of life as a continuum came to me later in life than it might for others. I did, after all, have a very long career with the same company. Yes, my job titles and responsibilities changed dramatically over twenty-nine years, just as Men's Wearhouse changed dramatically over those same years. But it was, by today's standards, an extraordinarily long career.

In a sense, even my decision to retire was a continuum, albeit a much shorter one than my career. At some point, I no longer saw myself working at Men's Wearhouse. And I saw that the best thing for my *self* was to start thinking about something else to do with my life. By then, the individual accomplishments had become part of the collective soup, and the line between my thoughts and contributions and those of others had faded away for me. I needed and wanted to do something else with my life. Off and on for several years before I made the actual decision, I'd spoken about retiring—mostly to myself. Initially, I was sure that I needed to devise a post-Men's Wearhouse plan while I was still working, so that I would feel less lost when the time finally came. Then it occurred to me: I wouldn't be doing the company or myself any favors by musing about being elsewhere *while* I was still at Men's Wearhouse, so I stopped thinking about it. I trusted that I'd know when the time to retire was at hand—or at least near.

In July of 2001, I had a clear sense that it was at hand. Facing retirement head-on was on my to-do list, as well as a long overdue conversation that I needed to have with a once-close friend, with whom I had lost contact over the years. On my way to the office one day, I decided to just go ahead and have that conversation. It was far less difficult than I had imagined it was going to be. On the contrary—it was great. With one to-do down and another to go, when I arrived at work, I proceeded to George's office, sat down with him, and told him that I was ready to retire. No doubt my experiences with yoga and mediation helped me to sense that this to-do list had to be shortened and gave me the perspective to know what to say, how to say it, hold my truth, and be calm all at the same time.

George and I had a warm, truly genuine conversation about what all these years had been like for each of us and for both of us. "So when are you thinking you want to do this?" George asked. My best guess was sometime between two days and two years, and I told him so. George was amenable to it, although he asked that it not be two days.

In November of 2001, I went to a retreat in the middle of the Arizona desert to try to sort many things out. I had been battling with my usual demons—mostly around fear—fear of relationships, fear of failure, fear of not knowing "what was next." Against the backdrop of the events of September 11th, the importance of making the best use of life called for attention. The retreat was recommended by a psychologist I trusted and deeply respected. So I went, with no expectations and a fair amount of trepidation.

One week into the ten-day retreat, while at lunch with three other people and discussing something not even closely connected to me or to my future retirement, a little voice whispered in my left ear, "You can't get out of there soon enough." There was no doubt about it—after a week of no TV, radio, phones, faxes, or newspapers, after literally being taken apart and put back together psychologically, and after intense meditation, that little voice was *very, very clear.* And that was it. I retired in January of the following year. I relied on my intuition to guide me to a decision I had wrestled with in another part of my being for a long time. The little, but very loud, voice didn't hurt, either. The voice was, for me, an amazing example how tuned in one can get when one is very quiet on many levels. And through this process, I saw very clearly how the end of one continuum is connected to the beginning of the next.

Living with Change

One of the big differences between the Boomer generation and that of their children is the career path. Boomers have tended to stay at the same job for most of, if not all of, their entire careers. At the least, they have stayed within the same industry. Now it is a given that those starting out will work at several different jobs over the course of their work career, and it's more than likely that they will change industries as well. Many will change fields entirely. As we've often heard, this generation needs the learning skills to prepare them for jobs that don't even exist yet. All of these changes make for a shift in reality that's important to understand: to cope with the job changes of the future, you're going to have to be comfortable with both the concept of change and the *practice* of change.

> *Be comfortable with both the concept of change and the practice of change.*

Change is a constant reminder that you are alive. The world we inhabit is always changing— more rapidly than ever. Indeed, change is inevitable and an absolute necessity for the survival of our species and our planet. Therefore, it is in your best interest to get comfortable with change and to be able to do it quickly, seamlessly, and in a way that best suits you. How do you deal with change? You can change that too: like so much else in life, it's a process and something to continually work on and refine.

The continuum of your life varies by situation. For example, at any one moment you can be at the beginning of personal transformation, in the middle of considering a big job change, or at the end of a relationship. In a certain sense, they're all separate and have to be treated as such in order to deal with them. But at the same time, and in a more important way, they're all part of a thematic ribbon—your personal development and the reminder that change is constant.

Life without a Manual

Life is a learning adventure. And that's a good thing, for most of the really important parts of life aren't taught in any formal sense.

You learn by learning how to learn—by experiencing, by making mistakes, and by succeeding. You also learn by observing others—by seeing others make their own mistakes, and by seeing others succeed. As always, keep your eyes, mind, and heart open. The rest of this section presents a few areas to watch and to appreciate about your life and others' lives.

Life Is a Privilege. Regardless of your personal beliefs as to how mankind came into existence, one way or another life itself is a miracle—and a gift. You can use your gift of life any way you wish. You can choose to take it for granted, ride a wave of indifference, and hope for the best. Although that is a choice, it's probably not the best one. Another choice is to take the gift and "pay it forward" by leveraging your intelligence, insight, and experience into an opportunity for self-improvement and the improvement of others.

Life Comes with Responsibilities. First, you have to take responsibility for yourself. Then you have to reach outside yourself to help improve the lives of others and to leave the world in a little better shape than it was when you entered it.

Life Is a Challenge. Every day offers new challenges. Your life and these challenges require that you show up every day, ready to engage with the challenges.

Life Is Not Static. What is true and meaningful today might not be tomorrow. Life is knowing where you are in each and every moment (also known as being present).

Life Is a Process. Life is not a destination. There is no "there" there. Everything is all here—now.

Recognizing Fear and Overcoming It

Why do people resist change? First, it's human nature, especially when the change does not involve some immediate benefit. We all get rooted (and rutted) in who we are and what we do, and when our comfortable ways get threatened, our first reaction is to balk. When someone *else* comes along with an idea for doing something differently, our first reaction is usually, "Why? I've been doing it this way for …" In a situation where change is required, people involved will usually demand a reason for it. By nature, people prefer stability—and change represents a loss of stability. It has been said that there are only two things that are certain in life: death and taxes. I'd add one more thing—*change.*

The second reason for resisting change is fear. Fear is a natural reaction to change, but in the long run, it is not the reaction that serves us best. Pay attention to your fears; they hold enormous potential lessons. What kind of fear do most of us experience? Here's a sampling.

Fear of the Unknown. Nothing is easier to comprehend or live with than what you already know—even sometimes when what you know you *also* know isn't in your best interest. Fear can control us, or we can control it. Instead of letting the word *fear* have control, think of it as simply standing for, "False Evidence Appearing Real." If you can train your mind to *expect* the unexpected, you can let go of fear.

Stepping out into that place where you have less comfort and fewer expectations may seem frightening, but on another level, it is also fascinating. Forget the false evidence and go with the fascination.

Fear of Making Mistakes. No one *wants* to make a mistake. Mistakes can be embarrassing or induce feelings of guilt. But we are human, and we *all* make mistakes. Lots of them.

Fear of Guilt. Guilt is another ally of ego. The ego wants you to feel shame and blame for every mistake—big or little—that happens in your life. If you assume that on a moment-to-moment basis you are doing your best, you can stop guilt in its tracks. Relinquish guilt—you created it, you can destroy it.

Fear of Loss. Usually people fear losing something of importance or value, like money, friendships, freedom, or security. Also, people fear losing something they don't yet have or something they might really want to have. Instead of fearing loss, look forward to what you might *gain* by making any change.

Fear of Criticism. If you're being asked to change something, try not to assume it's because what is current is *wrong*. Try looking at it as *different*, instead of wrong—thus eliminating the voice of judgment. Stop criticizing yourself and others. When you criticize, you set up a hierarchy of "better than and worse than." The antidote for criticism is acceptance. Accept your own fallibility and the fallibility of others. When you forgive yourself, you set yourself on a path to learn to forgive others.

When you experience fear, instead of retreating, keep this in mind: fear is your soul's way of telling you that there is a great learning experience in front of you. If you have the voices of fear, worry, and doubt swimming around in your head, how are you doing to tame those voices? First, learn to accept that they are there. Second, remember that *you're* in charge—not the voices. Third, think about the fact that fear, worry, and doubt can be great motivators. Their purpose is to call upon your inner reserves and resources to experiment—to go outside your own box.

Resistance is one more visitation on your soul by your ego. Resistance is the ego's way of defending an opposite point of view. The ego doesn't like change and will do all that it can to keep you mired in your current situation, regardless of whether it's working for you. Pay attention to resistance. Resistance is also your body being stubborn. When you feel resistance, your body and your mind might be at odds with what you *think* you want or need to do. The body usually wins and says, "No" and you resist. Try letting the mind win once in awhile. Instead of thinking, try feeling—what feels good or right in the particular situation?

Practicing Patience; Finding Flexibility

As a society, we have been trained to expect instant gratification in the form of rewards or acknowledgment. Consequently, we give up easily to frustration when things don't happen the way we want or when we want them to. It's another aspect of the misadvertisement of life. Your life is not a sixty-minute television drama, where all loose

174

ends miraculously get tied up at the end of the hour. The reality is this: just because the world moves fast doesn't mean that *you* always have to move fast with it. And the rewards or results that you might get are not necessarily on your timeline.

Patience is the ability to sit and wait for the outcome that *you* desire—in your own time and without becoming frantic. Patience is the same as trust; we are patient to the degree that we perceive that everything is in its right time, its right place, and moving in the right direction. Everything in your life is not going to fall into place immediately or perfectly—so watching, listening, staying calm and patient, and making alterations will help you to stay on course.

In the practice of yoga, you can often experience physical resistance. Some days your body is not as pliable as others. On those days, you learn to first back off a little and keep breathing, as a way to find out whether the resistance is coming from your mind or your body.

While on the surface yoga is all about physical flexibility, at its core, yoga also teaches flexibility in life. By breathing and being present, you can train yourself to take life as it comes at you, but at your own speed and with the willingness and capability to make adjustments when necessary. Emotional and mental flexibility—the ability to be able to quickly choose from different options in the face of changing conditions—is the hallmark of a mature nervous system and the hallmark of a mature human being. To be able to, at any moment, abandon all fear, all predisposed notions, and all sense of safety can allow you to be truly free. But it takes courage.

Being emotionally and mentally flexible means knowing that you don't know everything, and realizing that there is more knowledge in front of you than inside you. You don't know what the other person knows. There's a lot to learn by just listening.

Embracing Change

If life is change and resistance to it, how do we get through? Here are two ideas to help you get comfortable with change and be able to take it in with an open heart and an open mind.

LEARN TO ACCEPT CHANGE

Take a deep breath, smile, and know that like it or not—for that matter, accept it or not—change is all around us. You are far from alone in this. It's part of the fabric of our society. Take a look at the things that have changed in your life whether you wanted them to or not. The most obvious one is that you have gotten older. Be more open to the fact that there is nothing you can do to prevent a lot of the other changes in your life. Realizing that change is a fundamental part of your life will make accepting change less scary and stressful.

Start with small changes. There's change, and there's *CHANGE*. It's like the difference between decorating your apartment and moving to another city. Think small before you think big. Try the following everyday, stress-free changes for a while, and you might then find dealing with the bigger changes a little easier:

- Change some of the music you listen to.
- Change some of the websites that you frequent.
- Change your morning routine.
- Change a few items in your wardrobe.

By *doing* things a little differently, you will then be able to *experience* things differently and discover new ways to think, to see, and to allow change to begin to happen. While the above might seem like insignificant changes, once you train your mind to get comfortable with them, you'll notice that you can get comfortable with some slightly bigger changes. Go easy—it's a process, but the more that you do it, the better you'll get at it. Understand that there is knowledge sitting in all corners—often even the least likely ones. The key is to be open to the idea and to listen—not just to me in this book, but to the next wild hair and the next idea. Just because an idea or a thought doesn't conform to your picture of the world doesn't mean it's not valid.

After you've taken the small changes, before you know it, one day you'll actually find yourself *changing your mind*. Yes, it's amazing, but it will happen. You'll find yourself on one side of an issue, and the next thing you know—bam! You're on the other side. You're actually looking at all sides of an issue instead of digging in your heels on your position. It's an invigorating and exciting process. Push yourself by starting with the small changes. Try to experience at least one thing as new every day.

> *Just because an idea or a thought doesn't conform to your picture of the world doesn't mean it's not valid.*

CHANGE YOUR WORDS; CHANGE YOUR OUTLOOK

As the poet Derek Walcott wrote (in "Codicil"), "To change your language you must change your life." How about turning that around: to change your life, change your words. I've already suggested that you delete some phrases and words from your everyday speech. Now I suggest adding some in. **Stop!** Think about the phrases "up until now," and "aside from that." If you can train yourself to say them any time a new idea or thought comes into your mind, or any time you are presented a new thought or idea by someone else, you'll automatically be more open.

How often do you come to a "new" situation with your "old" thought paradigm? "Up until now" is your reminder that every situation, although it may be similar to another one, is inherently different. "Aside from that" is your reminder that ideas are big things. Although you might disagree with a *part* of someone else's idea, if you don't allow yourself to get attached to that part, you can then move into the space where you can embrace the entire thought that someone else has. By doing this, you can learn to embody change. And you can learn to *create* change, by transcending your past and by creating a new and unfettered slate for your present and future.

Here are two other words to consider: "I wonder." Think about sending an "I wonder" out to the universe as a way to come up with a way to deal with change, and as a way to also come up with a new idea or, for that matter, to solve a problem. Picture the situation or problem and say, even just to yourself, "I wonder." You can make the "I wonder" be "I wonder how am I going to be with the change?" or "I wonder, what would a solution look like?" Sending an "I wonder" to the universe is essentially the first step in visualizing something entirely new.

Think of the old expression, "I'll believe it when I see it." There are circumstances when this phrase and the reporter's adage to "Believe half of what you see and none of what you hear" may be justified, but not when you're looking for ways to embody change or arrive at solutions to problems. In those cases, what about instead of thinking that you'll believe it when you see it, start thinking that you'll *see it* when you *believe it.*

Wait! There's one more way to change your words to change your outlook. It's actually more of a question—one that my father used to ask me. When you find yourself struggling or resisting change, ask yourself: "What's the worst that can happen?" Chances are that even the worst scenario is not that bad. And couldn't the reward be greater than the struggle or the resistance?

Lesson Learned: Look Both Ways—and Listen

I started this chapter describing my decision to retire. There's another piece to it. Roughly a month before I retired, I met a woman who was about my age (and therefore also a Boomer), who had retired five years earlier. I really wanted to know what to expect, and although I was prepared for anything, I also knew I wasn't prepared for *everything.* Her comment to me was: "For the first three years or so, you're going to feel like you're walking around in the desert." I really didn't get what she meant until I actually lived through it. And she was right. Finding a new beginning takes time and effort, no matter what your experience level.

In a certain way, that time reminded me of an old black-and-white photograph that was taken of me at the Men's Wearhouse store one (of one), circa 1973. The photo encapsulated the beginning of a new continuum in my life way back when. In it I have hair on top of my head instead of my face, and I'm wearing a bow tie and a very busy nylon shirt. I'm standing next to a clunky old cash register with a rather dazed look on my face, not looking at the camera—or at anything in particular, for that matter. In the background is the store—vinyl asbestos tile floor, colored flags hanging off of a maze of steel bars, and signs that shout: "Double Knit Sport Jackets $27.75," and "Men's Suits $44.75." A friend of mine who saw that picture once said, "Did you realize at the time that Men's Wearhouse was going to turn out the way that it did?" I thought it was a pretty funny question and answered, "Do I *look* like someone who did?" Of course I didn't know it then—how could I have? I wasn't seeing into the future; I was more concerned with making ends meet. But on some level, I did have an inkling, so a more accurate answer is yes—and no.

I was young and open to possibilities. I was aware enough to be a container of receptivity—to be open enough for ideas, change, criticism, and overall knowledge. I was able to live with an enormous amount of change—from moving halfway across the country, to encountering resistances at the ad agency, to experiencing a new work environment. I stayed flexible and patient. It was all a self-taught and self-managed process, one that paid great dividends not only then, but in the years to come.

I realized *something* at the time, and looking back over the time and the effort, I'm not at all surprised by the company's success. Over the years, it had little to do with my contribution or me, as more and more had to do with the legacy created by the next generation of leaders. I *am* surprised at how so many other people—bankers, vendors, the soothsayers on Wall Street, and even some of our own employees—were surprised. And therein lies an important lesson. The lesson is to listen and pay attention, beginning with yourself. Had I listened to others' doubts and the kernels of self-doubt inside my own head, would I have prevailed? Probably not. You just never know. But in my case, listening to my stronger inner voice was certainly worth the risk.

Looking back, I'd like to say I paid full attention and by doing so, made my transition to retirement easier. But I was well used to being busy and, for the first few weeks after I retired, I got very busy right away. Soon enough, I found myself mad because I felt like my time—my precious time—was being eaten up by too many people asking for too many things of me. Then I realized that since *I* had contacted *them,* the person I needed to be mad at was myself. After calming down and meditating, I was able to realize that I was the one who was in control. So I redirected my efforts on getting involved in projects that fell into three categories and three categories only: they had to be fun, they had to be interesting, and they had to result in "greater good" somewhere along the line.

Having made those decisions and taken back the control, I remembered more of the uncertainty of the early days at Men's Wearhouse. Back when my continuum at the company had barely begun to play out, and the success of the company was nowhere near a sure thing, was it all luck? With the benefit of hindsight, I long ago came to realize that my success had nothing to do with luck. It had to do with the design for my own life—a design that changed over time.

9

Designing Your Luck;
Finding Your Place

LUCK DOESN'T JUST HAPPEN. THE saying, "The harder I work, the luckier I get" has been attributed to, among others, movie mogul Samuel Goldwyn, professional golfer Gary Player, and real estate developer Donald Trump, three very successful people who designed their own luck through hard work and persistence and with clear and definite goals for their lives. At some point, they realized that if they wanted to attain those goals, it was only going to be one way—through hard work. Ask any collection of successful people how they got to where they are, and you're bound to get the same answer—hard work. And you'll also probably find that their success had absolutely nothing to do with luck.

Luck by Design

My journey on the path to my "luck" began early, with a series of decisions, each of which led to another series of events unfolding.

183

After moving from Hazleton to Houston, I wound up on the steps of Men's Wearhouse. A short detour to my "dream" job at an advertising agency convinced me that the reality of that dream was far less than what I had expected. I then made a fundamental decision about where I wanted to be (Men's Wearhouse) and began to design my goals more consciously. I took risks, and I worked hard. I worked *very* hard. I succeeded—with a lot of help. And I failed—sometimes by myself, sometimes with a lot of help as well. When I failed, I recovered, kept getting up, and kept showing up. I was with Men's Wearhouse as it rose from a single store with a hand-painted wooden sign to a nationally known business with over five hundred stores. I retired from the company at the absolute perfect time for me and for what I wanted to do with the design for the rest of my life.

> *You're going to have to create your luck through your own hard work and design.*

The lesson? I created my luck—by design. And if I did it, *you* can do it.

If you want a rich, meaningful, and successful life for yourself, you're going to have to create your luck through your own hard work and design. This book has been dedicated to showing you how to do that, step by step. In this last chapter, I leave you with a few thoughts to help you piece it all together. The thoughts are not dissimilar to those back in the first chapter. Now, with the benefit of the knowledge you've gained in reading this far, you can better design your own luck and gain control of your life.

THE RESPONSIBILITY IS YOURS

If you haven't figured it out already, know the following: you are responsible for your own life and for what happens in your own life.

Yes, there is always the unexpected, both good and bad, but for the day-to-day events that occur, every bit of it is your responsibility and under your control. How do you keep things under your control?

First, make sure that you always have the ability to choose. You attain this by deciding whether you're going to be reactive or responsive. Choosing to be reactive is akin to saying, "Whatever happens, happens." Being responsive means that you take control over what happens and take the initiative to change the circumstances around things that might not be working for you. Choose to be responsive.

The second way to keep things under your control is to stay present, as described in chapter 3, "Everything Counts." Simply put, you can't let the outside world or any person around you tell you how you should think, feel, or act. Learn to trust your own intuition. It's your life and your design; own it.

Finally, dispel the notion that if left alone, problems will solve themselves. In fact, it's quite the contrary—generally problems that are left alone feed on themselves and become larger and less fixable. If things down the road are going to be better, *you* are going to have to make them better by the decisions and actions that you make *today.* There is no promise from any otherworldly source that you are being looked after or taken care of. Your life is one big experiment with many twists and turns, but certainly with no promises. Staying in control of your life means dealing with problems as they come up— as uncomfortable as that might be.

The best that you can do day to day is to keep showing up and learn to ride with everything, especially the rough spots, knowing and reminding yourself that you'll be just fine, even though there are no guarantees. That's a lot for one sentence, but trusting that it's the best path to follow *is* a great place to start. The lessons you've already read in this book should help clarify the idea as well.

Taking the Responsibility

If the responsibility is yours, how are you going to *take* that responsibility? The process begins with creating goals and actions for yourself. You can begin that process by creating your own "Life Design." Perhaps you've read a book or an article that has suggested a similar idea—maybe by creating a personal mission statement, or a list of goals—and perhaps you have decided not to do it, because you thought the idea was silly or too time consuming. It's neither. Establishing your own Life Design is an example of *action*, as opposed to *intention*. We all have ideas about what we'd like to do with our lives, but unless you commit those ideas to words, they will be just a lot of random thoughts, generally resulting in little or no action.

At some point in life, we all can feel stuck, adrift, or have the nagging feeling that "there must be more to life than this." If you truly want to begin to design your own luck, creating your Life Design is a great start. Before you begin, here are three recommendations:

1. Be specific. When thinking about where you'd like to be at some point in time (otherwise known as "there"), *define* "there." Too often people create goals that they really can't get their arms around. Examples would be, "I want to be

successful … I want to be happy … I want to retire at an early age …" I suggest a much sturdier and grounded "there." What is *your* definition of success? What is *your* definition of happiness? What *age* is in your retirement plan? Creating a Life Design is more than creating goals; it's creating *reachable* and *sustainable* goals. How do you know what is reachable and sustainable? You start by really knowing yourself, not only your strengths, but your weaknesses as well. You continue by (once again) getting comfortable with the fact that the answers are in your hands.

2. Remember that this Life Design is for your eyes only. Be honest and open. This is your own exercise, for *your* benefit. Don't write as if someone else were going to see it or comment on it.

3. Understand that your Life Design is not permanent. It is subject to change at any moment—by you.

If you want to print out a template for working through the Life Design process, you'll find one on my website: www.richiegoldman. com. If you prefer your own form, you'll need six pieces of paper.

- At the top of the first sheet, write: "These are the principles and ideas that are really important to me." Over the course of a week or two, write down those thoughts, ideas, and phrases that come to mind. Read them over right before you go to sleep to help your subconscious work. Think about and affirm everything you think you are and who you would like to become. Don't hold back: remember that anything is possible *when you allow it to be possible.*

- On the second sheet, write a list of "things that I'd be willing to change about myself in order to attain my goals."
- On the third, write a list of "things that I will not compromise in order to attain my goals."

Divide the remaining three pages into three columns each (work, physical, spiritual). For each question, you'll be describing what you want to be doing for work, and where you'd like to be in your life—as relates to your physical and spiritual place.

- Label the fourth page as: "This is what I'd like to be doing in one year."
- Label the fifth page as: "This is what I'd like to be doing in five years."
- And label the sixth page as: "This is what I'd like to be doing in ten years."

Once you've created your Life Design worksheets, you will have taken a giant step in taking responsibility for yourself. The next step is to replace intention (your Life Design statement) with action (what you actually to do about it).

Keep your Life Design where you can refer to it often. Reflect upon what you've written, and refine it when necessary. It is a living and pliable document, the blueprint for your life, and will require modifications as your life unfolds.

Make a conscious effort to live by your Life Design—to lead an intentional, rather than accidental, life. Focusing on your Life Design will keep you moving toward designing your luck.

Pain Is Inevitable; Suffering Is Optional

In his moving book, *The Last Lecture,* Randy Pausch writes: "No matter how bad things are, you can always make them worse" (page 88). Pausch, who was diagnosed with terminal pancreatic cancer and given only months to live, decided to make the most out of the time he had left. He decided to make things better and created a legacy for his wife, his children, and the millions of lives he touched with his lecture at Carnegie Mellon (which has since been broadcast widely via television and the Internet) and book. Pausch's intellect, abiding optimism, and sense of fun all shine through, both in the lecture and the book, immortalizing his role as hero and mentor to many.

No matter who you are and no matter how you live your life, you can be guaranteed that you will, at some point in your life, experience the following:

- You are going to be anxious.
- You are going to have fear.
- You are going to experience doubt.
- You are going to squander an opportunity.
- You are going to have regret.
- You are going to have your heart broken.
- You are going to experience the death of a close friend or family member.
- You are going to be disappointed by someone close.
- You are going to disappoint someone close.

How you manage and how you conduct your life after these negative experiences is all about your recovery—how you get back up when you fall down. To begin with, you can turn these events into life-altering experiences by demonstrating:

- Honesty
- Integrity
- Courage
- Strength
- Resiliency
- Growth
- Humility

Life is a constant process of recovery. It is when you're in pain that you learn the most about yourself and the most about your survival, humility, and ability to get back up and put yourself together. When you don't recover, you get stuck. When you get stuck, you lose the chance in the moment to learn and to grow. You also lose the chance to take control your life. When you don't recover, you fall victim to the event and lose control. Worse still, the less that you can recover in that instance, the less that you'll be *able* to recover the next time you need to. As a consequence, your world will continue to get smaller and smaller. No matter what the pain or how deeply it cuts, at some point after the initial shock wears off, you are going to have to develop a plan for recovery.

How do you recover? When something doesn't go the way you plan, crying a lot, complaining, or pointing the finger elsewhere isn't going to help. Ultimately, you're going to have to pick yourself back up. Part of the design for your life is how you get back up, and whether you choose to suffer (to make things worse) or to recover (to try to make things better). There is no universal cure-all for life's negative experiences. Each one has to be dealt with in its own time and space. But what you have read in the earlier chapters is a great foundation for you. When you can take every low point in your life as a learning experience, you will have added one more step in your ability to create your own luck by design.

The most painful and yet the greatest learning experience for me was in my painful life transition, back in 1998 (described in chapter 7). And now, years later, when I look back on it, I'm able to thank the universe and thank myself for the opportunity to learn and grow.

Why Are You Here?

At first glance, this might seem like an odd place in the book to be bringing up such big questions as why we are here on this planet, in this time, and why we are here individually. The questions that then might arise are what are we going to do, what is each of us going to do, and what are *you* going to do?

You might be wondering, "Why didn't he bring this up earlier?" The answer? Without the foundation that the book has presented, you might not be thinking about this question at the level that you are now. Sure, over the years you might have asked yourself why are you here, but my hope is that now, with the context and content of this book, you're prepared to think about this question in a more meaningful way.

Once you've begun to create your luck by design, you then have to ask, "What am I going to do with my life and my newfound luck?" That question might *then* bring up the next question: "Why am I here?"

Personally, I doubt that I was put on this planet to clothe Baby Boomer men. But through the process of helping to build Men's Wearhouse, I learned a lot about myself and about others in terms of how we all work, think, and share a wide variety of life experiences. Having been a part of Men's Wearhouse, I began to get a peek at why I am here. During the same period of time, I also began a series of personal explorations, completely separate from the company. These included such diverse topics as "Renewal," a three-day course I took at the Houstonian Hotel in 1980; "Learning to Feel," a weekend seminar at the Esalen Institute in Big Sur, California, in 1994; several yoga retreats; and of course, the desert experience in 2001.

The next steps for me have been the creation of the idea of this book, then the actual writing of it—intention, then action. It's my message to the next generation—my little piece of the puzzle that I'll leave behind. I don't know where it will all lead next, and that's part of the wonder of my life at this point.

Each of us has our own specific "true calling," an answer to the question, "Why am I here?" We need to feel that we are doing something worthwhile, that we are making a positive contribution to the planet. Sadly, many of us feel stalled or on standby, and we tend to sabotage ourselves with self-doubt, fear, and insecurities. But know that you are here on this earth at this time for several reasons. Broadly put, you are here to discover why you are here and what your purpose is; to find and tap into your divine source; to improve the world around you; to take care of yourself; and to have fun in the process.

LIVE AND DISCOVER

You are here to live the incredible experience of life that you've been given. Life itself is the discovery of why you are here. We are all flawed creatures who need to experience life in all of its capacities—good and bad. We have to make mistakes and feel failure in order to appreciate the imperfect world we live in. How you choose to live that experience is one of the fundamental challenges of your life. There are no universal answers—what matters is that you find the ones that work for you.

> *There are no universal answers—what matters is that you find the ones that work for you.*

You are on your life journey to fulfill your own sacred contract. This contract is something you are born to connect with—it is your reason and purpose for being alive. It is the essence of who you are; it is part of the path you are meant to travel during your lifetime. Your journey to find your sacred contract is just that—a journey. It's all about process and all about journey.

You are here to discover your "divine source." As children, perhaps even as adults, we think (or hope) that there is some divine spirit watching over us, making sure that all of the evils of the world don't happen to us, making sure that wrongs are righted, and making sure that we become our best person. It's a comforting thought, though (at least so far) unproven. In the meantime, how about this for comfort: the "divine source" isn't "out there"—it's *inside of you*. It's that place within that you will find when you slow down and get really quiet and really present. It's the place where you remember the life lessons

193

that you have learned through your successes and failures. Another place to find your divine source is when you are teaching others. It is in this moment that you can run your own "reality check." There is no better way to find out if you have learned a lesson than by trying to teach it to someone else. Perhaps the clearest examples of passing on the lesson are through being a mentor or a parent. The former was covered in chapter 6, and the latter is something I haven't discussed too much up until now.

I can vividly recall the wonderful days with my daughter Emily when she was a little one. She was full of wonder, discovery, and excitement. And I've had the great fortune to experience the light of a child all over again—twenty-seven years later in life—with my second daughter, Ava. Extraordinary as my children are, I believe that all children can exude a magnificent sense of awe about all that is around them—every day being an experiment in the wonderment of life.

If you're not a parent, or not planning to become a parent, you can experience the same awe by watching kids. They can be nieces or nephews, godchildren, or cousins, or they can be kids that you interact with in the process of being a volunteer. No matter what the way, find a way, and get involved with kids. Your experience in doing this could be life-altering, for both of you. Not convinced? *Stop!* Stop, just for a moment, and think about a child's eyes, the openness and innocence you can see there. Children are born innocent, loving, and trusting; their sense of self, the world, and others is barely forming. For most children, the world is a safe place, and they readily trust themselves and others. Assuming no crisis of upbringing, children start out trusting and untainted, able to believe anything, especially anything of a positive nature. As just one manifestation of this, consider the fact that children also believe in the unbelievable—Santa Claus, the Easter Bunny, the Tooth Fairy, and Garden Fairies.

Why do children believe? What is it that enables them to blindly accept? *Lack of conditioning.* In a child's world, *every day* is a new experience, and the world is filled with nonstop wonder and first-time experiences. There is little "always" and "never." Children's uncomplicated lives are filled with endless experimentation and joy.

Why don't adults believe? *Conditioning.* Adults have trouble having experiences that are really new, because every experience reminds them, in some way, of a previous experience. The result of that previous experience makes it almost impossible to accept the unbelievable. Adults have had experiences that chipped away at their trust and faith in themselves and others. How can you counteract that? Reconnect with your innocence, your inner light, by observing a child's unguarded serenity, self-awareness, and free spirit. A child's energy can teach us to let go, trust, and connect with ourselves completely in the moment.

> *Reconnect with your innocence, your inner light.*

LEAVE FOOTPRINTS

You are here to leave footprints. Do your best to leave a path of learning and love for others to follow. Those "others" *should* be the ones closest to you and *can* also be nameless others who might cross your path. In leaving these footprints, and having an impact, it is also important to remember that you are both significant and insignificant.

You Are Significant. Realize and accept that you make a difference, and what you do over the course of your life makes a difference. We all make some sort of contribution, whether big or small, intentional or inadvertent. Every action has some sort of reaction. So if you live consciously, you increase your opportunities to make a positive difference. In contrast, if you don't give a damn, don't create meaningful relationships, and destroy many things that cross your path, you'll make a difference, all right—just a negative one. The very fact that you're here is quite remarkable, and although we all take it for granted practically all of the time, it's important to take a deep breath every now and then, look up into a blue sky, and be appreciative.

You Are Also Insignificant. After you're done looking up at the sky, remember that the world doesn't revolve around you, your ideas, or anything else that you might be involved with. Don't get too caught up with yourself. You are one of billions. Make your mark as your way of thanking the great beyond for the fact that you're here—no more, no less.

You Have a Gift. Each of us has a gift for another—the gift of ourselves. I call that gift generativity. You are here to create generativity by expanding the awareness of other people. You work and you live to teach and to help create a better world, to take your own knowledge and experiences and share them with your peers and with the next generation. You won't live forever, so you must seek to build a better world that you can live in and leave behind a positive legacy for the few people you know and the many people you don't. And every time you give, you're contributing to the legacy you're leaving.

We *all* have the capacity to be generative in different ways—as parents, teachers, mentors, leaders, friends, neighbors, volunteers, and citizens. It's not only in our nature, but it's also incumbent on us to do so. Here are a few ideas:

- Do something kind for yourself. Loving-kindness begins with knowing how to love yourself.
- Do something kind for someone else.
- Be grateful.
- Smile—for no particular reason. (You may well brighten someone else's day. If nothing else, people will wonder what you're up to.)
- Do something—do anything—differently than how you normally do.
- Make some music. (Even if that only means singing at the top of your lungs in the shower or in your car.)
- Ask someone else's opinion. Listen to it.
- Change your point of view.
- Admit that you made a mistake.
- Give some money away—to a charity, a school, or a friend in need.
- Become a mentor.
- Volunteer. You can volunteer your time, your expertise, or just about anything that you know that someone else might not know or might need.

- Forgive someone.
- Buy a gift for someone for no particular reason.

There are limitless other ways to practice generativity. Just as in making changes, you may find it easier to start small, build the habits, and then increase your ways of giving.

TAKE CARE OF YOURSELF

You have to take care of yourself. Seriously. I have written a lot in this book about service to others, but the first and most important place for this kind of service is to yourself. *Talk to yourself.* Don't get the wrong idea here. I'm not suggesting that you mumble to yourself while wandering aimlessly in public. What I'm suggesting is that you talk to yourself every day—with patience and kindness.

Patience begins with how you treat yourself. If you can't speak to yourself with kindness, it's unlikely that you'll be able to be kind to others. Practice talking to yourself in a loving and kind way all of the time. Eventually, this voice of kindness and compassion will become second nature as you're talking to yourself and interacting with others, and you'll be better equipped to open yourself up to all of the wonderful possibilities of who you are and who you are meant to be.

Another way to take care of yourself is to *have fun.* Learn to smile, laugh, and just be silly. Used at the appropriate time, these practices—smiling, laughing, being silly—can deflate tension and remind you that you are human like nothing else. And you'll just *feel better* when you're having (and sharing) fun. Yes, it's important to take life seriously, but it's equally important to not take all of life seriously all of the time. Go out there and have a good time.

At the end of the day when you ask, "Why am I here?" there is no standard one-size-fits-all answer. It's really just about you, and for you to find out. But on the road to finding out—if you travel that road with a conscious mind, an open and kind heart, with presence and intention—you will find the deeper meaning in everything you do, and it will dramatically improve your own power to be the person you *want* to be, and the person you were *destined* to be. You will be able to experience a happier and more fulfilling life, and in turn be more relaxed with yourself and your surroundings. This will enable you to attain greater success in all of your endeavors, be they personal or professional. Your personal, inside happiness can mitigate a great deal of unhappiness that may cross your path. Your full-time job is to be the generator of being whole, healed, happy, and healthy. From this place, your contribution has the greatest potential. How do you find all of this? Through continuous introspection and through living an authentic and empathic life. You will find it through continuous internal dialogue. You will also find it by trial and error and through external dialogue with your friends, family, and co-workers. It might take a lifetime to find this, but the journey is what your life is all about, and it's the most important journey you will ever take.

Lesson Learned: Making a Difference

Have you thought about incorporating the practice of generativity into your life? I have another suggestion about generativity to expand on one I gave earlier in this chapter. This variation may seem a little more difficult than the others. Whenever you are asked to, give money to people on the street who ask for it. *Stop!* You may have to re-read that sentence: Whenever you are asked to, give money to people on the street who ask for it.

Does it seem like a radical idea to give money to people on the street who ask for it, whenever they ask? What is this recommendation doing here? How is giving money away part of a lesson learned? It has to do with being present. It has to do with having a sense and awareness of those around us. It has to do with giving back. "But they're just going to use the money to buy drugs and/or alcohol," you might say. Maybe yes, maybe no. The point is, *you don't know.* We share this planet with all people. We don't know what brought a homeless person to this point, nor do we really know where that person's next meal is coming from. It is not ours to tell. Try to not be judgmental. Try to the right thing, look that person in the eye, and give a dollar or two.

Helping the homeless one-on-one like this is gratifying, but on a small scale. The city of San Francisco has taken it one step further with the creation of Project Homeless Connect (PHC). It was founded on the premise that people working in City Hall could better serve the community if they got out from behind their desks, at least once in a while, to see what was *really* happening in the community. The brainchild of San Francisco's mayor, **Gavin Newsom**, and his Deputy Chief of Staff, Alex Tourk, PHC is a partnership of the public and private sectors. Its goal? To create positive change in dealing with the homeless—changes that the city government either can't implement

200

or doesn't have the money to implement by itself. The event itself is held about every six weeks, generally at the Bill Graham Civic Auditorium. It is, in a sense, "one-stop shopping" for the "clients" (as opposed to "homeless people")—a place where they can come and get food, clothing, arrangements for shelter, as well as psychological assistance, eyewear, or assistance in finding relatives. It's whatever the "clients" want.

While the origins of PHC were inside of City Hall, it soon became a volunteer effort staffed by average citizens, professional people, and businesses, all trying to lend a hand. The board of PHC created the nonprofit organization to raise the money needed to sustain it. The board is made up of people like myself who go to various community leaders and businesses to raise money to support the infrastructure and to raise awareness of PHC in the Bay Area.

PHC has been a runaway success—so much so that the idea has been taken and used in over 150 communities across the United States, including Denver, Minneapolis, and New York, as well as in Australia, Canada, and Puerto Rico. It is a classic example of how people working together with the same goal can create something great, without letting ego or desire for credit get in the way, and how all great things begin with one visionary idea.

The world works in mysterious ways. People can, without extraordinary effort, help to change a sour lemon into refreshing lemonade. And sometimes, having fun, doing good, and creating generativity can all come in one package. This is what I've witnessed personally in PHC. The camaraderie of the volunteers—people of all ages and backgrounds—is amazing to see. They are doing work that is very gratifying to them personally, and at the same time, they're having fun together. Their clients—also people of all ages and backgrounds—may be receiving more respect and positive attention than they have had in weeks. They all—volunteers and clients, alike—have smiles on their faces and gratitude in their hearts. And at the end of the day, one can be nothing less than appreciative of one's place on earth.

Your gift of generativity begins with the exploration of your inner self—discovering who you are and then finding the parts of yourself that you want to share and leave with others. The embodiment of your gift might come from your more practical side; it might come from your dream side. And remember, if you don't try to live your dream, you'll never know if it's right or what positive effects it might have, for you and for the world.

RICHARD E. GOLDMAN

PS...

You are here. Here at the end of this book. Here in this moment. Here to take over your life. A few parting thoughts:

There is a difference between hope and faith. Abandon hope. Always have faith. First, have faith in yourself and your abilities. You have the power, the knowledge, and the fundamental ability to make anything happen. Find that place deep inside of yourself that you know is there. That part that you might have hidden for a long time—the part that might you fear because of its power. Now is the time to use it. You are about to venture out into a world that you inherited— make it better. Make it safer. Make it more loving and caring than anything that you ever might have imagined.

Have faith in other people as well. Don't succumb to the media's lowest common denominator of dumbness, meanness, and "gotcha" mentality. Rise above it and soar to your own greatness. Do you want to take back your life? Take it back through fundamental kindness, fairness, and respect, one person at a time. Take it back by having faith that even the tallest buildings are built one brick at a time. Kindness, fairness, and respect are contagious. Spread them around. Do you want to take back your country? It's been said that the United States is the last best hope on earth. You are the last best hope for the United States. As I noted in the Open Letter at the beginning of this book, the problems that we all face in the world aren't the result of any one person. And they won't be solved by any one person. But maybe, just maybe as the result of your reading this book, a spark has been generated in you to go out there and make your best effort at resolving the problems.

We Boomer parents, who grew up with the Cold War, were taught to prepare for the worst—nuclear annihilation. We did so by building fallout shelters. Your worst is certainly scary as well, but here's a thought: instead of preparing for the worst, why not prepare for possibilities? Prepare for the *best case*, because to a great extent, you *can* control it.

You already have everything you need to make it happen.

Go MAKE SOME LUCK HAPPEN!

At the end of most yoga classes, after the final savasana (a resting pose), there is often a moment of thought or prayer, and the instructor usually ends by gently bowing to the participants and saying, "Namaste." This is Sanskrit for, "I bow to the light that is you." It's a way of seeing and acknowledging the special qualities that each of us has. It is a way to appreciate and embrace the abundant potential and endless possibilities in every person whose path you cross—your partner, spouse, child, parent, co-worker, boss, customer, and above all, yourself.

This is the end of *this* journey for me. It is also the beginning of a new journey for me, as well as a new journey for you ...

Namaste ...

References

Cleary, Thomas, trans. *Zen Lessons: The Art of Leadership*. (Boston: Shambhala Publications, 1989).

Farhi, Donna. *Yoga Mind, Body, & Spirit*. (New York: Henry Holt and Company, LLC, 2000).

Gafni, Marc. *Soul Prints: Your Path to Fulfillment*. (New York: Fireside, a division of Simon & Schuster, 2002).

Kabat-Zinn, Jon. *Wherever You Go, There You Are: Mindfulness Meditation in Everyday Life*. (New York: Hyperion, 1994).

Keen, Andrew. *The Cult of the Amateur: How Today's Internet Is Killing Our Culture*. (New York: Doubleday, a division of Random House, 2007).

Kundera, Milan. *Slowness*. (New York: HarperCollins, 1996).

Kundtz, David. *Stopping*. (Berkeley: Conari Press, 1998).

MacKenzie, Gordon. *Orbiting the Giant Hairball: A Corporate Fool's Guide to Surviving with Grace*. (New York: Viking Penguin, 1998).

Pausch, Randy. *The Last Lecture*. With Jeffrey Zaslow. (New York: Hyperion, 2008).

Peters, Tom, and Robert Waterman. *In Search of Excellence: Lessons from America's Best-Run Companies*. (New York: Warner, 1982).

Strand, Clark. *The Wooden Bowl: Simple Meditation for Everyday Life.* (New York: Hyperion, 1998).

von Oech, Roger. *A Whack on the Side of the Head: How You Can Be More Creative.* 25th Anniversary Edition, revised and updated. (New York: Business Plus, 2008).

Acknowledgments

I HAVE TAKEN ON MANY partners in the process of writing this book and living my life. I want and need to thank them, and at the risk of showing favoritism, I'll do so alphabetically. Granted, my alphabetization—by first name—is unusual. And it feels right to me, for it underscores my thanks to my father and my wife—first and last.

Aaron Goldman, my father. For giving me the wings to fly and instilling in me the fundamental and vital sense of fairness.

Advisory Board. For your insight, input, and interest. You've made this a much better book.

Charlie Bresler. A great leader and a great friend.

Cheryl Malakoff. Who pulled me out of more spiritual holes than I could ever begin to articulate, and who was my "ghost editor." A true joy and wonder.

Dan Goldman, my brother. Some great stories of our early years didn't make it into this book, but it was fun writing them and thinking about our childhood together.

Emily Goldman, my daughter. For having the guts to call this thing a book long before I did and setting me straight about what it was about. It's great to learn from your kids.

Eric Lane. Another terrific leader and friend, Eric inherited one of my jobs (General Merchandise Manager) and greatly improved on my efforts.

George Zimmer. A very important person in my life.

Ivan Cury. A patient teacher of the "biz" of making commercials. The movie rights for this book are yours.

Janet Hunter, my editor. You "got it" and me right away. You kept me focused, yet gave me enough rope to creatively swing. It's been a pleasure and an honor to work with you.

Jayme Maxwell. Jayme inherited my job as the head of Marketing and Advertising and did it better. Your style, tenacity, and sense for simply what is right have meant a lot to me.

Jordan Morganstein. An inspiration, a teacher, and a believer in Men's Wearhouse from the early years. Also one of the most honest people I've ever met. I miss you and think of you often.

Kim Grubbs. Thank you for just listening and pushing me when I needed it.

Kristen Feenstra. You showed up when I needed you most and gave me an appreciation for yoga that I never would have discovered otherwise.

Lonnie Hanzon. Amazing artist, incredible inspiration, but more than anything else, a wonderful friend.

Mary Zubrow, my sister. Not only are you my sister, but you are also my very good friend. How great is that?

Men's Wearhouse, my work family. While you aren't all mentioned by name, your spirit and your contributions have made the company successful, and they have made my writing this possible—and, I trust, worthwhile.

Morgan-James, my publisher. Everyone at Morgan-James. And a special thanks to David Hancock, for having faith in this book while it was barely an outline.

Reba Goldman, my mother. I don't know how you managed to raise the three of us and keep your sanity, but you did, and we all think of you often.

Samuel Goldman, my grandfather. I hardly knew you, but somehow I did, and your voice and spirit are part of my soul.

Traci Mitchell Goldman, my wife. For your unconditional love and support, and for knowing when to leave me alone and when not to. I've learned a lot from you by just observing.

About the Author

BORN IN HAZLETON, PENNSYLVANIA, Richie Goldman graduated from Rutgers University in 1972 with a BA in English. The following year, he moved to Houston, Texas, with his degree, his car, a bit of advertising experience, and $300 in hand. After a series of "lucky" decisions, he met George Zimmer and went on to help create Men's Wearhouse, one of the largest men's apparel retail companies in North America. While at Men's Wearhouse, Goldman was the general merchandise manager for many years and was responsible for the marketing and advertising of all brands. In 1992, Men's Wearhouse went public (NYSE: MW). During his tenure, Forbes Magazine recognized Men's Wearhouse as one of the "100 Best Companies to Work For" and Men's Wearhouse was named "Retailer of the Decade" by MR Magazine, the leading national trade magazine for menswear retailing.

Since his retirement from Men's Wearhouse in 2002, Goldman has shared his managing, marketing, and professional expertise in numerous ventures, consulting with retailers and manufacturers across the country. He is a founding Board Member of San Francisco Connect, the innovative public-private effort to eliminate/control homelessness in San Francisco (sfconnect.org), and is a former board member of The Jewish Community High School of San Francisco. He has been a board member, investor, and consultant to Benefit Magazine, a magazine dedicated to philanthropy in the greater Bay Area. He has also worked on the political campaigns of several candidates, most notably Gavin Newsom, both in 2003 and 2007. He was on the Board of Trustees at Mills College from 1999-2005, and is currently on the Board of Overseers for the Graduate School of International Business and Finance at Brandeis University. He is a founding member of the Milton S. Friedman Lecture Series at Rutgers University. He has spoken on Wall Street, to business groups, and to audiences in high schools and universities about his experiences at Men's Wearhouse, in business, and in life.

Luck by Design: Certain Success in an Uncertain World is Goldman's first book—and he is already at work on his next. Goldman and his wife, Traci, live in northern California with their daughter, Ava. Much to their delight, Goldman's older daughter, Emily, and her daughter, Zaia, live nearby.

Printed in the United States
129097LV00001B/166-348/P

STAND TALL

Provided
by
Oakland PTO

2003-2004

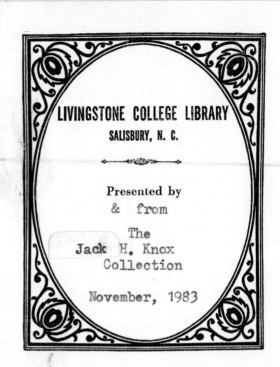

BOOKS BY MARJORIE KINNAN RAWLINGS

Cross Creek

When the Whippoorwill—

The Yearling

Golden Apples

South Moon Under

CHARLES SCRIBNER'S SONS

The Yearling

The Yearling

by

Marjorie Kinnan Rawlings

With pictures by
N. C. Wyeth

CHARLES SCRIBNER'S SONS · NEW YORK

1944

Illustrations

vii

Illustrations

The Yearling

Chapter I

A COLUMN of smoke rose thin and straight from the cabin chimney. The smoke was blue where it left the red of the clay. It trailed into the blue of the April sky and was no longer blue but gray. The boy Jody watched it, speculating. The fire on the kitchen hearth was dying down. His mother was hanging up pots and pans after the noon dinner. The day was Friday. She would sweep the floor with a broom of ti-ti and after that, if he were lucky, she would scrub it with the corn shucks scrub. If she scrubbed the floor she would not miss him until he had reached the Glen. He stood a minute, balancing the hoe on his shoulder.

The clearing itself was pleasant if the unweeded rows of young shafts of corn were not before him. The wild bees had found the chinaberry tree by the front gate. They burrowed into the fragile clusters of lavender bloom as greedily as though there were no other flowers in the scrub; as though they had forgotten the yellow jessamine of March; the sweet bay and the magnolias ahead of them in May. It occurred to him that he might follow the swift line of flight of the black and gold bodies, and so find a bee-tree, full of amber honey. The winter's cane syrup was gone and most of the jellies. Finding a bee-tree was nobler work than hoeing, and the corn could wait another day. The afternoon was alive with a soft stirring. It bored into him as the bees bored into the chinaberry blossoms, so that he must be gone across the clearing, through the pines and down the road to the running branch. The bee-tree might be near the water.

He stood his hoe against the split-rail fence. He walked down the cornfield until he was out of sight of the cabin.

The Yearling

He swung himself over the fence on his two hands. Old Julia the hound had followed his father in the wagon to Grahamsville, but Rip the bull-dog and Perk the new feice saw the form clear the fence and ran toward him. Rip barked deeply but the voice of the small mongrel was high and shrill. They wagged deprecatory short tails when they recognized him. He sent them back to the yard. They watched after him indifferently. They were a sorry pair, he thought, good for nothing but the chase, the catch and the kill. They had no interest in him except when he brought them their plates of table scraps night and morning. Old Julia was a gentle thing with humans, but her worn-toothed devotion was only for his father, Penny Baxter. Jody had tried to make up to Julia, but she would have none of him.

"You was pups together," his father told him, "ten year gone, when you was two year old and her a baby. You hurted the leetle thing, not meanin' no harm. She cain't bring herself to trust you. Hounds is often that-a-way."

He made a circle around the sheds and corn-crib and cut south through the black-jack. He wished he had a dog like Grandma Hutto's. It was white and curly-haired and did tricks. When Grandma Hutto laughed and shook and could not stop, the dog jumped into her lap and licked her face, wagging its plumed tail as though it laughed with her. He would like anything that was his own; that licked his face and followed him as old Julia followed his father. He cut into the sand road and began to run east. It was two miles to the Glen, but it seemed to Jody that he could run forever. There was no ache in his legs, as when he hoed the corn. He slowed down to make the road last longer. He had passed the big pines and left them behind. Where he walked now, the scrub had closed in, walling in the road with dense sand pines, each one so thin it seemed to the boy it might make kindling by itself. The road went up an incline. At the top he stopped. The April sky was framed by the tawny sand and the pines. It was as blue as his homespun shirt, dyed

2

with Grandma Hutto's indigo. Small clouds were stationary, like bolls of cotton. As he watched, the sunlight left the sky a moment and the clouds were gray.

"There'll come a little old drizzly rain before night-fall," he thought.

The down grade tempted him to a lope. He reached the thick-bedded sand of the Silver Glen road. The tar-flower was in bloom, and fetter-bush and sparkleberry. He slowed to a walk, so that he might pass the changing vegetation tree by tree, bush by bush, each one unique and familiar. He reached the magnolia tree where he had carved the wild-cat's face. The growth was a sign that there was water nearby. It seemed a strange thing to him, when earth was earth and rain was rain, that scrawny pines should grow in the scrub, while by every branch and lake and river there grew magnolias. Dogs were the same everywhere, and oxen and mules and horses. But trees were different in different places.

"Reckon it's because they can't move none," he decided. They took what food was in the soil under them.

The east bank of the road shelved suddenly. It dropped below him twenty feet to a spring. The bank was dense with magnolia and loblolly bay, sweet gum and gray-barked ash. He went down to the spring in the cool darkness of their shadows. A sharp pleasure came over him. This was a secret and a lovely place.

A spring as clear as well water bubbled up from nowhere in the sand. It was as though the banks cupped green leafy hands to hold it. There was a whirlpool where the water rose from the earth. Grains of sand boiled in it. Beyond the bank, the parent spring bubbled up at a higher level, cut itself a channel through white limestone and began to run rapidly down-hill to make a creek. The creek joined Lake George, Lake George was a part of the St. John's River, the great river flowed northward and into the sea. It excited Jody to watch the beginning of the ocean. There were other beginnings, true, but this one was his own. He liked to think that no one came here but himself and the wild animals and the thirsty birds.

He was warm from his jaunt. The dusky glen laid cool hands on him. He rolled up the hems of his blue denim breeches and stepped with bare dirty feet into the shallow spring. His toes sank into the sand. It oozed softly between them and over his bony ankles. The water was so cold that for a moment it burned his skin. Then it made a rippling sound, flowing past his pipe-stem legs, and was entirely delicious. He walked up and down, digging his big toe experimentally under smooth rocks he encountered. A school of minnows flashed ahead of him down the growing branch. He chased them through the shallows. They were suddenly out of sight as though they had never existed. He crouched under a bared and overhanging live-oak root where a pool was deep, thinking they might reappear, but only a spring frog wriggled from under the mud, stared at him, and dove under the tree root in a spasmodic terror. He laughed.

"I ain't no 'coon. I'd not ketch you," he called after it.

A breeze parted the canopied limbs over him. The sun dropped through and lay on his head and shoulders. It was good to be warm at his head while his hard calloused feet were cold. The breeze died away, the sun no longer reached him. He waded across to the opposite bank where the growth was more open. A low palmetto brushed him. It reminded him that his knife was snug in his pocket; that he had planned as long ago as Christmas, to make himself a flutter-mill.

He had never built one alone. Grandma Hutto's son Oliver had always made one for him whenever he was home from sea. He went to work intently, frowning as he tried to recall the exact angle necessary to make the mill-wheel turn smoothly. He cut two forked twigs and trimmed them into two Y's of the same size. Oliver had been very particular to have the cross-bar round and smooth, he remembered. A

4

wild cherry grew half-way up the bank. He climbed it and cut a twig as even as a polished pencil. He selected a palm frond and cut two strips of the tough fiber, an inch wide and four inches long. He cut a slit lengthwise in the center of each of them, wide enough to insert the cherry twig. The strips of palm frond must be at angles, like the arms of a windmill. He adjusted them carefully. He separated the Y-shaped twigs by nearly the length of the cherry cross-bar and pushed them deep into the sand of the branch bed a few yards below the spring.

The water was only a few inches deep but it ran strongly, with a firm current. The palm-frond mill-wheel must just brush the water's surface. He experimented with depth until he was satisfied, then laid the cherry bar between the twigs. It hung motionless. He twisted it a moment, anxiously, helping it to fit itself into its forked grooves. The bar began to rotate. The current caught the flexible tip of one bit of palm frond. By the time it lifted clear, the rotation of the bar brought the angled tip of the second into contact with the stream. The small leafy paddles swung over and over, up and down. The little wheel was turning. The flutter-mill was at work. It turned with the easy rhythm of the great water-mill at Lynne that ground corn into meal.

Jody drew a deep breath. He threw himself on the weedy sand close to the water and abandoned himself to the magic of motion. Up, over, down, up, over, down—the flutter-mill was enchanting. The bubbling spring would rise forever from the earth, the thin current was endless. The spring was the beginning of waters sliding to the sea. Unless leaves fell, or squirrels cut sweet bay twigs to drop and block the fragile wheel, the flutter-mill might turn forever. When he was an old man, as old as his father, there seemed no reason why this rippling movement might not continue as he had begun it.

He moved a stone that was matching its corners against his sharp ribs and burrowed a little, hollowing himself a nest for his hips and shoulders. He stretched out one arm and laid his head on it. A shaft of sunlight, warm and thin like a light patchwork quilt, lay across his body. He watched the flutter-mill indolently, sunk in the sand and the sunlight. The movement was hypnotic. His eyelids fluttered with the palm-leaf paddles. Drops of silver slipping from the wheel blurred together like the tail of a shooting star. The water made a sound like kittens lapping. A rain frog sang a moment and then was still. There was an instant when the boy hung at the edge of a high bank made of the soft fluff of broom-sage, and the rain frog and the starry dripping of the flutter-mill hung with him. Instead of falling over the edge, he sank into the softness. The blue, white-tufted sky closed over him. He slept.

When he awakened, he thought he was in a place other than the branch bed. He was in another world, so that for an instant he thought he might still be dreaming. The sun was gone, and all the light and shadow. There were no black boles of live oaks, no glossy green of magnolia leaves, no pattern of gold lace where the sun had sifted through the branches of the wild cherry. The world was all a gentle gray, and he lay in a mist as fine as spray from a waterfall. The mist tickled his skin. It was scarcely wet. It was at once warm and cool. He rolled over on his back and it was as though he looked up into the soft gray breast of a mourning dove.

He lay, absorbing the fine-dropped rain like a young plant. When his face was damp at last and his shirt was moist to the touch, he left his nest. He stopped short. A deer had come to the spring while he was sleeping. The fresh tracks came down the east bank and stopped at the water's edge. They were sharp and pointed, the tracks of a doe. They sank deeply into the sand, so that he knew the doe was an old one and a large. Perhaps she was heavy with fawn. She had come down and drunk deeply from the spring, not seeing him where he slept. Then she had scented him. There

6

JODY AND THE FLUTTER-MILL

was a scuffled confusion in the sand where she had wheeled in fright. The tracks up the opposite bank had long harried streaks behind them. Perhaps she had not drunk, after all, before she scented him, and turned and ran with that swift, sand-throwing flight. He hoped she was not now thirsty, wide-eyed in the scrub.

He looked about for other tracks. The squirrels had raced up and down the banks, but they were bold, always. A raccoon had been that way, with his feet like sharp-nailed hands, but he could not be sure how recently. Only his father could tell for certain the hour when any wild things had passed by. Only the doe had surely come and had been frightened. He turned back again to the flutter-mill. It was turning as steadily as though it had always been there. The palm-leaf paddles were frail but they made a brave show of strength, rippling against the shallow water. They were glistening from the slow rain.

Jody looked at the sky. He could not tell the time of day in the grayness, nor how long he may have slept. He bounded up the west bank, where open gallberry flats spread without obstructions. As he stood, hesitant whether to go or stay, the rain ended as gently as it had begun. A light breeze stirred from the southwest. The sun came out. The clouds rolled together into great white billowing feather bolsters, and across the east a rainbow arched, so lovely and so various that Jody thought he would burst with looking at it. The earth was pale green, the air itself was all but visible, golden with the rain-washed sunlight, and all the trees and grass and bushes glittered, varnished with the rain-drops.

A spring of delight boiled up within him as irresistibly as the spring of the branch. He lifted his arms and held them straight from his shoulders like a water-turkey's wings. He began to whirl around in his tracks. He whirled faster and faster until his ecstasy was a whirlpool, and when he thought he would explode with it, he became dizzy and closed his eyes and dropped to the ground and lay flat in the broom-

7

sage. The earth whirled under him and with him. He opened his eyes and the blue April sky and the cotton clouds whirled over him. Boy and earth and trees and sky spun together. The whirling stopped, his head cleared and he got to his feet. He was light-headed and giddy, but something in him was relieved, and the April day could be borne again, like any ordinary day.

He turned and galloped toward home. He drew deep breaths of the pines, aromatic with wetness. The loose sand that had pulled at his feet was firmed by the rain. The return was comfortable going. The sun was not far from its setting when the long-leaf pines around the Baxter clearing came into sight. They stood tall and dark against the red-gold west. He heard the chickens clucking and quarreling and knew they had just been fed. He turned into the clearing. The weathered gray of the split-rail fence was luminous in the rich spring light. Smoke curled thickly from the stick-and-clay chimney. Supper would be ready on the hearth and hot bread baking in the Dutch oven. He hoped his father had not returned from Grahamsville. It came to him for the first time that perhaps he should not have left the place while his father was away. If his mother had needed wood, she would be angry. Even his father would shake his head and say, "Son——" He heard old Cæsar snort and knew his father was ahead of him.

The clearing was in a pleasant clatter. The horse whinnied at the gate, the calf bleated in its stall and the milch cow answered, the chickens scratched and cackled and the dogs barked with the coming of food and evening. It was good to be hungry and to be fed and the stock was eager with an expectant certainty. The end of winter had been meager; corn short, and hay, and dried cow-peas. But now in April the pastures were green and succulent and even the chickens savored the sprouts of young grass. The dogs had found a nest of young rabbits that evening, and after such tid-bits the scraps from the Baxter supper table were a matter of some indifference. Jody saw old Julia lying under the wagon, worn out from her miles of trotting. He swung open the front paling gate and went to find his father.

Penny Baxter was at the wood-pile. He still wore the coat of the broadcloth suit that he had been married in, that he now wore as badge of his gentility when he went to church, or off trading. The sleeves were too short, not because Penny had grown, but because the years of hanging through the summer dampness, and being pressed with the smoothing iron and pressed again, had somehow shrunk the fabric. Jody saw his father's hands, big for the rest of him, close around a bundle of wood. He was doing Jody's work, and in his good coat. Jody ran to him.

"I'll git it, Pa."

He hoped his willingness, now, would cover his delinquency. His father straightened his back.

"I near about give you out, son," he said.

"I went to the Glen."

"Hit were a mighty purty day to go," Penny said. "Or to go anywhere. How come you to take out such a fur piece?"

It was as hard to remember why he had gone as though it had been a year ago. He had to think back to the moment when he had laid down his hoe.

"Oh." He had it now. "I aimed to foller the honey-bees and find a bee-tree."

"You find it?"

Jody stared blankly.

"Dogged if I ain't forgot 'til now to look for it."

He felt as foolish as a bird-dog caught chasing field mice. He looked at his father sheepishly. His father's pale blue eyes were twinkling.

"Tell the truth, Jody," he said, "and shame the devil. Wa'n't the bee-tree a fine excuse to go a-ramblin'?"

Jody grinned.

"The notion takened me," he admitted, "afore I studied on the bee-tree."

"That's what I figgered. How come me to know, was when I was drivin' along to Grahamsville, I said to myself, 'There's Jody now, and the hoein' ain't goin' to take him too long. What would I do this fine spring day, was I a boy?' And then I thought, 'I'd go a-ramblin'.' Most any-where, long as it kivered the ground."

A warmth filled the boy that was not the low golden sun. He nodded.

"That's the way I figgered," he said.

"But your Ma, now," Penny jerked his head toward the house, "don't hold with ramblin'. Most women-folks cain't see for their lives, how a man loves so to ramble. I never let on you wasn't here. She said, 'Where's Jody?' and I said, 'Oh, I reckon he's around some'eres.'"

He winked one eye and Jody winked back.

"Men-folks has got to stick together in the name o' peace. You carry your Ma a good bait o' wood now."

Jody filled his arms and hurried to the house. His mother was kneeling at the hearth. The spiced smells that came to his nose made him weak with hunger.

"That ain't sweet 'tater pone, is it, Ma?"

"Hit's sweet 'tater pone, and don't you fellers be too long a time now, piddlin' around and visitin'. Supper's done and ready."

He dumped the wood in the box and scurried to the lot. His father was milking Trixie.

"Ma says to git done and come on," he reported. "Must I feed old Cæsar?"

"I done fed him, son, sich as I had to give the pore feller." He stood up from the three-legged milking stool. "Carry in the milk and don't trip and waste it outen the gourd like you done yestiddy. Easy, Trixie——"

He moved aside from the cow and went to the stall in the shed, where her calf was tethered.

"Here, Trixie. Soo, gal——"

The cow lowed and came to her calf.

"Easy, there. You greedy as Jody."

He stroked the pair and followed the boy to the house. They washed in turn at the water-shelf and dried their hands and faces on the roller towel hanging outside the kitchen door. Ma Baxter sat at the table waiting for them, helping their plates. Her bulky frame filled the end of the long narrow table. Jody and his father sat down on either side of her. It seemed natural to both of them that she should preside.

"You-all hongry tonight?" she asked.

"I kin hold a barrel o' meat and a bushel o' biscuit," Jody said.

"That's what you say. Your eyes is bigger'n your belly."

"I'd about say the same," Penny said, "if I hadn't learned better. Goin' to Grahamsville allus do make me hongry."

"You git a snort o' 'shine there, is the reason," she said.

"A mighty small one today. Jim Turnbuckle treated."

"Then you shore didn't git enough to hurt you."

Jody heard nothing; saw nothing but his plate. He had never been so hungry in his life, and after a lean winter and slow spring, with food not much more plentiful for the Baxters than for their stock, his mother had cooked a supper good enough for the preacher. There were poke-greens with bits of white bacon buried in them; sand-buggers made of potato and onion and the cooter he had found crawling yesterday; sour orange biscuits and at his mother's elbow the sweet potato pone. He was torn between his desire for more biscuits and another sand-bugger and the knowledge, born of painful experience, that if he ate them, he would suddenly have no room for pone. The choice was plain.

"Ma," he said, "kin I have my pone right now?"

She was at a pause in the feeding of her own large frame. She cut him, dexterously, a generous portion. He plunged into its spiced and savory goodness.

"The time it takened me," she complained, "to make that pone—and you destroyin' it before I git my breath——"

"I'm eatin' it quick," he admitted, "but I'll remember it a long time."

Supper was done with. Jody was replete. Even his father, who usually ate like a sparrow, had taken a second helping.

"I'm full, thank the Lord," he said.

Ma Baxter sighed.

"If a feller'd light me a candle," she said, "I'd git shut o' the dishwashin' and mebbe have time to set and enjoy myself."

Jody left his seat and lit a tallow candle. As the yellow flame wavered, he looked out of the east window. The full moon was rising.

"A pity to waste light, ain't it," his father said, "and the full moon shinin'."

He came to the window and they watched it together.

"Son, what do it put in your head? Do you mind what we said we'd do, full moon in April?"

"I dis-remember."

Somehow, the seasons always took him unawares. It must be necessary to be as old as his father to keep them in the mind and memory, to remember moon-time from one year's end to another.

"You ain't forgot what I told you? I'll swear, Jody. Why, boy, the bears comes outen their winter beds on the full moon in April."

"Old Slewfoot! You said we'd lay for him when he come out!"

"That's it."

"You said we'd go where we seed his tracks comin' and goin' and criss-crossin', and likely find his bed, and him, too, comin' out in April."

"And fat. Fat and lazy. The meat so sweet, from him layin' up."

"And him mebbe easier to ketch, not woke up good."

"That's it."

"When kin we go, Pa?"

"Soon as we git the hoein' done. And see bear-sign."

"Which-a-way will we begin huntin' him?"

"We'd best to go by the Glen springs and see has he come out and watered there."

"A big ol' doe watered there today," Jody said. "Whilst I was asleep. I built me a flutter-mill, Pa. It run fine."

Ma Baxter stopped the clatter of her pots and pans.

"You sly scaper," she said. "That's the first I knowed you been off. You gittin' slick as a clay road in the rain."

He shouted with laughter.

"I fooled you, Ma. Say it, Ma, I got to fool you oncet."

"You fooled me. And me standin' over the fire makin' potato pone——"

She was not truly angry.

"Now, Ma," he cajoled her, "suppose I was a varmint and didn't eat nothin' but roots and grass."

"I'd not have nothin' then to rile me," she said.

At the same time he saw her mouth twist. She tried to straighten it and could not.

"Ma's a-laughin'! Ma's a-laughin'! You ain't riled when you laugh!"

He darted behind her and untied her apron strings. The apron slipped to the floor. She turned her bulk quickly and boxed his ears, but the blows were feather-light and playful. The same delirium came over him again that he had felt in the afternoon. He began to whirl around and around as he had done in the broom-sage.

"You knock them plates offen the table," she said, "and you'll see who's riled."

"I cain't he'p it. I'm dizzy."

"You're addled," she said. "Jest plain addled."

It was true. He was addled with April. He was dizzy with Spring. He was as drunk as Lem Forrester on a Saturday night. His head was swimming with the strong brew made up of the sun and the air and the thin gray rain. The flutter-mill had made him drunk, and the doe's coming, and his father's hiding his absence, and his mother's making him a pone and laughing at him. He was stabbed with the candle-light inside the safe comfort of the cabin; with the moonlight around it. He pictured old Slewfoot, the great black outlaw bear with one toe missing, rearing up in his winter bed and tasting the soft air and smelling the moonlight, as he, Jody, smelled and tasted them. He went to bed in a fever and could not sleep. A mark was on him from the day's delight, so that all his life, when April was a thin green and the flavor of rain was on his tongue, an old wound would throb and a nostalgia would fill him for something he could not quite remember. A whip-poor-will called across the bright night, and suddenly he was asleep.

Chapter II

ENNY BAXTER lay awake beside the vast sleeping bulk of his wife. He was always wakeful on the full moon. He had often wondered whether, with the light so bright, men were not meant to go into their fields and labor. He would like to slip from his bed and perhaps cut down an oak for wood, or finish the hoeing that Jody had left undone.

"I reckon I'd ought to of crawled him about it," he thought.

In his day, he would have been thoroughly thrashed for slipping away and idling. His father would have sent him back to the spring, without his supper, to tear out the flutter-mill.

"But that's it," he thought. "A boy ain't a boy too long."

As he looked back over the years, he himself had had no boyhood. His own father had been a preacher, stern as the Old Testament God. The living had come, however, not from the Word, but from the small farm near Volusia on which he had raised a large family. He had taught them to read and write and to know the Scriptures, but all of them, from the time they could toddle behind him down the corn rows, carrying the sack of seed, had toiled until their small bones ached and their growing fingers cramped. Rations had been short and hookworm abundant. Penny had grown to maturity no bigger than a boy. His feet were small, his shoulders narrow, his ribs and hips jointed together in a continuous fragile framework. He had stood among the Forresters one day, like an ash sapling among giant oaks.

Lem Forrester looked down at him and said, "Why, you leetle ol' penny-piece, you. You're good money, a'right, but hit jest don't come no smaller. Leetle ol' Penny Baxter——"

The name had been his only one ever since. When he voted, he signed himself "Ezra Ezekial Baxter," but when he paid his taxes, he was put down as "Penny Baxter" and made no protest. But he was a sound amalgam; sound as copper itself; and with something, too, of the copper's softness. He leaned backward in his honesty, so that he was often a temptation to store-keepers and mill-owners and horse-traders. Store-keeper Boyles at Volusia, as honest as he, had once given him a dollar too much in change. His horse being lame, Penny had walked the long miles back again to return it.

"The next time you came to trade would have done," Boyles said.

"I know," Penny answered him, "but 'twa'n't mine and I wouldn't of wanted to die with it on me. Dead or alive, I only want what's mine."

The remark might have explained, to those who puzzled at him, his migration to the adjacent scrub. Folk who lived along the deep and placid river, alive with craft, with dug-outs and scows, lumber rafts and freight and passenger vessels, side-wheel steamers that almost filled the stream, in places, from bank to bank, had said that Penny Baxter was either a brave man or a crazy one to leave the common way of life and take his bride into the very heart of the wild Florida scrub, populous with bears and wolves and panthers. It had been understandable for the Forresters to go there, for the growing family of great burly quarrelsome males needed all the room in the county, and freedom from any hindrance. But who would hinder Penny Baxter?

It was not hindrance— But in the towns and villages, in farming sections where neighbors were not too far apart, men's minds and actions and property overlapped. There were intrusions on the individual spirit. There were friendliness and mutual help in time of trouble, true, but there were bickerings and watchfulness, one man suspicious of another. He had grown from under the sternness of his father into a world less direct, less honest, in its harshness, and therefore more disturbing.

He had perhaps been bruised too often. The peace of the vast aloof scrub had drawn him with the beneficence of its silence. Something in him was raw and tender. The touch of men was hurtful upon it, but the touch of the pines was healing. Making a living came harder there, distances were troublesome in the buying of supplies and the marketing of crops. But the clearing was peculiarly his own. The wild animals seemed less predatory to him than people he had known. The forays of bear and wolf and wild-cat and panther on stock were understandable, which was more than he could say of human cruelties.

In his thirties he had married a buxom girl, already twice his size, loaded her in an ox-cart along with the rudiments of housekeeping, and jogged with her to the clearing, where with his own hands he had reared a cabin. He had chosen his land as well as a man might choose in the brooding expanse of scrawny sand pines. He had bought of the Forresters, who lived a safe four miles away, high good land in the center of a pine island. The island was called by such a name, in an arid forest, because it was literally an island of long-leaf pines, lifted high, a landmark, in the rolling sea that was the scrub. There were other such islands scattered to the north and west, where some accident of soil or moisture produced patches of luxuriant growth; even of hammock, the richest growth of all. Live oaks were here and there; the red bay and the magnolia; wild cherry and sweet gum; hickory and holly.

A scarcity of water was the only draw-back to the location. The water level lay so deep that wells were priceless. Water for inhabitants of Baxter's Island must come, until bricks and mortar were cheaper, from the great sink-hole on the western boundary of the hundred-acre tract. The sink-hole was a phenomenon common to the Florida limestone regions. Underground rivers ran through such sections. The bubbling springs that turned at once into creeks and runs were outbreaks of these. Sometimes a thin shell of surface soil caved in and a great cavern was revealed, with or without a flow of water. The sink-hole included with Penny Baxter's land contained, unfortunately, no flowing spring. But a pure filtered water seeped day and night through the high banks and formed a pool at the bottom. The Forresters had tried to sell Penny poor land in the scrub itself, but with cash to back him, he had insisted on the island.

He had said to them, "The scrub's a fitten place for the game to raise, and all the wild things. Foxes and deer and panther-cats and rattlesnakes. I cain't raise young uns in a pure thicket."

The Forresters had slapped their thighs and roared with laughter from their beards.

Lem had bellowed, "How mainy ha' pennies is in a penny? You'll do good, be you daddy to a fox-cub."

Penny could hear him now, after all the years. He turned over in his bed, cautiously, not to awaken his wife. He had indeed planned boldly for sons and daughters, moving in prolific plenty among the long-leaf pines. The family had come. Ora Baxter was plainly built for child-bearing. But it had seemed as though his seed were as puny as himself.

"Or Lem put a mouth on me," he thought.

The babies were frail, and almost as fast as they came, they sickened and died. Penny had buried them one by one in a cleared place among the black-jack oaks, where the poor loose soil made the digging easier. The plot grew in size until he was compelled to fence it in against the vandalism of hogs and pole-cats. He had carved little wooden tombstones for all. He could picture them now, standing white and straight in the moonlight. Some of them had names: Ezra Jr.; Little Ora; William T. The others bore only such legends as Baby Baxter, aged 3 mos. 6 days. On one, Penny had scratched laboriously with his pocket-knife, "She never saw the light of day." His mind moved back down the years, touching them, as a man touches fence-posts in his passing.

There had been a hiatus in the births. Then, when the loneliness of the place had begun to frighten him a little, and his wife was almost past the age of bearing, Jody Baxter was born and thrived. When the baby was a toddling two-year-old, Penny had gone to the war. He had taken his wife and child to the river, to live with his crony, Grandma Hutto, for the few months he expected to be away. He had come back at the end of four years with the mark of age on him. He had gathered up his wife and boy and taken them back to the scrub with gratitude for its peace and isolation.

Jody's mother had accepted her youngest with something of detachment, as though she had given all she had of love and care and interest to those others. But Penny's bowels yearned over his son. He gave him something more than his paternity. He found that the child stood wide-eyed and breathless before the miracle of bird and creature, of flower and tree, of wind and rain and sun and moon, as he had always stood. And if, on a soft day in April, the boy had prowled away on his boy's business, he could understand the thing that had drawn him. He understood, too, its briefness.

His wife's bulk stirred and she made a sound in her sleep. He would act on any such occasion, he knew, as a bulwark for the boy against the mother's sharpness. The whip-poor-will flew farther into the forest and took up his lament again, sweet with distance. The moonlight moved beyond the focus of the bedroom window.

"Leave him kick up his heels," he thought, "and run away. Leave him build his flutter-mills. The day'll come, he'll not even care to."

Chapter III

JODY opened his eyes unwillingly. Sometime, he thought, he would slip away into the woods and sleep from Friday until Monday. Daylight was showing through the east window of his small bedroom. He could not be certain whether it was the pale light that had awakened him, or the stirring of the chickens in the peach trees. He heard them fluttering one by one from their roost in the branches. The daylight lay in orange streaks. The pines beyond the clearing were still black against it. Now in April the sun was rising earlier. It could not be very late. It was good to awaken by himself before his mother called him. He turned over luxuriously. The dry corn shucks of his mattress rustled under him. The Dominick rooster crowed boisterously under the window.

"You crow now," the boy said. "See kin you rout me out."

The bright streaks in the east thickened and blended. A golden flush spread as high as the pines, and as he watched, the sun itself lifted, like a vast copper skillet being drawn to hang among the branches. A light wind stirred, as though the growing light had pushed it out of the restless east. The sacking curtains eddied out into the room. The breeze reached the bed and brushed him with the cool softness of clean fur. He lay for a moment in torment between the luxury of his bed and the coming day. Then he was out of his nest and standing on the deerskin rug, and his breeches were hanging handily, and his shirt right side out by good fortune, and he was in them, and dressed, and there was not any need of sleep, or anything but the day, and the smell of hot cakes in the kitchen.

20

The Yearling

"Hey, ol' Ma," he said at the door. "I like you, Ma."

"You and them hounds and all the rest o' the stock," she said. "Mighty lovin' on a empty belly and me with a dish in my hand."

"That's the way you're purtiest," he said, and grinned.

He went whistling to the water-shelf and dipped into the wooden bucket to fill the wash-basin. He sousled his hands and face in the water, deciding against the strong lye soap. He wet his hair and parted and smoothed it with his fingers. He took down the small mirror from the wall and studied himself a moment.

"I'm turrible ugly, Ma," he called.

"Well, there ain't been a purty Baxter since the name begun."

He wrinkled his nose at the mirror. The gesture made the freckles across the bridge blend together.

"I wisht I was dark like the Forresters."

"You be proud you ain't. Them fellers is black as their hearts. You a Baxter and all the Baxters is fair."

"You talk like I wasn't no kin to you."

"My folks runs to fairness, too. They ain't none of 'em puny, though. Iffen you'll learn yourself to work, you'll be your Pa all over."

The mirror showed a small face with high cheek bones. The face was freckled and pale, but healthy, like a fine sand. The hair grieved him on the occasions when he went to church or any doings at Volusia. It was straw-colored and shaggy, and no matter how carefully his father cut it, once a month on the Sunday morning nearest the full moon, it grew in tufts at the back. "Drakes' tails," his mother called them. His eyes were wide and blue. When he frowned, in close study over his reader, or watching something curious, they narrowed. It was then that his mother claimed him kin.

"He do favor the Alverses a mite," she said.

Jody turned the mirror to inspect his ears; not for

cleanliness, but remembering the pain of the day when Lem Forrester had held his chin with one vast hand and pulled his ears with the other.

"Boy, your ears is set up on your head like a 'possum's," Lem said.

Jody made a leering grimace at himself and returned the mirror to the wall.

"Do we got to wait for Pa to eat breakfast?" he asked.

"We do. Set it all in front of you and there'd likely not be enough left for him."

He hesitated at the back door.

"And don't you slip off, neither. He ain't but to the corn-crib."

From the south, beyond the black-jacks, he heard the bell-like voice of old Julia, giving tongue in great excitement. He thought he heard, too, his father, giving her a command. He bolted away before his mother's sharp voice could stop him. She, too, had heard the dog. She followed to the door and called after him.

"Don't you and your Pa be gone too long now, follerin' that fool hound. I'm o' no mind to set around waitin' breakfast and you two piddlin' around in the woods."

He could no longer hear either old Julia or his father. He was in a frenzy for fear the excitement was over; the intruder gone and perhaps dog and father with it. He crashed through the black-jacks in the direction from which the sounds had come. His father's voice spoke, close at hand.

"Easy, son. What's done 'll wait for you."

He stopped short. Old Julia stood trembling, not in fear but in eagerness. His father stood looking down at the crushed and mangled carcass of black Betsy, the brood sow.

"He must of heered me darin' him," Penny said. "Look careful, boy. See do you see what I see."

The sight of the mutilated sow sickened him. His father was looking beyond the dead animal. Old Julia had her sharp nose turned in the same direction. Jody walked a few paces and examined the sand. The unmistakable tracks made his blood jump. They were the tracks of a giant bear. And from the print of the right front paw, as big as the crown of a hat, one toe was missing.

"Old Slewfoot!"

Penny nodded.

"I'm proud you remembered his track."

They bent together and studied the signs and the direction in which they had both come and gone.

"That's what I call," Penny said, "carryin' the war into the enemy's camp."

"None o' the dogs bayed him, Pa. Lessen I didn't hear, for sleepin'."

"None of 'em bayed him. He had the wind in his favor. Don't you think he didn't know what he was doin'. He slipped in like a shadow and done his meanness and slipped out afore day."

A chill ran along Jody's backbone. He could picture the shadow, big and black as a shed in motion, moving among the black-jacks and gathering in the tame and sleeping sow with one sweep of the great clawed paw. Then the white tusks followed into the backbone, crushing it, and into the warm and palpitating flesh. Betsy had had no chance even to squeal for help.

"He'd a'ready fed," Penny pointed out. "He ate no more'n a mouthful. A bear's stomach is shrunk when he first comes outen his winter bed. That's why I hate a bear. A creetur that kills and eats what he needs, why, he's jest like the rest of us, makin' out the best he kin. But an animal, or a person either, that'll do harm jest to be a-doin'—— You look in a bear's face and you'll see he's got no remorse."

"You aim to carry in old Betsy?"

"The meat's bad tore up, but I reckon there's sausage left. And lard."

Jody knew that he should feel badly about old Betsy, but

all that he could feel was excitement. The unwarranted kill, inside the sanctuary of the Baxter acres, had made a personal enemy of the big bear that had evaded all the stock owners for five years. He was wild to begin the hunt. He acknowledged to himself, as well, a trace of fear. Old Slewfoot had struck close to home.

He took one hind leg of the sow and Penny the other. They dragged it to the house with Julia reluctant at their heels. The old bear-dog could not understand why they did not set out at once on the chase.

"I'll swear," Penny said, "I'm daresome to break the news to your Ma."

"She'll rare for certain," Jody agreed.

"Betsy was sich a fine brood sow. My, she was fine."

Ma Baxter was waiting for them by the gate.

"I been a-callin' and I been a-callin'," she hailed them. "What you got there, piddlin' around so long? Oh dear goodness, oh dear goodness—my sow, my sow."

She threw her arms toward the sky. Penny and Jody passed through the gate and back of the house. She followed, wailing.

"We'll hang the meat to the cross-piece, son," Penny said. "The dogs'll not reach it there."

"You might tell me," Ma Baxter said. "The least you kin do is tell me, how come her dead and tore to ribbons right under my nose."

"Old Slewfoot done it, Ma," Jody said. "His tracks was certain."

"And them dogs asleep right here in the clearin'?"

The three had already appeared, nosing about the fresh smell of the blood. She threw a stick in their direction.

"You no-account creeturs! Hornin' in on our rations and leavin' sich as this to happen."

"Ain't a dog borned as smart as that bear," Penny said.

"They could of barked."

She threw another stick and the dogs slunk away.

The Yearling

The family went to the house. In the confusion, Jody went first into the kitchen, where the smell of breakfast tortured him. His mother could not be too disturbed to notice what he was doing.

"You git right back here," she called, "and wash your dirty hands."

He joined his father at the water-shelf. Breakfast was on the table. Ma Baxter sat, swaying her body in distress, and did not eat. Jody heaped his plate. There were grits and gravy, hot cakes, and buttermilk.

"Anyway," he said, "we got meat to eat for a whiles now."

She turned on him.

"Meat now, and none this winter."

"I'll ask the Forresters out of a sow," Penny said.

"Yes, and be beholden to them rascals." She began to wail again. "That blasted bear— I'd like to git my hands on him."

"I'll tell him when I see him," Penny said mildly between mouthfuls.

Jody burst out laughing.

"That's right," she said. "Make a fun-box outen me."

Jody patted her big arm.

"Hit jest come to me, Ma, how you'd look—you and ol' Slewfoot mixin' it."

"I'd bet on your Ma," Penny said.

"Nobody but me don't take life serious," she lamented.

Chapter IV

ENNY pushed back his plate and stood up from the table.

"Well, son, we got our day's work laid out for us."

Jody's heart fell. Hoeing——

"We stand a right good chancet o'comin' up with that bear today."

The sun was bright again.

"Fetch me my shot-bag and my powder horn. And the tinder horn."

Jody jumped to bring them.

"Look at him move," his mother said. "To see him hoe, you'd think he was a snail. Say 'huntin' ' and he's quick as a otter."

She went to the kitchen safe and took out one of the few remaining glasses of jelly. She spread the jelly on the left-over stack of hot cakes and tied them in a piece of cloth and dropped them in Penny's knapsack. She took the remains of the sweet potato pone and set aside a piece for herself, then added the pone, wrapped in a fragment of paper, to the knapsack. She looked again at the pone she had saved, and with a quick motion dropped it in the sack with the other.

"This ain't much dinner," she said. "Mebbe you'll be soon back."

"Don't look for us 'til you see us," Penny said. "Anyways, no man never starved to death in a day."

"To hear Jody tell it," she said, "he kin starve to death about a hour after breakfast."

Penny swung the knapsack and tinder horn over his shoulder.

26

The Yearling

"Jody, take the big knife and go cut a good strip offen that 'gator tail."

The meat, dry-cured for the feeding of the dogs, hung in the smoke-house. Jody ran to it and swung open the heavy timbered door. The smoke-house was dark and cool, odorous with the smell of hams and bacons, dusty with the ash of hickory. The rafters, studded with square-headed nails for the hanging of meats, were now almost bare. Three shoulders of ham hung, lean and withered, and two bacon sides. A haunch of jerked venison swung beside the smoked alligator meat. Old Slewfoot had indeed done damage. Betsy the brood-sow would have filled the room with her plump progeny by the coming fall. Jody hacked away a piece of alligator. The meat was dry but tender. He touched his tongue to it. Its saltiness was not unpleasing. He joined his father in the yard.

At sight of the old muzzle-loading shotgun, Julia lifted her voice in a wail of delight. Rip shot from under the house to join her. Perk, the new feice, wagged his tail stupidly and without understanding. Penny patted the dogs in turn.

"You'll likely not be so merry, time the day be done," he told them. "Jody-boy, you best put on your shoes. Hit'll be rough goin', places."

It seemed to Jody that he would burst if there was further delay. He dashed in to his room and routed out his heavy cowhide brogans from under the bed. He slipped his feet into them and raced after his father as though the hunt would be done and over before he reached him. Old Julia was loping ahead, her long nose against the trail of the bear.

"The trail'll not be too cold, Pa? Reckon he won't be gone too fur yonder to ketch up with him?"

"He'll be fur yonder, but we got a heap better chancet o' ketchin' up with him, do we let him take it easy and give him time to lay up. A bear that knows he's follered moves a sight faster'n one that figgers the world's his own, to prowl and feed in."

The Yearling

The trail led south through the black-jacks. After the rain of the afternoon before, the great nubbed tracks made a plain pattern across the sand.

"He's got a foot like a Georgia nigger," Penny said.

The black-jacks ended as though they had been sown by hand and there had been no more seed in the sack. The land was lower and the growth was of large pines.

"Pa, how big you reckon he be?"

"He's big. He ain't full weight right now, account of his stomach bein' shrunk up from layin' up, and empty. But look at that track. Hit's sizable enough to prove him. And look at the way it's deeper at the back. A deer track'll prove the same. A deer or bear that's fat and heavy'll sink in that-a-way. A leetle ol' light doe or yearlin' 'll walk tippy-toed, and you'll not see more than the front of their hooves. Oh, he's big."

"You'll not be scairt when we come up with him, Pa?"

"Not lessen things goes mighty wrong. I'm fearful, always, for the pore dogs. They're the scapers gits the worst of it."

Penny's eyes twinkled.

"I don't reckon you'll be scairt, son?"

"Not me." He thought a moment. "But if I was to be scairt, must I climb a tree?"

Penny chuckled.

"Yes, son. Even if you ain't scairt, hit's a good place to watch the ruckus."

They walked in silence. Old Julia moved certainly. Rip the bulldog was content to follow at her heels, snuffing where she snuffed, stopping when she hesitated. She blew through her soft nose when the grasses tickled it. The feice made dashes to one side or another and once tore wildly after a rabbit that bolted from under his nose. Jody whistled after him.

"Leave him go, son," Penny told him. "He'll join up agin when it comes to him he's lonesome."

The Yearling

Old Julia gave a thin high wail and looked over her shoulder.

"The wise old scaper's changin' his direction," Penny said. "Likely he's headin' for the saw-grass ponds. Iffen that's his notion, we kin mebbe slip around and surprise him."

Some understanding came to Jody of the secret of his father's hunting. The Forresters, he thought, would have plunged after old Slewfoot the moment they had found his kill. They would have shouted and bellowed, their pack of dogs would have bayed until the scrub echoed with it, for they encouraged them in it, and the wary old bear would have had full warning of their coming. His father got game, ten to their one. The little man was famous for it.

Jody said, "You shore kin figger what a creetur'll do."

"You belong to figger. A wild creetur's quicker'n a man and a heap stronger. What's a man got that a bear ain't got? A mite more sense. He cain't out-run a bear, but he's a sorry hunter if he cain't out-study him."

The pines were becoming scattering. There was suddenly a strip of hammock land, and a place of live oaks and scrub palmettos. The undergrowth was thick, laced with cat-briers. Then hammock, too, ended, and to the south and west lay a broad open expanse that looked at first sight to be a meadow. This was the saw-grass. It grew knee-deep in water, its harsh saw-edged blades rising so thickly that it seemed a compact vegetation. Old Julia splashed into it. The rippling of the water showed the pond. A gust of air passed across the open area, the saw-grass waved and parted, and the shallow water of a dozen ponds showed clearly. Penny watched the hound intently. The treeless expanse seemed to Jody more stirring than the shadowy forest. At any moment the great black form might rear itself high.

He whispered, "Will we cut around?"

Penny shook his head. He answered in a low voice.

"Wind's wrong. Don't seem to me like he's headin' acrost it, nohow."

29

The Yearling

The hound splashed in a zigzag trail where solid ground edged the saw-grass. Here and there the scent was lost in the water. Once she dipped her head to lap, not in thirst, but for the very taste of the trail. She moved confidently down the middle of the pond. Rip and Perk found their short legs too deep in muck for comfort. They retreated to higher ground and shook themselves, watching Julia anxiously. Perk barked shortly, and Penny slapped him, for quiet. Jody stepped cautiously behind his father. A blue heron flew low over him without warning, and he started. The pond water was cold an instant against his legs, his breeches were clammy, the muck sucked at his shoes. Then the water was comfortable, and it was good to walk in the wet coolness, leaving sandy whirlpools behind.

"He's feedin' on the fire-plant," Penny murmured.

He pointed to the flat arrow-shaped leaves. Edges showed jagged tooth-marks. Others were bitten clear of the stalk.

"Hit's his spring tonic. A bear'll make for it first thing, time he comes out in the spring." He leaned close and touched a leaf whose ragged edge was turning brown. "Dogged if he wa'n't here a night ago, too. That's how come him to have appetite for a nip o' pore old Betsy."

The hound too paused. The scent lay now, not underfoot, but on the reeds and grasses where the strong-smelling fur had brushed. She laid her long nose against a bulrush and stared into space, then, satisfied as to direction, splashed due south at a lively pace. Penny spoke now freely.

"He's done feedin'. Old Julia says he's clippin' it for home."

He moved to higher land, keeping the hound in sight. He walked briskly, chatting.

"Many's the time I've seed a bear feedin' on the fire-plant in the moonlight. He'll snort and shuffle, and splash and grunt. He'll rip them leaves offen the stems and cram 'em in his ugly ol' mouth like a person. Then he'll nose along and chaw, like a dog chawin' grass. And the night-birds cryin' over him, and the bull-frogs hollerin' like nigger-dogs, and the Mallards callin' 'Snake! Snake! Snake!' and the drops o' water on the leaves o' the fire-plant shinin' bright and red as a bull-bat's eyes——"

It was as good as seeing it, to hear Penny tell of it.

"I'd shore love to see a bear feedin' on the fire-plant, Pa."

"Well, you live long as me, and you'll see that and a heap more things is strange and curious."

"Did you shoot 'em, Pa, while they was feedin'?"

"Son, I've helt back my shot and contented myself with watchin' many a time when creeturs was feedin' harmless and innocent. It goes agin me to crack down at sich a time. Or when creeturs is matin'. Now and agin, when it was git meat or the Baxters go hongry, I've done what I've no likin' to do. And don't you grow up like the Forresters, killin' meat you got no use for, for the fun of it. That's evil as the bears. You hear me?"

"Yes, sir."

Old Julia gave a sharp cry. The trail cut at right angles, to the east.

"I feared it," Penny said. "The bay——"

The red bay thicket seemed impenetrable. This land of sudden changes gave good cover for the game. Old Slewfoot in his careless feeding had never been far from shelter. The bay saplings stood as close together as the palings of a stockade. Jody wondered how the bear had managed to work his bulk among them. But here and there the saplings thinned, or were young and limber, and he could see, plainly marked, a common trail. Other creatures had used it. Tracks crossed and crisscrossed. Wild-cat had followed deer, lynx had followed wild-cat, and all about were the paw-prints of the small things, 'coons and rabbits and 'possums and skunks, feeding cautiously aside from their predatory kin.

Penny said, "I reckon I best load."

He clucked to Julia to wait for him. She lay down knowingly to rest and Rip and Perk dropped willingly beside her.

The Yearling

Jody had been carrying the powder horn over his shoulder. Penny opened it and shook a measure of powder down the muzzle. From his shot-bag he pulled a wisp of dried black Spanish moss, inserted it for wadding, and packed it with the ramrod. He dropped in a measure of low-mould shot, more wadding, and at the last, a cap, and used the ramrod lightly again.

"All right, Julia. Git him."

The morning's trailing had been a leisurely business; a pleasant jaunting rather than a hunt. Now the dark bay thicket closed in over their heads, jorees flew from the denseness with an alarming whir of wings, the earth was soft and black, and there were scurryings and rustlings on either side in the bushes. On the trail, a bar of sunlight lay occasionally where the thicket parted. The scent, for all the comings and goings, was not confused, for the taint of bear hung heavy in the leafy tunnel. The short fur of the bulldog stood on end. Old Julia ran swiftly. Penny and Jody were forced to stoop to follow. Penny swung the muzzle-loader in his right hand, its barrel tipped at an angle, so that if he stumbled and the charge went off, he would not touch the running dogs before him. A branch crashed behind and Jody clutched at his father's shirt. A squirrel ran chattering away.

The thicket thinned. The ground dropped lower and became a swamp. The sunlight came through in patches as big as a basket. There were giant ferns here, taller than their heads. One lay crushed where the bear had moved across it. Its spiced sweetness lay heavy on the warm air. A young tendril sprang back into an upright position. Penny pointed to it. Slewfoot, Jody understood, had passed not many minutes before. Old Julia was feverish. The trail was food and drink. Her nose skimmed the damp ground. A scrub jay flew ahead, warning the game, and crying *"Plick-up-wha-a-a."*

The swamp dipped to a running branch no broader than a fence post. The print of the nubbed foot spanned it. A water moccasin lifted a curious head, then spun down-stream

The Yearling

in smooth brown spirals. Across the branch, palmettos grew. The great track continued across the swamp. Jody noticed that the back of his father's shirt was wet. He touched his own sleeve. It was dripping. Suddenly Julia bayed and Penny began to run.

"The Creek!" he shouted. "He's tryin' to make the Creek!"

Sound filled the swamp. Saplings crashed. The bear was a black hurricane, mowing down obstructions. The dogs barked and bayed. The roaring in Jody's ears was his heart pounding. A bamboo vine tripped him and he sprawled and was on his feet again. Penny's short legs churned in front of him like paddles. Slewfoot would make Juniper Creek before the dogs could halt him at bay.

A clear space opened at the creek's bank. Jody saw a vast black shapeless form break through. Penny halted and lifted his gun. On the instant, a small brown missile hurled itself at the shaggy head. Old Julia had caught up with her enemy. She leaped and retreated, and in the moment of retreat, was at him again. Rip darted in beside her. Slewfoot wheeled and slashed at him. Julia flashed at his flank. Penny held his fire. He could not shoot, for the dogs.

Old Slewfoot was suddenly, deceptively, indifferent. He seemed to stand baffled, slow and uncertain, weaving back and forth. He whined, like a child whimpering. The dogs backed off an instant. The moment was perfect for a shot and Penny swung his gun to his shoulder, drew a bead on the left cheek, and pulled the trigger. A harmless pop sounded. He cocked the hammer again and pulled the trigger once more. The sweat stood out on his forehead. Again the hammer clicked futilely. Then a black storm broke. It roared in on the dogs with incredible swiftness. White tusks and curved claws were streaks of lightning across it. It snarled and whirled and gnashed its teeth and slashed in every direction. The dogs were as quick. Julia made swift sorties from the rear, and when Slewfoot wheeled to rake at her, Rip leaped for the hairy throat.

The Yearling

Jody was in a paralysis of horror. He saw that his father had cocked the hammer again and stood half-crouching, licking his lips, fingering the trigger. Old Julia bored in at the bear's right flank. He wheeled, not on her, but on the bulldog at his left. He caught him sideways and sent him sprawling into the bushes. Again Penny pulled the trigger. The explosion that followed had a sizzling sound, and Penny fell backward. The gun had back-fired.

Rip returned to his attempts for the bear's throat and Julia took up her worrying from the rear. The bear stood again at bay, weaving. Jody ran to his father. Penny was already on his feet. The right side of his face was black with powder. Slewfoot shook free of Rip, whirled to Julia and caught her to his chest with his cupped claws. She yelped sharply. Rip hurled himself at the back and buried his teeth in the hide.

Jody screamed, "He's killin' Julia!"

Penny ran desperately into the heart of the fracas. He jammed the gun-barrel in the bear's ribs. Even in her pain, Julia had taken a grip on the black throat above her. Slewfoot snarled and turned suddenly and plunged down the bank of the creek and into the deep water. Both dogs kept their hold. Slewfoot swam madly. Only Julia's head showed above water, below the bear's snout. Rip rode the broad back with bravado. Slewfoot made the far bank and scrambled up its side. Julia loosed her hold and dropped limply on the earth. The bear plunged toward the dense thicket. For a moment more Rip stayed with him. Then, confused, he too dropped away and turned back uncertainly to the creek. He snuffed at Julia and sat down on his haunches and howled across the water. There was a crashing in the distant undergrowth, then silence.

Penny called, "Here, Rip! Here, Julia!"

Rip wagged his stumpy tail and did not stir. Penny lifted his hunting horn to his lips and blew caressingly. Jody saw Julia lift her head, then fall back again.

THE FIGHT WITH OLD SLEWFOOT

Penny said, "I got to go fetch her."

He slipped off his shoes and slid down the bank into the water. He struck out strongly. A few yards from shore the current laid hold of him as though he were a log and shot him down-stream at a fierce clip. He struggled against it, fighting for distance. Jody saw him stagger to his feet far down the run, wipe the water from his eyes and push his way back up the shore to his dogs. He leaned to examine the hound, then gathered her under one arm. This time he went some distance up-stream before taking to the creek. When he dropped into the water, stroking with his free arm, the current picked him up and deposited him almost at Jody's feet. Rip paddled behind him, landed and shook himself. Penny laid the old hound down gently.

"She's bad hurt," he said.

He took off his shirt and trussed the dog in it. He tied the sleeves together to make a sling and hoisted it on his back.

"This settles it," he said. "I got to git me a new gun."

The powder burn on his cheek had already turned into a blister.

"What's wrong, Pa?"

"Near about ever'thing. The hammer's loose on the cylinder. I knowed that. I been havin' to cock it two-three times right along. But when it back-fired, that belongs to mean the main-spring's got weak. Well, le's git goin'. You tote the blasted ol' gun."

The procession started homeward through the swamp. Penny cut north and west.

"Now I'll not rest 'til I git that bear," he said. "Jest give me a new gun—and time."

Suddenly Jody could not endure the sight of the limp bundle in front of him. There were tricklings of blood down his father's thin bare back.

"I want to go ahead, Pa."

Penny turned and eyed him.

"Don't go gittin' faintified on me."

"I kin break a trail for you."

"All right. Go ahead. Jody—take the knapsack. Git you some bread. Eat a bite, boy. You'll feel better."

Jody fumbled blindly in the sack and pulled out the parcel of pancakes. The brierberry jelly was tart and cool on his tongue. He was ashamed to have it taste so good. He bolted several of the cakes. He handed some to his father.

"Rations is mighty comfortin'," Penny said.

A whine sounded in the bushes. A small cringing form was following them. It was Perk, the feice. Jody kicked at him in a fury.

"Don't bother him," Penny said. "I suspected him all along. There's dogs is bear-dogs and there's dogs jest isn't bear-dogs."

The feice dropped in at the end of the line. Jody tried to break trail, but fallen trees lay, thicker than his body, and would not be stirred. Bull-briers, tougher than his father's muscles, snared him, and he could only push his way around them or crawl beneath. Penny with his burden had to shift for himself. The swamp was close and humid. Rip was panting. The pancakes lay soothingly in Jody's belly. He reached in the knapsack for the sweet potato pone. His father refused his share and Jody divided it with Rip. The little feice, he thought, deserved nothing.

It was good to clear the swamp at last and come into the open pine woods. Even the scrub that followed after for a mile or two seemed light and penetrable. Pushing through the low scrub oaks, the scrub palmettos, the gallberry bushes and the ti-ti was less laborious than crossing the swamp. It was late afternoon when the high pines of Baxter's Island showed ahead. The procession filed down the sand road from the east and into the clearing. Rip and Perk ran ahead to the hollowed cypress watering trough kept for the chickens. Ma Baxter sat rocking on the narrow veranda, a mound of mending in her lap.

"A dead dog and no bear, eh?" she called.

The Yearling

"Not dead yit. Git me water and rags and the big needle and thread."

She rose quickly to help. Jody was always amazed at the capability of her great frame and hands when there was trouble. Penny laid old Julia down on the veranda floor. She whimpered. Jody bent to stroke her head and she bared her teeth at him. He trailed his mother disconsolately. She was tearing an old apron into strips.

"You kin fetch the water," she told him, and he scurried to the kettle.

Penny returned to the veranda with an armful of crocus sacks to make a bed for the hound. Ma Baxter brought the surgical equipment. Penny unwrapped his blood-soaked shirt from the dog and bathed the deep gashes. Old Julia made no protest. She had known claws before. He sewed the two deepest cuts and rubbed pine gum into all of them. She yelped once and then was silent as he worked. A rib, he said, was broken. He could do nothing for that, but if she lived, it would mend. She had lost much blood. Her breath came short. Penny gathered her up, bed and all.

Ma Baxter demanded, "Now where you carryin' her?"

"To the bedroom. I got to watch her tonight."

"Not to my bedroom, Ezra Baxter. I'll do for her what's got to be done, but I'll not have you poppin' in and outen the bed all night, wakin' me. I didn't half sleep, last night."

"Then I'll sleep with Jody and bed Julia there," he said. "I'll not leave her alone in no shed tonight. Fetch me cold water, Jody."

He carried her to Jody's room and laid her in the corner on the pile of sacking. She would not drink, or could not, and he opened her mouth and poured water down her dry throat.

"Leave her rest now. We'll go do our chores."

The clearing possessed this evening a strange coziness. Jody gathered the eggs from the hay-mow, milked the cow and turned the calf in to her, and cut wood for his mother. Penny, as always, went to the sink-hole with a wooden ox-yoke supporting two wooden buckets over his thin shoulders. Ma Baxter cooked supper of poke-greens and dried cow-peas. She fried a frugal slice of the fresh pork.

"A piece o' bear meat 'd go mighty good tonight," she lamented.

Jody was hungry but Jenny had little appetite. He left the table twice to offer Julia food, which she rejected. Ma Baxter rose heavily to clear the table and wash the dishes. She asked for no details of the hunt. Jody longed to talk of it, to cast away the spell of the tracking, and the fight, and the fear that had struck him. Penny was silent. No one noticed the boy and he dipped deeply into the dish of cow-peas.

The sun set red and clear. Shadows lay long and black in the Baxter kitchen.

Penny said, "I'm wore out. I could do with bed."

Jody's feet were raw and blistered from the cowhide shoes. "Me, too," he said.

"I'll set up a whiles," Ma Baxter said. "I ain't done much today, excusin' fret and worry, and mess with the sausage."

Penny and Jody went to their room. They undressed on the side of the narrow bed.

"Now if you was big as your Ma," Penny said, "we couldn't lay in it without somebody fell on the floor."

There was room enough for the two thin bony bodies. The red faded from the west and the room was dusky. The hound slept and whimpered in her sleep. The moon rose, an hour past the full, and the small room lay in a silver brightness. Jody's feet burned. His knees twitched.

Penny said, "You wakeful, son?"

"I cain't stop walkin'."

"We went a fur piece. How you like bear-huntin', boy?"

"Well—" He rubbed his knees. "I like thinkin' about it."

"I know."

"I liked the trackin' and the trailin'. I liked seein' the saplin's broke down, and the ferns in the swamp."

"I know."

The Yearling

"I liked old Julia bayin' now and agin——"

"But the fightin's right fearsome, ain't it, son?"

"Hit's mighty fearsome."

"Hit's sickenin', the dogs gittin' bloodied and sich as that. And son, you ain't never seed a bear kilt. But mean as they be, hit's someway piteeful when they go down and the dogs tears their throats and they cry out just like a person, and lay down and die before you."

Father and son lay in silence.

"If the wild creeturs'd only leave us be," Penny said.

"I wisht we could kill 'em all off," Jody said. "Them that steals offen us and does us harm."

" 'Tain't stealin', in a creetur. A creetur's got his livin' to make and he makes it the best way he kin. Same as us. Hit's panther nature and wolf nature and bear nature to kill their meat. County lines is nothin' to them, nor a man's fences. How's a creetur to know the land's mine and paid for? How's a bear to know I'm dependin' on my hogs for my own rations? All he knows is, he's hongry."

Jody lay staring into the brightness. Baxter's Island seemed to him a fortress ringed around with hunger. Now in the moonlight eyes were shining, red and green and yellow. The hungry would dart in to the clearing in swift forays, and kill and eat and slink away again. Pole-cats and 'possums would raid the hen-roost, wolf or panther might slay the calf before daylight, old Slewfoot might come again to murder and feed.

"A creetur's only doin' the same as me when I go huntin' us meat," Penny said. "Huntin' him where he lives and beds and raises his young uns. Hit's a hard law, but it's the law. 'Kill or go hongry.' "

Yet the clearing was safe. The creatures came, but they went away again. Jody began to shiver and could not tell why.

"You cold, son?"

"I reckon."

He saw old Slewfoot wheel, and slash and snarl. He saw

39

old Julia leap, and be caught and crushed, and hold on, and then fall away, broken and bleeding. But the clearing was safe.

"Move close, son. I'll warm you."

He edged closer to his father's bones and sinews. Penny slipped an arm around him and he lay close against the lank thigh. His father was the core of safety. His father swam the swift creek to fetch back his wounded dog. The clearing was safe, and his father fought for it, and for his own. A sense of snugness came over him and he dropped asleep. He awakened once, disturbed. Penny was crouched in the corner in the moonlight, ministering to the hound.

Chapter V

PENNY said at breakfast, "Well, it's trade for a new gun, or court trouble."

Old Julia was better. Her wounds were clean, without swelling. She was exhausted from loss of blood and wanted only to sleep. She had lapped a little milk from the gourd Penny held for her.

"How you aim to buy a new gun," Ma Baxter asked, "and not money scarcely for taxes?"

"I said 'trade'," Penny corrected.

"Ary day you git the best of a trade, I'll eat my wash-pot."

"Now Ma, I wouldn't even crave to beat a man. But there's trades where all is satisfied."

"What you got to trade with?"

"The feice."

"Who'd have him?"

"He's a good ketch-dog."

"Good to ketch biscuits."

"You know as good as I do, the Forresters is fools for dogs."

"Ezra Baxter, do you go tradin' with the Forresters, you'll do good to come home wearin' your breeches."

"Well, that's where me and Jody is headin' for, today."

Penny spoke with a firmness against which the bulk of his wife was sheer air. She sighed.

"All right. Leave me without nobody to split my wood or fetch me water or care do I drop in my tracks. Go. Take him."

"I ain't never left you without wood nor water."

Jody listened anxiously. He would rather visit the Forresters than eat.

"Jody has got to mix with men and learn the ways o' men," Penny said.

"The Forresters' is a fine place to begin. Do he learn from them, he'll learn to have a heart as black as midnight."

"He might learn from them, not to. Anyways, that's where we're goin'."

He rose from the table.

"I'll fetch water and Jody, you go split a good bait o' wood."

"You want to tote lunch?" she called after him.

"I'd not insult my neighbors that-a-way. We'll noon with them."

Jody hurried to the wood-pile. Every blow of the axe on that fat pine brought him closer to the Forresters and his friend Fodder-wing. He split a plentiful amount and carried enough to the kitchen to fill his mother's wood-box. His father had not yet returned from the sink-hole with his load of water. Jody hurried to the lot and saddled the horse. If the horse were ready and waiting, they might get off before his mother discovered some fresh pretext for detaining him. He saw Penny coming down the sand road from the west, bowed under the ox-yoke with the two heavy wooden buckets brimming with water. He ran to help him ease the load to the ground, for a lack of balance would tumble the buckets head-long, and the tedious hauling would have to be done all over again.

"Cæsar's saddled," he said.

"And the woods is a-fire, I take it." Penny grinned. "All right. Leave me put on my tradin' coat and tie up Rip and git my gun and we're long gone."

The saddle had been bought of the Forresters, having proved a trifle small for any of their great butts. It held Penny and Jody together in comfort.

"Git in front, son. But do you keep out-growin' me, you'll be obliged to ride behind, for I cain't see the road before me. Here, Perk! Heel up."

The Yearling

The feice fell in behind. He stopped once and looked back over his shoulder.

"I hope it's your last look," Penny told him.

Cæsar, well rested, went into a steady trot. His old back was broad, the saddle was wide, and riding so, with his father braced behind him, was as comfortable, Jody thought, as a rocking chair. The sand road was a sunny ribbon, leaf-shadowed. West, by the sink-hole, the road forked, one branch continuing on to Forresters' Island, the other turning north. Ancient axe-marks on venerable long-leaf pines blazed the turn to the northerly trail.

"Did you or the Forresters make them blazes?" Jody asked.

"Them was cut before me and the Forresters was ever heered tell of. Why, son, some's so deep, and them pines grows so slow, I'd not be surprised was some of 'em Spanish blazes. That teacher never learned you no history last year? Why, boy, the Spaniards made this trail. This right here, that we're leavin' now, is the old Spanish trail clear acrost Floridy. It split back near Fort Butler. The south un goes to Tampa. Hit's the Dragoon trail. This un here's the Black Bear."

Jody turned big eyes to his father.

"You reckon the Spaniards fit the bears?"

"I reckon they had to, when they stopped to camp. They had Injuns to fight and bears and panther-cats. Same as us, only we ain't got the Injuns."

Jody stared about him. The pine-woods were suddenly populous.

"Is there any Spaniards hereabouts now?"

"There's nary a man livin', Jody, has even heered his grandpappy say he'd ever seed a Spaniard. The Spaniards come from acrost the ocean, and went tradin' and fightin' and marchin' acrost Floridy, and no man knows where they're gone."

The business of the spring woods went forward leisurely in the golden morning. Red-birds were mating, and the crested

43

males were everywhere, singing until Baxter's Island dripped with the sweetness of the sound.

"Hit's better'n fiddlin' and guitarin', ain't it?" Penny said.

Jody came back to the scrub with a start. He had been halfway across the ocean with the Spaniards.

The sweet gums were in full new leaf. The flowers of red-bud and jessamine and dogwood had come and gone, but huckleberries and ti-ti and dog-tongue were in full bloom. The road ran to the west through a mile of tender green, of white and rosy blossoming. Wild honey-bees hummed in the small lacelike flowers of the St. Augustine grapes. The road narrowed past an abandoned clearing. Cæsar slowed to a walk. The scrub closed in around them. Scrub oak and gallberry and myrtle bushes brushed their legs. The growth was thick and low and there was only occasional shade. The April sun was high and strong. Cæsar was sweating and the stirrup leathers rubbed and squeaked.

Two miles of the way were hot and silent. Only jorees darted among the bushes. A fox crossed, dragging his brush, and a yellow shape that might have been a wild-cat shot almost invisibly into the myrtle. Then the road widened, the vegetation withdrew, and the landmark that was the tall trees of Forresters' Island lifted ahead. Penny dismounted and picked up the feice and mounted again, holding the dog in his arms.

Jody said, "Why you totin' him?"

"Jest never you mind."

They passed into hammock, cool and deep, arched with palms and live oaks. The road wound about and the weathered gray of the Forrester cabin showed under a giant oak. A pond shone beyond and below it.

Penny said, "Now don't you torment Fodder-wing."

"I don't never torment him. He's my friend."

"That's good. He's the second settin' and he ain't to blame for hatchin' out peculiar."

"He's my best friend. Except Oliver."

The Yearling

"You better stick to Oliver. His tales is tall as Fodder-wing's, but at least he knows when he's lyin'."

Suddenly the quiet of the forest exploded. A commotion broke loose inside the cabin. The sound came of chairs hurled across its width, a large object crashed, glass shattered, heavy feet stamped on the plank floor and the voices of male Forresters beat against the walls. A female voice shrilled above the tumult. The door flew wide and a pack of dogs streamed into the open. Ma Forrester flailed at them with a hearth-broom as they raced for safety. Her sons crowded behind her.

Penny called, "Hit safe for a feller to git down here?"

The Forresters roared greetings to the Baxters and commands to the dogs. Ma Forrester lifted her gingham apron in both hands and waved it up and down like a flag. The shouts of welcome were so mingled with orders to the dogs that Jody was uncomfortable, faintly uncertain of the reception.

"Git down and come in! Git away, you blasted bacon-thieves! Hi-yuh! Howdy! Git to tarnation!"

Ma Forrester swooped after the dogs and they scattered into the forest.

"Penny Baxter! Jody! Git down and come in!"

Jody dropped to the ground and she thumped him on the back. She smelled of snuff and of wood-smoke. The odor did not offend him but he was obliged to think of the delicate sweet scent of Grandma Hutto. Penny dismounted. He held the feice tenderly. The Forresters milled about him. Buck led the horse away to the corral. Mill-wheel caught Jody up and swung him over one shoulder and to the ground again, as though he swung a puppy.

Beyond, down the cabin steps, Jody saw Fodder-wing hurrying toward him. The humped and twisted body moved in a series of contortions, like a wounded ape. Fodder-wing lifted his walking stick and waved it. Jody ran to meet him. Fodder-wing's face was luminous.

He cried, "Jody!"

45

The Yearling

They stood, embarrassed and delighted.

A sense of pleasure came over Jody that he felt with no one else. His friend's body was no more unnatural to him than the body of a chameleon or a 'possum. He took the word of grown folks that Fodder-wing was witless. He himself would have known better than to do the thing that had given Fodder-wing his name. The youngest Forrester had conceived the idea that if he could attach himself to something light and airy, he could float from the roof-tree of the barn as gently as any bird. He had attached great bundles of fodder, cow-pea hay, to his arms, and jumped. He had survived, miraculously, adding a few broken bones further to contort the hunch-backed frame with which he had been born. It was a crazy thing to do, of course. Yet privately, Jody felt, something of the sort might work. He had, himself, often thought of kites, very large kites. And some secret understanding was his of the crippled boy's longing for flight; for lightness; for a moment's freedom from his body, earthbound and bent and stumbling.

He said, "Hey."

Fodder-wing said, "I got a baby 'coon."

He had, always, a new pet.

"Le's go see it."

Fodder-wing led him back of the cabin to a collection of boxes and cages that sheltered his changing assortment of birds and creatures.

"My eagle died," Fodder-wing said. "He was too wild to pen."

The pair of black swamp rabbits was not new.

"They won't raise no young uns," Fodder-wing complained. "I'm fixin 'to turn 'em a-loose."

A fox-squirrel worked an endless treadle

"I'll give him to you," Fodder-wing offered. "I kin git me another."

Jody's hopes lifted and fell.

"Ma won't let me keep nothin'."

46

His heart swelled, aching for the fox-squirrel.

"Here's the 'coon. Here, Racket!"

A black nose protruded between narrow slats. A tiny black paw, like a nigger baby's hand, reached out. Fodder-wing lifted a slat and brought out the 'coon. It clung to his arm and gave a strange chirring cry.

"You kin hold him. He'll not bite you."

Jody cuddled the 'coon against him. He thought he had never seen or touched a thing so delightful. The gray fur was as soft as his mother's outing flannel nightgown. The pointed face was masked across the eyes with a black bar. The bushy tail was beautifully ringed. The 'coon nibbled at his flesh and cried again.

"He wants his sugar-teat," Fodder-wing said maternally. "Le's take him to the house whilst the dogs is out. He's mighty skeert o' the dogs, but he'll git used to 'em. He don't like no commotion."

"What was you-all fightin' about," Jody asked, "when we come up?"

"I wasn't into it," Fodder-wing said with disdain. "It was them."

"What was it?"

"One o' the dogs wet in the middle o' the floor. They couldn't agree whose dog 'twas, done it."

Chapter VI

T HE 'coon sucked greedily at his sugar-teat. He lay on his back, cupped in Jody's arm, and clutched the sugar-filled cloth with his fore feet. He closed his eyes blissfully. His small paunch was already round with milk and shortly he pushed the sugar-teat away and scrambled to be free. Jody lifted him to his shoulder. The 'coon parted his hair and felt along his neck and ears with his small, restless hands.

"His hands is never still," Fodder-wing said.

Pa Forrester spoke from the shadows beyond the hearth. Jody had not noticed him, he sat so quiet.

"I had me a 'coon when I were a young un," he said. "Hit were gentle as a kitten for two yare. Then one day hit bit a chunk outen my shin." He spat into the fire. "This un'll grow up to bite. Hit's 'coon nature."

Ma Forrester came into the cabin and went to her pots and pans. Her sons trooped in behind her; Buck and Mill-wheel, Gabby and Pack, Arch and Lem. Jody looked puzzled at the dried and wizened pair that had bred these mountain-ous men. They were all much alike, except Lem and Gabby. Gabby was shorter than the rest and not unduly bright. Lem alone was clean-shaven. He was as tall as any of them, but thinner, and not so dark, and had the least to say. He often sat apart, brooding and sulky, while Buck and Mill-wheel, the most boisterous, caroused.

Penny Baxter came in, lost among them. Pa Forrester continued his discourse on the nature of 'coons. No one listened but Jody, but the old man relished his own words.

"That 'coon'll grow up to where he's big as a dog. He'll whop ary dog on the yard. A 'coon lives for one thing, to whop a dog. He'll lie on his back in the water and fight a hull pack o' dogs. He'll drown 'em, one by one. And bite? A 'coon'll bite one more time after he's dead."

Jody was torn between the desire to follow him, and his interest in the talk of the other Forresters. He was surprised to see that his father still carried the worthless feice tenderly in his arms. Penny crossed the room.

"Howdy, Mr. Forrester. Proud to see you. How's your health?"

"Howdy, sir. I'm right smart tol'able, seein' as how I be near about done for. Truth to tell, I'd ought to be dead this minute and gone to glory, but I keep puttin' it off. Seems like I'm better acquainted here."

Ma Forrester said, "Set down, Mr. Baxter."

Penny drew a rocker and sat down.

Lem Forrester called across the room, "Your dog lame?"

"Why, no. I've never knowed him to go lame. I jest figger on keepin' him outen the jaws o' them blood-hounds o' yourn."

"Valuable, eh?" Lem asked.

"Not him. He ain't wuth a good twist o' t'baccy. Don't you-all aim to detain him when I leave here, for he's not wuth stealin'."

"You takin' mighty good keer of him, iffen he's that sorry."

"So I be."

"You had him on bear?"

"I've had him on bear."

Lem came close and breathed down heavily.

"Do he track good? Do he holt a bear at bay?"

"He's mighty sorry. Sorriest bear-dog I ever owned or fol-lered."

Lem said, "I never heered a man run down his own dog that-a-way."

Penny said, "Well, I'll admit he's likely-lookin', and most ary man'd want him, lookin' at him, and I jest wouldn't put no notion o' tradin' in your minds, for you'd git fooled and cheated."

"You figger on huntin' some on your way back?"

"Why, a man allus has huntin' in his mind."

"Hit's mighty quare you toted a dog along wouldn't be no good to you."

The Forresters looked about at one another. They fell silent. Their black eyes were riveted on the feice.

"The dog's no good and my old muzzle-loadin' shotgun is no good," Penny said. "I'm in a pure fix."

The black eyes darted to the walls of the cabin, where the Forrester arms hung. The array, Jody thought, would stock a gun-shop. The Forresters made good money trading horses, selling venison and making moonshine. They bought guns as other men would buy flour and coffee.

"I never heered tell o' you failin' to git meat," Lem said.

"I failed yestiddy. My gun wouldn't shoot and when it did, hit back-fired."

"What was you huntin'?"

"Old Slewfoot."

A roar broke.

"Where's he feedin'? Which-a-way did he come from? Where's he gone?"

Pa Forrester thumped the floor with his cane.

"You fellers shut up and leave Penny tell it. He cain't tell a thing, and you-all bellerin' like bulls."

Ma Forrester banged a pot-lid and lifted a pan of corn-bread as big, Jody thought, as a syrup kettle. The good smells from the hearth were overwhelming.

She said, "Don't git Mr. Baxter started 'til he's et. Where's your manners?"

"And where's your manners," Pa Forrester reproached his sons, "not givin' comp'ny the chancet to wet his whistle afore dinner?"

Mill-wheel went into a bedroom and returned with a

demi-john. He pulled out the corn-cob stopper and handed the jug to Penny.

"You'll excuse me," Penny said, "if I don't drink deep. I ain't got as big a place to put it as you fellers."

They laughed uproariously. Mill-wheel passed the jug about the room.

"Jody?"

Penny said, "He ain't old enough."

Pa Forrester said, "Why, I were weaned on it."

Ma Forrester said, "Pour me a noggin. In my cup."

She ladled food into pans big enough to wash in. The long trenchered table was covered with steam. There were dried cow-peas boiled with white bacon, a haunch of roast venison, a platter of fried squirrel, swamp cabbage, big hominy, biscuits, cornbread, syrup and coffee. A raisin pudding waited at the side of the hearth.

"If I'd of knowed you was comin'," she said, "I'd of cooked somethin' fitten. Well, draw up."

Jody looked at his father to see whether he too was excited by the savory plenty. Penny's face was somehow grave.

"All this here is fine enough for the governor," he said.

Ma Forrester said uncomfortably, "I reckon you folks gives thanks, to your table. Pa, hit won't hurt you none to ask a blessin', long as we got comp'ny."

The old man looked about unhappily and folded his hands.

"Oh Lord, once more Thou hast done see fit to bless our sinnin' souls and bellies with good rations. Amen."

The Forresters cleared their throats and fell to. Jody sat opposite his father, and between Ma Forrester and Fodder-wing. He found his plate piled high. Buck and Mill-wheel slipped choice morsels to Fodder-wing. He passed them on under the table to Jody. The Forresters ate with concentration, silent for once. The food melted away before them. An argument arose between Lem and Gabby. Their father pounded on the table with his withered fist. They protested a moment at the intervention, then subsided. Pa Forrester leaned close to Penny and murmured in a low voice.

"My boys is rough, I know. They don't do what they ought. They drink a heap and they fight and ary woman wants to git away from 'em has got to run like a doe. But I'll say this for 'em—they ain't nary one of 'em has ever cussed his mammy or his pappy at the table."

Chapter VII

PA FORRESTER said, "Well, neighbor, let's have the news about that tormented bear."

Ma Forrester said, "Yes, and you scapers git the dishes washed afore you git too deep into it, too."

Her sons rose hurriedly, each with his own plate and some larger dish or pan. Jody stared at them. He would as soon have expected them to tie ribbons in their hair. She tweaked his ear on her way to her rocker.

"I got no girls," she said. "If these fellers wants me to cook for 'em, they kin jest clean up after me."

Jody looked at his father, pleading mutely that this piece of heresy be not taken home to Baxter's Island. The Forresters made short work of the dishes. Fodder-wing hobbled after them, gathering the scraps for all the animals. Only by feeding the pack of dogs himself could he be sure of saving tid-bits for his pets as well. He smiled to himself, that there would be so much today to take to them. There was even enough cold food left for supper. Jody gaped at the abundance. The Forresters finished their work in a clatter, and hung the iron pots and kettles on nails near the hearth. They drew up their cowhide chairs and hand-hewn benches around Penny. Some lit corn-cob pipes and others shaved parings of tobacco from dark plugs. Ma Forrester lipped a little snuff. Buck picked up Penny's gun and a small file and began to work on the loose hammer.

"Well," Penny began, "he taken us plumb by surprise."

Jody shivered.

"He slipped in like a shadow and killed our brood-sow.

Laid her open, end to end, and only ate a mouthful. Not hongry. Jest low-down and mean."

Penny paused to light his own pipe. The Forresters bent to him with blazing splinters of fat pine.

"He come as quiet as a black cloud, into the wind. Made a circle to git his wind right. So quiet, the dogs never heered nor scented him. Even this un—even this un—" he leaned to stroke the feice at his feet—"was fooled."

The Forresters exchanged glances.

"We set out after breakfast, Jody and me and all three o' the dogs. We tracked that bear acrost the south scrub. We tracked him along the edge o' the saw-grass ponds. We tracked him thu Juniper Bay. We tracked him thu the swamp, the trail gittin' hotter and hotter. We come up with him——"

The Forresters gripped their knees.

"We come up with him, men, right smack at the edge o' Juniper Creek, where the water flows swiftest and deepest."

The story, Jody thought, was even better than the hunt. He saw it all again, the shadows and the fern, the broken palmettos and the running branch water. He was bursting with the excitement of the story. He was bursting, too, with pride in his father. Penny Baxter, no bigger than a dirt-dauber, could out-hunt the best of them. And he could sit, as he sat now, weaving a spell of mystery and magic, that held these huge hairy men eager and breathless.

He made the fight an epic thing. When his gun back-fired, and old Slewfoot crushed Julia to his breast, Gabby swallowed his tobacco and rushed to the fire-place, spitting and choking. The Forresters clenched their fists, and sat precariously at the edges of their seats, and listened with their mouths open.

"Gawd," Buck breathed, "I'd o' loved to o' been there."

"And where's Slewfoot gone?" Gabby begged.

"No man knows," Penny told them.

PENNY TELLS THE STORY OF THE BEAR FIGHT

There was silence.

Lem said at last, "You ain't never oncet mentioned that dog you got there."

"Don't press me," Penny said. "I done told you he's wuthless."

"I notice he come outen it in mighty good shape. Not a mark on him, is there?"

"No, there's nary mark on him."

"Takes a mighty clever dog to fight a bear and not git ary scratch on him."

Penny puffed on his pipe.

Lem rose and walked to him, towering over him. He cracked his knuckles. He was sweating.

"I want two things," he said hoarsely. "I want to be in at the death o' ol' Slewfoot. And I want that dog there."

"Oh my, no," Penny said mildly. "I'd not cheat you, tradin' him."

"No use lyin' to me. Name your trade."

"I'll trade you old Rip, instead."

"Think you're foxy. I got better dogs than Rip right now."

Lem went to the wall and took down from its nails a gun. It was a London Fine Twist. The double barrels shone. The stock was walnut, warm and glowing. The twin hammers were jaunty. The fittings were chased and intricate. Lem swung it to his shoulder, sighted it. He handed it to Penny.

"Right from England. No more muzzle-loadin'. Fill your own shell-cases easy as spittin'. Stick your shells in—breech her—cock her—Bam! Bam! Two shots. Shoots as true as a eagle flies. Swap even."

"Oh my, no," Penny said. "This here gun is valuable."

"There's more where it come from. Don't argue with me, man. When I want a dog, I want a dog. Take the gun for him or by God I'll come and steal him."

"Well, all right, then," Penny said, "if that's the way it

stands. But you got to promise before witnesses not to beat the very puddin' outen me after you've hunted him."

"Shake." A hairy paw closed over Penny's hand. "Here, boy!"

Lem whistled to the feice. He took him by the scruff of the neck and led him outside, as though fearful even now of losing him.

Penny teetered in his chair. He balanced the gun indifferently across his knees. Jody could not take his eyes from its perfection. He was filled with awe that his father had outwitted a Forrester. He wondered if Lem would keep his promise. He had heard of the intricacies of trading, but it had never occurred to him that one man could get the best of another by the simple expedient of telling him the truth.

Talk went on into the afternoon. Buck had tightened up Penny's old muzzle-loader so that he thought it could be counted on. The Forresters were unhurried; unoccupied. Tales were told of old Slewfoot's smartness; of other bears before him; but none so clever as he. Chases were described in every detail. Dogs twenty years dead were called by name and by performance. Fodder-wing grew tired of them and wanted to go to the pond and fish for minnows. But Jody could not bear to leave this telling of old tales. Pa and Ma Forrester chirped and shrilled occasionally, then dozed off in between, like sleepy crickets. At last their infirmities took them over, and they slept soundly, side by side in their rockers, their dried old frames stiff even in their slumber. Penny stretched and rose.

He said, "I hate to leave good comp'ny."

"Spend the night. We'll have a fox-chase."

"I thank you, but I don't like to leave my place without no man on it."

Fodder-wing tugged at his arm.

"Leave Jody stay with me. He ain't half seed my things."

Buck said, "Leave the young un stay, Penny. I got to go to Volusia tomorrow. I'll ride him by your place."

56

The Yearling

"His Ma'll rare," Penny said.

"That's what Ma's is good for. Eh, Jody?"

"Pa, I'd be mighty proud to stay. I ain't played none in a long while."

"Not since day before yestiddy. Well, stay, then, if these folks is shore you're welcome. Lem, don't kill the boy if you try out the feice afore Buck gits him home to me."

They shouted with laughter. Penny shouldered the new gun with his old one and went for his horse. Jody followed. He reached out one hand and stroked the smoothness of the gun.

"If 'twas anybody in the world but Lem," Penny murmured, "I'd be too shamed to go home with it. I've owed Lem a trimmin' since he named me."

"You told him the truth."

"My words was straight, but my intentions was crooked as the Ocklawaha River."

"What'll he do when he finds out?"

"He'll want to tear me down. And after that, I'm hopin' he'll laugh. Good-by, son, 'till tomorrer. Be good now."

The Forresters followed to see him off. Jody waved after his father with a new sense of aloneness. He was almost tempted to call him back; to run after him and climb up in the saddle and ride home with him to the snugness of the clearing.

Fodder-wing called, "The 'coon's fishin' in a puddle, Jody! Come see!"

He ran to watch the 'coon. It was paddling about in a small pool of water, feeling with its human hands for something only instinct told it could be there. He played with Fodder-wing and the 'coon the rest of the afternoon. He helped to clean the squirrel's box and build a cage for a crippled red-bird. The Forresters had game chickens, as wild as themselves. The hens laid their eggs all over the adjacent woods, in brierberry tangles, under piles of brush, and the snakes ate as many as the hens hatched. He went with

Fodder-wing to collect the eggs. A hen was setting. Fodder-wing gave her the eggs they had gathered. There were fifteen in all.

"This un's a good mother," he said. It appeared that he took charge of all such matters.

Again Jody longed for something of his own. Fodder-wing would give him the fox squirrel, even, he believed, the baby 'coon. But past experience had taught him not to aggravate his mother with another mouth, no matter how small, to feed. Fodder-wing talked to the setting hen.

"You stay on the nest now, you hear me? You hatch all them eggs into biddies. I want yellow biddies this time. None o' them black uns."

They turned back toward the cabin. The 'coon came crying to meet them. It scrambled up Fodder-wing's crooked legs and back and snugged down, clasping his neck. It closed its small white teeth over his skin and shook its head with pretended ferocity. Fodder-wing let Jody carry it to the cabin. It looked up at him with inquiring bright eyes, aware of his strangeness; then accepted him. The Forresters had scattered over their land at chores which they took leisurely, in their stride. Buck and Arch drove the penned cows and their calves to the pond to water. Mill-wheel fed the string of horses in the corral. Pack and Lem had disappeared into the dense woods north of the cabin; perhaps, Jody speculated, to their still. There was ease and abundance here, as well as violence. There were so many of them to do things. Penny Baxter carried the work of a clearing almost as large as theirs, alone. Jody remembered guiltily the unhoed rows of corn he had left behind him. But Penny would not mind finishing them.

Pa and Ma Forrester were still asleep in their chairs. The sun was red in the west. Darkness came quickly into the cabin, for the live oaks kept out light that would have been still bright at the Baxters' clearing. One by one the brothers trooped into the cabin. Fodder-wing started up the fire on

the hearth to heat the left-over coffee. Jody saw Ma Forrester open one careful eye, then close it again. Her sons
piled the cold food on the table with a clatter that would
have awakened an owl in the daytime. She sat up and
prodded Pa Forrester in the ribs and joined the rest at
their supper. This time they cleaned every platter. There
was not even food left for the dogs. Fodder-wing mixed a
pan of cold cornbread with a bucket of clabber and took it
outside for them. He swung crookedly from side to side, tilt-
ing the bucket, and Jody ran to help him.

After supper, the Forresters smoked and talked of horses.
The cattle-men in the county, and farther to the west, were
complaining of a scarcity. Wolves and bears and panthers
had raised havoc with the spring's colts. The traders who
came usually from Kentucky with strings of horses had not
appeared. The Forresters agreed that it would be profitable
to go north and west and trade for cattle ponies. Jody and
Fodder-wing lost interest in the talk and went into a corner
to play mumblede-peg. Ma Baxter would never have allowed
pocket knives to be flipped into her clean smooth floors.
Here, a few splinters more or less could make no difference.
Jody sat up erect from the game.

"I know something I bet you don't know."

"What?"

"The Spaniards used to cross the scrub right in front of
our gate."

"Why, I knowed that." Fodder-wing hunched close and
began to whisper excitedly. "I've seed 'em."

Jody stared at him.

"What you seed?"

"I've seed the Spaniards. They're tall and dark and have
shiny helmets and they ride black horses."

"You couldn't see 'em. There ain't none left. They've done
left here, jest like the Injuns."

Fodder-wing closed one eye wisely.

"That's what folks tell you. You listen to me. Next time

you go west o' your sink-hole—you know that big magnolia? With dogwood all around it? You look behind that magnolia. There's allus a Spaniard on a black horse ridin' past that magnolia."

The hair stiffened on Jody's neck. This was, of course, another of Fodder-wing's tales. This was why his father and mother said Fodder-wing was crazy. But he longed to believe it. It would do no harm at least to look behind the magnolia.

The Forresters stretched and knocked out their pipes or spat out their tobacco. They went into their bedrooms, dropping their suspenders and loosening their breeches. There was a bed for each, for no two of them could sleep together in any double bed. Fodder-wing led Jody to his own bed in a shed-like room under the kitchen eaves.

"You kin have the pillow," he told him.

Jody wondered if his mother would ask him if he had washed his feet. How freely the Forresters lived, he thought, tumbling into bed without it. Fodder-wing began a tall tale about the end of the world. It was empty and dark, he said, with only clouds to ride on. At first Jody was interested. Then the tale became dull and rambling. He dropped off to sleep and dreamed of Spaniards, riding clouds instead of horses.

He awakened with a start late in the night. Din filled the cabin. His first thought was that the Forresters were fighting again. But the shouts held a community of purpose, and Ma Forrester called encouragement. A door was banged open and several of the dogs were halloo-ed inside. A light shone in the doorway of Fodder-wing's room and the dogs and men poured in. The men were stark naked, and they looked thinner and less bulky, but they seemed as tall as the cabin. Ma Forrester held a lighted tallow candle. Her grasshopper frame was lost inside a long gray flannel nightgown. The dogs shot under the bed and out again. Jody and Fodder-wing scrambled to their feet. No one troubled to explain the commotion. The boys followed after the hunt. It led through every room and ended with a mad exit of the dogs through the torn mosquito netting that covered one window.

"They'll git him outside," Ma Forrester said, suddenly placid. "Pesky varmint."

"Ma's got the best ear for varmints," Fodder-wing said proudly.

"I guess anybody'd hear him did he come scratchin' around their bed-post," she said.

Pa Forrester hobbled into the room on his cane.

"The night's near about done," he said. "I'd ruther have a snort o' whiskey than sleep agin."

Buck said, "Pa, you got the most sense for sich a ol' buzzard."

He went to a cupboard and brought out the demi-john. The old man uncorked it and tipped it back and drank.

Lem said, "Don't take no sense to crave liquor. Give it here."

He took a deep draught and passed the jug on. He wiped his mouth and rubbed his bare stomach. He went to the wall and felt along it for his fiddle. He twanged the strings carelessly, then sat down and began to scrape a tune.

Arch said, "You ain't got that right," and brought his guitar and sat on the bench beside him.

Ma Forrester set the candle on the table.

She asked, "You naked jay-birds fixin' to set up 'till day?"

Arch and Lem were deep in their chords and no one answered her. Buck took his mouth-organ from a shelf and began a tune of his own. Arch and Lem stopped to listen, then fell in with his melody.

Pa Forrester said, "Dog take it, that's purty."

The demi-john went around again. Pack brought out his Jew's-harp and Mill-wheel his drum, Buck changed his plaintive song for a lively dance tune, and the idle music swung into full volume. Jody and Fodder-wing dropped on the floor between Lem and Arch.

Ma Forrester said, "Now you needn't think I aim to go to bed and miss nothin'."

She unbanked the fire on the hearth and threw on fat-wood and moved the coffee-pot close.

"You hootin' owls 'll eat breakfast soon this mornin' or I'll know why," she said. She winked at Jody. "Kill two birds with one stone. Have a frolic and git breakfast done with."

He winked back at her. He felt bold and gay and tremulous. He could not understand how his mother could disapprove of such frolicksome people.

The music was out of tune and thunderous. It sounded like all the wild-cats in the scrub rounded up together, but it had a rhythm and a gusto that satisfied the ear and soul. The wild chords went through Jody as though he too were a fiddle and Lem Forrester drew long fingers across him.

Lem said to him in a low voice, "Iffen I only had my sweetheart here, to sing and dance."

Jody asked brashly, "Who-all's your sweetheart?"

"My leetle ol' Twink Weatherby."

"Why, she's Oliver Hutto's gal."

Lem lifted his fiddle-bow. Jody thought for an instant he meant to strike him. Then he went on with his fiddling, but his eyes smoldered.

"You say that agin in your life, boy, and you'll not have a tongue left to say it with. Understand?"

"Yes, Lem. Could be I was wrong," he added eagerly.

"I'm jest tellin' you."

He felt depressed a while, and disloyal to Oliver. Then the music caught him up again as though a great gust of wind lifted him across the tree-tops. The Forresters went from dance-tunes to songs, and Pa and Ma Forrester joined the singing with shrill, wavering voices. Daylight came, and the mocking-birds in the live oaks sang so clear and loud the Forresters heard them, and laid down their pieces, and saw the dawn in the cabin.

The Yearling

Breakfast covered the table with some scantiness, for a Forrester breakfast, for Ma had been too much occupied to do much cooking. The men pulled on only their breeches, for the food was ready and smoking. After breakfast, they washed above their beards, and put on their boots and shirts, and went leisurely about their day's business. Buck saddled his big roan stallion and swung Jody up behind him on the rump, for there was not room for a feather with him in the saddle.

Fodder-wing followed limping to the edge of the clearing, with the raccoon on his shoulder, and waved his stick in farewell until they were out of sight. Jody rode home with Buck to Baxter's Island and waved after him as he went on. He was still in a daze. It was only as he swung open the gate under the chinaberry that he remembered he had forgotten to look behind the magnolia tree for a Spaniard riding.

Chapter VIII

ODY clicked the gate behind him. The unmistakable smell of roasting meat filled the air. He ran around the side of the cabin. Resentment was mixed with his eagerness. Resisting the open kitchen door, he hurried to his father. Penny stepped out of the smoke-house and hailed him.

The truth, a tangled pain and pleasure, was before him. A large deer hide was stretched on the smoke-house wall.

Jody wailed, "You been huntin' and didn't wait on me." He stamped his foot. "I ain't never goin' to leave you go off without me agin."

"Easy, son, 'till you hear. Be proud things come so bountiful."

His wrath cooled. Curiosity bubbled like a spring.

"Tell me quick, Pa, how come."

Penny sat down on his heels in the sand. Jody dropped flat beside him.

"A buck, Jody. I near about run him down."

Again he was furious.

"Why'n't it wait 'till I got home?"

"Didn't you pleasure yourself at the Forresters? You cain't git all your 'coons up one tree."

"Hit could of waited. They ain't never enough time. Hit go too fast."

Penny laughed.

"Well, son, you nor me nor no man, ain't never yit learnt to halt it."

"Were the buck runnin'?"

"Jody, I'll declare. I ain't never had meat stand and wait for me, the way that buck stood in the road. He didn't pay

64

the horse no mind. Jest stood there. My first thought was, ' 'Tarnation, and me with no shells to my new gun.' Then I unbreeched the gun and looked in, and bless Heaven, I mought o' knowed a Forrester would have ary gun full-loaded. There was two shells in the gun, and there stood the buck, jest waitin'. I cracked down and he dropped. Right in the road, handy as a sack o' meal. I h'isted him over old Cæsar's rump and away we goed. Tell you what come to me. 'Me bringin' in venison,' I figgered, 'Ma won't crawl me for leavin' Jody with Fodder-wing.' "

"What did she say when she seed the new gun and the meat?"

"She said, 'If 'twas anybody but a honest fool like you, I'd swear you'd been out thievin'.' "

They chuckled together. The odors from the kitchen were savory. The hours with the Forresters were forgotten. There was no reality but the day's dinner. Jody went into the kitchen.

"Hey, Ma. I'm home."

"Well, must I laugh or cry?"

Her ample figure was bent over the hearth. The day was warm and sweat ran down her heavy neck.

"We got us a shootin' Pa, ain't we, Ma?"

"Yes, and a good thing, too, with you off all the time."

"Ma——"

"What is it?"

"We eatin' venison today?"

She turned from the fire.

"Merciful Heaven, don't you ever think o' nothin' but your empty belly?"

"You cook venison so good, Ma."

She was mollified.

"We eatin' it today. I was feared it'd not keep, and the weather warm."

"The liver'll not keep, neither."

"Well, for pity's sake, we cain't eat ever'thing to oncet.

If you'll fill my wood-box this evenin', could be we'd eat liver tonight."

He prowled among the dishes.

"Git outen my kitchen, lessen you want to torment me to death. Then what'd you do for dinner?"

"I'd cook it."

"Yes, you and the dogs."

He ran out of the house to his father.

"How's old Julia?"

It seemed to him he had been away a week.

"Doin' fine. Give her a month, and she'll have ol' Slew-foot hollerin'."

"Is the Forresters aimin' to he'p us hunt him?"

"We never come to no agreement. I'd ruther they hunted their way and leave me hunt mine. I don't much care who gits him, long as we keep him offen our stock."

"Pa, I never told you. I was scairt when the dogs was fightin' him. I was too scairt even to run."

"Hit didn't pleasure me none, neither, when I found I didn't have me a gun."

"But you told it to the Forresters like as if we was mighty bold-hearted."

"Well, son, that's what makes a tale."

Jody examined the deer hide. It was large and handsome, red with spring. The game seemed for him to be two different animals. On the chase, it was the quarry. He wanted only to see it fall. When it lay dead and bleeding, he was sickened and sorry. His heart ached over the mangled death. Then when it was cut into portions, and dried and salted and smoked; or boiled or baked or fried in the savory kitchen or roasted over the camp-fire, it was only meat, like bacon, and his mouth watered at its goodness. He wondered by what alchemy it was changed, so that what sickened him one hour, maddened him with hunger, the next. It seemed as though there were either two different animals or two different boys.

The Yearling

The hides did not change. They kept their aliveness. Whenever he stepped with bare feet on the soft deer-skin beside his bed, he half expected to feel it start under him. Penny, small body though he was, had a scattering of black hair across his thin chest. As a boy, he had slept naked in winter in a bear-skin, with the fur next to him. Ma Baxter said he had grown hair on his chest from so sleeping. It was her joke, but Jody half believed it.

The clearing was filled as abundantly as the Forresters'. His mother had ground the slaughtered sow into sausage. Stuffed casings hung in the smoke-house. A slow hickory fire smoked under them. Penny left his work to drop a few chips of wood on the smoldering embers.

Jody said, "Must I chop wood or finish hoein' the corn?"

"Now, Jody, you know good and well I couldn't let the weeds take the corn. I finished the hoein'. Wood's the thing."

He was glad to go to the wood-pile, for if he did not do something to occupy his mind, hunger would force him to gnaw the dogs' alligator meat or pick up the chickens' scraps of cornbread. The time went slowly at first, and he was tormented with the desire to follow his father's activities. Then Penny disappeared in the mule lot and Jody swung the axe without distraction. He carried an armful of wood to his mother as an excuse to see how dinner was progressing. He was relieved to see it on the table. She was pouring the coffee.

"Call your Pa," she said. "And wash them turrible hands. I'll guarantee you ain't touched water since you left home."

Penny came at last. The ham of venison filled the center of the table. He drew his carving knife with maddening deliberation across the meat.

Jody said, "I'm so hongry, my belly thinks my throat is cut."

Penny laid down the knife and looked at him.

Ma Baxter said, "Now if that ain't a purty somethin' to say. Where'd you learn to say that?"

"Well, that's what the Forresters say."

"I knowed it. That's the kind o' thing you learn o' them low-down rascals."

"They ain't low-down, Ma."

"Ever' one of 'em's lower'n a doodle-bug. And black-hearted to boot."

"They ain't black-hearted. They're purely friendly. Ma, they fiddle and play and sing better'n the fiddlers' convention. We was up long before day, singin', and frolickin'. It was fine."

"That's all right if they got nothin' better to do."

Meat was before them, piled high on the plates. The Baxters fell to.

Chapter IX

A SOFT rain fell in the night. The April morning that followed was clear and luminous. The young corn lifted pointed leaves and was inches higher. The cow-peas in the field beyond were breaking the ground. The sugar-cane was needle-points of greenness against the tawny earth. It was strange, Jody thought, whenever he had been away from the clearing, and came home again, he noticed things that he had never noticed before, but that had been there all the time. Young mulberries were clustered along the boughs, and before he went to the Forresters' he had not even seen them. The Scuppernong grapevine, a gift from his mother's kin in Carolina, was in bloom for the first time, fine and lace-like. The wild golden bees had found its fragrance, and were standing on their heads to guzzle its thin honey.

For two days he had filled his stomach so richly that this morning he felt a little languid and was not truly hungry. His father was up and out ahead of him, as usual. Breakfast was ready in the kitchen and his mother was tending the sausages in the smoke-house. The woodbox was low and Jody idled outside to fill it. He was in a mood for work, but it must be something gentle and unhurried. He made two leisurely trips to fill the woodbox. Old Julia was dragging herself around in search of Penny. Jody stooped to stroke her head. She seemed to share the sense of well-being that filled the clearing; or perhaps she understood that she had been spared a time longer to run through swamp and scrub and hammock. She wagged her long tail and stool quiet under his petting. The deepest wound was still raw and angry, but the others were healing. Jody saw his father, moving across the road toward the house from the barns and lot. He dangled a strange object. He called to Jody.

"I got a mighty cur'ous somethin'."

Jody ran to him. The limp object was an animal, at once strange and familiar. It was a raccoon, but instead of being the usual iron-gray, it was all a creamy white. He could not believe his eyes.

"How come it white, Pa? Is it a ol' grand-daddy 'coon?"

"That's what's so cur'ous. A 'coon don't never git to where he's white-headed. No sir, hit's one o' them rare things the books calls a albino. Borned white. And look, them rings on its tail, them that's due to be dark, they ain't no more'n cream-colored."

They crouched in the sand and examined the 'coon.

"Were it in the trap, Pa?"

"In the trap. Bad hurted but not dead. I'll declare, I hated a-killin' of it."

Jody felt a sense of loss, that he had not known the albino 'coon alive.

"Leave me tote him, Pa."

He cradled the dead animal in his arms. The pale fur seemed softer than the ordinary. The belly fur was as soft as the fluff of new-hatched biddies. He stroked it.

"I'd of loved to of ketched him leetle, Pa, and raised him."

"He'd of been a purty pet, a'right, but likely jest as mean as ary other 'coon."

They turned in at the gate and around the side of the house to the kitchen.

"Fodder-wing said none of his 'coons wasn't never per-tickler mean."

"Yes, but a Forrester wouldn't scarcely notice if he was to git bit."

"Likely he'd bite right back, eh, Pa?"

They laughed together, picturing their neighbors. Ma Baxter met them at the door. Her face brightened, seeing the animal.

70

"You got him. Good. That's what's been goin' with my hens."

"But Ma," Jody protested. "Look at him. He's white. He's a cur'ossity."

"He's a thievin' varmint right on," she said indifferently. "Is the hide wuth more'n usual?"

Jody looked at his father. Penny was deep in the wash-basin. He opened one bright eye among the soap-suds and winked at his son.

"Likely ain't wuth a nickel," he said carelessly. "Jody's been a-wantin' of a leetle knapsack. Jest as good to leave him use up the hide."

Next to having the albino 'coon alive, nothing could be finer than a knapsack of the soft curious fur. Jody's mind was full of it. He could not eat his breakfast. He wanted to show his gratitude.

"I kin clean the water troughs, Pa," he said.

Penny nodded.

"I keep hopin' each year, come spring, to hire us a deep well dug. Then them water troughs could fill with trash and welcome. But bricks is mighty high."

"I'd not know what 'twas, not to be sparin' o' my water," Ma Baxter said. "For twenty years, I been sparin'."

"Now be patient, Ma," Penny said.

His face furrowed. Jody knew that the lack of abundant water was a trial to his father, and a greater hardship than for mother or son. Jody was held accountable for wood, but it was Penny himself who slung the ox yoke across his narrow shoulders, hung the great hewn cypress buckets at either end, and trudged up and down the sandy road from the clearing to the sink-hole, where seepage alone built pools of water, amber-colored from leaf-mould, and filtered by the sand. It was as though the labor were Penny's apology to his family for having established them on land so arid, when creeks and rivers and good wells flowed not many miles away. For the first time, Jody wondered why his father had chosen to inhabit this place. Thinking of the pools on the steep side of the sink-hole that must be cleared, he was almost tempted to wish that they lived on the river, with Grandma Hutto. Yet the clearing, the island of tall pines, made up the world. Life in other places was only a tale that was told, as Oliver Hutto told of Africa and China and Connecticut.

His mother said, "You better put a biscuit-two and some meat in your pocket. You ain't et."

He filled his pockets.

"You know what I wisht I had, Ma? A pouch like a 'possum, to tote things."

"The Lord put your stomach inside you o' purpose. He meant you to put your rations inside you when your Ma sets 'em on the table."

He rose and ambled to the door.

Penny said, "You git on to the sink-hole, son, and I'll foller time I've skinned out your 'coon hide."

The day was bright and windy. Jody took a grubbing hoe from the shed behind the house and strolled toward the road. The mulberry trees by the fence were a sharp green. His mother's favorite hen clucked to her biddies from the slat coop. He scooped up a small ball of yellow down and held it against his cheek, its cheepings shrill in his ear. He released it and it scurried for shelter under the fat hen's wings. The yard would soon need hoeing.

The walk from the front steps to the gate needed hoeing, too. The walk was bordered with cypress slats, but the weeds crept under and over, and grew impudently among the Amaryllis that lined the pathway. The lavender petals of the chinaberry blooms were falling. Jody scuffed his bare toes through them and went through the gate. He hesitated. The barns were tempting. There might be a new hatching of biddies. The calf might have a different look from yesterday. And if he could think of a good reason to give himself for prowling about, the increasingly unwelcome job of cleaning the water troughs might be that much longer postponed.

The Yearling

Then it occurred to him that if he finished the cleaning in short order, he might be through for the day. He swung the grubbing hoe over his shoulder and set off at a trot toward the sink-hole.

The end of the world, he thought, might be like the sink-hole. Fodder-wing had said that it was empty and dark, with only clouds to ride on. But no one knew. Certainly reaching it must feel as it felt to reach the edge of the sink-hole. Jody wished that he had been the first to discover it. He turned the corner of the fence now. He left the road and took the trail. It was narrow, hemmed in by briers. He pretended that he did not know there was a sink-hole. He passed a dogwood tree. It was a landmark. He closed his eyes and whistled carelessly. He put his feet ahead of him slowly. In spite of his determination, in spite of squeezing his eyelids tight, he could not make himself go farther with his eyes shut. He opened them and walked with a sense of relief the last few steps to the edge of the great limestone sink.

A small world lay at his feet. It was deep and concave, like a great bowl. Fodder-wing said that a bear as big as God had scooped out a pawful of earth to get a lily-root. Jody knew the truth from his father. It was only that underground rivers ran through the earth and swirled and eddied beneath the surface, and changed their courses. This was especially so where there were streaks of limestone, as here. The limestone was soft and crumbling before the air touched and hardened it. Sometimes, without reason, without warning, after long rains, perhaps, a section of earth sank in, gently and almost without sound, and a deep cavity marked the place where once had run, darkly and unseen, a river. Sometimes the sink-hole was a few feet only in depth and width. Baxter's sink-hole was sixty feet deep. It was so wide that Penny's old muzzle-loader could not hit a squirrel from one side to the other. The sink-hole was as round as though it had been dug so on purpose. Staring into it, it seemed to Jody that the truth of its fashioning was more fantastic than the tales of Fodder-wing.

The hole was older than Penny Baxter. Penny said he could remember when the trees that lined its steep banks were no larger much than saplings. Now they were of great size. A magnolia that grew half-way up the east bank had a trunk as broad as the mill-stone with which the Baxters ground their meal. A hickory was as thick as a man's thigh. A live oak spread its branches across half the sink-hole. Smaller trees, sweet gum and dogwood, ironwood and holly, grew lushly up and down the banks. Palmettos thrust tall spears among them. Giant ferns grew from top to bottom. Jody looked down into a great cupped garden, feathered with green leaves, cool and moist and, always, mysterious. The sink-hole was set in the arid scrub, at the core of the pine island, like a lush green heart.

The trail to the bottom of the sink-hole led down the west bank. It was worn deep into the sand and limestone by the years of Penny Baxter's feet, leading his stock to water. In the dryest weather, there was a continual seepage which dripped down the banks and came to gather at the bottom in a shallow pool. This water was stagnant, and clouded by the comings and goings of the animals who watered there. Only Penny's hogs used it for drinking and wallowing. For the other stock, and for his own family's use, Penny had an ingenious arrangement. Up the east, or opposite, bank from the trail, he had cut out of the limestone strata a series of troughs to catch and hold the filtered seepage. The lowest trough was shoulder-high from the bottom of the sink-hole. Here he led the cow and calf to water, and his horse. Here in his young manhood he had led the yoke of cream-colored oxen with which he had cleared his land. A few yards higher up, he had cut a pair of deeper troughs. Here his wife brought her block and paddle and came to do her washing. A portion of the bank bore a milky whitewash from the years of her soap-suds. For her annual quilt-washing, she caught rain water.

At the last, high above the stock trough and the wash troughs, lay a deep, narrow trough that gathered water used only for cooking and drinking. The bank above was so steep that none of the larger animals disturbed the water. The deer that came, the bears, the panthers, all used the west trail and watered either at the pool itself, or at the stock trough. Squirrels drank from the upper trough, and occasionally a wild-cat, but for the most it was untouched by anything but Penny's gourd, dipping into it to fill his cypress buckets.

Jody jolted down the trail, bracing himself against the steepness with the grubbing hoe. It made a clumsy stock, catching in the wild grape vines. The descent always excited him. Step by step the banks lifted above him. Step by step he passed the tops of trees. A breath of wind eddied into the green bowl, stirring waves of coolness. The leaves fluttered their thin hands. The ferns bent a moment to the ground. A red-bird swung in an arc across the sink-hole. It turned and dropped down to the pool, like a bright leaf falling. Seeing the boy, it whirred up and away. Jody knelt by the pool.

The water was clear, for the hogs were feeding to the north in the marshy prairies, and had no need of the sink-hole. A small green frog eyed the boy from a partly submerged twig. The nearest water was a couple of miles away. It seemed amazing that frogs should travel so far, to settle in a small and distant pool. He wondered if the first frog migrants had known that there was water here, when they hopped to the rim of the sink-hole and hesitated on their green haunches. Penny said that once in rainy weather he had seen a line of frogs in single file, like marching soldiers, crossing the dry flat-woods. Did they move blindly or with knowledge? Penny did not know. Jody flipped a frond of fern into the pool and the frog dove and hid himself in the soft muck.

The Yearling

A sense of aloneness that was not lonely came to the boy. He decided that when he was grown he would build himself a little house beside the pool. The animals would become used to it, and he would look out of the windows on moonlit nights and see them drinking.

He crossed the flat floor of the sink-hole and climbed a few feet to reach the stock trough. It was awkward, bringing the grubbing hoe over his shoulder and into the trough. He discarded it and went at his work with his two hands. An accumulation of leaves and sand had left a thick layer. He dug and scraped vigorously. He worked against the creeping moisture, trying to hold the trough dry and empty for an instant. The seepage had returned by the time he took his hands away. The limestone trough was white and clean. He left it with satisfaction and moved higher up the bank to the more laborious work of scouring out the larger wash troughs. Constant use kept these comparatively free from leaves, but the soap-suds in time made them slippery. He climbed a sweet gum and gathered an armful of Spanish moss. It made good scouring material. He scooped sand from a bare spot on the bank and used it with the moss.

He was tired when he reached the drinking trough at the top. The incline was so steep that by resting his belly flat against the bank, he needed only to lower his head, like a fawn, to drink. He ran his tongue up and down the length of the trough. He darted it in and out and leaned back to watch the ripples. He wondered whether a bear lapped water like a dog or sucked it in like a deer. He imagined himself a bear and drank both ways, deciding. Lapping was slower, but he choked when he sucked the water in. He could not decide. Penny would know how a bear drank. He had probably actually seen them.

Jody buried his face completely in the water. He turned it from side to side, so that first one cheek and then the other was laved and cooled. He stood on his head in the trough, resting his weight on the palms of his hands. He tried to see how long he could hold his breath. He made bubbles. He heard his father's voice at the bottom of the sink-hole.

"Son, how come that water to feel so good to you? Put the same thing in the wash-basin, you act like 'twas something nasty."

He turned, dripping.

"Pa, I never heered you comin'."

"You had your dirty leetle ol' face too deep in what your pore Pa was fixin' to take a drink of."

"I wa'n't dirty, Pa. The water ain't riled."

"I ain't that thirsty."

Penny climbed the bank and examined the lower troughs. He nodded. He leaned over the rim of the wash trough and chewed a twig.

"I declare," he said, "your Ma purely shocked me when she said 'twenty years'. I jest hadn't never set down and reckoned the time. The years has slipped by me, one by one, me not noticin' nor countin'. Ever' spring, I'd figger to git your Ma a well dug. Then I'd need a ox, or the cow'd bog down and perish, or one o' the young uns'd put in and die and I'd have no heart for well-diggin', and medicine to pay for. Bricks so turrible high— When I begun diggin' oncet, and got no water at thirty feet, I knowed I was in for it. But twenty years is too long to ask ary woman to do her washin' on a seepage hillside."

Jody listened gravely.

He said, "We'll git her a well one day."

"Twenty years—" Penny repeated. "But always somethin' interferin'. And the war— And then the land to be cleared all over agin."

He stood leaning against the trough, looking backward along the years.

"When I first come here," he said, "when I picked this place and come to it, I hoped——"

The morning's question came to Jody's mind again.

"How come you to pick it, Pa?"

"Well, I picked it because—" His face puckered, his mind seeking words. "I jest craved peace, was all." He smiled. "Out here I got it, excusin' the bears and panthers and wolves and wild-cats—and now and agin, your Ma."

They sat in silence. The squirrels began to stir in the tree-tops. Suddenly Penny poked Jody in the ribs with his elbow.

"Look at that scaper, peekin' at us."

He pointed to a sweet gum. A half-grown raccoon was peering around the side of the trunk, a dozen feet from the ground. It saw itself observed and pulled back out of sight. In an instant the masked face looked again.

Penny said, "I reckon we be as cur'ous to the creeturs as they be to us."

"How come some is skeert and some is bold?"

"That I don't know. It depend, likely, on how young a creetur is scairt. They don't seem to be no rule for it. I mind me, oncet, I'd been huntin' all mornin'—this were over on Wild-cat Prairie—and I set down under a live oak and made me a leetle fire to warm me and cook me a bit o' bacon. Well, whilst I was settin' there, a fox walked right up t'other side o' the fire and laid down. I looked at him and he looked at me. I figgered mebbe he were hongry. I takened a piece o' meat and I jobbed it on a long stick and I helt it out to him. I helt it right over his nose. Now a fox is mighty wild and I ain't never knowed one to git that hongry to where he wouldn't run. And you know that fox laid there right on, lookin' at me, and never et nor run."

"I'd love to of seed him. What you figger made him lay there, Pa, lookin' at you?"

"Hit's been a puzzlement to me all these years since it happened. All I kin figger is, the dogs had run him until he got heated and his brains was cooked. I figger, for some reason, that fox were cold-out crazy."

The 'coon had moved into full view.

Jody said, "Pa, I wisht I had me somethin' to pet and play with, like Fodder-wing. I wisht I had me a 'coon, or a bear cub, or sich as that."

The Yearling

Penny said, "You know how your Ma rares. I'd not mind it, for I love the creeturs. But times has been hard and rations scarce, and your Ma's the one to say."

"I'd love a baby fox, or a baby panther. Kin you tame 'em, do you git 'em young?"

"You kin tame a 'coon. You kin tame a bear. You kin tame a wild-cat and you kin tame a panther." He pondered. His mind went back to his father's sermons. "You kin tame arything, son, excusin' the human tongue."

Chapter X

ODY lay comfortably ill, recovering from the fever. His mother called it the fever, so he did not argue. He thought privately that too many half-ripe brierberries might have something to do with his ailment. Treatment for such things was always much more violent than treatment for the fever. His mother had observed his shaking, had laid her big hand on his forehead and said, "Git into the bed. You got chills and fever." He had said nothing.

She came into the room now with a cup of steaming liquid. He eyed it anxiously. For two days she had been giving him lemon-leaf tea. It was aromatic and pleasant. When he had grumbled about its tartness, she had added a teaspoon of jelly to it. He wondered if now, in the mysterious wisdom that sometimes descended on her, she had discovered the truth. If she guessed that his trouble had been the colic, the medicine she held would be either snake-root tonic, or a blood purifier made from Queen's Delight, both of which he abominated.

"If your Pa'd only plant me a root o' fever grass," she said, "I could git both o' you well o' the fever in no time. 'Tain't decent, not havin' fever-grass in the yard."

"What you got in the cup, Ma?"

"None o' your business. Open your mouth."

"I got a right to know. Supposin' you kilt me and I never knowed what medicine you give me."

"Hit's mullein tea, if you got to know. Hit come to me, could be you was comin' down with the measles."

" 'Tain't the measles, Ma."

"How do you know?" You ain't never had 'em. Open your

mouth. If 'tain't the measles, this here won't hurt you. If 'tis the measles, hit'll bring out the rash."

The thought of bringing out a rash was tempting. He opened his mouth. She grasped him by the hair and poured half the cupful down his throat. He sputtered and fought.

"I won't take no more. 'Tain't the measles."

"Well, you'll die if 'tis, and the rash don't break out."

He opened his mouth again and took the rest of the mullein tea. It was bitter, but not nearly as bad as some of her concoctions. The bitter brew she made from pomegranate peelings, or that from pitcher-plant root, was infinitely worse. He lay back on his moss-stuffed pillow.

"If 'tis the measles, Ma, how soon will the rash come?"

"Soon as you git to sweatin' from the tea. Kiver up."

She left the room and he resigned himself to waiting for the sweat. Being sick was something of a treat. He would not willingly go through the first night again, when cramps had tied him in knots. But the convalescence, the solicitude of his mother and his father, was definitely pleasant. He felt a faint sense of guilt that he had not told about the brierberries. She would have given him a purge, and it would all have been over with by the next morning. Penny had done all the work of the clearing alone for two days. He had hitched old Cæsar to the plow and plowed over the sugar-cane and hilled it up, had worked the corn and the cow-peas and the small patch of tobacco. He had hauled water from the sink-hole, cut wood, fed and watered the stock.

But perhaps, Jody speculated, he did have the fever. Perhaps he was coming down with the measles. He felt his face and stomach. There was no rash yet, no sweat. He flounced back and forth in the bed to hurry the heating. He realized that he felt as well as ever; better, actually, than before the plenitude of meat had tempted him into over-eating. He recalled the quantities of fresh sausage and of venison that he had eaten without his mother's stopping him. Perhaps after all the brierberries had had nothing to do with it. He was sweating at last.

He called, "Hey, Ma, come see! The sweat's done come."

She came to him and examined him.

"You feel as good as I do," she said. "Git outen that bed."

He threw back the covers and stepped out onto the deer-skin rug. For a moment he was light-headed.

"You feel all right?" she asked.

"Yessum. Sort o' weakified."

"Well, you ain't et nothin'. Git into your shirt and breeches and come git you some dinner."

He dressed quickly and followed her to the kitchen. The food was still warm. She laid out biscuits for him, and a plate of hash, and poured him a cup of sweet milk. She watched him eat.

"I hoped you'd git up a leetle mite pacified," she said.

"Kin I have some more hash, Ma?"

"I should say not. You've et enough now, to fill a alligator."

"Where's Pa?"

"To the lot, I reckon."

He strolled in search of him. Penny was sitting idly, for once, on the gate.

"Well, son," he said, "you look right peert."

"I feel good."

"You ain't got the measles, or the child-bed fever, or the smallpox?" The blue eyes twinkled.

Jody shook his head.

"Pa——"

"Yes, son."

"I don't figger there was nothin' ailded me but green brierberries."

"That's about what I figgered. I never said nothin' to your Ma, for she's death on a belly-full of green brierberries."

Jody sighed with relief.

Penny said, "I been settin' here studyin'. The moon'll be

right in a hour-two. What say you and me git us a couple o' bobs and go fishin'?"

"In the creek?"

"I sort o' crave to fish some o' them saw-grass ponds over where ol' Slewfoot was feedin'."

"I'll bet we kin ketch us a cattywampus in one o' them ponds."

"We kin sure pleasure ourselves tryin'."

They went together to the shed back of the house to gather their paraphernalia. Penny discarded an old hook and rigged two new ones. He cut short hairs from the tail of the deer he had shot and made lures of the gray and white wisps. He tied them invisibly to the fish-hooks.

"If I was a fish, I'd strike at this myself," he said.

He went to the house and spoke briefly with his wife.

"Me and Jody is goin' bobbin' for bass."

"I thought you was give out and Jody was ailin'."

"That's why we're goin' fishin'," he said.

She followed to the door and watched after them.

"If you don't git no bass," she called, "ketch me a leetle bream I kin fry crisp and eat bones and all."

"We'll not come back without somethin'," he promised.

The afternoon was warm but the way seemed short. In a way, Jody thought, fishing was better than hunting. It was not so exciting, but neither was there terror. The heart beat at a reasonable cadence. There was time to look about, and see the increase of green leaves in the live oaks and magnolias. They stopped at a familiar pond. It was shallow from too long dryness. Penny found a grasshopper and threw it into the water. There was no strike; no hungry swirl of waters.

"I'm feered the fish has died outen here," he said. "These leetle ol' ponds in the middle o' no-where has allus been a puzzlement to me. I cain't see how the fish lives here, year on year."

He caught another grasshopper and hurled it without result.

"The pore fish," he said. "Helpless in a world o' their own. 'Stead o' fishin' for 'em, I'd ought to come out here and feed 'em."

He lifted his bamboo rod over his shoulder.

"Mebbe the Lord figgers the same about me," he chuckled. "Mebbe he looks down and says, 'There's Penny Baxter tryin' to make out on that clearin'.' " He added, "But hit's a good clearin'. Likely the fish is as content as me."

Jody said, "Look, Pa, there's people."

Human beings were a stranger sight in the lonely place of live oak islands and saw-grass ponds and prairies, than the creatures. Penny shaded his eyes. A file of half a dozen men and women was entering the scrub road they had just left behind.

"Hit's the Minorcans," he said. "Huntin' gophers."

Jody saw now the sacks over their shoulders. The small dusty land-turtles, whose deep burrows were an indication of the poorest soil, were the last food most inhabitants of the scrub considered edible.

"I've allus wondered," Penny said, "didn't they make a medicine mebbe outen the gophers. Don't seem like they'd come here clear from the coast to hunt them things jest to eat."

"Let's slip back clost and look at 'em," Jody said.

"I'd not pry on the pore things," Penny said. "The Minorcans is a people was mighty bad put upon. My father knowed their hull history. A English feller carried 'em to New Smyrna, over by the ocean and the Indian River. He promised 'em a pure Heaven and put 'em to work. And when times got bad and the crops failed, he left 'em to nigh about starve to death. There wasn't many left."

"Is they like gypsies?"

"No, for gypsies is wild. The men is dark, like gypsies, but the women is fair when they're young. They mind their own business and live peaceable."

The procession disappeared into the scrub. Jody tingled,

and the hair stirred on the back of his neck. It was like seeing Spaniards. It was as though phantoms, dark and shadowy, and not men and women, had passed before him, weighted with their strange burden of gophers and injustice.

Penny said, "Now the bass had ought to be thick as tadpoles in that pond right over there."

They were in territory a little west of the prairie's rim where old Slewfoot had fed on fire-plant. Dry weather had sucked up much of the water and the marsh had broad areas that were now firm and dry. The ponds showed plainly. They had withdrawn from the saw-grass and only lily pads troubled the water's surface. A Blue Peter ran across them, bright with yellow legs and painted face. A slight breath of air rippled across the marsh and the water rippled under it. The lily pads tipped, an instant, their broad shining leaves to the glint of the sun.

"Jest enough of a riffle," Penny said, "and the moon jest right."

He fastened lengths of line to the two poles and attached the deer-hair bobs.

"Now you work your bob acrost the north end and I'll try the south. Don't make no fuss, walkin'."

Jody stood a moment to watch his father make an expert cast across the pond. He marveled at the skill of the knotted hands. The bob lay at the edge of a cluster of lily pads. Penny began to jerk it slowly across the water. It dipped and bobbed with the irregular rhythm of a live insect. There was no strike and Penny drew in his line and cast again in the same place. He called to invisible fish, lurking near the weedy bottom.

"Now Grandpappy, I kin see you settin' there on your stoop." He jerked the bob more slowly. "You better lay down your pipe and come git your dinner."

Jody tore himself from the fascination of his father's performance and moved to his end of the pond. He cast badly for a time, tangling his line and laying his bob in the most unlikely places; over-reaching the narrow pond and enmeshing the hook in the tough saw-grass. Then something of harmony came to him. He felt his arm swing in a satisfying arc. His wrist flexed at the proper moment. He laid the bob exactly where he had meant to, at the edge of a patch of switch-grass.

Penny called, "Mighty nice, son. Leave it lay jest a minute. Then git ready the first second you jerk it."

He had not known his father was watching. He was tense. He jerked his pole cautiously and the bob flipped across the water. There was a swirl, a silver form shot half clear of the water, an open mouth as big as a cock-pot enveloped the bob. A weight like a millstone dropped at the end of his line, fought like a wild-cat, and pulled him off-balance. He braced himself against the frenzy to which he was irrevocably attached.

Penny called, "Take it easy. Don't let him git under them bonnets. Keep the tip o' your pole up. Don't give him no slack."

Penny left him to the struggle. His arms ached from the strain. He was afraid to tug too hard for fear of breaking the line. He dared not yield an inch for fear a sudden slackness would tell of the loss of the giant. He longed for magic words from his father, indicating some miracle by which he might land his fish and be done with the torment. The bass was sulking. It made a dash for the grasses, where it might tangle the line around their stems and so rip free. It came to Jody that if he walked around the edge of the pond, keeping a taut line, he might lead the bass into shallow water and flounder him at the edge. He worked cautiously. He was tempted to drop the pole and clutch the line itself and come to grips with his adversary. He began to walk away from the pond. He gave his pole a heave and landed the bass, flouncing, in the grass. He dropped the pole and ran, to move the catch to a final safety. The bass would weigh ten pounds. Penny came to him.

The Yearling

"Boy, I'm proud of you. Nobody couldn't of handled him better."

Jody stood panting. Penny thumped him on the back, as excited as he. He looked down, unbelieving, at the stout form and the great maw.

"I feel as good as if 'twas ol' Slewfoot," he said, and they grinned together and pummeled each other's backs.

"Now I got to go beat you," Penny said.

They took separate ponds. Penny called that he was licked and beaten. He began fishing for Ma Baxter's bream with a hand-line and bonnet worms. Jody cast and cast again, but there was never the mad swirl of waters, the great leap, the live and struggling weight. He caught a small bass and held it up to show his father.

"Throw him back," Penny called. "We don't need him for eatin'. Leave him to grow up big as t'other one. Then we'll come back agin and ketch him."

Jody put the small fish back reluctantly and watched it swim away. His father was stern about not taking more of anything, fish or game, than could be eaten or kept. Hope of another monster dwindled as the sun finished its spring arc of the daylight sky. He cast leisurely, taking his pleasure in his increasing dexterity of arm and wrist. The moon was now wrong. It was no longer feed-time. The fish were not striking. Suddenly he heard his father whistle like a quail. It was the signal they used together in squirrel hunting. Jody laid down his pole and looked back to make sure he could identify the tuft of grass where he had covered his bass from the rays of the sun. He walked cautiously to where his father beckoned.

Penny whispered, "Foller me. We'll ease up clost as we dare."

He pointed. "The whoopin' cranes is dancin'."

Jody saw the great white birds in the distance. His father's eye, he thought, was like an eagle's. They crouched on all fours and crept forward slowly. Now and then Penny dropped flat on his stomach and Jody dropped behind him.

The Yearling

They reached a clump of high saw-grass and Penny motioned for concealment behind it. The birds were so close that it seemed to Jody he might touch them with his long fishing pole. Penny squatted on his haunches and Jody followed. His eyes were wide. He made a count of the whooping cranes. There were sixteen.

The cranes were dancing a cotillion as surely as it was danced at Volusia. Two stood apart, erect and white, making a strange music that was part cry and part singing. The rhythm was irregular, like the dance. The other birds were in a circle. In the heart of the circle, several moved counter-clock-wise. The musicians made their music. The dancers raised their wings and lifted their feet, first one and then the other. They sank their heads deep in their snowy breasts, lifted them and sank them again. They moved soundlessly, part awkwardness, part grace. The dance was solemn. Wings fluttered, rising and falling like out-stretched arms. The outer circle shuffled around and around. The group in the center attained a slow frenzy.

Suddenly all motion ceased. Jody thought the dance was over, or that the intruders had been discovered. Then the two musicians joined the circle. Two others took their places. There was a pause. The dance was resumed. The birds were reflected in the clear marsh water. Sixteen white shadows reflected the motions. The evening breeze moved across the saw-grass. It bowed and fluttered. The water rippled. The setting sun lay rosy on the white bodies. Magic birds were dancing in a mystic marsh. The grass swayed with them, and the shallow waters, and the earth fluttered under them. The earth was dancing with the cranes, and the low sun, and the wind and sky.

Jody found his own arms lifting and falling with his breath, as the cranes' wings lifted. The sun was sinking into the saw-grass. The marsh was golden. The whooping cranes were washed with gold. The far hammocks were black. Darkness came to the lily pads, and the water blackened.

THE DANCE OF THE WHOOPING CRANES

The Yearling

The cranes were whiter than any clouds, or any white bloom of oleander or of lily. Without warning, they took flight. Whether the hour-long dance was, simply, done, or whether the long nose of an alligator had lifted above the water to alarm them, Jody could not tell, but they were gone. They made a great circle against the sunset, whooping their strange rusty cry that sounded only in their flight. Then they flew in a long line into the west, and vanished.

Penny and Jody straightened and stood up. They were cramped from the long crouching. Dusk lay over the saw-grass, so that the ponds were scarcely visible. The world was shadow, melting into shadow. They turned to the north. Jody found his bass. They cut to the east, to leave the marsh behind them, then north again. The trail was dim in the growing darkness. It joined the scrub road and they turned once more east, continuing now in a certainty, for the dense growth of the scrub bordered the road like walls. The scrub was black and the road was a dark gray strip of carpet, sandy and soundless. Small creatures darted across in front of them and scurried in the bushes. In the distance, a panther screamed. Bull-bats shot low over their heads. They walked in silence.

At the house, bread was baked and waiting, and hot fat was in the iron skillet. Penny lighted a fat-wood torch and went to the lot to do his chores. Jody scaled and dressed the fish at the back stoop, where a ray of light glimmered from the fire on the hearth. Ma Baxter dipped the pieces in meal and fried them crisp and golden. The family ate without speaking.

She said, "What ails you fellers?"

They did not answer. They had no thought for what they ate nor for the woman. They were no more than conscious that she spoke to them. They had seen a thing that was unearthly. They were in a trance from the strong spell of its beauty.

Chapter XI

HE fawns were being born. Jody saw through the scrub the delicate tracery of their small pointed hooves. Wherever he went, to the sink-hole, for wood into the black-jacks south of the lot, to the traps Penny was obliged to keep about for varmints, he walked with eyes on the ground, watching for signs of their comings and their goings. The larger hoof-marks of the does usually preceded them. But the does were wary. Often the doe-sign was in one place, where the mother had fed alone, and the wavering fawn-sign was some distance away, where the infant had been left in the greater safety of heavy cover. Often there were twin fawns. When Jody found the double set of tracks he could scarcely contain himself.

He thought always then, "I could leave one for the mammy and take one for myself."

He broached the matter to his mother one evening.

"Ma, we got milk a-plenty. Cain't I git me a leetle ol' fawn for a pet for me? A spotted fawn, Ma. Cain't I?"

"I should jest say not. What you mean, milk a-plenty? They ain't a extry drop left from sun to sun."

"It could have my milk."

"Yes, and fatten the blasted fawn and you grow up puny. Much as we all got to do, what on earth do you want with one o' them things, blayting around here day and night?"

"I want one. I want a 'coon, but I know a 'coon gits mischievous. I'd love a bear cub, but I know they're liable to be mean. I jest want something—" he puckered his face so that his freckles ran together—"I jest want something all my own. Something to foller me and be mine." He struggled for words. "I want something with dependence to it."

90

His mother snorted.

"Well, you'll not find that no-where. Not in the animal world nor in the world o' man. Now Jody, I'll not have you pesterin' me. You say another word, 'fawn' or ' 'coon' or 'bear cub,' and I'll take a bresh to you."

Penny listened quietly from his corner.

In the morning he said, "We'll go hunt us a buck today, Jody. Likely we'll find a fawn beddin'. Hit's near about as much pleasure seein' 'em wild, as havin' 'em tame."

"Will we take both dogs?"

"Nobody but old Julia. She ain't had a work-out since she was hurt. A slow hunt'll do her good."

Ma Baxter said, "That last venison didn't last no time. But we did jerk right smart of it, come to think of it. Git a few hams in the smoke-house and hit'll look natural agin."

Her good nature rose and fell with the food supply.

Penny said, "Jody, looks like you've fell heir to the old muzzle-loader. But don't git too put out now, do it fail you like it failed me."

He could not imagine being impatient about it. It was enough to have the use of it for himself. His mother had sewed the cream-colored 'coonskin into a knapsack for him. He filled it with shot and caps and wadding and filled the powder horn.

Penny said, "Ma, I been studyin'. I jest about got to go to Volusia to git me shell cases. Lem only th'owed in a few shells with the gun. And I'd love some rale coffee. I've had a bait o' them wild coffee beans."

"Me, too," she agreed. "And I need me some thread and a paper o' needles."

"Now the bucks," he said, "seems to be feedin' toward the river. I been seein' a perfect shower o' tracks headin' that-a-way. I believe me and Jody kin hunt on in that direction, and do we git us a buck or two, we kin trade the saddles and haunches to Volusia for what we need. Then we kin say 'Howdy' to Grandma Hutto."

She frowned.

"You'll git to visitin' with that sassy old woman and like as not you'll be gone a couple o' days. I think you'd ought to leave Jody with me."

Jody squirmed and looked at his father.

Penny said, "We'll be back tomorrer. How's Jody to learn to hunt and be a man if his daddy don't carry him along and learn him?"

"Hit's a good excuse," she said. "Hit's jest men-folks likin' to prowl off together."

"Then you come make the hunt with me, sweetheart, and leave Jody here."

Jody laughed out. The picture of his mother's great frame pushing through the bay-heads made him shout in spite of himself.

"Oh, go on," she said, and laughed. "Git it over and done with."

"You know you enjoy gittin' shut of us now and agin," Penny told her.

"Hit's my only rest," she admitted. "Leave me Grandpa's gun loaded."

The ancient Long Tom, Jody thought, was more of a menace to her than to any intruders. She was an inaccurate and incompetent shot, and the gun was as fallible as Penny's muzzle-loader, but he could understand the comfort to her of its presence. He brought it from the shed for his father to load, grateful that she had not demanded his own newly acquired piece.

Penny whistled to old Julia and the man and boy and hound set out eastward in mid-morning. The May day was warm and close. The sun beat down through the scrub. The small hard leaves of the scrub oaks were flat pans to hold the heat. The sand burned Jody's feet through his cowhide shoes. In spite of the heat, Penny walked at a fast gait. It was all Jody could do to follow him. Julia loped ahead. There was as yet no scent. Penny stopped once and stared about the horizon.

The Yearling

Jody asked, "What you see, Pa?"

"Nothin', son, and very leetle o' that."

A mile east of the clearing, he changed his direction. There were suddenly deer tracks in a great plenty. Penny studied them, for size and sex and freshness.

"Here's two big ol' bucks travelin' together," he said at last. "They come this way before day."

"How kin you tell about tracks so?"

"Jest by bein' used to 'em."

Jody could see little difference between them and some of the other hoof-marks. Penny stooped and traced them with his finger.

"Now you know to tell a doe from a buck. A doe's track is pointed and fine. And ary one kin tell how fresh a track be, for a old track has sand blowed into it. And now if you'll notice, a deer's toes is spraddled when he's runnin'. They're close together when he walks." He indicated the fresh tracks to the hound. "Here, Julia, git him!"

Julia bent her long nose to the trail. It led out of the scrub, toward the south-east, into an open area of gallberry flats. Here was bear sign as well.

Jody asked, "Must I shoot a bear, do I git the chancet?"

"Bear or buck, hit's all right. Jest be sure you got a good chancet. Don't go wastin' your shot."

The flats were not hard going, but the sun was blazing. The gallberry bushes ended and there was a welcome stretch of pines. The shadows were cooling. Penny pointed out a bear gnaw. It was a clawed area on a tall pine tree, shoulder high to a man. The resin dripped from it.

"I've watched a bear at it," Penny said, "many a time. He'll stretch up and he'll claw. He'll turn his head sideways and he'll nag and gnaw. Then he'll back up and rub his shoulders agin the resin. Some folks says it's to keep the bees from stingin' when he robs a bee-tree, but I've allus figgered 'twas jest a way o' boastin'. A buck'll boast jest about the same way. He'll rub his head and horns agin a saplin' jest to prove hisself."

The Yearling

Julia lifted her nose and Penny and Jody stopped short. There was a commotion ahead. Penny motioned Julia to heel and they crept close. An opening showed and they halted. Twin bear cubs were high in a slim pine sapling, using it for a swing. The sapling was tall and limber and the yearling cubs were rocking it back and forth. Jody had swung in the same fashion. For an instant the cubs were not bears, but boys like himself. He would have liked to climb the sapling and rock with them. It bent half-way to the ground as they swung their weight, swayed upright again, then low on the other side. The cubs made now and then an amiable talking.

Julia could not resist barking. The cubs stopped their play, astonished, and stared down at the humans. They were not alarmed. It was their first sight of mankind and they seemed to feel, as Jody felt, only curiosity. They cocked their black furry heads from one side to the other. One scrambled to a higher limb, not for safety, but for a better view. He curled one arm around the sapling and gaped down below him. His black beady eyes were bright.

"Oh Pa," Jody begged, "let's ketch us one."

Penny himself was tempted.

"They're a mite big for tamin'." He brought himself to his senses. "Now what ails us? Jest how long would it take your Ma to run him off, and me and you with him?"

"Pa, look at him cut his eyes."

"That's likely the mean un. Of twin bear cubs, one'll be gentle and t'other'll be mean."

"Let's ketch the gentle un. Please, Pa."

The cubs craned their necks. Penny shook his head.

"Come along, boy. Le's git on with our hunt and leave 'em to their play."

He lingered behind while his father took up the bucks' trail again. He thought once that the cubs were about to come down the sapling to him, but they only scrambled about from one limb to another and turned their heads to watch him. He ached to touch them. He imagined them

94

sitting on their haunches and begging, as Oliver Hutto described trained bears as doing; nesting in his lap, warm and furry and intimate; sleeping on the foot of his bed; even under the covers with him, if the nights were cold. His father was almost out of sight under the pines. He ran after him. He looked back over his shoulder and waved his hand to the bear cubs. They lifted their black noses, as though the air might tell them, what their eyes had not, the nature of their observers. In their first sign of alarm, he saw them clamber down the sapling and slip away to the west beyond the gall-berries. He caught up to his father.

"Do you ever ask your Ma into leavin' you have sich as that," Penny told him, "you belong to git one young enough to train easy."

The thought was encouraging. The yearling cubs would indeed be large to handle.

"Now I never had nothin' much to pet nor play with, neither," Penny said. "There was sich a mess of us. Neither farmin' nor the Bible pays a man too good, and Pa was like your Ma, he jest wouldn't feed no creeturs. He done well to fill our bellies. Then he put in and died, and since I was the oldest rat in the barn, I had to look after the rest of 'em 'til they was old enough to shuffle around for theirselves."

"Well, a bear cub could near about make his own livin', couldn't he?"

"Yes—offen your Ma's chickens."

Jody sighed and applied himself with his father to the buck tracks. The pair of deer was keeping close together. It was odd, he thought, that the bucks could be so friendly through the spring and summer. Then when their horns were grown, and they began to run with the does in the autumn, they would drive the fawns away from the does, and battle fiercely. One buck was larger than the other.

"That un there's a buck big enough to ride," Penny said.

A patch of hammock joined the pines. Dogbane grew thickly here, lifting its yellow bells. Penny studied the multitude of tracks.

The Yearling

"Now boy," he said, "you been wantin' to see fawns. Me and Julia'll go on and make a circle. You climb up this here live oak and scrooch down in the branches and I believe you'll see somethin'. Hide your gun here in the bushes. You'll not want it."

Jody settled himself halfway up the live oak. Penny and Julia disappeared. The shade of the oak was cool. A light breeze moved through its leaves. Jody's shaggy hair was wet. He pushed it out of his eyes and wiped his face on his blue sleeve, then settled himself to quiet. Silence took over the scrub. Far away a hawk cried shrilly and was gone. No bird stirred in any branches. No creature moved or fed. No bees droned, or any insect. It was high noon. Everything living was resting in the heat of the sun's meridian. Everything except Penny and old Julia, who moved now somewhere among the scrub oaks and the myrtle. Bushes crackled below him. He thought his father was returning. He almost betrayed himself with a quick movement. A bleat sounded. A fawn was moving from under the protection of a low clump of palmettos. It must have been there all the time. Penny had known. Jody held his breath.

A doe bounded over the palmettos. The fawn ran to her, wobbling on unsteady legs. She bent her head to it and made a low sound in greeting. She licked its small anxious face. It was all eyes and ears. It was spotted. Jody had never seen one so young. The doe threw up her head and tasted the air with her wide nostrils. A taint lay on it of the human enemy. She kicked up her heels and made a sortie about the live oak. She discovered the trail of hound and man. She followed it backward and forward, throwing up her head at every few steps. She stopped and listened, her ears pricked tall above her great luminous eyes.

The fawn bleated. The doe quieted. She seemed satisfied that the danger had come and gone. The fawn nuzzled her full udders and began to nurse. It butted her bag with its knobby head and switched its short tail in a gluttonous ecstasy. The doe was not content. She broke away from it and moved directly underneath the live oak. The boughs below Jody obscured his view, but he could see that she had traced his scent to the tree and was lifting her head to locate him. Her nose followed the odor of his hands, the leather of his shoes, the sweat of his clothing, as surely as a man's eyes followed a blazed trail. The fawn followed, greedy for the warm milk. Suddenly the doe wheeled and kicked the fawn sprawling into the bushes. She cleared them in a great bound and galloped away.

Jody scrambled down from his perch and ran to the place where he had seen the fawn tumble. It was not there. He hunted the ground carefully. The tiny hoof-marks crossed and criss-crossed and he could not tell one track from another. He sat down disconsolately to wait for his father. Penny returned, red of face and wet with sweat.

"Well, son," he called, "what did you see?"

"A doe and a fawn. The fawn were right here all the while. He nursed his mammy and she smelled me and run off. And I cain't find the fawn no-where. You reckon Julia kin track him?"

Penny dropped down on the ground.

"Julia kin track ary thing that makes a trail. But don't let's torment the leetle thing. Hit's right clost this minute, and likely scairt to death."

"His mammy shouldn't of left him."

"That's where she was smart. Most ary thing would take out after her. And she's learned the fawn to lay up so still hit'll not git noticed."

"Hit was mighty cute spotted, Pa."

"Was the spots all in a line, or helter-skelter?"

"They was in a line."

"Then hit's a leetle ol' buck-fawn. Wasn't you proud to see it so clost?"

"I was proud, but I'd shore love to ketch him and keep him."

The Yearling

Penny laughed and opened his knapsack and took out the lunch. Jody protested. He was for once more anxious to hunt than to eat.

Penny said, "We got to noon somewhere, and a deer is mighty like to run over us right here. When you noon, you jest as good to noon where the game walks."

Jody brought his gun from its hiding place and sat down to eat. He was abstracted and only the flavor of fresh brier-berry jam brought him back to a consciousness of his food. The jam was thin and not sweet enough, sugar being scarce. Old Julia was still a little weak. She lay stretched out on her side. Her battle scars showed white against her dark hide. Penny lay on his back.

He said lazily, "Them two bucks is like to circle back through here to bed up right soon, if the wind don't change. If you was of a notion to go climb one o' them high pine trees about a quarter to the east, hit'd make a mighty good stand."

Jody picked up his gun and started away. He would give anything to bring down a buck alone.

Penny called after him, "Don't try for too long a shot. Take your time. And don't let the gun kick you outen the tree."

Tall scattered pines lifted ahead from a desolate flat of gallberry bushes. Jody chose one that commanded a view of a wide area. Nothing could cross in any direction without his seeing it. It was hard work to climb the straight trunk with the gun in one hand. His knees and shins were raw when he reached the lowest branches. He rested a moment then climbed as high as he dared in the tree-top. The pine swayed in an imperceptible breeze. It seemed alive, stirring with a breath of its own.

He recalled the bear cubs, rocking the sapling. He began to swing his tree-top, but it was over-balanced with his weight and that of his gun. It cracked ominously and he held quiet. He looked about him. He knew now how a hawk felt, surveying the world from high places. An eagle stared down as he was staring, high and wise and predatory and keen. He swung his head in a slow circle. For the first time he could believe that the world was round. By turning his head quickly, he could almost see the whole horizon at once.

He thought that his vision covered the entire area. He was startled to see movement. He had seen nothing approaching. But a large buck was feeding toward him. Early huckleberries were offering food. The buck was still out of range. He debated climbing down from the pine tree and stalking it, but knew that the animal, more alert than he, would be gone before he could lift his gun. He could only wait, and pray that it would feed within a reasonable distance. It moved with a maddening slowness.

For a time he thought it meant to feed away from him, to the south. Then it began to move directly toward him. He brought his gun up behind the shelter of the branches. His heart pounded. He could not tell for the life of him whether the deer was near or far. It loomed large, yet he was conscious that such details as eyes and ears were still not plain to him. He waited for what seemed an interminable period. The buck lifted his head. Jody drew a bead on the stout neck.

He pulled the trigger. At the instant that he did so, he realized that he had not made sufficient allowance for his height above the game. He had over-shot. Yet it seemed to him that he must have touched the animal, for it leaped into the air with something more than alarm. It cleared the gallberry bushes with a high bounding, making long cradled arcs. It passed directly under the pine-tree. If he had had his father's new double-barreled gun, he would have had another shot. In a few seconds he heard Penny's gun. He was quivering. He climbed down from the pine and pushed his way back to the patch of hammock. The buck lay in the shade of the live oak. Penny had already begun the dressing.

Jody called, "Did I hit him?"

"You hit him. You done a mighty good job. Like as not,

he'd of fell a piece on, but I takened a shot at him as he come by, jest to make sure. You was a mite high."

"I know it. The minute I shot, I knowed I was high."

"Well, that's the way you learn. Next time, you'll know. Now here's your shot, here, and there's mine."

Jody knelt down to examine the fine frame. Again, a sickness came over him at the sight of the glazed eyes and the bleeding throat.

He said, "I wisht we could git our meat without killin' it."

"Hit's a pity, a'right. But we got to eat."

Penny was working deftly. His hunting knife, a flat saw-file ground down to an edge, with only a corn-cob for handle, was not overly sharp, but he had already drawn the venison and cut off the heavy head. He skinned it below the knees, crossed the legs and tied them, slipped his arms through the junctures, and stood up with the carcass neatly balanced on his back for carrying.

"Now Boyles may want the hide when we skin it out at Volusia," he said, "but if you'd like to carry the hide to Grandma Hutto for a present, we'll jest refuse him."

"I reckon she'd be proud to have it for a rug, a'right. I wisht I'd shot it by myself, to give her."

"That's jest all right. The hide's yours. I'll carry her a fore-quarter, for my portion. She's got nobody but us to hunt for her, with Oliver gone to sea. That mindless Yankee hangs around her is no good for sich as that." Penny said innocently, "Now mebbe you'd ruther carry the hide to your sweetheart."

Jody scowled blackly.

"Pa, you know I got no sweetheart."

"You ain't goin' back on Eulalie after I seed you holdin' hands at the doin's?"

"I was not holdin' hands. It was a game they was playin'. If you say that agin, Pa, I'll jest die."

Penny seldom teased his son, but now and then an occasion was irresistible.

The Yearling

"Grandma's my sweetheart," Jody said.

"All right. I jest wanted to git it straight."

The sand road was long and hot. Penny was wet with sweat, but he walked easily under his burden.

Jody said, "Kin I tote it a ways?" but Penny shook his head.

"These fellers only fits a man's back," he said.

They crossed Juniper Creek, then, after two miles of narrow road, picked up the main road to the river and to Volusia. Penny stopped to rest. In late afternoon they passed Captain McDonald's house and Jody knew they were nearing Fort Butler. Around a bend in the road, the dry growth of pines and scrub oak disappeared. There was a new lushness. Sweet gums and bay were here, and, like sign-posts indicating the river, cypress. Wild azaleas were blooming late in the low places, and the passion flower opened its lavender corollas along the road.

They reached the St. John's River. It was dark and aloof. It seemed to slide toward the ocean indifferent to its own banks and to the men who crossed or used it. Jody stared at it. It was a pathway to the world. Penny shouted across it to summon the ferry from the Volusia side. A man crossed over for them with a rough raft of hewn logs. They crossed back, watching the slow sweep of the river current. Penny paid his ferriage and they walked up the curving shell road and into the Volusia store.

Penny hailed the proprietor, "Howdy, Mr. Boyles. How do this feller look to you?"

"Too good for the steam-boat. But Cap'll want it."

"What's venison worth?"

"The same. A dollar and a half a saddle. I'll swear, those city folks travelling up and down the river— Hollering for venison, and 'tain't half as good as pork, and you and me, we know it."

Penny hauled the deer to the big meat block and began the skinning.

"Yes," he agreed, "but if a feller's pot-bellied and cain't git out and shoot it for hisself, I reckon venison has a mighty fancy taste to him."

They laughed together. Penny was a welcome trader at the store, as much for his wit and his stories, as his business. Boyles himself was judge and arbiter and encyclopedia for the small community. He stood now in the close odorous dusk of his store like a captain in the hold of his ship. His wares included the necessities and scanty luxuries of the whole country-side, from plows, wagons, buggies and implements, through food staples to whiskey and hardware, dry goods and notions and medicines.

"Now one fore-quarter I'll call back by for tomorrer to carry home to my wife. T'other one goes to Grandma Hutto," Penny said.

"Bless her old soul," Boyles said. "Why I say 'old soul' I don't know. If a man's wife was as young-hearted as Grandma Hutto, why, living'd be a feast."

Jody walked along the length of the glass case under the counter. There were sweet crackers and an assortment of candies. There were Barlow knives and the new Rogers. There were shoe-strings, buttons, thread and needles. The coarser wares were on shelves that lined the walls. Buckets and pitchers, lard-oil lamps and basins, the new kerosene lamps, coffee pots and cast-iron skillets and Dutch ovens, nestled together like strange birds, fledglings in one nest. Beyond the utensils were the dress goods; calico and Osnaburg, denim and shoddy, domestic and homespun. A few bolts of alpaca and linsey and broadcloth were thick with dust. There was little sale for such luxuries, especially in the summer. At the back of the store were the groceries, hams and cheeses and bacons. There were barrels of sugar and flour and meal and grits and green coffee beans; sacks of potatoes; kegs of syrup; barrels of whiskey. Nothing here was tempting and Jody wandered back to the glass case. A rusty mouth organ lay on top of a pile of licorice strings. He was tempted for a moment to trade in his deer hide and buy the mouth organ, so that he could play to Grandma Hutto or accompany the Forresters. But Grandma would probably prefer the deer hide. Boyles called to him.

"Young man, your daddy doesn't come to trade too often. I'll treat you to a dime's worth of anything you take a notion to."

He looked over the assortment hungrily.

"I reckon the mouth organ's wuth more'n a dime."

"Well, yes, but it's been there a good while now. Take it and welcome."

Jody cast a last look at the candies. But Grandma Hutto would have sweets for him.

He said, "Thank you, sir."

Boyles said, "Your boy's mannerly, Mr. Baxter."

"He's right smart of a comfort," Penny said. "We lost so many young uns, I think sometimes I set too much store by him."

Jody glowed with a sense of virtue. He longed to be good and noble. He turned back of the counter to garner the reward of his character. He glanced up at a motion by the door. Boyles' niece, Eulalie, stood gaping at him. He was flooded instantly with hate. He hated her because his father had teased him. He hated her hair, hanging in tight pig-tails. He hated her freckles, more lavish than his own. He hated her squirrel-teeth, her hands, her feet, and every bone in her lank body. He leaned over swiftly and picked a small potato from a sack and lifted it. She eyed him venomously. Slowly, she flickered her tongue at him like a garter snake. She clasped two fingers over her nose in a gesture of malodorous disgust. He hurled the potato. It struck her on the shoulder and she retreated with shrieks of anguish.

Penny said, "Why, Jody."

Boyles advanced, frowning.

Penny said sternly, "Git right outen here. Mr. Boyles, he cain't have the mouth organ."

He went outside into the hot sunlight. He was humiliated. Yet if he had it to do over again, he would throw another potato at her, a larger one. When his business was done, Penny joined him.

He said, "I'm sorry you seed fit to shame me. Mebbe your Ma's right. Mebbe you hadn't ought to have no truck with the Forresters."

Jody scuffled his feet in the sand.

"I don't keer. I hate her."

"I don't know what to say. How on earth come you to do it?"

"I jest hate her. She made a face at me. She's ugly."

"Well, son, you cain't go thru life chunkin' things at all the ugly women you meet."

Jody spat unrepentant in the sand.

"Well," Penny said, "I don't know what Grandma Hutto'll say."

"Oh Pa, don't tell her. Please don't tell her."

Penny was ominously silent.

"I'll be mannerly, Pa."

"I don't know whether she'll take this hide from you now or not."

"Leave me have it, Pa. I'll not chunk nothin' at nobody agin, if you'll not tell Grandma."

"All right. This time. But don't let me ketch you at sich as that agin. Take your deer-hide."

His spirits lifted. The menacing cloud moved away. They turned north up a path that paralleled the river. Magnolias were in bloom along it. Beyond, there was a lane of oleanders. These too were blossoming. Red-birds flew ahead down the lane. The oleanders led to a gate in a white picket fence. Grandma Hutto's flower garden was a bright patchwork quilt thrown down inside the pickets. Her small white cottage was bound to the substantial earth with vines of honeysuckle and jessamine. Everything here was dear and familiar. Jody ran down the path through the garden;

through the patch of indigo, in feathery, rose-lavender bloom.

He called, "Hey! Grandma!"

Light steps sounded inside the cottage and she was on the door-step.

"Jody! You scamp."

He ran to her.

Penny called, "Don't knock her down, boy."

She braced her small frame. He squeezed her until she squeaked.

"You tormented bear cub," she said.

She began to laugh, and he tipped back his head to laugh with her and watch her face. It was pink and wrinkled. Her eyes were as black as gallberries. They opened and shut when she laughed, and the wrinkles rippled out from the sides. She shook up and down, and her small plump breast quivered like a quail dusting. Jody sniffed at her like a puppy.

He said, "Ummm, Grandma, you smell good."

Penny said, "That's more'n you kin say for us, Grandma. We're a dirty pair o' somebodies."

" 'Tain't nothin' but huntin' smell," Jody said. "Deer-hide and leaves and sich. And sweatin'."

"It's a dandy smell," she said. "I'm jest lonesome for boy-smell and man-smell."

Penny said, "Anyway, here's our excuse-us. Fresh venison."

"And the hide," Jody said. "For a rug for you. Hit's mine. I wounded it."

She lifted her hands in the air. Their gifts became at once of great value. It seemed to Jody that he could bring in a panther single-handed, in return for her approval. She touched meat and hide.

Penny said, "Now don't dirty them leetle hands."

She drew gallantry from men as the sun drew water. Her pertness enchanted them. Young men went away from her with a feeling of bravado. Old men were enslaved by her silver curls. Something about her was forever female and made all men virile. Her gift infuriated all women. Ma Baxter had returned to the clearing from her four years in her house with an acute dislike. The older woman returned it with good measure.

Penny said, "Leave me tote the meat to the kitchen. And I'd best tack the hide to your shed wall, to cure for you."

Jody called, "Here, Fluff!"

The white dog came racing. He bounded at Jody like a ball and leaped at his face to lick it.

Grandma said, "He's as proud to see you as if 'twas some of his kin-folks."

Fluff caught sight of old Julia, sitting sedately on her haunches. He stiffened and advanced to her. Julia sat without stirring, her long ears drooping.

Grandma said, "I like that dog. She looks jest like my Aunt Lucy."

Penny went to the rear of the cottage with the venison and the hide. They were all welcome here, father and son and battle-scarred hound. Jody felt more at home than when he returned to his own mother.

He said, "I reckon you wouldn't be so proud to see me, did you have to put up with me all the time."

Grandma chuckled.

"You've heard your Ma say that. Did she quarrel about you comin'?"

"Not so turrible as sometimes."

"Your father," she said tartly, "married a woman all Hell couldn't amuse."

She lifted a finger in the air.

"I'll bet you want to go swimmin'."

"In the river?"

"Smack in the river. When you come out, I'll give you clean clothes. Some of Oliver's."

She did not caution him against alligators or moccasins or against the river current. It was good to have it taken for granted that he had a little sense of his own. He ran down the path to the landing. The river flowed deep and dark. It made a rippling sound against the banks, but the great liquid heart of it moved silently. Only the swift progress of fallen leaves showed the current. Jody hesitated a moment on the wooden landing, then dove in. He came up gasping with the coldness and struck upstream. He kept close to the bank, where the current ran less swiftly.

He made almost no progress. The dark vegetation towered on either side of the river. He was pinned between banks of live oaks and cypresses. He pretended that an alligator was behind him and swam desperately. He passed one spot and then, laboriously, another, dog-paddling. He wondered if he could swim as far as the upper landing, where the ferry crossed and the river steamers halted. He fought his way toward it. A cypress knee offered anchorage and he clung to it and caught his wind. He set out again. The landing looked far away. His shirt and breeches interfered with his freedom. He wished he had gone in naked. Grandma would not have minded. He wondered what his mother would have said if he had told her the Forresters had played and sung naked.

He looked over his shoulder. Hutto's landing had disappeared around the bend. He was suddenly not happy in the fluid darkness. He turned around. The current caught him and he shot downstream. He struggled to approach the bank. Watery tentacles held him. He thought in a panic that he might be swept on to Volusia Bar, to great Lake George itself, even, perhaps, the sea. He fought blindly, reaching for whatever might be solid under him. He found himself grounding a little above the landing. In relief, he drifted cautiously down to it and climbed up on the wooden platform. He drew a deep breath. The panic left him and he was exhilarated by the cold water and the danger. Penny was on the landing.

His father said, "That were right smart of a tussle. Reckon I'll jest ease around the edge to git me my wash."

The Yearling

He dropped cautiously from the landing.

He said, "Now I don't aim to take my feet offen the ground. My day for capers is over."

He came out of the water shortly. They returned to the rear of the cottage. Grandma Hutto had clean clothes waiting for them. For Penny, there were garments of the long-dead Mr. Hutto, musty with age. For Jody, there were shirt and breeches that Oliver had worn and outgrown many years ago.

Grandma said, "They say you git to use things again, if you save them, ever' seven years. How many is two times seven, Jody?"

"Fourteen."

Penny said, "Don't ask him no further. That school teacher me and the Forresters boarded last winter didn't scarcely know, hisself."

"Well, lots of things is more important than book-learnin'."

"I know that, but a feller needs to know to read and write and figger. But Jody's gittin' along right good with what I kin make out to learn him."

They dressed in the shed. They smoothed back their hair with their hands and felt clean and strange in the borrowed clothing. Jody's freckled face shone. His tawny hair lay wet and smooth. They put on their own shoes and wiped away the dust with their discarded shirts. Grandma Hutto called to them and they went into the cottage.

Jody smelled its familiar odor. He had never been able to disentangle its elements. The sweet lavender she used on her clothing was plain. There were dried grasses in a jar before the fire-place. There was the unmistakable smell of honey, which she kept in a cupboard. There was pastry; tarts and cookies and fruit cakes. There was the smell of the soap she used on Fluff's fur. There was the pervasive scent of flowers from the garden outside the windows. And above it all, it came to him at last, lay the smell of the river. The river itself was fluid through the cottage and around it, leaving a whirl-

108

pool of odorous dampness and decaying fern. He looked through the open door. A path led through marigolds to the water. The river shone in the late sunlight, Guinea-gold, like the bright flowers. Its flow drew Jody's mind with it to the ocean, where Oliver rode the storms in ships, and knew the world.

Grandma brought Scuppernong wine and spice cakes. Jody was allowed a glass of wine. It was as clear as Juniper Springs. Penny smacked his lips over it, but Jody wished it was something sweeter, blackberry shrub, perhaps. He ate spice cakes absently, and stopped in shame to see that he had emptied the plate. This, at home, would be catastrophe. Grandma went to the cupboard and filled the plate again.

She said, "Don't you spoil your dinner."

"I never know, 'til it's too late."

She went to the kitchen and he followed her. She began to slice venison to broil. He frowned anxiously. The meat was no great treat to the Baxters. She opened the oven door and he became aware that other things were being cooked. She had an iron cook stove. Food from it was more mysterious than from the open hearth at home. The closed door concealed all manner of things behind its black bosom. The cake had dulled his appetite a little, but the good odors brought it back again.

He wandered back and forth from Grandma to his father. Penny sat sunk in quiet in a padded chair in the front room. Shadows lay over him and absorbed him. There was not here the excitement of a visit to the Forresters. There was instead a snugness that covered him like a warm quilt in winter. It was meat and drink to Penny, harassed at home by all his duties. Jody offered to help in the kitchen, but Grandma sent him away. He rambled into the yard and played with Fluff. Old Julia watched them wonderingly. Romping was as alien to her as to her master. Her black and tan face wore the solemnity of the work-dog.

Dinner was ready. Grandma Hutto was the only person

Jody knew who had a separate room to eat in. Every one else ate in the kitchen, from a scrubbed and bare pine table. Even as she brought in the food, he could not take his eyes from the white cloth and the blue plates.

Penny said, "Now we're a mighty sorry pair o' tramps to set down to all these purties."

But he joked and gossiped with Grandma with an ease he did not have at his own table.

He said to her, "I'm surprised your sweetheart ain't showed up yit."

Her black eyes snapped.

"Anybody but you said that, Penny Baxter, he'd get pitched in the river."

"The way you done pore Easy hisself, eh?"

"Pity he didn't drown. A man that don't know when he's insulted."

"You'll be obliged to take him yit, to give you the legal right to throw him out."

Jody laughed boisterously. He could not listen to them and eat at the same time. He found himself getting behind and settled down to steady eating. There was a bass, fresh from Easy's fish-trap in the river, baked whole with a savory stuffing. The Irish potatoes were a treat, after the Baxter sweet potatoes three times a day. There was early mutton corn. The Baxters seldom ate new corn, for all that was raised seemed more desperately needed for the stock. Jody sighed with his inability to hold everything. He concentrated on light bread and mayhaw jelly.

Penny said, "He'll be so spoiled, his Ma'll have to break him in like a new bird-dog."

After dinner they walked together through the garden to the river bank. Boats passed. The travellers waved to Grandma and she waved back. Toward sunset Easy Ozell turned into the path to the cottage to do the evening chores. Grandma eyed her approaching admirer.

"Now don't he look like the back end o' bad luck?"

The Yearling

Jody thought that Easy looked like a sick gray crane, with feathers draggled by the rain. His hair hung in gray wisps in his neck. He had a long thin gray mustache that drooped to his jaws. His arms hung like limp wings at his sides.

"Look at him," she said. "Tormented Yankee. His feet drag like a 'gator's tail."

"He shore ain't purty," Penny admitted, "but he's humble as a dog."

"I hate a pitiful man," she said. "And I hate anything is bow-legged. He's so bow-legged his breeches near about make a mark on the ground."

Easy shuffled back of the house. Jody heard him with the cow, and later at the wood-pile. When the evening's work was done, he came timidly to the front steps. Penny shook hands with him and Grandma nodded to him. He cleared his throat. Then as though his Adam's apple, working up and down, blocked his words, he gave up trying to speak and sat down on the bottom step. The talk flowed about him, and his gray face was bright with content. At twilight, Grandma disappeared inside the house. Easy rose stiffly to go.

He said to Penny, "My, if I could talk like you. Maybe she'd take to me better. You s'pose it's that, or won't she never forgive me, bein' a Yankee? If 'twas that, I'll declare, Penny, I'd spit on the flag."

"Well, you know a woman'll hold a idee like a 'gator'll hold a shoat. She cain't fergit the time the Yankees takened her needles and thread and she walked clean to St. Augustine with three hen's eggs to trade for a paper o' needles. Now if the Yankees had got beat, she'd mebbe forgive you."

"But I was beat, Penny. I myself was beat something awful. It was at Bull Run. You rebels whipped us something terrible. My, I hated it." His memories overcame him. He wiped his eyes. "You whipped us, and we was two to your one!"

He shuffled away.

"Now think o' that beat-down human aspirin' to Grandma," Penny said. "He's shore got a low eye for a high fence."

Inside the cottage, Penny tormented Grandma about Easy, as he had tormented Jody about Eulalie. But she gave back as good as she took, and the bout was good-natured. The subject reminded Jody of the matter that had been on his conscience.

He said, "Grandma, Lem Forrester said Twink Weatherby was his gal. I said she was Oliver's, and Lem didn't like it no leetle bit."

"Oliver'll likely take care o' Lem when he comes home," she said. "If a Forrester knows to fight fair."

She put them to bed in a room as white as the snow that Oliver told of. Jody stretched out beside his father between immaculate sheets.

He said, "Don't Grandma live nice?"

Penny said, "Hit's a way some women has." He added loyally, "But don't think hard o' your Ma for not doin' like Grandma. Your Ma ain't never had nothin' much to do with, and I'm to blame for that, not her. She cain't he'p it, livin' rough."

Jody said, "I wisht Grandma was really my Grandma. I wisht Oliver was shore enough kin."

"Well, folks that seems like kin-folks, is kin-folks. You ruther live here with Grandma?"

Jody pictured the cabin in the clearing. Hoot-owls would be crying, and perhaps the wolves would howl, or a panther scream. The deer would be drinking at the sink-hole, the bucks alone, the does with their fawns. The bear cubs would be curled up in their beds together. There was something at Baxter's Island that was better than white tablecloths and counterpanes.

"No, I'd not. I'd jest like to take Grandma home to live with us. But we'd have to make Ma mind her."

Penny chuckled.

"Pore boy," he said, "has got to grow up and learn women——"

Chapter XII

JODY heard the freight and passenger steamer pass the Hutto landing about daylight. He sat up in bed and looked out of the window. The lights of the steamer were pale under the early morning sky. The paddle wheels churned thickly through the water. The steamer blew its thin high whistle at Volusia. He thought he heard it stop and then go on up the river. Somehow, its passing concerned him. He could not go to sleep again. Outside in the yard old Julia growled. Penny stirred from his sleep. Watchfulness lived sentinel in his brain. Sounds no heavier than the wind aroused him.

He said, "The steamer stopped. Somebody's comin'."

Old Julia barked deeply, then whined and was still.

"Hit's somebody she knows."

Jody cried, "Hit's Oliver!" and jumped from the bed.

He ran naked through the cottage. Fluff awakened and dashed from his bed by Grandma's door, barking shrilly.

A voice shouted, "Turn out, you lazy landlubbers!"

Grandma ran from her bedroom. She had on a long white nightgown and a white nightcap. She fastened a shawl around her shoulders as she ran. Oliver took the steps in one bound like a buck and Jody and his mother were on him in a whirlwind. He lifted his mother by the waist and swung her. She thumped him with her small fists. Jody and Fluff yelped for attention. Oliver swung them in turn. Penny joined them sedately, fully dressed. They pumped hands in greeting. In the dim light of dawn, Oliver's teeth flashed white. Grandma's eye caught another flashing.

"Now you jest give me them ear-bobs, you pirate."

She stood on tip-toe to reach up to his ears. Gold hoops

swung from the lobes. She unscrewed them and put them in her own ears. He laughed and shook her and Fluff barked in a frenzy. In the tumult, Penny spoke.

"Lord save us, Jody, you're plumb naked."

Jody froze in his tracks. He turned to run. Oliver caught him. Grandma pulled the shawl from her shoulders and tied it around his waist.

She said, "I'd of run naked, too, if I'd had to. Oliver don't come home but twice a year, do he, boy?"

He said, "Hit was dark when I set out, anyways."

The commotion quieted. Oliver picked up his duffel-bag and carried it inside. Jody trailed him.

"Where you been to this time, Oliver? Did you see whales?"

Penny said, "Leave the man ketch his breath, Jody. He cain't turn out tales for young uns like a spring turns water."

But Oliver was bursting with his tales.

"That's what a sailor comes home for," he said. "To see his Ma and his gal and to tell lies."

His ship had been in the tropics. Jody tore himself away long enough to slip into his borrowed shirt and breeches. He called questions and Grandma called questions. The home-comer answered back and forth. Grandma dressed in a flowered dimity and arranged her silver curls with special care. She went to the kitchen to start breakfast. Oliver opened the mouth of his duffel-bag and dumped the contents in the middle of the floor.

Grandma said, "I can't look and cook at the same time."

Oliver said, "Then for the Lord's sake, Ma, cook."

"You're thin."

"I'm skin and bones, waitin' to get home to eat."

"Jody, come get that fire to roarin'. Slice that ham. Slice that bacon. Slice that venison."

She took bowls from cupboards, beat eggs and batter. Jody helped her, then ran back to Oliver. The sun rose and flooded the cottage. Oliver and Penny and Jody squatted on their haunches over the contents of the duffel-bag.

Oliver said, "I've got somethin' for everybody but Jody. Funny, I forgot him."

"You didn't. You ain't never yit forgot me."

"See can you pick out your present."

Jody passed over a roll of silk. That was of course for Grandma. He pushed aside Oliver's clothes, spiced and musty with strange foreign odors. A small packet was wrapped in flannel. Oliver took it out of his hands.

"That's for my gal."

A loose sack was filled with agates and translucent stones. Jody passed on. He lifted a parcel to his nose.

"T'baccy!"

"For your Pa. From Turkey."

"Why, Oliver." Penny opened it, marvelling. The rich aroma drifted across the room. "Why, Oliver. I cain't remember when I've had me a present."

Jody pinched a long narrow bundle. It was heavy and metallic.

"This is it!"

"You can't tell without seein' it."

Jody unwrapped the bundle madly. A hunting knife fell to the floor. The blade was keen and shining. Jody stared.

"Not a knife, Oliver——"

"Now if you'd rather have one of them ground-down files like your Pa has——"

Jody pounced. He swung the long blade to catch the light.

"There ain't nobody in the scrub," he said, "has got sich as that. Not even the Forresters has got sich a knife."

"That's what I figured. We can't let them black-beards get ahead of us."

Jody looked at the small flannel-swathed parcel Oliver held in one hand. He was torn between Oliver and the Forresters.

He burst out, "Oliver— Lem Forrester says Twink Weatherby is his gal."

Oliver laughed and tossed the parcel from one hand to the other.

He said, "No Forrester ever told the truth. Nobody takes my gal away from me."

Jody felt a wave of relief. He had told both Grandma and Oliver and washed his conscience clear, and Oliver was not disturbed. Then a memory came to him of Lem's dark face, brooding and sullen, as he scraped the strings of his fiddle. He put the picture from him. He sunk himself in the treasures his friend had brought home from far places across the sea.

Grandma, he noticed, did not touch her plate at breakfast. She kept Oliver's filled. Her bright eyes hovered over her son like hungry swallows. Oliver sat tall and straight at the table. His skin was bronzed where his shirt was open over his lean throat. His hair was sun-burned, with a red light in it. His eyes were the color which Jody imagined was the color of the sea, gray-blue, with a flashing of green. Jody ran his hand over his own snub nose and freckled skin. He felt surreptitiously across the back of his head, where the straw-colored drake's-tails stuck out stiffly. He was immensely dissatisfied with himself.

He asked, "Grandma, was Oliver borned good-lookin'?"

Penny said, "I kin answer that. I kin remember when he was uglier'n you and me both."

Oliver said complacently, "You'll grow up handsome as I am, Jody, if that's what's botherin' you."

"Jest half as handsome'd do," he said.

Oliver said, "I'll call you in to tell that to my gal today."

Grandma wrinkled her nose.

"Sailors belong to do their courtin' before they come home," she said.

"From what I hear," Penny offered, "sailors don't never quit courtin'."

"How about you, Jody?" Oliver asked. "You got a sweetheart yet?"

Penny said, "Why, ain't you heered, Oliver? Jody's sweet on Eulalie Boyles."

116

Jody felt a murderous fury creep over him. He wanted to roar like the Forresters and frighten every one with his rage. He stuttered.

"I—I hate girls. I hate Eulalie most of all."

Oliver said innocently, "Why, what's the matter with her?"

"I hate her ol' twitchy nose. She looks like a rabbit."

Oliver and Penny shouted and slapped each other.

Grandma said, "Now quit tormentin' the boy, both of you. Can't you remember that fur back, yourselves?"

His venom melted under his gratitude to her. Grandma was the only one who ever stood up for him. No, he thought, that was not true. Penny himself usually helped him fight his battles. When his mother was unreasonable, Penny always said, "Leave him be, Ory. I remember when I were a boy—" It came to him that his father only teased him here, in the hands of friends. When he needed help, Penny never failed him. He grinned.

He said to his father, "I jest dare you tell Ma I got a gal. She'd rare worse'n if I had me a varmint."

Grandma said, "Your Ma rares at you, do she?"

"At me and Pa both. Worse at Pa."

"She don't appreciate him," she said. "She jest don't know any better." She sighed. "A woman has got to love a bad man once or twice in her life, to be thankful for a good one."

Penny stared modestly at the floor. Jody was consumed with curiosity as to whether Mr. Hutto had been good or bad. He dared not ask. At any rate, Mr. Hutto had been so long dead that he supposed it no longer mattered. Oliver rose and stretched his long legs.

Grandma said, "You leavin' me, the very minute you get home?"

"Just for a little while. I got to go around and get acquainted in the neighborhood again."

"That little yellow-headed Twink, eh?"

"Sure." He leaned over her and tousled her curls. "Penny, you-all ain't goin' home today?"

"We got to do our tradin' and head for the scrub, Oliver. I hate it, I hate to miss the Sat'day frolic. We come on a Friday so's to git our venison to Boyles in time for the north boat today. And 'tain't right to leave Ory alone too long."

"No," Grandma said. "A panther might get her."

Penny looked at her quickly, but she was arranging the folds of her apron with great care.

Oliver said, "Well, see you over the river."

He was gone, slapping his sailor's cap on the back of his head. His whistle sounded after him. Jody was desolate. Something would happen to keep him from hearing Oliver's tales. He could feel it. He would have liked to sit on the river bank all morning while Oliver yarned. He had never had enough. Oliver told a tale or two, and some one came, or Oliver stopped to do something else, and never finished.

"I ain't never yit had me a bait o' stories," he said.

Grandma said, "I've never had him long enough, neither."

Penny loitered over his leaving.

"I hate to leave," he said, "pertickler, now Oliver's here."

"I miss Oliver worse," she said, "when he's here, and away from me, than when he's at sea."

Jody said, "Hit's Twink. Hit's gals does it. I don't never aim to have no gal."

He was resentful of Oliver's leaving them. The four of them made a close community, and Oliver had torn it to tatters. Penny basked in the peace of the cottage. He filled his pipe again and again with the foreign tobacco.

He said, "I do hate it, but we got to go. We got our tradin' to do, and hit's a fur piece home, a-foot."

Jody walked along the river bank and threw sticks for Fluff. He saw Easy Ozell running toward the cottage.

Easy called, "Git your Pa quick. Don't let Mis' Hutto hear."

The Yearling

Jody ran through the garden and called his father. Penny came outside.

Easy panted, "Oliver's fightin' the Forresters. He took a crack at Lem outside the store and all them fightin' Forresters come down on him. They're killin' him."

Penny ran for the store. Jody could not keep up with him. Easy trailed behind both of them.

Penny called over his shoulder, "I hope we kin settle it afore Grandma gits into it with a gun."

Jody called, "Pa, we fightin' for Oliver?"

"We're fightin' for whoever's takin' a lickin' and that's Oliver."

Jody's brain whirled like a wind-mill.

He said, "Pa, you said no man couldn't live on Baxter's Island without the Forresters was his friends."

"I said so. But I ain't goin' to see Oliver hurt."

Jody was numb. It seemed to him that Oliver deserved his punishment. He had gone away and left them, to see a girl. He was almost glad the Forresters were after him. Perhaps Oliver would come home from the fight and be done with his nonsense. Twink Weatherby— Jody spat into the sand. He thought of Fodder-wing. He could not bear never to be friends with him again.

He called to his father's back, "I ain't goin' to fight for Oliver."

Penny did not answer. His short legs churned. The fight was in the sandy road in front of the Boyles store. A cloud of dust rose ahead, like a whirlwind in the heat of summer. Jody heard the shouting of the watchers before he could make out the figures of the fighters. All of Volusia was there.

Penny panted, "That white 'possumed crowd don't keer who's kilt, long as they git to see a fight.'

Jody saw Twink Weatherby on the outer circle. Men and women all called her pretty, but he wanted to tear out her soft yellow curls, one by one. Her small pointed face was white. Her wide blue eyes were fixed on the fighters. She twisted a handkerchief around and around in her fingers. Penny pushed his way through the crowd. Jody followed behind him. He clutched at his father's shirt.

It was true. The Forresters were killing Oliver. Oliver was fighting three of them at once, Lem and Mill-wheel and Buck. He looked like a buck deer Jody had once seen, wounded and bleeding, with the dogs tearing flesh from its throat and shoulders. Blood and sand covered his face. He was boxing warily, trying to take on one Forrester at a time. Lem and Buck rushed in on him together. Jody heard a heavy fist crack against bone. Oliver dropped in the sand. The crowd roared.

Jody's mind whirled in confusion. Oliver deserved it, for leaving the cottage and going to a girl. But three against one was never fair. Even when the dogs bayed a bear or panther, it seemed to him an uneven matter. The Forresters, his mother said, were black-hearted. He had never believed her. They sang and drank and frolicked and guffawed. They fed him lavishly and slapped him on the back and gave him Fodder-wing to play with. Was this black-hearted, for three to fight together against one? Yet Mill-wheel and Buck were fighting for Lem, keeping his girl for him. Was not that good? Was that not loyal? Oliver came to his knees, then wavered to his feet. He smiled through the dirt and blood. Jody's stomach turned over. Oliver was being killed.

Jody jumped on Lem's back. He clawed at his neck and thumped his head. Lem shook him off and turned and sent him sprawling. His face stung from the impact of the big hand. His hip ached from the fall.

Lem snapped, "You keep outen this, you leetle panther."

Penny called loudly, "Who's judgin' this fight?"

Lem said, "We're judgin' it."

Penny pushed in front of him. His voice was high against the shouting.

"If it take three men to whop one, I say that one is the better man."

Lem advanced on him.

THE FIGHT AT VOLUSIA

He said, "I'm o' no mind to kill you, Penny Baxter. But I'll smack you flat as a skeeter if you don't git outen my way."

Penny said, "Fair is fair. If you aim to kill Oliver, shoot him honest and hang for murder. But be men."

Buck shuffled his feet in the sand.

He said, "We'd of fit him one at a time, but he lit right in."

Penny pressed his advantage.

"Whose fight is it? Who done what to who?"

Lem said, "He come back stealin', that's what he done."

Oliver wiped his sleeve across his face.

He said, "It's Lem that tried to steal."

"Steal what?" Penny pounded one fist inside the other. "Hounds, hogs, guns, or hosses?"

On the outer rim, Twink Weatherby began to cry.

Oliver said in a low voice, "This is no place to tell it, Penny."

"Then be this the place to fight it out? Like a pack o' dogs fightin' in the road? You two fellers fight it out alone another day."

Oliver said, "I'll fight a man anywhere, that says what Lem said."

Lem said, "And I'll say it again."

They started together. Penny pushed between them. He seemed to Jody like a small stout pine tree, bending against a hurricane. The crowd roared. Lem drew back his fist and struck Oliver over Penny's head. The blow sounded like the crack of a rifle. Oliver crumpled like a rag doll to the sand and lay still. Penny brought his knuckles under Lem's jaw. Buck and Mill-wheel came at him from the sides. Lem sunk his fist in Penny's ribs. Jody moved with a fury that caught him up from the outside, like a strong wind. He sunk his teeth in Lem's wrist. He kicked the big shins. Lem turned, like a bear annoyed by a puppy. He knocked Jody clear of his feet. It seemed to him that Lem struck him again in mid-air. He saw Oliver sway to his feet. He saw Penny's arms swinging like flails. He heard a roaring. It was close at first, then it faded. He dropped into blackness.

Chapter XIII

JODY thought, "I dreamed the fighting."

He stared at the ceiling in Grandma Hutto's spare bedroom. A freight steamer was thrashing up-stream. He heard the side-wheel paddles drinking the swift current of the river. They gulped great wet mouthfuls and let it spill out again. The steamer blew for the Volusia landing. He must certainly have only now awakened in the morning. The steamer's chugging filled the river bed and beat against the western wall that was the scrub. He had had a nightmare about Oliver Hutto, coming home to fight the Forresters. He turned his head to look out of the window and watch the passing vessel. A sharp pain shot through his neck and shoulder. He could only turn his head part-way. Memory went through him, thrusting like the pain.

He thought, "The fighting was true."

It was afternoon. The sun shone in the west across the river. A bright band lay across the counterpane. The pain stopped, but he felt faint and dizzy. There was movement in the room. A rocker creaked.

Grandma Hutto said, "His eyes are open."

He tried to turn his head toward her voice but could not, without pain. She leaned over him.

He said, "Hey, Grandma."

She spoke, not to him, but to his father.

"He's tough as you. He's all right."

Penny appeared on the other side of the bed. One wrist was bandaged and one eye was black. He grinned at Jody.

He said, "We was a big help, you and me."

A cold wet cloth slipped from Jody's forehead. Grandma took it away and laid her hand in its place. She reached her fingers back of his head and felt carefully for the source of pain. It was in his left jaw, where Lem had struck him, and in the back of his head, where he had hit the sand. It eased under her slow manipulation.

She said, "Say somethin', so I'll know your brains ain't jellied."

"I cain't think o' nothin' to say." He added, "Ain't it past dinner-time?"

Penny said, "The only serious hurt could come to him, is likely his belly."

He said, "I ain't hongry. I jest seed the sun and I was wonderin'."

She said, "That's all right, Punkin."

He asked, "Where's Oliver?"

"In the bed."

"Is he bad hurted?"

"Not bad enough to learn him sense."

"I don't know now," Penny said. "One more clip, and he'd not of had much left to learn with."

"Anyway, he's spoiled his pretty looks so no yellow-headed thing'll look at him for a while."

"You women is right smart hard on one another," Penny said. "Seems to me 'twas Oliver and Lem done most o' the lookin'."

Grandma rolled up the cold cloth and left the bedroom.

Penny said, " 'Twa'n't noways fair, gittin' a young un knocked dead. But I'm proud you was man enough to mix in it, when you seed a friend in trouble."

Jody stared at the sunlight.

He thought, "The Forresters are my friends, too."

As though he read his thoughts, Penny said, "This'll likely end neighborin' with the Forresters."

A twinge of pain shot from Jody's head into the pit of his stomach. He could not give up Fodder-wing. He decided that he would slip away some time and call to Fodder-wing from the bushes. He pictured the secret meeting. Perhaps they would be discovered and Lem would whip them both to death. Then Oliver would be sorry he had fought because of Twink Weatherby. Jody was more resentful at Oliver than at the Forresters. Something of Oliver that had belonged to him, and to Grandma, had been taken away and given to the yellow-headed girl who wrung her hands over the fighting.

Yet if he had it to do over again, he would still have to help Oliver. He recalled a wild-cat that the dogs had torn to pieces. Wild-cats deserved what they got. Yet at one moment, when the snarling mouth had gaped wide in agony, and the evil eyes had filmed in dying, he had been stabbed with pity. He had cried out, longing to help the creature in its torture. Too much pain was unjust. Too many against one were unjust. That was why it had been necessary to fight for Oliver, even if it lost him Fodder-wing. He closed his eyes, satisfied. Everything was all right when he understood it.

Grandma came into the bedroom with a tray.

"Now, Punkin, see can you sit up."

Penny slipped his hands under the pillow and Jody eased up slowly. He was stiff and sore, but he felt no worse than the time he had fallen out of the chinaberry tree.

Penny said, "I wisht pore Oliver had got off this light."

Grandma said, "He's lucky he didn't get his fine nose broke."

He ate his way painfully toward a plate of gingerbread. Because of the soreness, he was forced to leave a square. He looked at it.

Grandma said, "I'll save that for you."

Penny said, "Ain't it a treat, to have a woman reads your mind and then agrees with it."

"I mean."

Jody lay against his pillow. Violence broke into peace, and tore the world to tatters, and then, suddenly, all was peaceful again.

Penny said, "I got to be pushin' on. Ory'll be rarin'."

He stood in the doorway. He was a little stooped. He looked lonely.

Jody said, "I want to go with you."

Penny's face grew bright.

He said, "Now, boy." He was eager. "You shore you're fitten? Tell you what I'll do. Borry Boyles' ol' mare, the one goes home alone. We'll ride her back and turn her a-loose."

Grandma said, "Ora'll feel better about him, if he goes with you. I know what happens to Oliver where I can see him, ain't near as bad as what happens out of my sight."

Jody eased his body from the bed. He was dizzy. His head felt large and full. He was tempted to sink back on the smooth sheets.

Penny said, "Jody's a man, if I do say it."

He straightened and went to the door.

"Must I say good-by to Oliver?"

"Why, shore, but don't let on how bad he looks. He's proud."

He went to Oliver's room. Oliver's eyes were swollen shut, as though he had fallen in a nest of wasps. One cheek was purple. A white bandage was tied around his head. His lips were puffed. The fine sailor was laid low, and all because of Twink Weatherby.

Jody said, "Good-by, Oliver."

Oliver did not answer. Jody softened.

"I'm sorry Pa and me didn't git there quicker."

Oliver said, "Come here."

Jody went close to the bed.

"You do somethin' for me? Go tell Twink I'll meet her at the old grove Tuesday about dusk-dark."

Jody was frozen.

He burst out, "I won't do it. I hate her. Ol' yellow-headed somethin'."

"All right. I'll send Easy."

Jody scuffled the rug with one foot.

Oliver said, "I thought you were my friend."

Being friends, he thought, was a nuisance. Then he remembered the hunting knife and was filled with gratitude and shame.

"Well, all right. I don't want to, but I'll tell her."

Oliver laughed from the bed. He would laugh, Jody thought, if he lay dying.

"Good-by, Oliver."

"Good-by, Jody."

He left the room. Grandma was waiting.

He said, "It come out kind o' disappointin', didn't it, Grandma? Oliver fightin', and all."

Penny said, "Boy, be civil."

Grandma said, "The truth's civil enough. When bears with sore heads go courtin', there's always trouble. As long as this is the end and not the beginning——"

Penny said, "You know where to send for me."

They went down the path through the garden. Jody looked back over his shoulder. Grandma stood waving after them.

Penny stopped at Boyles' store for his supplies and for his forequarter of venison. Boyles was willing to lend the mare, if Penny would strap a length of good buckskin for boot laces on the saddle when he sent her home, in payment. The supplies, flour and coffee and powder and lead and shell cases for the new gun, were dropped in a sack. Boyles went to his lot and brought out the mare, saddled with a blanket.

"Don't turn her loose 'til morning," he said. "She can outrun a wolf, but I wouldn't want a panther dropping on her."

Penny turned away to lift his sacks. Jody sidled close to the storekeeper. He was reluctant to have his father know Oliver's secret.

He whispered, "I got to see Twink Weatherby. Where do she live?"

"What you want of her?"

"I got somethin' to say to her."

The Yearling

Boyles said, "A heap of us have something to say to her. Well, you'll have to bide your time. The young lady's put a kerchief on her yellow curls and slipped off on the freight boat to Sanford."

Jody felt a satisfaction as great as though he had driven her away himself. He borrowed a piece of paper and a thick pencil and printed a note to Oliver. It was laborious work, for his father's teachings had been supplemented only by one brief winter of instruction from the itinerant school teacher. He wrote:

Dear ollever; yor ol twinkk has dun gode up the rivver. im gladd. yor frend jody.

He read it over. He decided in favor of a greater kindness. He crossed out "im gladd" and wrote in its place "im sorry." He felt virtuous. Something of the old glow for Oliver came back to him. Perhaps he could still hear his tales.

Crossing to the scrub side on the ferry, he stared down into the swift river. His thoughts were as turbulent as the current. Oliver had never failed him before. The Forresters were after all as rough as his mother insisted. He felt deserted. But he was sure Fodder-wing would not change. The gentle mind in the twisted body would be as aloof from the quarrel as his own. His father, of course, stood as unchangeable as the earth.

Chapter XIV

THE quail were nesting. The fluted covey call had been silent for some time. The coveys were dividing into pairs. The cocks were sounding the mating call, clear and sweet and insistent.

One day in mid-June Jody saw a cock and a hen run from the grape arbor with the scuttling hurry of paternity. He was wise enough not to follow them, but prowled about under the arbor until he found the nest. It held twenty cream-colored eggs. He was careful not to touch them, for fear the quail might desert them, as guineas did. A week later he went to the arbor to look at the progress of the Scuppernongs. They were like the smallest pellets of shot, but they were green and sturdy. He lifted a length of vine, imagining the dusty golden grapes in the late summer.

There was a stirring at his feet, as though the grass had exploded. The setting was hatched. The young quail, each no bigger than the end of his thumb, scattered like small wind-blown leaves. The mother quail cried out, and made alternate sorties after the brood, in defense, and at Jody, in attack. He stood quiet, as his father had taught him to do. The hen gathered her young together and took them away through the tall broom-sage grasses. Jody ran to find his father. Penny was working the field peas.

"Pa, the quail has hatched under the Scuppernong. And the grapes is makin'."

Penny rested on the plow handles. He was wet with sweat. He looked across the field. A hawk flew low, quartering.

He said, "If the hawks don't git the quail, and the 'coons don't git the Scuppernongs, we'll have a mighty good meal, about first frost."

128

Jody said, "I hate the hawks eatin' the quail, but I don't someway mind the 'coons eatin' the grapes."

"That's because you love quail-meat more'n you love grapes."

"No, 'tain't. Hit's because I hate hawks and I love 'coons."

"Fodder-wing learned you that," Penny said, "with all them pet 'coons."

"I reckon so."

"The hogs come up yit, boy?"

"Not yit."

Penny frowned.

"I purely hate to think the Forresters has trapped 'em. But they ain't never stayed off so long. If 'twas bears, they wouldn't all be gone to oncet."

"I been as far as the old clearin', Pa, and the tracks goes on west from there."

"Time I git done workin' these peas, we're jest obliged to take Rip and Julia and go track 'em."

"What'll we do, do the Forresters have 'em trapped?"

"Whatever we got to do, when the time comes."

"Ain't you skeert to face the Forresters agin?"

"No, for I'm right."

"Would you be skeert if you was wrong?"

"If I was wrong, I wouldn't face 'em."

"What'll we do, do we git beat up agin?"

"Take it for our share and go on."

"I'd ruther let the Forresters keep the hogs."

"And go without meat? A black eye'll quiet down a heap quicker'n a empty belly. You want to beg off goin'?"

He hesitated.

"I reckon not."

Penny turned back to his cultivating.

"Then go tell your Ma please Ma'am to fix us early supper."

Jody went to the house. His mother was rocking and sewing on the shady porch. A small blue-bellied lizard scuttled from under her chair. Jody grinned, thinking how quickly she would heave her frame from the rocker if she had known.

"Please, Ma'am, Pa says to fix us supper right now. We got to go huntin' the hogs."

"About time."

She finished her seam leisurely. He dropped on the step below her.

"We likely got to face the Forresters, Ma, if they got 'em trapped."

"Well, face 'em. Black-hearted thieves."

He stared at her. She had been furious at both him and his father because they had fought the Forresters at Volusia.

He said, "We're like to git beat up and bloodied agin, Ma."

She folded her sewing impatiently.

"Well, pity on us, we got to have our meat. Who'll git it if you don't?"

She went into the house. He heard her thumping the lid on the Dutch oven. He was confused. His mother talked much of "duty." He had always hated the very word. Why was it his duty to let the Forresters maul him again, to recover the hogs, if it had not been his duty to let them maul him in order to help his friend Oliver? It seemed more honorable to him to bleed for a friend than for a side of bacon. He sat idly, listening to the fluttered whirring of mockingbirds in the chinaberry. The jays were chasing the red-birds out of the mulberry trees. There was a squabble for food even in the safety of the clearing. But it seemed to him there was always enough here for every one. There was food and shelter for father and mother and son; for old Cæsar; for Trixie and her spotted calf; for Rip and Julia; for the chickens, clucking and crowing and scratching; for the hogs, grunting in at evening for a cob of corn; for the song-birds in the trees, and the quail nesting under the arbor; for all of these, there was enough at the clearing.

Out in the scrub, the war waged ceaselessly. The bears

and wolves and panthers and wild-cats all preyed on the deer. Bears even ate the cubs of other bears, all meat being to their maws the same. Squirrels and wood-rats, 'possums and 'coons, must all scurry for their lives. Birds and small furred creatures cowered in the shadow of hawk and owl. But the clearing was safe. Penny kept it so, with his good fences, with Rip and old Julia, with a wariness that seemed to Jody to be unsleeping. Sometimes he heard a rustling in the night, and the door opened and closed, and it was Penny, slipping back to his bed from a silent hunt for some marauder.

There was intrusion back and forth, as well. The Baxters went into the scrub for flesh of deer and hide of wild-cat. And the predatory animals and the hungry varmints came into the clearing when they could. The clearing was ringed around with hunger. It was a fortress in the scrub. Baxter's Island was an island of plenty in a hungry sea.

He heard the trace chains clanking. Penny was returning to the lot along the fence row. Jody ran ahead to open the lot gates for him. He helped with the unharnessing. He climbed the ladder into the loft and pitched down a forkful of cowpea hay into Cæsar's manger. There was no more corn and would not be until the summer's crop was made. He found a pile of hay with the dried peas still clinging to it and threw it down for Trixie. There would be more milk in the morning for both the Baxters and the spotted calf. The calf was inclined to leanness, for Penny was weaning it from the cow. The loft was heavy with heat, trapped under the thick hand-hewn slabs of the shingled roof. The hay crackled with a dry sweetness. It tickled his nostrils. He lay down in it a moment, abandoning himself to the resiliency. He was no more than comfortable when he heard his mother call. He scrambled down from the loft. Penny had finished milking. They went to the house together. Supper was on the table. There were only clabber and cornbread, but there was enough.

Ma Baxter said, "You fellers try to git a shot at some meat while you're off."

Penny nodded.

"I'm totin' my gun o' purpose."

They set off to the west. The sun was still above the tree-tops. There had been no rain for several days, but now cumulus clouds were piled low in the north and west. From the east and south, a steel grayness crept toward the glaring brilliance of the west.

Penny said, "A good rain today'd near about leave us lay by the corn."

There was no breeze. The air lay over the road like a thick down comforter. It seemed to Jody that it was something that could be pushed away, if he could struggle up through it. The sand burned his bare calloused soles. Rip and Julia walked listlessly, heads down, tails sagging, their tongues dripping from open jaws. It was not easy to follow the tracks of the hogs where the loose soil had been so long dry. Penny's eye was keener here than Julia's nose. The hogs had fed through the black-jack, crossed the abandoned clearing, and then headed for the prairie, where lily roots could be dug, and pools of cool water could be muddied and wallowed in. They did not range so far when food could be had close at home. Now was a barren and parlous season. There was no mast yet, of pine or oak or hickory, except what could be rooted deep under the leaves from last year's falling. Palmetto berries were still too green, even for the undiscerning taste of a hog. Three miles from Baxter's Island Penny crouched to examine the trail. He picked up a grain of corn and turned it over in his hand. He pointed to the hoof-marks of a horse.

"They baited them hogs," he said.

He straightened his back. His face was grave. Jody watched him anxiously.

"Well, son, we're obliged to follow."

"Clare to the Forresters?"

"Clare to wheresomever the hogs be. Mought be, we'll find 'em in a pen some'eres."

The trail zigzagged where the hogs had weaved back and forth for the scattered corn.

Penny said, "I kin understand the Forresters fightin' Oliver and I kin understand them rompin' on you and me. But I be dogged if I kin understand cold-out meanness."

A quarter of a mile beyond stood a rough hog-trap. It had been sprung but the pen was now empty. It was made of untrimmed saplings and a limber sapling had been baited to spring the gate behind the crowding hogs.

"Them rascals was nearby, waitin'," Penny said. "That pen wouldn't hold a hog no time."

A cart had turned around in the sand to the right of the pen. The wheel tracks led down a dim scrub road toward Forresters' Island.

Penny said, "All right, boy. Here's our way."

The sun was near the horizon. The cumulus clouds were white puff-balls, stained with the red and yellow wash of the sunset. The south was filled with darkness, like the smoke of gunpowder. A chill air moved across the scrub and was gone, as though a vast being had blown a cold breath and then passed by. Jody shivered and was grateful for the hot air that fell in behind it. A wild grape-vine trailed across the thin-rutted road. Penny leaned to pull it aside.

He said, "When there's trouble waitin' for you, you jest as good go to meet it."

The rattler struck him from under the grape-vine without warning. Jody saw the flash, blurred as a shadow, swifter than a martin, surer than the slashing claws of a bear. He saw his father stagger backward under the force of the blow. He heard him give a cry. He wanted to step back, too. He wanted to cry out with all his voice. He stood rooted to the sand and could not make a sound. It was lightning that had struck, and not a rattler. It was a branch that broke, it was a bird that flew, it was a rabbit running——

Penny shouted, "Git back! Hold the dogs!"

The voice released him. He dropped back and clutched the dogs by the scruff of their necks. He saw the mottled shadow lift its flat head, knee-high. The head swung from side to side, following his father's slow motions. He heard the rattles hum. The dogs heard. They winded. The fur stood stiff on their bodies. Old Julia whined and twisted out of his hand. She turned and slunk down the trail. Her long tail clung to her hindquarters. Rip reared on his hind feet, barking.

As slowly as a man in a dream, Penny backed away. The rattles sung. They were not rattles— Surely it was a locust humming. Surely it was a tree-frog singing— Penny lifted his gun to his shoulder and fired. Jody quivered. The rattler coiled and writhed in its spasms. The head was buried in the sand. The contortions moved down the length of the thick body, the rattles whirred feebly and were still. The coiling flattened into slow convolutions, like a low tide ebbing. Penny turned and stared at his son.

He said, "He got me."

He lifted his right arm and gaped at it. His lips lifted dry over his teeth. His throat worked. He looked dully at two punctures in the flesh. A drop of blood oozed from each.

He said, "He was a big un."

Jody let go his hold on Rip. The dog ran to the dead snake and barked fiercely. He made sorties and at last poked the coils with one paw. He quieted and snuffed about in the sand. Penny lifted his head from his staring. His face was like hickory ashes.

He said, "Ol' Death goin' to git me yit."

He licked his lips. He turned abruptly and began to push through the scrub in the direction of the clearing. The road would be shorter going, for it was open, but he headed blindly for home in a direct line. He plowed through the low scrub oaks, the gallberries, the scrub palmettos. Jody panted behind him. His heart pounded so hard that he could not see where he was going. He followed the sound of his father's crashing across the undergrowth. Suddenly the denseness ended. A patch of higher oaks made a shaded clearing. It was strange to walk in silence.

Penny stopped short. There was a stirring ahead. A doe-deer leaped to her feet. Penny drew a deep breath, as though breathing were for some reason easier. He lifted his shotgun and leveled it at the head. It flashed over Jody's mind that his father had gone mad. This was no moment to stop for game. Penny fired. The doe turned a somersault and dropped to the sand and kicked a little and lay still. Penny ran to the body and drew his knife from its scabbard. Now Jody knew his father was insane. Penny did not cut the throat, but slashed into the belly. He laid the carcass wide open. The pulse still throbbed in the heart. Penny slashed out the liver. Kneeling, he changed his knife to his left hand. He turned his right arm and stared again at the twin punctures. They were now closed. The forearm was thick-swollen and blackening. The sweat stood out on his forehead. He cut quickly across the wound. A dark blood gushed and he pressed the warm liver against the incision.

He said in a hushed voice, "I kin feel it draw——"

He pressed harder. He took the meat away and looked at it. It was a venomous green. He turned it and applied the fresh side.

He said, "Cut me out a piece o' the heart."

Jody jumped from his paralysis. He fumbled with the knife. He hacked away a portion.

Penny said, "Another."

He changed the application again and again.

He said, "Hand me the knife."

He cut a higher gash in his arm where the dark swelling rose the thickest. Jody cried out.

"Pa! You'll bleed to death!"

"I'd ruther bleed to death than swell. I seed a man die——"

The sweat poured down his cheeks.

"Do it hurt bad, Pa?"

"Like a hot knife was buried to the shoulder."

The meat no longer showed green when he withdrew it. The warm vitality of the doe's flesh was solidifying in death. He stood up.

He said quietly, "I cain't do it no more good. I'm goin' on home. You go to the Forresters and git 'em to ride to the Branch for Doc Wilson."

"Reckon they'll go?"

"We got to chance it. Call out to 'em quick, sayin', afore they chunk somethin' at you or mebbe shoot."

He turned back to pick up the beaten trail. Jody followed. Over his shoulder he heard a light rustling. He looked back. A spotted fawn stood peering from the edge of the clearing, wavering on uncertain legs. Its dark eyes were wide and wondering.

He called out, "Pa! The doe's got a fawn."

"Sorry, boy. I cain't he'p it. Come on."

An agony for the fawn came over him. He hesitated. It tossed its small head, bewildered. It wobbled to the carcass of the doe and leaned to smell it. It bleated.

Penny called, "Git a move on, young un."

Jody ran to catch up with him. Penny stopped an instant at the dim road.

"Tell somebody to take this road in to our place and pick me up in case I cain't make it in. Hurry."

The horror of his father's body, swollen in the road, washed over him. He began to run. His father was plodding with a slow desperation in the direction of Baxter's Island.

Jody ran down the wagon trail to the myrtle thicket where it branched off into the main road to Forresters' Island. The road, much used, had no growth of weeds or grass to make a footing. The dry shifting sand caught at the soles of his feet and seemed to wrap clinging tentacles around the muscles of his legs. He dropped into a short dog-trot that seemed to pull more steadily against the sand. His legs moved, but his mind and body seemed suspended above them, like an empty box on a pair of cart-wheels. The road under him was a tread-mill. His legs pumped up and down, but he seemed to be passing the same trees and bushes again and again. His pace seemed so slow, so futile, that he came to a bend with a dull surprise. The curve was familiar. He was not far from the road that led directly into the Forrester clearing.

He came to the tall trees of the island. They startled him, because they meant that he was now so close. He came alive and he was afraid. He was afraid of the Forresters. And if they refused him help, and he got safely away again, where should he go? He halted a moment under the shadowy live oaks, planning. It was twilight. He was sure it was not time for darkness. The rain clouds were not clouds, but an infusion of the sky, and had now filled it entirely. The only light was a strand of green across the west, the color of the doe's flesh with the venom on it. It came to him that he would call to his friend Fodder-wing. His friend would hear him and come, and he might be allowed to approach close enough to tell his errand. It eased his heart to think of it, to think of his friend's eyes gentle with sorrow for him. He drew a long breath and ran wildly down the path under the oak trees.

He shouted, "Fodder-wing! Fodder-wing! Hit's Jody!"

In an instant now his friend would come to him from the house, crawling down the rickety steps on all fours, as he must do when in a hurry. Or he would appear from the bushes with his raccoon at his heels.

"Fodder-wing! Hit's me!"

There was no answer. He broke into the swept sandy yard.

"Fodder-wing!"

There was an early light lit in the house. A twist of smoke curled from the chimney. The doors and shutters were closed against the mosquitoes and against the night-time. The door swung open. In the light beyond, he saw the Forrester men rise to their feet, one after the other, as though the great trees in the forest lifted themselves by their roots and stirred toward him. He stopped short. Lem Forrester advanced to the stoop. He lowered his head and turned it a little sideways until he recognized the intruder.

"You leetle bastard. What you after here?"

Jody faltered, "Fodder-wing——"

"He's ailin'. You cain't see him no-ways."

It was too much. He burst out crying.

He sobbed, "Pa— He's snake-bit."

The Forresters came down the steps and surrounded him. He sobbed loudly, with pity for himself and for his father, and because he was here at last and something was finished that he had set out to do. There was a stirring among the men, as though the leavening quickened in a bowl of bread-dough.

"Where's he at? What kind o' snake?"

"A rattlesnake. A big un. He's makin' it for home but he don't know kin he make it."

"Is he swellin'? Where'd it git him?"

"In the arm. Hit's bad swelled a'ready. Please ride for Doc Wilson. Please ride for him quick, and I won't he'p Oliver agin you no more. Please."

Lem Forrester laughed.

"A skeeter promises he won't bite," he said.

Buck said, "Hit's like not to do no good. A man dies right now, bit in the arm. He'll likely be dead afore Doc kin git to him."

"He shot a doe-deer and used the liver to draw out the pizen. Please ride for Doc."

Mill-wheel said, "I'll ride for him."

Relief flooded him like the sun.

"I shore thank you."

"I'd he'p a dog, was snake-bit. Spare your thanks."

Buck said, "I'll ride on and pick up Penny. Walkin's bad for a man is snake-bit. My God, fellers, we ain't got a drop o' whiskey for him."

Gabby said, "Ol' Doc'll have some. If he's purty tol'able

sober, he'll have some left. If he's drunk all he's got, he kin blow his breath, and that'll make a powerful portion."

Buck and Mill-wheel turned away with torturing deliberation to the lot to saddle their horses. Their leisureliness frightened Jody as speed would not have done. If there was hope for his father, they would be hurrying. They were as slow and unconcerned as though they were burying Penny, not riding for assistance. He stood, desolate. He would like to see Fodder-wing just a moment before he went away. The remaining Forresters turned back up the steps, ignoring him.

Lem called from the door, "Git goin', Skeeter."

Arch said, "Leave the young un be. Don't torment him, and his daddy likely dyin'."

Lem said, "Die and good riddance. Biggety bantam."

They went into the house and closed the door. A panic came over Jody, that they did not mean, any of them, to help at all; that Buck and Mill-wheel had gone away to the corral for a joke, and were laughing at him there. He was forsaken, and his father was forsaken. Then the two men rode out and Buck lifted his hand to him, not unkindly.

"No use to fret, boy. We'll do what we kin. We don't hold nothin' agin folks in trouble."

They touched their heels to the horses' flanks and shot away. Lightness filled him where he had been heavy as lead. It was only Lem, then, who was an enemy. He settled his hate on him with satisfaction. He listened until the hoofbeats faded from his hearing, then set out down the road for home.

Now he was free to accept the facts. A rattlesnake had struck his father, who might die of it. But help was on the way, and he had done what he was supposed to do. His fear had a name, and was no longer quite so terrible. He decided not to try to run, but to walk steadily. He should have liked to ask the loan of a horse for himself, but dared not.

The Yearling

A pattering of rain passed over him. A hush followed. The storm might go around the scrub entirely, as often happened. There was a faint luminosity in the air around him. He had scarcely been conscious that he was carrying his father's gun. He swung it over one shoulder and walked rapidly where the road was firm. He wondered how long it would take Mill-wheel to reach the Branch. He wondered, not whether old Doc would be drunk, for that was known, but just how drunk he would be. If Doc could sit up in bed, he was considered fit to go.

He had been at Doc's place once when he was very young. He remembered still the sprawling house with wide veran-das, decaying, as old Doc was decaying, in the heart of a dense vegetation. He remembered the cockroaches and the lizards, as much at home inside the house as in the thick vines outside it. He remembered old Doc, deep in his cups, lying under a mosquito canopy, staring at the ceiling. When he was called, he sprawled to his feet and went about his business on uncertain legs, but with gentle heart and hands. He was known far and wide as a good doctor, drunk or no. If he could be reached in time, Jody thought, his father's life was certain.

He turned from the Forresters' lane into the road that ran east to his father's clearing. He had four miles ahead of him. On hard ground, he could make it in little over an hour. The sand was soft, and the very darkness seemed to hold him back and make his steps uneven. He would do well to reach home in an hour and a half, and it might take two. He broke now and then into a trot. The brightness in the air dropped into the darkness of the scrub like a water turkey dropping into the river. The growth on either side of the road pressed closer, so that the way was narrow.

He heard thunder in the east, and a flash of lightning filled the sky. He thought he heard foot-steps in the scrub oaks, but it was drops of rain, striking like shot on the leaves. He had never minded night or darkness, but Penny had always been in front of him. Now he was alone. He wondered, sickened, whether his father lay now in the road ahead of him, swollen with poison, or perhaps across Buck's saddle, if Buck had reached and found him. The lightning flashed again. He had sat with his father through many storms, under the live oaks. The rain had then been friendly, shutting them in together.

A snarl sounded in the bushes. Something incredibly swift flashed across the road in front of him and was gone, soundlessly. A musky taint lay on the air. He was not afraid of lynx or wild-cat, but a panther had been known to attack a horse. His heart thumped. He fingered the stock of his father's gun. It was useless, for Penny had shot both barrels, one at the rattler, one at the doe. He had his father's knife in his belt, and wished he had brought the long knife Oliver had given him. He had no scabbard for it, and it was dangerously sharp, Penny had said, to carry. When he was safe at home, lying under the grape arbor, or at the bottom of the sink-hole, he had pictured himself thrusting it with one sure plunge into the heart of bear or wolf or panther. There was no flush of pride now in the picture. A panther's claws were quicker than he.

Whatever the animal, it had gone its way. He walked more rapidly, stumbling in his haste. He thought he heard a wolf howl, but it was so far away that it might only have been the wind. The wind was rising. He heard it far off in the distance. It was as though it were blowing in another world, across a dark abyss. Suddenly it swelled. He heard it coming closer, like a moving wall. The trees ahead thrashed their limbs. The bushes rattled and flattened to the ground. There was a great roaring and the storm hit him like a blow.

He lowered his head and fought against it. He was drenched to the skin in an instant. The rain poured down the back of his neck and washed through his breeches. His clothes hung heavily and held him back. He stopped and turned his back to the wind and propped the gun at the side of the road. He took off his shirt and breeches and rolled them into a bundle. He took up the gun and went on naked through the storm. The rain on his bare skin made him feel clean and free. The lightning flashed and he was startled by his own whiteness. He felt suddenly defenceless. He was alone and naked in an unfriendly world; lost and forgotten in the storm and darkness. Something ran behind him and ahead of him. It stalked the scrub like a panther. It was vast and formless and it was his enemy. Ol' Death was loose in the scrub.

It came to him that his father was already dead, or dying. The burden of the thought was intolerable. He ran faster, to shake it off. Penny could not die. Dogs could die, and bears and deer and other people. That was acceptable, because it was remote. His father could not die. The earth might cave in under him in one vast sink-hole and he could accept it. But without Penny, there was no earth. Without him there was nothing. He was frightened as he had never been before. He began to sob. His tears ran salt into his mouth.

He begged of the night, as he had begged of the Forresters, "Please——"

His throat ached and his groins were shot with hot lead. The lightning showed an opening ahead of him. He had reached the abandoned clearing. He darted into it and crouched against the old rail fence for a moment's shelter. The wind washed over him more coldly than the rain. He shivered and rose and went on again. The stop had chilled him. He wanted to run, to warm himself, but he had strength only to plod slowly. The rain had packed the sand so that the walking was firm and easier. The wind lessened. The down-pour settled into a steady falling. He walked on in a dull misery. It seemed to him that he must walk forever, but suddenly he was passing the sink-hole and was at the clearing.

The Baxter cabin was bright with candles. Horses whinnied and pawed the sand. There were three tethered to the slat fence. He passed through the gate and into the cabin.

Whatever was, was done. There was no bustle to greet him. Buck and Mill-wheel sat by the empty hearth, tilted back in their chairs. They were talking casually. They glanced at him, said "Hey, boy," and went on with their talk.

"You wasn't here, Buck, when ol' man Twistle died o' snake-bite. Penny must o' been right about whiskey not doin' no good. Twistle were drunk as a coot when he stepped on the rattler."

"Well, do I ever git snake-bit, fill me full jest for luck. I'd ruther die drunk than sober, ary day."

Mill-wheel spat into the fireplace.

"Don't fret," he said. "You will."

Jody was faint. He dared not ask them the question. He walked past them and into his father's bedroom. His mother sat on one side of the bed and Doc Wilson sat on the other. Old Doc did not turn his head. His mother looked at him and rose without speaking. She went to a dresser and took out a fresh shirt and breeches and held them out to him. He dropped his wet bundle and stood the gun against the wall. He walked slowly to the bed.

He thought, "If he's not dead now, he'll not die."

In the bed, Penny stirred. Jody's heart leaped like a rabbit jumping. Penny groaned and retched. Doc leaned quickly and held a basin for him and propped his head. Penny's face was dark and swollen. He vomited with the agony of one who has nothing to emit, but must vomit still. He fell back panting. Doc reached inside the covers and drew out a brick wrapped in flannel. He handed it to Ma Baxter. She laid Jody's garments at the foot of the bed and went to the kitchen to heat the brick again.

Jody whispered, "Is he bad?"

"He's bad, a'right. Looks as if he'd make it. Then again, looks as if he won't."

Penny opened his puffed eyes. The pupils were dilated until his eyes seemed black. He moved his arm. It was swollen as thick as a bullock's thigh.

He murmured thickly, "You'll ketch cold,"

Jody fumbled for his clothes and pulled them on. Doc nodded.

"That's a good sign, knowin' you. That's the first he's spoken."

A tenderness filled Jody that was half pain, half sweetness. In his agony, his father was concerned for him. Penny could not die. Not Penny.

He said, "He's obliged to make it, Doc, sir." He added, as he had heard his father say, "Us Baxters is all runty and tough."

Doc nodded.

He called to the kitchen, "Let's try some warm milk now."

With hope, Ma Baxter began to sniffle. Jody joined her at the hearth.

She whimpered, "I don't see as we'd deserve it, do it happen."

He said, "Hit'll not happen, Ma." But his marrow was cold again.

He went outside for wood to hurry the fire. The storm was moving on to the west. The clouds were rolling like battalions of marching Spaniards. In the east, bright spaces showed, filled with stars. The wind blew fresh and cool. He came in with an armful of fatwood.

He said, "Hit'll be a purty day tomorrow, Ma."

"Hit'll be a purty day iffen he's yit alive when day comes." She burst into tears. They dropped on the hearth and hissed. She lifted her apron and wiped her eyes. "You take the milk in," she said. "I'll make Doc and me a cup o' tea. I hadn't et nothin', waitin' for you-all, when Buck carried him in."

He remembered that he had eaten lightly. He could think of nothing that would taste good. The thought of food on his tongue was a dry thought, without nourishment or relish. He carried the cup of hot milk carefully, balancing it in his hands. Doc took it from him and sat close to Penny on the bed.

"Now boy, you hold his head up while I spoon-feed him."

THE VIGIL

The Yearling

Penny's head was heavy on the pillow. Jody's arms ached with the strain of lifting it. His father's breathing was heavy, like the Forresters when they were drunk. His face had changed color. It was green and pallid, like a frog's belly. At first his teeth resisted the intruding spoon.

Doc said, "Open your mouth before I call the Forresters to open it."

The swollen lips parted. Penny swallowed. A portion of the cupful went down. He turned his head away.

Doc said, "All right. But if you lose it, I'm comin' back with more."

Penny broke into a sweat.

Doc said, "That's fine. Sweatin's fine, for poison. Lord of the jay-birds, if we weren't all out of whiskey, I'd make you sweat."

Ma Baxter came to the bedroom with two plates with cups of tea and biscuits on them. Doc took his plate and balanced it on his knee. He drank with a mixture of gusto and distaste.

He said, "It's all right, but 'tain't whiskey."

He was the soberest Jody had ever heard of his being.

"A good man snake-bit," he said mournfully, "and the whole county out of whiskey."

Ma Baxter said dully, "Jody, you want somethin'?"

"I ain't hongry."

His stomach was as queasy as his father's. It seemed to him that he could feel the poison working in his own veins, attacking his heart, churning in his gizzard.

Doc said, "Blest if he ain't goin' to keep that milk down."

Penny was in a deep sleep.

Ma Baxter rocked and sipped and nibbled.

She said, "The Lord watches the sparrer's fall. Mought be He'll take a hand for the Baxters."

Jody went into the front room. Buck and Mill-wheel had lain down on the deer-skin rugs on the floor.

Jody said, "Ma and Doc's eatin'. You-all hongry?"

Buck said, "We'd jest done et when you come. Don't pay

us no mind. We'll sleep here and wait-see how it comes out."

Jody crouched on his heels. He would have liked to talk with them. It would be good to talk of dogs and guns and hunting, of all the things that living men could do. Buck snored. Jody tiptoed back to the bedroom. Doc was nodding in his chair. His mother moved the candle from the bed-side and returned to her rocker. The runners swished a while and then were still. She too nodded.

It seemed to Jody that he was alone with his father. The vigil was in his hands. If he kept awake, and labored for breath with the tortured sleeper, breathing with him and for him, he could keep him alive. He drew a breath as deep as the ones his father was drawing. It made him dizzy. He was light-headed and his stomach was empty. He knew he would feel better if he should eat, but he could not swallow. He sat down on the floor and leaned his head against the side of the bed. He began to think back over the day, as though he walked a road backward. He could not help but feel a greater security here beside his father, than in the stormy night. Many things, he realized, would be terrible alone that were not terrible when he was with Penny. Only the rattle-snake had kept all its horror.

He recalled the triangular head, the lightning flash of its striking, the subsidence into alert coils. His flesh crawled. It seemed to him he should never be easy in the woods again. He recalled the coolness of his father's shot, and the fear of the dogs. He recalled the doe and the horror of her warm meat against his father's wound. He remembered the fawn. He sat upright. The fawn was alone in the night, as he had been alone. The catastrophe that might take his father had made it motherless. It had lain hungry and bewildered through the thunder and rain and lightning, close to the devastated body of its dam, waiting for the stiff form to arise and give it warmth and food and comfort. He pressed his face into the hanging covers of the bed and cried bitterly. He was torn with hate for all death and pity for all aloneness.

146

Chapter XV

JODY moved through a tortuous dream. With his father beside him, he fought a nest of rattlesnakes. They crawled across his feet, trailing their rattles, clacking lightly. The nest resolved itself into one snake, gigantic, moving toward him on a level with his face. It struck and he tried to scream but could not. He looked for his father. He lay under the rattler, with his eyes open to a dark sky. His body was swollen to the size of a bear. He was dead. Jody began to move backward away from the rattler, one agonized step at a time. His feet were glued to the ground. The snake suddenly vanished and he stood alone in a vast windy place, holding the fawn in his arms. Penny was gone. A sense of sorrow filled him so that he thought his heart would break. He awakened, sobbing.

He sat up on the hard floor. Day was breaking over the clearing. A pale light lay in streaks beyond the pine trees. The room was filled with grayness. For an instant he was still conscious of the fawn against him. Then he remembered. He scrambled to his feet and looked at his father.

Penny was breathing with a greater ease. He was still swollen and fevered, but he looked no worse than when the wild honey bees had stung him. Ma Baxter was asleep in her rocker with her head thrown far back. Old Doc lay across the foot of the bed.

Jody whispered, "Doc!"

Doc grunted and lifted his head.

"What is it—what is it—what is it?"

"Doc! Look at Pa!"

Doc shifted his body and eased himself on one elbow. He

blinked and rubbed his eyes. He sat up. He leaned over Penny.

"Lord o' the jay-birds, he's made it."

Ma Baxter said, "Eh?"

She sat upright.

"He dead?"

"Not by a long sight."

She burst out crying.

Doc said, "You sound like you're sorry."

She said, "You jest don't know what 'twould mean, him leavin' us here."

Jody had never heard her speak so gently.

Doc said, "Why, you got you another man here. Look at Jody, now. Big enough to plow and reap and do the huntin'."

She said, "Jody's a'right, but he ain't a thing but boy. Got his mind on nothin' but prowlin' and playin'."

He hung his head. It was true.

She said, "His Pa encourages him."

Doc said, "Well, boy, be glad you got encouragement. Most of us live our lives without it. Now, Ma'am, let's get some more milk down this feller, time he wakes."

Jody said eagerly, "I'll go milk, Ma."

She said with satisfaction, "About time."

He passed through the front room. Buck was sitting up on the floor, rubbing his head sleepily. Mill-wheel was still asleep.

Jody said, "Doc says Pa's done made it."

"I be dogged. I woked up, fixin' to go he'p bury him."

Jody went around the side of the house and took down the milk-gourd from the wall. He felt as light as the gourd. It seemed to him in his liberation that he might spread his arms and float over the gate like a feather. The dawn was still nebulous. A mocking-bird made a thin metallic sound in the chinaberry. The Dominick rooster crowed uncertainly. This was the hour at which Penny arose, allowing Jody to sleep a little later. The morning was still, with a faint fluttering of breeze through the tops of the tall pine trees. The sunrise reached long fingers into the clearing. As he clicked the lot-gate, doves flew from the pines with a whistling of wings.

He called exultantly after them. "Hey, doves!"

Trixie lowed, hearing him. He climbed into the loft for fodder for her. She was very patient, he thought, giving her milk in return for so poor a feeding. She munched hungrily. She lifted a hind leg once in threat when he was clumsy with the milking. He stripped two teats carefully, then turned the calf in with her to nurse on the other two. There was not as much milk as his father would have gotten from her. He decided that he would drink none himself so that his father might have all of it until he was well again.

The calf butted the sagging udders and sucked noisily. It was too big still to be nursing. The thought of the fawn returned to him. A leaden feeling came over him again. It would be desperate with hunger this morning. He wondered if it would try to nurse the cold teats of the doe. The open flesh of the dead deer would attract the wolves. Perhaps they had found the fawn and had torn its soft body to ribbons. His joy in the morning, in his father's living, was darkened and tainted. His mind followed the fawn and would not be comforted.

His mother took the milk-gourd without comment on the quantity. She strained the milk and poured a cupful and took it to the sick room. He followed her. Penny was awake. He smiled weakly.

He whispered thickly, "Ol' Death got to wait a while on me."

Doc said, "You belong to be kin to the rattlesnakes, man. How you done it without whiskey, I don't know."

Penny whispered, "Why, Doc, I'm a king snake. You know a rattler cain't kill a king snake."

Buck and Mill-wheel came into the room. They grinned.

Buck said, "You ain't purty, Penny, but by God, you're alive."

Doc held the milk to Penny's lips. He swallowed thirstily.

Doc said, "I can't take much credit for savin' you. Your time just hadn't come to make a die of it."

Penny closed his eyes.

He said, "I could sleep a week."

Doc said, "That's what I want you to do. I can't do no more for you."

He stood up and stretched his legs.

Ma Baxter said, "Who'll do the farmin' and him asleep?"

Buck said, "What's he got, belongs to be done?"

"Mostly the corn, needs another workin' to be laid by. The 'taters needs hoein', but Jody's right good at hoein', do he choose to stick to it."

"I'll stick, Ma."

Buck said, "I'll stay and work the corn and sich."

She was flustered.

She said stiffly, "I hates to be beholden to you."

"Hell, Ma'am, they ain't too many of us shiftin' for a livin' out here. I'd be a pore man, didn't I not stay."

She said meekly, "I'm shore obliged. If the corn don't make, we jest as good all three to die o' snake-bite."

Doc said, "This is the soberest I've waked up since my wife died. I'd be proud to eat breakfast before I go."

She bustled to the kitchen. Jody went to build up the fire.

She said, "I never figgered I'd be beholden to a Forrester."

"Buck ain't exactly a Forrester, Ma. Buck's a friend."

"Hit do look that-a-way."

She filled the coffee-pot with water and added fresh coffee to the grounds.

She said, "Go to the smoke-house and git that last side o' bacon. I'll not be out-done."

He brought it proudly. She allowed him to slice the meat.

He said, "Ma, Pa shot a doe and used the liver to draw out the pizen. He bled hisself and then laid on the liver."

"You should of carried back a haunch o' the meat."

"There wasn't no time to figger on sich as that."

"That's right, too."

"Ma, the doe had a fawn."

"Well, most does has fawns."

"This un was right young. Nigh about new-borned."

"Well, what about it? Go set the table. Lay out the brier-berry jelly. The butter's right strong but it's yit butter. Lay it out, too."

She was stirring up a cornpone. The fat was sizzling in the skillet. She poured in the batter. The bacon crackled in the pan. She turned and flattened the slices, so that they would brown evenly. He wondered if they would ever be able to fill up Buck and Mill-wheel, accustomed to the copiousness of Forrester victuals.

He said, "Make a heap o' gravy, Ma."

"Iffen you'll do without your milk, I'll make milk-gravy."

The sacrifice was nothing.

He said, "We could of kilt a chicken."

"I studied on it, but they're all too young or too old."

She turned the cornpone. The coffee began to boil.

He said, "I could of shot some doves or some squirrels this mornin'."

"A fine time to think of it. Go tell the men-folks to wash theirselves and come to table."

He called them. The three men went outside to the water-shelf and slapped water over their faces, dabbled their hands. He brought them a clean towel.

Doc said, "Blest if I don't get hungry when I'm sober."

Mill-wheel said, "Whiskey's a food. I could live on whis-key."

Doc said, "I've near about done it. Twenty years. Since my wife died."

Jody was proud of the table. There were not as many different dishes as the Forresters served, but there was enough of everything. The men ate greedily. At last they pushed away their plates and lit their pipes.

Mill-wheel said, "Seems like Sunday, don't it?"

The Yearling

Ma Baxter said, "Sickness allus do seem like Sunday, someway. Folks settin' around, and the men not goin' to the field."

Jody had never seen her so amiable. She had waited to eat until the men were done, for fear of their not having plenty. She sat now eating with relish. The men chatted idly. Jody allowed his thoughts to drift back to the fawn. He could not keep it out of his mind. It stood in the back of it as close as he had held it, in his dreaming, in his arms. He slipped from the table and went to his father's bedside. Penny lay at rest. His eyes were open and clear, but the pupils were still dark and dilated.

Jody said, "How you comin', Pa?"

"Jest fine, son. Ol' Death gone thievin' elsewhere. But wa'n't it a close squeak!"

"I mean."

Penny said, "I'm proud of you, boy, the way you kept your head and done what was needed."

"Pa——"

"Yes, son."

"Pa, you recollect the doe and the fawn?"

"I cain't never forget 'em. The pore doe saved me, and that's certain."

"Pa, the fawn may be out there yit. Hit's hongry, and likely mighty skeert."

"I reckon so."

"Pa, I'm about growed and don't need no milk. How about me goin' out and seein' kin I find the fawn?"

"And tote it here?"

"And raise it."

Penny lay quiet, staring at the ceiling.

"Boy, you got me hemmed in."

"Hit won't take much to raise it, Pa. Hit'll soon git to where it kin make out on leaves and acorns."

"Dogged if you don't figger the farrest of ary young un I've ever knowed."

152

"We takened its mammy, and it wa'n't no-ways to blame."

"Shore don't seem grateful to leave it starve, do it? Son, I ain't got it in my heart to say 'No' to you. I never figgered I'd see daylight, come dawn today."

"Kin I ride back with Mill-wheel and see kin I find it?"

"Tell your Ma I said you're to go."

He sidled back to the table and sat down. His mother was pouring coffee for every one.

He said, "Ma, Pa says I kin go bring back the fawn."

She held the coffee-pot in mid-air.

"What fawn?"

"The fawn belonged to the doe we kilt, to use the liver to draw out the pizen and save Pa."

She gasped.

"Well, for pity sake——"

"Pa say hit'd not be grateful, to leave it starve."

Doc Wilson said, "That's right, Ma'am. Nothing in the world don't ever come quite free. The boy's right and his daddy's right."

Mill-wheel said, "He kin ride back with me. I'll he'p him find it."

She set down the pot helplessly.

"Well, if you'll give it your milk— We got nothin' else to feed it."

"That's what I aim to do. Hit'll be no time, and it not needin' nothin'."

The men rose from the table.

Doc said, "I don't look for nothing but progress, Ma'am, but if he takes a turn for the worse, you know where to find me."

She said, "Well. What do we owe you, Doc? We cain't pay right now, but time the crops is made——"

"Pay for what? I've done nothing. He was safe before I got here. I've had a night's lodging and a good breakfast. Send me some syrup when your cane's ground."

"You're mighty good, Doc. We been scramblin' so, I didn't know folks could be so good."

"Hush, woman. You got a good man there. Why wouldn't folks be good to him?"

Buck said, "You reckon that ol' horse o' Penny's kin keep ahead o' me at the plow? I'm like to run him down."

Doc said, "Get as much milk down Penny as he'll take. Then give him greens and fresh meat, if you can get it."

Buck said, "Me and Jody'll tend to that."

Mill-wheel said, "Come on, boy. We got to git ridin'."

Ma Baxter asked anxiously, "You'll not be gone long?"

Jody said, "I'll be back shore, before dinner."

"Reckon you'd not git home a-tall," she said, "if 'twasn't for dinner-time."

Doc said, "That's man-nature, Ma'am. Three things bring a man home again—his bed, his woman, and his dinner."

Buck and Mill-wheel guffawed. Doc's eye caught the cream-colored 'coonskin knapsack.

"Now ain't that a pretty something? Wouldn't I like such as that to tote my medicines?"

Jody had never before possessed a thing that was worth giving away. He took it from its nail, and put it in Doc's hands.

"Hit's mine," he said. "Take it."

"Why, I'd not rob you, boy."

"I got no use for it," he said loftily. "I kin git me another."

"Now I thank you. Every trip I make, I'll think, 'Thank you, Jody Baxter.'"

He was proud with old Doc's pleasure. They went outside to water the horses and feed them from the scanty stock of hay in the Baxter barn.

Buck said to Jody, "You Baxters is makin' out and that's about all, ain't it?"

Doc said, "Baxter's had to carry the work alone. Time the boy here gets some size to him, they'll prosper."

Buck said, "Size don't seem to mean much to a Baxter."

The Yearling

Mill-wheel mounted his horse and pulled Jody up behind him. Doc mounted and turned away in the opposite direction. Jody waved after him. His heart was light.

He said to Mill-wheel, "You reckon the fawn's yit there? Will you he'p me find him?"

"We'll find him, do he be alive. How you know it's a he?"

"The spots was all in a line. On a doe-fawn, Pa says the spots is ever' which-a-way."

"That's the female of it."

"What you mean?"

"Why, females is on-accountable."

Mill-wheel slapped the horse's flank and they broke into a trot.

"This female business. How come you and your Pa to pitch into us, when we was fightin' Oliver Hutto?"

"Oliver was gittin' the wust of it. Hit didn't seem right, a hull passel o' you-all whoppin' Oliver."

"You right. Hit were Lem's gal and Oliver's gal. They should of fit it out alone."

"But a gal cain't belong to two fellers at oncet."

"You jest don't know gals."

"I hate Twink Weatherby."

"I'd not look at her, neither. I got a widder-woman at Fort Gates, knows how to be faithful."

The matter was too complicated. Jody gave himself over to thoughts of the fawn. They passed the abandoned clearing.

He said, "Cut to the north, Mill-wheel. Hit were up here Pa got snake-bit and kilt the doe and I seed the fawn."

"What was you and your daddy doin' up this road?"

Jody hesitated.

"We was huntin' our hogs."

"Oh— Huntin' your hogs, eh? Well, don't fret about them hogs. I jest got a idee they'll be home by sundown."

"Ma and Pa'll shore be proud to see 'em come in."

"I had no idee, you-all was runnin' so tight."

"We ain't runnin' tight. We're all right."

The Yearling

"You Baxters has got guts, I'll say that."

"You reckon Pa'll not die?"

"Not him. His chitlin's is made o' iron."

Jody said, "Tell me about Fodder-wing. Is he shore enough ailin'? Or didn't Lem want I should see him?"

"He's purely ailin'. He ain't like the rest of us. He ain't like nobody. Seems like he drinks air 'stead o' water, and feeds on what the wild creeturs feeds on, 'stead o' bacon."

"He sees things ain't so, don't he? Spaniards and sich."

"He do, but dogged if they ain't times he'll make you think he do see 'em."

"You reckon Lem'll leave me come see him?"

"I'd not risk it yit. I'll git word to you one day when mebbe Lem's gone off, see?"

"I shore crave to see Fodder-wing."

"You'll see him. Now whereabouts you want to go, huntin' that fawn? Hit's gittin' right thick up this trail."

Suddenly Jody was unwilling to have Mill-wheel with him. If the fawn was dead, or could not be found, he could not have his disappointment seen. And if the fawn was there, the meeting would be so lovely and so secret that he could not endure to share it.

He said, "Hit's not fur now, but hit's powerful thick for a horse. I kin make it a-foot."

"But I'm daresome to leave you, boy. Suppose you was to git lost, or snake-bit, too?"

"I'll take keer. Hit'll take me likely a long time to find the fawn, if he's wandered. Leave me off right here."

"All right, but you go mighty easy now, pokin' in them palmeeters. This is rattlesnake Heaven in these parts. You know north here, and east?"

"There, and there. That fur tall pine makes a bearin'."

"That's right. Now do things go wrong again, you or Buck, one, ride back for me. So long."

"So long, Mill-wheel. I'm shore obliged."

He waved after him. He waited for the sound of the

156

hooves to end, then cut to the right. The scrub was still. Only his own crackling of twigs sounded across the silence. He was eager almost past caution, but he broke a bough and pushed it ahead of him where the growth was thick and the ground invisible. Rattlers got out of the way when they had a chance. Penny had gone farther into the oak thicket than he remembered. He wondered for an instant if he had mistaken his direction. Then a buzzard rose in front of him and flapped into the air. He came into the clearing under the oaks. Buzzards sat in a circle around the carcass of the doe. They turned their heads on their long scrawny necks and hissed at him. He threw his bough at them and they flew into an adjacent tree. Their wings creaked and whistled like rusty pump-handles. The sand showed large cat-prints, he could not tell whether of wild-cat or of panther. But the big cats killed fresh, and they had left the doe to the carrion birds. He asked himself whether the sweeter meat of the fawn had scented the air for the curled nostrils.

He skirted the carcass and parted the grass at the place where he had seen the fawn. It did not seem possible that it was only yesterday. The fawn was not there. He circled the clearing. There was no sound, no sign. The buzzards clacked their wings, impatient to return to their business. He returned to the spot where the fawn had emerged and dropped to all fours, studying the sand for the small hoof-prints. The night's rain had washed away all tracks except those of cat and buzzards. But the cat-sign had not been made in this direction. Under a scrub palmetto he was able to make out a track, pointed and dainty as the mark of a ground-dove. He crawled past the palmetto.

Movement directly in front of him startled him so that he tumbled backward. The fawn lifted its face to his. It turned its head with a wide, wondering motion and shook him through with the stare of its liquid eyes. It was quivering. It made no effort to rise or run. Jody could not trust himself to move.

The Yearling

He whispered, "It's me."

The fawn lifted its nose, scenting him. He reached out one hand and laid it on the soft neck. The touch made him delirious. He moved forward on all fours until he was close beside it. He put his arms around its body. A light convulsion passed over it but it did not stir. He stroked its sides as gently as though the fawn were a china deer and he might break it. Its skin was softer than the white 'coonskin knapsack. It was sleek and clean and had a sweet scent of grass. He rose slowly and lifted the fawn from the ground. It was no heavier than old Julia. Its legs hung limply. They were surprisingly long and he had to hoist the fawn as high as possible under his arm.

He was afraid that it might kick and bleat at sight and smell of its mother. He skirted the clearing and pushed his way into the thicket. It was difficult to fight through with his burden. The fawn's legs caught in the bushes and he could not lift his own with freedom. He tried to shield its face from prickling vines. Its head bobbed with his stride. His heart thumped with the marvel of its acceptance of him. He reached the trail and walked as fast as he could until he came to the intersection with the road home. He stopped to rest and set the fawn down on its dangling legs. It wavered on them. It looked at him and bleated.

He said, enchanted, "I'll tote you time I git my breath."

He remembered his father's saying that a fawn would follow that had been first carried. He started away slowly. The fawn stared after him. He came back to it and stroked it and walked away again. It took a few wobbling steps toward him and cried piteously. It was willing to follow him. It belonged to him. It was his own. He was light-headed with his joy. He wanted to fondle it, to run and romp with it, to call to it to come to him. He dared not alarm it. He picked it up and carried it in front of him over his two arms. It seemed to him that he walked without effort. He had the strength of a Forrester.

158

The Yearling

His arms began to ache and he was forced to stop again.
When he walked on, the fawn followed him at once. He
allowed it to walk a little distance, then picked it up again.
The distance home was nothing. He could have walked all
day and into the night, carrying it and watching it follow.
He was wet with sweat but a light breeze blew through the
June morning, cooling him. The sky was as clear as spring
water in a blue china cup. He came to the clearing. It was
fresh and green after the night's rain. He could see Buck
Forrester following old Cæsar at the plow in the cornfield.
He thought he heard him curse the horse's slowness. He
fumbled with the gate latch and was finally obliged to set
down the fawn to manage it. It came to him that he would
walk into the house, into Penny's bedroom, with the fawn
walking behind him. But at the steps, the fawn balked and
refused to climb them. He picked it up and went to his
father. Penny lay with closed eyes.

Jody called, "Pa! Lookit!"

Penny turned his head. Jody stood beside him, the fawn
clutched hard against him. It seemed to Penny that the boy's
eyes were as bright as the fawn's. His face lightened, seeing
them together.

He said, "I'm proud you found him."

"Pa, he wa'n't skeert o' me. He were layin' up right where
his mammy had made his bed."

"The does learns 'em that, time they're borned. You kin
step on a fawn, times, they lay so still."

"Pa, I toted him, and when I set him down, right off he
follered me. Like a dog, Pa."

"Ain't that fine? Let's see him better."

Jody lifted the fawn high. Penny reached out a hand and
touched its nose. It bleated and reached hopefully for his
fingers.

He said, "Well, leetle feller. I'm sorry I had to take away
your mammy."

"You reckon he misses her?"

"No. He misses his rations and he knows that. He misses somethin' else but he don't know jest what."

Ma Baxter came into the room.

"Look, Ma, I found him."

"I see."

"Ain't he purty, Ma? Lookit them spots all in rows. Lookit them big eyes. Ain't he purty?"

"He's powerful young. Hit'll take milk for him a long whiles. I don't know as I'd of give my consent, if I'd knowed he was so young."

Penny said, "Ory, I got one thing to say, and I'm sayin' it now, and then I'll have no more talk of it. The leetle fawn's as welcome in this house as Jody. It's hissen. We'll raise it without grudgment o' milk or meal. You got me to answer to, do I ever hear you quarrelin' about it. This is Jody's fawn jest like Julia's my dog."

Jody had never heard his father speak to her so sternly. The tone must hold familiarity for his mother, however, for she opened and shut her mouth and blinked her eyes.

She said, "I only said it was young."

"All right. So it is."

He closed his eyes.

He said, "If ever'body's satisfied now, I'd thank you to leave me rest. Hit puts my heart to jerkin', to talk."

Jody said, "I'll fix its milk, Ma. No need you should bother."

She was silent. He went to the kitchen. The fawn wobbled after him. A pan of morning's milk stood in the kitchen safe. The cream had risen on it. He skimmed the cream into a jug and used his shirt sleeve to wipe up the few drops he could not keep from spilling. If he could keep the fawn from being any trouble to his mother, she would mind it less. He poured milk into a small gourd. He held it out to the fawn. It butted it suddenly, smelling the milk. He saved it precariously from spilling over the floor. He led the fawn outside to the yard and began again. It could make nothing of the milk in the gourd.

160

The Yearling

He dipped his fingers in the milk and thrust them into the fawn's soft wet mouth. It sucked greedily. When he withdrew them, it bleated frantically and butted him. He dipped his fingers again and as the fawn sucked, he lowered them slowly into the milk. The fawn blew and sucked and snorted. It stamped its small hooves impatiently. As long as he held his fingers below the level of the milk, the fawn was content. It closed its eyes dreamily. It was ecstasy to feel its tongue against his hand. Its small tail flicked back and forth. The last of the milk vanished in a swirl of foam and gurgling. The fawn bleated and butted but its frenzy was appeased. Jody was tempted to go for more milk, but even with his father's backing he was afraid to press his advantage too far. A doe's bag was as small as a yearling heifer's. Surely the fawn had had as much as its mother could have given it. It lay down suddenly, exhausted and replete.

He gave his attention to a bed for it. It would be too much to ask, to bring it into the house. He went to the shed behind the house and cleaned out a corner down to the sand. He went to the live oaks at the north end of the yard and pulled down armfuls of Spanish moss. He made a thick bed in the shed. A hen was on a nest close by. Her bright beady eyes watched him dubiously. She finished her laying and flew through the door, cackling. The nest was a new one, with six eggs in it. Jody gathered them carefully and took them to his mother in the kitchen.

He said, "You'll be proud to git these, Ma. Extry eggs."

"Hit's a good thing they's somethin' extry around to eat."

He ignored the comment.

He said, "The new nest is right next to where I fixed the fawn's bed. In the shed, where it'll not bother nobody."

She did not answer and he went outside where the fawn lay under a mulberry tree. He gathered it up and carried it to its bed in the dark shed.

"Now you belong to do whatever I tell you," he said. "Like as if I was your mammy. I tell you to lay here 'til I come git you agin."

The fawn blinked its eyelids. It groaned comfortably and dropped its head. He tiptoed from the shed. No dog, he thought, could be more biddable. He went to the wood-pile and shaved fine splinters of fatwood for kindling. He arranged the pile neatly. He gathered an armful of black-jack oak and took it to his mother's wood-box in the kitchen.

He said, "Was it all right, Ma, the way I skimmed the cream?"

"Hit was all right."

He said, "Fodder-wing's ailin'."

"Is?"

"Lem wouldn't leave me see him. Lem's the only one is mad at us, Ma. On account of Oliver's gal."

"Uh-huh."

"Mill-wheel said he'd leave me know and I could slip in some time and see Fodder-wing when Lem ain't around."

She laughed.

"You're talkified as a old woman today."

She passed him on her way to the hearth and touched his head lightly.

She said, "I feel right good, myself. I never figgered your Pa'd see daylight today."

The kitchen was filled with peace. There was a clanking of harness. Buck passed through the gate from the field and crossed the road to the lot to put up old Cæsar for the noon hour.

Jody said, "I best go he'p him."

But it was the fawn that drew him from the contentment of the house. He slipped into the shed to marvel at its existence and his possession. When he returned with Buck from the lot, chattering of the fawn, he beckoned him to follow.

He said, "Don't skeer him. There he lies——"

Buck was not as satisfying as Penny in his response. He had seen so many of Fodder-wing's pets come and go.

"He'll likely go wild and run off," he said, and went to the water-shelf to wash his hands before dinner.

The Yearling

A chill came over Jody. Buck was worse than his mother to take away pleasure. He lingered a moment with the fawn, stroking it. It moved its sleepy head and nuzzled his fingers. Buck could not know of the closeness. It was all the better for being secret. He left the fawn and went to the basin and washed, too. The touch of the fawn had left his hands scented with a faint grassy pungency. He hated to wash it away, but decided that his mother might not find it as pleasant.

His mother had wet and combed her hair for dinner, not with coquetry, but with pride. She wore a clean sacking apron over her brown calico.

She said to Buck, "With only Penny to do, we ain't got the rations plentiful like you folks. But we do eat clean and decent."

Jody looked quickly to see if Buck would take offense. Buck ladled grits into his plate and scooped a hole in the center for the fried eggs and gravy.

"Now Miss Ory, don't fret about me. Jody and me'll slip off this evenin' and git you a mess o' squirrels and mebbe a turkey. I seed turkey sign the fur edge o' the pea field."

Ma Baxter filled a plate for Penny, and added a cup of milk.

"You take it to him, Jody."

He went to his father. Penny shook his head at the plate.

"Hit look jest plain nasty to me, son. Set up there and feed me a spoon o' the grits, and the milk. Hit wearies me to lift my arm."

The swelling had left his face, but his arm was still three times its normal size, and his breath came heavily. He swallowed a few mouthfuls of the soft hominy and drank the milk. He motioned the plate away.

"You gittin' along all right with your baby?"

Jody reported on the moss bed.

"You picked a good place. What you fixin' to name him?"

"I jest don't know. I want a name is real special."

The Yearling

Buck and Ma Baxter came into the bedroom and sat down to visit. The day was hot and the sun high and there was no hurry for anything.

Penny said, "Jody's in a tight for a name for the new Baxter."

Buck said, "Tell you, Jody, when you see Fodder-wing, he'll pick a name. He's got a ear for sich things, jest like some folks has got a ear for fiddle music. He'll pick you a name is purty."

Ma Baxter said, "Go eat your dinner, Jody. That spotted fawn has takened your mind off your rations."

The opportunity was choice. He went to the kitchen and heaped a plate with food and went to the shed. The fawn was still drowsy. He sat beside it and ate his dinner. He dipped his fingers in the grease-covered grits and held them out to it, but it only snuffed and turned its head away.

He said, "You better learn somethin' besides milk."

The dirt daubers buzzed in the rafters. He scraped his plate clean and set it aside. He lay down beside the fawn. He put one arm across its neck. It did not seem to him that he could ever be lonely again.

Chapter XVI

HE fawn took up much of Jody's time. It tagged him wherever he went. At the woodpile, it interfered with the swing of his axe. The milking had been assigned to him. He was forced to bar the fawn from the lot and it stood by the gate, peering between the bars, and bleated until he had finished. He stripped Trixie's teats until she kicked in protest. Each cupful of milk meant more nourishment for the fawn. It seemed to him that he could see it growing. It stood firm on its small legs and leaped and tossed its head and tail. He romped with it until they dropped together in a heap to rest and cool themselves.

The days were hot and humid. Penny sweat in his bed. Buck came dripping from the fields. He discarded his shirt and worked naked to the waist. His chest was thick with black hair. The perspiration glistened on it like rain drops on black dried moss. When she was sure he would not call for it, Ma Baxter washed and boiled the shirt and hung it in the scalding sunshine.

She said with satisfaction, "There's that much of him, now, won't stink."

Buck filled the Baxter cabin until it bulged.

Ma Baxter said to Penny, "First sight I catch o' that beard and chest in the mornin's, I take a start, for I think a bear's got in the house."

She was appalled at the amount of food he bolted three times a day. She could scarcely complain, since he more than made it up with the work he was doing and the game with which he supplied her. In the week he had been at the clearing, he had worked out the corn, the cow-peas and the sweet potatoes. He had cleared two acres of new ground to the west, between the pea-field and the sink-hole. He had cut down a dozen oaks and pines and sweet gums and innumerable saplings, burned the stumps and trimmed the fallen trees, so that Jody and Penny on the cross-cut saw might cut the limbs and trunks for fire-wood.

He said, "You plant Sea Island cotton on that new ground, come spring, and you'll make you a crop."

Ma Baxter said suspiciously, "You-all has got no cotton."

He said easily, "Us Forresters ain't farmers. We'll do the clarin', we'll plow a field now and agin, but it's our nature to make a livin' what I reckon you'd call rough and easy."

She said primly, "Rough ways lands folks in trouble."

He said, "You ever know my granddaddy? They called him Trouble Forrester."

She could not dislike him. He was as good-natured as a dog. She could only say to Penny in the privacy of night, "He works like a ox, but he's so tormented black. Ezra, he's black as a buzzard."

"Hit's his beard," Penny said. "Did I have a black beard like that un, I mought not look like no buzzard, but I'd shore look like a crow."

Penny's strength was slow in returning. The swelling from the poisoning had gone down. The skin was sloughing away where the rattler had struck him and he had cut the wounds to make the envenomed blood flow more freely. But at the least exertion, he was nauseated, and his heart pumped like the paddle-wheels on the river steamers, and he gasped for breath and must lie flat to recover himself. He was all wiry nerves, strung like harp-strings on a frail wooden body.

To Jody, the presence of Buck was a stimulation so great that he was feverish with it. The fawn alone would have had him delirious. The two together kept him in a daze, wandering from Penny's room to wherever Buck was working, to wherever the fawn might be, and around again.

His mother said, "You'd ought to be noticin' all what Buck is doin', so you kin do it when he's gone."

The Yearling

There was a tacit understanding among the three of them that Penny was to be spared.

The morning of the eighth day that Buck had been at the clearing, he called Jody to the cornfield. Vandals had visited it during the night. Half a row of corn had been stripped of its ears. Mid-way of the row lay a pile of corn-husks.

Buck said, "You know what done that?"

" 'Coons?"

"Hell, no. Foxes. Foxes love corn gooder'n I do. Two-three o' them bushy-tailed scapers come in last night and had them a pure picnic."

Jody laughed out.

"A fox picnic! I'd love to of seed it."

Buck said sternly, "You'd ought to be out at night with your gun, keepin' 'em out. Now we'll git 'em tonight. You got to learn to be serious. And this evenin' we'll rob that bee-tree by the sink-hole, and that'll learn you how to do that."

Jody went through the day impatiently. A hunt with Buck had a different quality from a hunt with his father. There was an excitement in anything the Forresters did that made him nervous and high-keyed. There was noise and confusion. A hunt with Penny held a satisfaction that was of more than the chase. There was always time to see a bird fly over, or to listen to a 'gator, bellowing in the swamp. He wished that Penny were able to be about, to rob the bee-tree with them; to go on the trail of the robber foxes. In mid-afternoon, Buck came from the new ground. Penny was sleeping.

Buck said to Ma Baxter, "I'll want a lard-pail and a axe and a heap o' rags to burn for smudges."

There were not many rags in the Baxter household. Clothes were worn and patched and mended until they dropped in ribbons. Flour sacks went into aprons and dish-towels and chair-backs that she embroidered on winter evenings; into backs for her patch-work quilts. Buck looked disgustedly at the small handful she gave him.

He said, "Well, reckon we kin use moss."

She said, "Don't you-all git stung, now. My grand-pappy got hisself stung oncet to where he was in the bed a fort-night."

"If we git stung, hit shore won't be o' purpose."

He started across the yard with Jody beside him. The fawn was close behind.

"You want your blasted baby to git stung to death? Then shut him up."

Jody led the fawn reluctantly to the shed and closed the door. He hated to be separated from it, even for honey-hunting. It seemed unjust that Penny should not be along. He had had his eye on the bee-tree all spring. He had waited for the proper time, when the bees should have gathered their nectar from the yellow jessamine, from the mulberry and the holly, the palmetto bloom and the chinaberry, the wild grapes and the peaches, and from the hawthorn and the wild plum. There would still be bloom from which they might make their own winter store. The red bay and the loblolly were in full blossom. There would soon be sumac and goldenrod and asters.

Buck said, "You know who'd purely love to be gittin' honey with us? Fodder-wing. He'll work amongst the bees so quiet, you'd figger they was makin' him a present o' the honey-comb."

They reached the sink-hole.

Buck said, "I don't see how you-all have made out, totin' your water so fur. If I wasn't about to be leavin', I'd shore he'p you dig a well nigh to the house."

"You fixin' to leave?"

"Well, yes. I'm fretted about Fodder-wing. And I ain't never lived this long without whiskey."

The bee-tree was a dead pine. Mid-way up its height, the wild honey-bees flew in and out of a deep cavity. It stood at the north edge of the sink-hole. Buck stopped by the live oaks to pull down armfuls of green Spanish moss. At the base of the pine he pointed to a pile of dried grass and feathers.

"The wood-ducks tried to nest there," he said. "They'll see a hole in a tree, and don't matter do it belong to a Lord God woodpecker, or one o' them big woodpeckers with a ivory bill, or a swarm o' bees, they'll take a notion to it and they'll try to nest in the hole. The bees has done drove these uns out."

He began to chop at the base of the dead pine. High in the air a humming sounded like a den of rattlers, far distant and turbulent. The blows of the axe echoed back and forth across the sink-hole. Squirrels, quiescent in the oaks and palm trees, began to chatter at the disturbance. Scrub jays cried shrilly. The pine shook. The humming grew into a roar. The bees sung across their heads like small shot.

Buck called, "Light me a smudge, boy. Be peert."

Jody made a loose ball of moss and rags and opened Buck's tinder horn. He struggled with flint and steel. Penny was so expert at starting a fire that it occurred to Jody in a panic that he had never done it himself. The sparks flashed to the scorched rags that constituted the tinder, but he blew them so violently that they flickered out almost as soon as they touched the cloth. Buck dropped the axe and ran to him and took the materials from him. He rubbed flint and steel together as vigorously as Jody had done, but he blew on the spark-touched rags with a judiciousness amazing in a Forrester. The rags blazed and he touched the fire to the moss. It began to smoke without blazing.

Buck ran back to the pine and put his muscles behind the axe. Its bright blade ate into the decayed center of the tree. Its long fibers split and ripped and shivered. The pine roared in the air as though a voice had come to it to cry out with in its falling. It crashed to earth and the bees were a cloud across its dead gaping heart. Buck snatched up the smudge and darted in as quick, for all his size, as a weasel. He stuffed the smoking ball into the cavity with one thrust and ran madly. He looked more than ever like a lumbering bear. He let out a howl and slapped at his chest and shoulders. Jody had to laugh at him. Then a needle-point of fire stabbed his own neck.

Buck shouted, "Git down the sink-hole! Git to the water!"

They scrambled down the steep bank. The seepage pool at the bottom was shallow for lack of rains. The water did not quite cover them when they lay in it. Buck scooped up handfuls of mud and plastered Jody's hair and neck with it. His own thatch was a thick enough protection. A few bees followed and swung back and forth persistently. After a time Buck raised himself cautiously.

He said, "They're due to be quiet now. But ain't we a pair o' hogs."

Their breeches, their faces, their shirts, were caked with mud. It was not yet wash-day and Jody led the way up the south wall of the sink-hole to the wash-troughs. They sousled their clothes in one and washed themselves from the other.

Buck said, "What you grinnin' about?"

Jody shook his head. He could imagine his mother saying, "If it takes bees to git a Forrester clean, I'll hive 'em a swarm."

Buck had half a dozen stings but Jody had escaped with two. They approached the bee tree cautiously. The smudge had been properly placed. The bees were drugged with the heavy smoke. They swarmed slowly around the cavity, searching for their queen.

Buck split a wider opening and used his sheath knife to hack away the edges. He cleaned away trash and splinters and reached in with the knife. He turned, amazed.

"Great day! They's a wash-tub o' honey here. The tree's full."

He brought out a slab, golden and dripping. The comb was rough and dark, but the honey was paler than fine syrup. They filled the lard-pail and carried it between them to the house. Ma Baxter gave them a cypress tub to take back with them.

Buck said, "Now a wash tub o' biscuits is all more is needed."

The return load was heavy. It was the largest yield, Buck said, he had ever seen from a bee-tree since he was a boy.

He said, "When I go home tomorrer and tell my folks, they'll not believe me."

She said slowly, "I reckon you'll want to carry some back with you."

"No more'n I kin carry in my belly. I got my eye on two-three trees in the swamp. Do they fail me, I'm like to come beggin'."

Ma Baxter said, "You've been mighty neighborly. Mebbe some day we'll have a plenty and kin do for you."

Jody said, "I wish you'd not go, Buck."

The big man shoved him playfully.

"With me gone, you'll not have no time to nuss that fawn."

Buck was plainly restless. He shuffled his feet at supper and paced up and down afterward. He looked at the sky.

He said, "A good clare night for ridin'."

Jody said, "How come you anxious all to oncet?"

Buck paused in his pacing.

"I git that-a-way. I like to come and I like to go. Wherever I be, I'm content a while, and then I jest someway ain't content no more. When me and Lem and Mill-wheel goes off hoss-tradin' to Kentucky, I'll swear, I figger I'll bust 'till I git home agin." He paused and stared into the sunset. He added in a low voice, "And I'm right smart fretted about Fodder-wing. I got a feelin' here—" he thumped his hairy chest—"he ain't doin' good."

"Wouldn't somebody of come?"

"That's it. If they didn't know your Pa was bad off, they'd of ridden over jest to say Howdy. They figgered your Pa needed he'p and they'd not like to toll me away, was the news bad or worrisome."

He waited nervously for dark. He wanted to be done with

his job, and gone. Penny was as good a night-hunter as any Forrester. Jody was tempted to brag of the varmints his father had disposed of, but that might cut him out of a night-prowl with Buck. He held his tongue. He helped Buck prepare the fatwood splinters for the fire-pan.

Buck said, "My Uncle Cotton had red hair. They was a heap of it, stood up like a haystack, and red as a fightin' cock's comb. He was fire-huntin' one night, and the handle was a mite short, and a spark from the pan set his hair a-fire. And you know when he hollered to Pa for he'p, Pa didn't pay him no mind. He jest thought the moon had done rose and was shinin' through Uncle Cotton's hair."

Jody gaped.

"Is that true, Buck?"

Buck whittled busily.

"Now if you was to tell me a tale," he said, "I'd not ask you no sich of a question."

Penny called from his bedroom.

"I cain't stand it. I'm o' good notion not to leave you go without me."

They came to his room.

"If 'twas a panther hunt you was goin' on," he said, "I'll swear I'd feel good enough to go with you."

Buck said, "Now I'd jest carry you on a panther hunt, did I have my dogs."

"Why, my pair'll out-hunt your whole pack." He asked innocently, "How did you-all come out with that sorry dog I traded you?"

Buck drawled, "Why, that dog's proved out the fastest and the finest and the hardest-huntin' and the fearlessest of ary dog we've ever had on the place. All he needed was men to train him."

Penny chuckled.

He said, "I'm proud you was smart enough to make somethin' outen him. Where's he now?"

"Well, he was so blasted good, he put t'other dogs so to

shame, Lem couldn't abide it, and he hauled off and shot him and buried him in the Baxter cemetery one night."

Penny said gravely, "I noticed the new grave and I figgered you-all had give outen buryin'-ground. I'll whittle a head-stone, time I git my strength. I'll carve on it, 'Here lies a Forrester, mourned by all his kin.'"

He grinned broadly and slapped the covers of his bed.

"Give in, Buck," he said, "give in."

Buck wiped his beard.

"All right," he said, "I'll take it for funnin'. But don't look to Lem to take it for ary thing but a cold-out insult."

Penny said, "No hard feelin's. I got none, and I hope you-all'll hold none, Lem nor nobody."

"Lem's different. He takes things personal."

"That grieves me. I pitched into the fight betwixt him and Oliver because they was too many of you on one side."

Buck said, "Well, blood's thicker'n water. We fight amongst ourselves now and agin, but when it's us and t'other feller, we allus fight on the same side o' the creek. But me and you has got no call to fall out."

Words began fights and words ended them.

Jody asked, "If fellers didn't say quarrelin' things, would they put in to fight?"

Penny said, "I'm feered so. I oncet seed a pair o' deef dummies havin' it. But they do say they got a sign language, and likely one passed the insult in a sign."

Buck said, "Hit's male nature, boy. Wait 'til you git to courtin' and you'll git your breeches dusted many a time."

"But nobody but Lem and Oliver was courtin', and here all us Baxters and all you Forresters was in to it."

Penny said, "They's no end to what a man'll fight for. I even knowed a preacher takened off his coat and fit ary man wouldn't agree to infant damnation. All a feller kin do, is fight for what he figgers is right, and the devil take the hindmost."

Buck said, "Listen. I think I heered a fox bark then in the hammock."

At first the night seemed silent. Then sounds drifted like clouds into their hearing. An owl hooted. A tree-frog scraped his fiddle and predicted rain.

Buck said, "There he be."

A thin bark sounded in the distance, shrill and mournful.

Buck said, "Now wouldn't that be music to my pore dogs? Wouldn't they sing to that sopranner?"

Penny said, "If you and Jody don't clean out the litter tonight, bring your dogs on the next moon and we'll have us a chase."

Buck said, "Let's us git goin', Jody. That yipper'll about make the cornfield time we do." He picked up Penny's shotgun from the corner. "I'll borry this tonight. Seems to me I've seed it before."

"Jest don't bury it beside the dog," Penny said. "Hit's ralely a good gun."

Jody packed his muzzle-loader over his shoulder. He went out with Buck. The fawn heard him and bleated from the shed. They walked under the mulberries and crossed the split-rail fence into the cornfield. Buck walked north down the first row. At the far end of the field he began walking across the ends of the rows. He stopped at each row and focussed the light from the fire-pan down the length of the field. Mid-way he stopped. He turned and nudged Jody. Where the light came to rest, two fiery green agates caught the light.

He murmured, "Slip half-way up the row. I'll keep the light on him. Don't git in the path o' the light. When his eyes looks as big as a shillin', give it to him, right between 'em."

Jody crept forward, hugging the corn at his left. The green lights were extinguished a moment, then stared again. He lifted his gun and allowed the light from the blazing splinters in the fire-pan to slip down the barrel. He pulled the trigger. The gun, as always, knocked him off balance. He started to run forward to ascertain his hit, but Buck hissed at him.

"Psst. You got him. Leave him lay. Come back."

He crept along the row. Buck handed him the shotgun.

"They's likely another here clost."

They crept from row to row. This time he saw the glowing eyes before Buck saw them. He advanced down the row as before. The shotgun was a delight to handle. It was lighter than the old muzzle-loader, not so long, and easier to sight. He shot with a feeling of confidence. Again Buck called him back and he retreated. But though they combed the rows carefully, and worked around the west end of the field and flashed the light down the corn rows from the south, there were no more bright green eyes.

Buck said aloud, "That's the crop for tonight. Let's see what we got."

Both shots had killed. One was a dog-fox and one a vixen, fat with Baxter corn.

Buck said, "Now they got a litter off in a den some'eres, but they'll be part-growed and kin make out by theirselves. Come fall, we'll have us a fox-chase."

The foxes were gray and in good condition, with full brushes. Jody carried them in complacently.

Approaching the cabin, they heard a commotion. Ma Baxter shrieked.

Buck said, "Your Ma wouldn't romp on your Pa while he was ailin', would she?"

"She don't never romp on him with nothin' but talkin'."

"I'd a heap ruther a woman tore me down with a lighter'd knot, than speakin' sharp."

Close to the cabin, they heard Penny shout.

Buck said, "Why, boy, the woman's killin' him."

Jody said, "Somethin's after the fawn!"

The yard itself was not often disturbed by anything more dangerous than the small varmints. Buck hurdled the fence

and Jody vaulted it after him. A light shone from the doorway. Penny stood there dressed only in his breeches. Ma
Baxter was beside him, flapping her apron. Jody thought he
saw a dark form move off into the night, toward the grape
arbor, followed by the dogs, baying.

Penny called, "Hit's a bear! Git him! Git him 'fore he
makes the fence!"

Sparks showered from the fire-pan as Buck ran. The light
reached out to a lumbering body galloping to the east under
the peach trees.

Jody shouted, "Give me the fire-pan, Buck, and you do
the shootin'."

He felt frightened and incompetent. They exchanged on
the run. At the fence the bear turned at bay. He slashed at
the dogs. His eyes and teeth shone in the spasmodic light.
Then he turned to clamber over the fence. Buck shot. The
bear tumbled. The dogs broke into a tumult. Penny came
running. The light showed a kill. The dogs made a pretense
of having done the job, and bayed and attacked proudly.
Buck was smug.

He said, "This feller'd not of come around if he'd knowed
they was a Forrester on the place."

Penny said, "He smelt things set him so wild, he'd not
of noticed the hull tribe of you."

"What was that?"

"Jody's fawn and the new honey."

"Did he git to the fawn, Pa? Oh Pa, the fawn ain't hurt?"

"He never got to him. The door by luck was closed. Then
he must of winded the honey and come traipsin' around by
the stoop. I figgered it was you-all comin' back and I didn't
pay no mind until he knocked the cover offen the honey. I
could of shot him down right at the door, but here I was and
no gun. All me and Ory could do was holler, but I reckon it
was the fiercest hollerin' he'd ever run into, and he lit out."

Jody was weak at thought of what might have happened
to the fawn. He ran to the shed to comfort it, and found it

drowsy and unconcerned. He stroked it gratefully, then returned to the men and the bear. It was a two-year-old male, in good condition. Penny insisted on helping with the dressing. They dragged the carcass to the back yard and skinned it out by the light of the fire-pan; quartered it and hung the meat in the smoke-house.

Buck said, "Now I will beg a pail o' the fat for Ma, to make her some bear grease and cracklin's. There's things she jest won't fry without bear grease, and the old soul says bear cracklin's and sweet pertaters rests so easy on her gums. Why, them four teeth o' hers could chomp on 'em all day."

Ma Baxter developed generosity with the plenitude.

She said, "And a big piece o' the liver goes to pore leetle Fodder-wing. Hit'll give him strength."

Penny said, "I'm only sad this ain't old Slewfoot. My, wouldn't I love to draw the knife down his thievin' backbone."

The foxes could wait to be skinned until morning, for the meat would be used only to cook for the chickens, with pepper, for a tonic.

Buck said, "Did old man Easy Ozell ever ask you to come eat one o' his fox pilaus?"

Penny said, "He done so. And I said, 'No, thank you, Easy, I'll jest wait until you cook one o' your dogs.'"

Penny was thriving on the excitement. He sat on his heels beside Buck and exchanged tales of foxes and of dogs, of strange foods and the stranger people who ate them. The yarns for once failed to hold Jody's interest. He was anxious for every one to go to bed. At last Penny's new-found energy failed him, and he washed his hands and cleaned his skinning knife and joined his wife in the bed. Buck was wound up to talk half the night. Jody knew the signs and pretended to go to sleep on his pallet on the floor of his small room. Buck had been occupying his bed, his long hairy legs hanging unsupported a quarter of its length. Buck sat on the edge of the

bed and talked until the lack of audience discouraged him.
Jody heard him yawn and pull off his trousers and lie down
on the corn shucks mattress on the creaking slats.

He waited until a deep rumbling snore sounded. Then he
slipped from the house and groped his way to the shed. The
fawn stood up at the sound. He felt his way to it and threw
his arms around its neck. It nuzzled his cheek. He picked it up
and carried it to the door. It had grown so fast in the brief
time he had had it, that it was all he could do to carry it.
He tiptoed into the yard with it and set it down. It followed
him willingly. He crept into the house, keeping one hand on
its smooth hard head to guide it. Its sharp heels clicked on
the wooden floor. He lifted it again and stepped cautiously
past his mother's bedroom and into his own.

He lay down on his pallet and drew the fawn down beside
him. He often lay so with it in the shed, or under the live
oaks in the heat of the day. He lay with his head against its
side. Its ribs lifted and fell with its breathing. It rested its
chin on his hand. It had a few short hairs there that prickled
him. He had been cudgeling his wits for an excuse to bring
the fawn inside at night to sleep with him, and now he had
one that could not be disputed. He would smuggle it in and
out as long as possible, in the name of peace. On the inevitable day when he should be discovered, what better reason was there than the menace—the constant danger, he
would point out—of bears?

Chapter XVII

THERE was not a field of sweet potatoes, but an endless sea. Jody looked behind him at the rows he had finished hoeing. They were beginning to make a respectable showing, but the rows unfinished seemed to stretch to the horizon. The July heat simmered on the earth. The sand was scalding to his bare feet. The leaves of the sweet potato vines curled upward, as though the dry soil, and not the sun, were burning them. He pushed back his palmetto hat and wiped his face with his sleeve. By the sun, it must be nearly ten o'clock. His father had said that if the sweet potatoes were hoed by noon, he might go in the afternoon to see Fodder-wing, and get a name for the fawn.

The fawn lay in the hedge-row in the shade of an elderberry bush. It had been almost a nuisance when he began his work. It had galloped up and down the sweet potato beds, trampling the vines, and knocking down the edges of the beds. It had come and stood in front of him in the direct path of his hoeing, refusing to move, to force him to play with it. The wide-eyed, wondering expression of its first weeks with him had given way to an alert awareness. It had as wise a look as old Julia. Jody had almost decided that he would have to lead it back and shut it up in the shed, when of its own accord it sought the shade and lay down.

It lay watching him from the corner of one big eye, its head in its favorite position, twisted back against its own shoulder. Its small white tail flicked now and then and its spotted hide rippled, shaking off flies. If it would stay quiet, he could make better time at the hoeing. He liked to work with it near. It gave him a comfortable feeling that he had never had before in the company of a hoe. He attacked the weeds again lustily, and was pleased with himself to see his own progress. The rows fell away behind him. He whistled tunelessly.

He had thought of many names for the fawn, had called it by each in turn, but not one pleased him. All the names by which the dogs of his acquaintance had been called, Joe and Grab, Rover and Rob, on down the line, all were inadequate. It had such a light way of walking, "tippy-toed" as Penny put it, that he would have named it Twinkle-toes and called it "Twink" for short, but that reminded him of Twink Weatherby and spoiled the name. "Tip" itself would not do, because Penny had once had an ugly and vicious bull-dog by the name. Fodder-wing would not fail him. He had a great gift for naming his own pets. He had Racket the raccoon, Push the 'possum, Squeak the squirrel, and Preacher, the lame red-bird, who sang from his perch, "Preacher, preacher, preacher!" Fodder-wing said the other red-birds came to him from the forest to be married, but Jody had heard other red-birds sing the same words. At any rate, it was a good name.

He had done a great deal of work in the two weeks since Buck had gone home. Penny's strength was returning, but every now and then he became faint and dizzy and his heart pounded. Penny was sure it was the lingering effect of the rattlesnake venom, but Ma Baxter believed it was the fever, and dosed him with lemon-leaf tea. It was good to have him up and about again, with the cold fear gone. Jody tried to remember to spare him. It was so good to have the fawn, to be relieved of the dull lonely ache that had overtaken him so often, that he was filled with gratitude for his mother's tolerance of its presence. There was no question but that it did require a great deal of milk. It undoubtedly got in her way. It came into the house one day and discovered a pan of cornbread stirred up, ready for baking. It had cleaned the pan. Since then it had eaten—green leaves, cornmeal mixed with water, bits of biscuit, almost anything. It had to be shut in the shed when the Baxters ate. It butted and bleated and knocked dishes out of their hands. When Jody and Penny laughed at it, it tossed its head knowingly. The dogs at first had baited it, but they were now tolerant. Ma Baxter was tolerant, but she was never amused. Jody pointed out its charms.

"Ain't his eyes purty, Ma?"

"They see a pan o' cornbread too fur."

"Well, ain't he got a cute, foolish tail, Ma?"

"All deer's flags looks the same."

"But Ma, ain't it cute and foolish?"

"Hit's foolish, a'right."

The sun crept toward its zenith. The fawn came into the sweet potatoes and nibbled a few tender vines, then returned to the hedge-row and found a new place of shade under a wild cherry tree. Jody checked his work. He had a row and a half yet undone. He would have liked to go to the house for a drink of water, but that would cut down his remaining time too sharply. Perhaps dinner would be late. He pulled the hoe as fast as he dared without cutting the vines. When the sun stood over-head, he had finished the half-row, and the full row stretched mockingly before him. In a moment now his mother would beat on the iron ring by the kitchen door and he would have to stop. Penny had made it plain that there would be no quarter as to time. If the hoeing was not finished by dinner time, there would be no visit to Fodder-wing. He heard steps on the other side of the fence. Penny was standing there, watching him.

"A heap o' 'taters, ain't it, son?"

"Hit's a mort of 'em."

"Hard to think, this time next year, there'll not be one left. That baby o' yours there, under the cherry tree, he'll be wantin' his share of 'em. Remember the time we had, two year gone, keepin' the deer out?"

"Pa, I cain't make it. I ain't scarcely stopped all mornin', and I've yet got a row."

"Well now, I tell you. I ain't fixin' to let you off, for I said I'd not. But I'll strike a bargain. You go fetch fresh water for your Ma from the sink-hole, and I'll finish the 'taters this evenin'. Climbin' the walls o' that sink-hole purely beats me. Now that's a fair deal."

Jody dropped the hoe and started on a run for the house to get the water-buckets.

Penny called after him, "Don't try to tote 'em plumb full. A yearling ain't got a buck's strength."

The buckets alone were heavy. They were of hand-hewn cypress, and the ox-yoke from which they hung was of white oak. Jody hung the yoke over his shoulders and trotted down the road. The fawn loped after him. The sink-hole was dark and still. There was more sunlight in the early morning and at evening, than at noon, for the thick leaves of the trees cut off the overhead sun. The birds were still. Around the sandy rim of the sink-hole they were nooning and dusting themselves. In late afternoon they would fly down for water. The doves would come, and the jorees, the red-birds and the bee-martins, the mocking-birds and the quail. He could not be too hurried to run down the steep slope to the bottom of the great green bowl. The fawn followed and they splashed together across the pool. The fawn bent its head to drink. He had dreamed of this.

He said to it, "Some day I'll build me a house here. And I'll git you a doe, and we'll all live here by the pool."

A frog leaped and the fawn backed away. Jody laughed at it and ran up the slope to the drinking trough. He leaned over it to drink. The fawn, following, drank with him, sucking up the water and moving its mouth up and down the length of the trough. At one moment its head was against Jody's cheek and he sucked in the water with the same sound as the fawn, for the sake of companionship. He lifted his head and shook it and wiped his mouth. The fawn lifted its head, too, and the water dropped from its muzzle.

Jody filled the buckets with the gourd dipper that hung

on the rim of the trough. Against his father's warning, he filled them nearly full. He would like to walk into the yard with them. He crouched and bent his shoulders under the yoke. When he straightened, he could not rise against the weight. He dipped out part of the water and was able to stand and pull his way up the remainder of the slope. The wooden yoke cut into his thin shoulders. His back ached. Halfway home, he was obliged to stop and set down the buckets and pour out more of the water. The fawn dipped its nose inquisitively into one of the buckets. Fortunately, his mother need not know. She could not understand how clean the fawn was, and would not admit how sweet it smelled.

They were at dinner when he reached the house. He lifted the buckets to the water shelf and shut up the fawn. He filled the water pitcher from the fresh buckets and took it in to the table. He had worked so hard and was so hot and tired that he was not particularly hungry. He was glad of this and was able to set aside a large portion of his own dinner for the fawn. The meat was a pot-roast from the bear's haunch, pickled in brine for keeping. It was a trifle coarse, with long fibers, but the flavor, he thought, was better than beef and almost as good as venison. He made his meal on the meat, with a helping of collard greens, and saved all his cornpone and his milk for the fawn.

Penny said, "We was mighty lucky 'twas a young bear like this un come scaperin' under our noses. Had it of been a big ol' male, we couldn't of et the meat this time o' year. The bears mates in July, Jody, and allus remember the meat o' the males ain't fitten when they're matin'. Don't never shoot one then unless it's botherin' you."

"Why ain't the meat fitten?"

"Now I don't know. But when they're courtin', they're mean and hateful——"

"Like Lem and Oliver?"

"—like Lem and Oliver. Their gorge rises, or their spleen, and seems like the hatefulness gits right into their flesh."

Ma Baxter said, "A boar hog's the same. Only he's that-a-way the year around."

"Well Pa, do the male bears fight?"

"They'll fight turrible. The female'll stand off and watch the fightin——"

"Like Twink Weatherby."

"—like Twink Weatherby, and then she'll go off with the one wins the fight. They'll stay in pairs all through July, mebbe into August. Then the males goes off and the cubs is borned in February. And don't you think a male, like ol' Slewfoot, won't eat them cubs do he come on 'em. That's another reason I hate bears. They ain't natural in their affections."

Ma Baxter said to Jody, "You look out, now, walkin' to Forresters' today. A matin' bear's a thing to shun."

Penny said, "Jest keep your eyes open. You're all right as long as you see a creetur first and don't take him by surprise. Even that rattlesnake that got me, why, I takened him by surprise and he wasn't no more'n lookin' out for hisself."

Ma Baxter said, "You'd stick up for the devil hisself."

"I reckon I would. The devil gits blamed for a heap o' things is nothin' but human cussedness."

She asked suspiciously, "Jody finish his hoein' like he belonged to?"

Penny said blandly, "He finished his contract."

He winked at Jody and Jody winked back. There was no use in trying to explain the difference to her. She was outside the good male understanding.

He said, "Ma, kin I go now?"

"Let's see. I'll need a mite o' wood toted in——"

"Please don't think up nothin' long to do, Ma. You wouldn't want I should be so late gittin' home tonight the bears'd git me."

"You be later'n dark gittin' home and you'll wish 'twas a bear had you, 'stid o' me."

He filled the wood-box and was ready to go. His mother

made him change his shirt and comb his hair. He fretted at the delay.

She said, "I jest want them dirty Forresters to know there's folks does live decent."

He said, "They ain't dirty. They jest live nice and natural and enjoy theirselves."

She sniffed. He let out the fawn from the shed, fed it from his hand, held the pan of milk mixed with water for it to drink, and the two set off. The fawn ran sometimes behind him, sometimes ahead, making short forays into the brush, bounding back to him in an alarm that Jody was sure was only pretended. Sometimes it walked beside him, and this was best. He laid his hand, then, lightly on its neck, and fitted the rhythm of his two legs to its four. He imagined that he was another fawn. He bent his legs at the knees, imitating its walk. He threw his head up, alertly. A rabbit-pea vine was in blossom beside the road. He pulled a length of it and twined it around the fawn's neck for a halter. The rosy blooms made the fawn so pretty that it seemed to him even his mother would admire it. If it faded before he returned, he would make a fresh halter on the way home.

At the cross-roads near the abandoned clearing, the fawn halted and lifted its nostrils into the wind. It pricked up its ears. It turned its head this way and that, savoring the air. He turned his own nose in the direction on which it seemed to settle. A strong odor came to him, pungent and rank. He felt the hair prickle on the back of his neck. He thought he heard a low rumbling sound and then a snapping that might be of teeth. He was tempted to turn tail and head for home. Yet he would always wonder what the sounds had been. He moved one step at a time around the turn in the road. The fawn stayed motionless behind him. He stopped short.

Two male bears were moving slowly ahead down the road, a hundred yards distant. They were on their hind legs, walking like men, shoulder to shoulder. Their walk seemed almost a dance, as when couples in the square dance moved side by side to do a figure. Suddenly they jostled each other, like wrestlers, and lifted their forepaws, and turned, snarling, each trying for the other's throat. One raked his claws across the other's head and the snarls grew to a roar. The fighting was violent for a few moments, then the pair walked on, boxing, jostling, parrying. The wind was in Jody's favor. They could never smell him. He crept down the road after them, keeping his distance. He could not bear to lose sight of them. He hoped they would fight to a finish, yet he should be terrorized if one should end the fight and turn his way. He decided that they had been fighting for a long time and were exhausted. There was blood in the sand. Each attack seemed less violent than the others. Each shoulder-to-shoulder walking was slower paced. As he stared, a female walked out of the bushes ahead with three males following her. They turned silently into the road and walked on in single file. The fighting pair swung their heads a moment, then fell in behind. Jody stood until the procession passed from sight, solemn and ludicrous and exciting.

He turned and ran back to the cross-roads. The fawn was nowhere to be seen. He called and it emerged from the scrub growth at the side of the road. He took the Forresters' road and ran down it. Now that it was over, he shook at his own boldness. But it was done now, and he would follow again, for all men were not privileged to see the creatures in their private moments.

He thought, "I've seen a thing."

It was good to become old and see the sights and hear the sounds that men saw and heard, like Buck and his father. That was why he liked to lie flat on his belly on the floor, or on the earth before the camp-fire, while men talked. They had seen marvels, and the older they were, the more marvels they had seen. He felt himself moving into a mystic company. He had a tale now of his own to tell on winter evenings.

The Yearling

His father would say, "Jody, tell about the time you seed the two male bears fightin' down the road."

Above all, he could tell Fodder-wing. He ran again, for pleasure in his hurry to tell his friend his story. He would surprise him. He would walk up to Fodder-wing in the woods, or back of the house among his pets, or to his bed, if he were still ailing. The fawn would walk beside him. Fodder-wing's face would shine with its strange brightness. He would hunch his twisted body close and put out his gentle and crooked hand and touch the fawn. He would smile, to know that he, Jody, was content. After a long time Fodder-wing would speak, and what he said would be perhaps peculiar, but it would be beautiful.

Jody reached the Forrester land and hurried under the live oaks into the open yard. The house was somnolent. There was no curl of smoke from the chimney. There were no dogs in sight, but a hound was howling from the dog-pen at the rear. The Forresters were probably all sleeping through the heat of the early afternoon. But when they slept in the day-time, they overflowed the house, out to the veranda, under the trees. He stopped and called.

"Fodder-wing! Hit's Jody!"

The hound whined. A chair scraped on the board floor inside the house. Buck came to the door. He looked down at Jody and passed his hand over his mouth. His eyes were unseeing. It seemed to Jody that he must be drunk.

Jody faltered, "I come to see Fodder-wing. I come to show him my fawn."

Buck shook his head as though he would shake away a bee that annoyed him, or his thoughts. He wiped his mouth again.

Jody said, "I come special."

Buck said, "He's dead."

The words had no meaning. They were only two brown leaves that blew past him into the air. But a coldness followed their passing, and a numbness took him. He was confused.

187

He repeated, "I come to see him."

"You come too late. I'd of fotched you, if there'd been time. There wasn't time to fotch ol' Doc. One minute he was breathin'. The next minute he jest wa'n't. Like as if you blowed out a candle."

Jody stared at Buck and Buck stared back at him. The numbness grew into a paralysis. He felt no sorrow, only a coldness and a faintness. Fodder-wing was neither dead nor alive. He was, simply, nowhere at all.

Buck said hoarsely, "You kin come look at him."

First Buck said that Fodder-wing was gone, like candle-light, and then he said that he was here. None of it made sense. Buck turned into the house. He looked back, compelling Jody with his dull eyes. Jody lifted one leg after the other and mounted the steps. He followed Buck into the house. The Forrester men sat all together. There was a one-ness about them, sitting so, motionless and heavy. They were pieces of one great dark rock, broken into separate men. Pa Forrester turned his head and looked at Jody as though he were a stranger. Then he turned it away again. Lem and Mill-wheel looked at him. The others did not stir. It seemed to Jody that they saw him from over a wall they had built against him. They were unwilling to hold the sight of him. Buck groped for his hand. He led him toward the large bedroom. He started to speak. His voice broke. He stopped and gripped Jody's shoulder.

He said, "Bear up."

Fodder-wing lay with closed eyes, small and lost in the center of the great bed. He was smaller than when he had lain sleeping on his pallet. He was covered with a sheet, turned back beneath his chin. His arms were outside the sheet, folded across his chest, the palms of the hands falling outward, twisted and clumsy, as in life. Jody was frightened. Ma Forrester sat by the side of the bed. She held her apron over her head and rocked herself back and forth. She flung down the apron.

She said, "I've lost my boy. My pore crookedy boy."

She covered herself again and swayed from side to side. She moaned, "The Lord's hard. Oh, the Lord's hard."

Jody wanted to run away. The bony face on the pillow terrified him. It was Fodder-wing and it was not Fodder-wing. Buck drew him to the edge of the bed.

"He'll not hear, but speak to him."

Jody's throat worked. No words came. Fodder-wing seemed made of tallow, like a candle. Suddenly he was familiar.

Jody whispered, "Hey."

The paralysis broke, having spoken. His throat tightened as though a rope choked it. Fodder-wing's silence was intolerable. Now he understood. This was death. Death was a silence that gave back no answer. Fodder-wing would never speak to him again. He turned and buried his face against Buck's chest. The big arms gripped him. He stood a long time.

Buck said, "I knowed you'd hate it fearful."

They left the room. Pa Forrester beckoned to him. He went to his side. The old man stroked his arm. He waved at the circle of brooding men.

He said, "Ain't it quare now? We could of spared nigh ary one o' them fellers. The one we cain't spare was the one was takened." He added brightly, "And him a swiveled, no-account thing, too."

He sank back in his rocking chair, pondering the paradox.

Jody bruised them all with his presence. He wandered outside into the yard. He roamed to the back of the house. Fodder-wing's pets were here, caged and forgotten. A five-months' bear cub, brought no doubt to amuse him in his illness, was chained to a stake. It had walked its dusty circle, around and around, until its chain was tangled and it was held tight against the stake. Its water-pan was overturned and empty. At sight of Jody, it rolled on its back and cried with a sound like a human baby. Squeak the squirrel ran his endless treadle. His cage had neither food nor water. The 'possum was asleep in its box. Preacher the redbird hopped on his one good leg and pecked at the bare floor of his cage. The raccoon was not in sight.

Jody knew where Fodder-wing kept sacks of peanuts and corn for his creatures. His brothers had made him a little feed-box and kept it filled for him. Jody fed the small things first and watered them. He approached the bear cub cautiously. It was small and roly-poly, but he was not too certain what use it might make of its sharp claws. It whimpered and he reached out one arm to it. It wrapped all four legs around it and clung desperately. It rubbed its black nose against his shoulder. He untangled it and pulled away from it and straightened its chain and brought it a pan of water. It drank again and again, then took the pan from him with its paws like the hands, he thought, of a nigger baby, and turned the last few cool drops on its stomach. He could have laughed aloud if he were not so heavy with sadness. But it relieved him to care for the animals, to give them, for the time, the comfort that their master could never offer them again. He wondered sorrowfully what would become of them.

He played abstractedly with them. The sharp joy that he had once felt when Fodder-wing shared them was muted. When Racket, the raccoon, came in from the forest with its queer, uneven gait, and recognized him, and climbed up his leg to his shoulder, and made its plaintive, chirring cry, and parted his hair with its thin, restless fingers, he longed so painfully for Fodder-wing that he had to lie on his belly and beat his feet in the sand.

The ache turned into a longing for the fawn. He got up and brought a handful of peanuts for the 'coon, to keep it occupied. He went in search of the fawn. He found it behind a myrtle bush, where it had been able to watch unobserved. He thought it might be thirsty, too, and he offered it water in the bear cub's pan. The fawn sniffed and would not drink. He was tempted to feed it a handful of corn from the Forresters' abundance, but decided it would not be honest to do so. Probably its teeth were still too tender to chew the hard kernels in any case. He sat down under a live oak and held the fawn close to him. There was a comfort in it not to be found in the hairy arms of Buck Forrester. He wondered if his pleasure in Fodder-wing's creatures had been dissipated because Fodder-wing was gone, or because the fawn now held all he needed of delight.

He said to it, "I'd not trade you for all of 'em, and the cub to boot."

A gratifying feeling of faithfulness came over him, that the enchantment of the creatures he had so long coveted could not deflect his affections from the fawn.

The afternoon was endless. It came to him that something was unfinished. The Forresters ignored him, yet, somehow, he knew they expected him to stay. Buck would have said good-by to him if he were supposed to go. The sun dropped behind the live oaks. His mother would be angry. Yet he was waiting for something, if only dismissal by a sign. He was bound to Fodder-wing, tallow-white in the bed, and a thing waited that would set him free. At dusk the Forresters filed out of the house and went in silence about their chores. Smoke drifted from the chimney. The smell of fat pine blended with frying meat. He trailed after Buck, driving the cows to water.

He offered, "I done fed and watered the bear cub and the squirrel and them."

Buck touched a switch to a heifer.

He said, "I remembered them oncet today, and then my mind went black agin."

Jody said, "Kin I he'p?"

"They's a plenty of us here, to do. You could wait on Ma like Fodder-wing done. Keep up her fire and sich as that."

He went reluctantly into the house. He avoided the sight

of the bedroom door. It was drawn almost closed. Ma Forrester was at the hearth. Her eyes were red. She stopped
every few moments to touch them with the corner of her
apron. Her straggly hair had been wet and brushed back
smooth and neat, as though in honor of a guest.

He said, "I come to he'p."

She turned with a spoon in her hand.

She said, "I been standin' here thinkin' about your Ma.
She's burrit as many as I got."

He fed the fire unhappily. He was increasingly uneasy.
Yet he could not go. The meal was as meager as the Baxters'
own. Ma Forrester set the table indifferently.

She said, "Now I forgot to make coffee. They'd drink
coffee when they'd not eat."

She filled the pot and set it on the coals. The Forrester
men came one by one to the back porch and washed their
hands and faces and combed their hair and beards. There
was no talk, no joking and jostling, no noisy stamping. They
trooped in to the table like men in a dream. Pa Forrester
came in from the bedroom. He looked about him wonderingly.

He said, "Ain't it quare——"

Jody sat down next to Ma Forrester. She served the plates
with meat, then began to cry.

She said, "I counted him in, same as always. Oh my
Lord, I counted him in."

Buck said, "Well now, Ma, Jody'll eat his portion and
mebbe grow up big as me. Eh, boy?"

The family rallied. For a few minutes they ate hungrily.
Then a nauseating fullness came over them and they pushed
away their plates.

Ma Forrester said, "I got no heart to clean up tonight,
nor you neither. Jest stack the plates 'til after tomorrer
mornin'."

Release, then, would come in the morning. She looked
at Jody's plate.

The Yearling

She said, "You ain't et your biscuits nor drinked your milk, boy. What ailded 'em?"

"That's for my fawn. I allus save him some o' my dinner."

She said, "You pore lamb." She began to cry again. "Wouldn't my boy of loved to seed your fawn. He talked about it and he talked about it. He said, 'Jody's got him a brother.'"

Jody felt the hateful thickening of his throat. He swallowed.

He said, "That's how come me to be here. I came for Fodder-wing to name my fawn."

"Why," she said, "he named it. Last time he talked about it, he give it a name. He said, 'A fawn carries its flag so merry. A fawn's tail's a leetle white merry flag. If I had me a fawn, I'd name him "Flag." "Flag the fawn," is what I'd call him.'"

Jody repeated, "Flag."

He thought he would burst. Fodder-wing had talked of him and had named the fawn. There was happiness tangled with his grief that was both comforting and unbearable.

He said, "I reckon I best go feed him. I best go feed Flag."

He slid from his chair and went outside with the cup of milk and the biscuits. Fodder-wing seemed close and living.

He called, "Here, Flag!"

The fawn came to him and it seemed to him that it knew the name, and had perhaps always known it. He soaked the biscuits in the milk and fed them to it. Its muzzle was soft and wet in his hand. He went back into the house and the fawn followed.

He said, "Kin Flag come in?"

"Bring him right in and welcome."

He sat down stiffly on Fodder-wing's three-legged stool in the corner.

Pa Forrester said, "Hit'd pleasure him, you comin' to set up with him tonight."

193

That, then, was the thing expected of him.

"And 'twouldn't scarcely be decent, buryin' him in the mornin' without you was here. He didn't have no friend but you."

Jody cast off his anxiety over his mother and father like a too-ragged shirt. It was of no importance, in the face of matters so grave. Ma Forrester went into the bedroom to take the early vigil. The fawn nosed about the room, smelling of one man after the other, then came and lay down beside Jody. Darkness came tangibly into the house, adding its heaviness to theirs. They sat smothered under the thick air of sorrow that only the winds of time could blow away.

At nine o'clock Buck stirred and lit a candle. At ten o'clock a horse and rider clattered into the yard. It was Penny on old Cæsar. He dropped the reins over its head and came into the house. Pa Forrester, as head of the house, rose and greeted him. Penny looked about at the dark faces. The old man pointed to the half-open bedroom door.

Penny said, "The boy?"

Pa Forrester nodded.

"Gone—or goin'?"

"Gone."

"I feered it. Hit come over me, that was what was keepin' Jody away."

He laid one hand on the old man's shoulder.

"I feel for you."

He spoke to one man after the other. He looked directly at Lem.

"Howdy, Lem."

Lem hesitated.

"Howdy, Penny."

Mill-wheel gave him his chair.

Penny asked, "When did it happen?"

"Jest at dawn today."

"Ma goed in to see would he eat a bite o' breakfast."

"He'd been layin' punishin' a day-two, and we'd had ol' Doc, but he seemed to be mendin'."

The talk broke over Penny in a torrent. The relief of words washed and cleansed a hurt that had been in-growing. He listened gravely, nodding his head from time to time. He was a small staunch rock against which their grief might beat. When they finished and fell quiet, he talked of his own losses. It was a reminder that no man was spared. What all had borne, each could bear. He shared their sorrow, and they became a part of his, and the sharing spread their grief a little, by thinning it.

Buck said, "Likely Jody'd like to set up with him alone a whiles."

Jody was in a panic when they took him into the room and turned away to close the door. Something sat in a far dark corner of the room and it was the same thing that had prowled the scrub the night his father had been bitten.

He said, "Would it be all right, did Flag come, too?"

They agreed that it was seemly and the fawn was brought to join him. He sat on the edge of the chair. It was warm from Ma Forrester's body. He crossed his hands in his lap. He looked furtively at the face on the pillow. A candle burned on a table at the head of the bed. When the flame flickered, it seemed that Fodder-wing's eyelids fluttered. A light breeze stirred through the room. The sheet seemed to lift, as though Fodder-wing were breathing. After a time the horror went away and he could sit back in the chair. When he leaned far back, Fodder-wing looked a little familiar. Yet it was not Fodder-wing who lay, pinched of cheek, under the candle-light. Fodder-wing was stumbling about outside in the bushes, with the raccoon at his heels. In a moment he would come into the house with his rocking gait, and Jody would hear his voice. He stole a look at the crossed, crooked hands. Their stillness was implacable. He cried to himself, soundlessly.

The wavering candle was hypnotic. His eyes blurred. He

roused himself, but a moment came when his eyes would not open. Death and the silence and his sleep were one.

He awakened at daylight to a heaviness of spirit. He heard a sound of hammering. Some one had laid him across the foot of the bed. He was wide awake instantly. Fodder-wing was gone. He slid from the bed and into the big room. It was empty. He went outside. Penny was nailing a cover on a fresh pine box. The Forresters stood about. Ma Forrester was crying. No one spoke to him. Penny drove the last nail.

He asked, "Ready?"

They nodded. Buck and Mill-wheel and Lem moved forward.

Buck said, "I kin tote it alone."

He swung the box to his shoulder. Pa Forrester and Gabby were missing. Buck set out toward the south hammock. Ma Forrester followed him. Mill-wheel took hold of her arm. The others dropped in behind them. The procession filed slowly to the hammock. Jody remembered that Fodder-wing had a grape-vine swing here, under a live oak. He saw Pa Forrester standing beside it. They had spades in their hands. A raw hole gaped in the earth. The mounded soil beside it was dark with wood-mould. The hammock was light with the dawning, for the sunrise reached out luminous fingers parallel with the earth and covered it with brightness. Buck set down the coffin and eased it into the opening. He stepped back. The Forresters hesitated.

Penny said, "The father first."

Pa Forrester lifted his spade and shovelled earth on the box. He handed the spade to Buck. Buck threw a few clods. The spade passed from one to the other of the brothers. There was a tea-cupful of earth remaining. Jody found the spade in his hands. Numb, he scooped the earth and dropped it on the mound. The Forresters looked at one another.

Pa Forrester said, "Penny, you've had Christian raising. We'd be proud, did you say somethin'."

THE BURIAL OF FODDER-WING

The Yearling

Penny advanced to the grave and closed his eyes and lifted his face to the sunlight. The Forresters bowed their heads.

"Oh Lord. Almighty God. Hit ain't for us ignorant mortals to say what's right and what's wrong. Was ary one of us to be a-doin' of it, we'd not of brung this pore boy into the world a cripple, and his mind teched. We'd of brung him in straight and tall like his brothers, fitten to live and work and do. But in a way o' speakin', Lord, you done made it up to him. You give him a way with the wild creeturs. You give him a sort o' wisdom, made him knowin' and gentle. The birds come to him, and the varmints moved free about him, and like as not he could o' takened a she wild-cat right in his pore twisted hands.

"Now you've done seed fit to take him where bein' crookedy in mind or limb don't matter. But Lord, hit pleasures us to think now you've done straightened out them legs and that pore bent back and them hands. Hit pleasures us to think on him, movin' around as easy as ary one. And Lord, give him a few red-birds and mebbe a squirrel and a 'coon and a 'possum to keep him comp'ny, like he had here. All of us is somehow lonesome, and we know he'll not be lonesome, do he have them leetle wild things around him, if it ain't askin' too much to put a few varmints in Heaven. Thy will be done. Amen."

The Forresters murmured "Amen." Sweat stood on their faces. They came to Penny one by one and wrung his hand. The raccoon came running and ran across the fresh-turned earth. It cried and Buck lifted it to his shoulder. The Forresters turned and trooped back to the house. They saddled Cæsar and Penny mounted. He swung Jody up behind him. Jody called the fawn and it came from the bushes. Buck came from the rear of the house. He had a small wire cage in his hand. He handed it up to Jody on the horse's rump. It held Preacher, the lame red-bird.

He said, "I know your Ma wouldn't leave you keep ary o'

the creeturs, but this feller'll make out on pure crumbs. Hit's
for you to remember him by."

"I thank you. Good-by."

"Good-by."

Cæsar jogged down the road toward home. They did not
speak. Cæsar dropped into a walk and Penny did not disturb
him. The sun rose high. Jody's arm ached from holding the
little cage in the air. The Baxter clearing came into sight.
Ma Baxter had heard the horse's hooves and was at the gate.

She called out, "Hit's enough to be fretted about one, then
you both go off and stay gone."

Penny dismounted and Jody slid down.

Penny said, "Easy, Ma. We had a duty. Pore leetle ol'
Fodder-wing died and we he'ped bury him."

She said, "Well— Pity 'twa'n't that great quarrelin' Lem."

Penny turned Cæsar out to graze and came to the house.
Breakfast had been cooked but was now cold.

He said, "Ne' mind. Jest warm the coffee."

He ate abstractedly.

He said, "I never seed a family take a thing so hard."

She said, "Don't tell me them big rough somebodies took
on."

He said, "Ory, the day may come when you'll know the
human heart is allus the same. Sorrer strikes the same all
over. Hit makes a different kind o' mark in different places.
Seems to me, times, hit ain't done nothin' to you but sharpen
your tongue."

She sat down abruptly.

She said, "Seems like bein' hard is the only way I kin
stand it."

He left his breakfast and went to her and stroked her hair.

"I know. Jest be a leetle mite easy on t'other feller."

Chapter XVIII

UGUST was merciless in its heat, but it was, mercifully, leisurely. There was little work to be done and no great hurry about the doing of that little. There had been rains and the corn had come to maturity. It was drying on the stalks and could soon be broken for curing. Penny estimated that he would have a good yield, perhaps as much as ten bushels to the acre. The sweet potato vines grew lushly. The Kaffir corn for the chickens was ripening, its long heads like sorghum. The sunflowers along the fence, also for the chickens, had heads as big as plates. The cow-peas were abundant. They made the staple food, with the meat of some game, almost every day. There would be a fine stand of cow-pea hay for use through the winter months. The field of pindars was not doing so well, but because of the killing by old Slewfoot of Betsy the brood sow, there were not many shoats to fatten. The Baxter hogs had come mysteriously home, and with them a young brood sow. Its mark had been changed from the Forrester mark to the Baxter. Penny accepted it as the peace offering for which it was intended.

The red ribbon cane had made a fair stand. The Baxters looked forward to autumn and the frosts, when sweet potatoes would be dug, hogs butchered, corn ground into meal, and the cane would be ground and the juice boiled into syrup, and plenty would replace the meagerness. There was enough to eat, even now in the leanest season, but there was no variety, no richness, no comfortable feeling of ample reserve stores. They lived from day to day, with meal and flour and fat meat short, dependent on Penny's chance shots at deer and turkey and squirrel. He trapped a fat 'possum in the yard one night, and dug a mess of the new sweet potatoes to roast with it, for a special treat. It was an extravagance, for the potatoes were small and immature.

The sun laid a heavy hand on the scrub and on the clearing. Ma Baxter's bulk suffered with the heat. Penny and Jody, lean and clean-limbed, felt the temperature only in an increasing reluctance to move rapidly, or often. They did the chores together in the morning, milked the cow, fed the horse, chopped wood for cooking, brought water from the sink-hole, and then were through until the evening. Ma Baxter cooked hot dinner at noon, then banked the fire on the hearth with ashes; and supper was cold, consisting of the noon surplus.

Jody was conscious always of Fodder-wing's absence. Living, Fodder-wing had been with him, in the back of his mind, a friendly presence to which he might turn in his thoughts, if not in reality. But Flag grew miraculously, day by day, and that was comfort enough. Jody thought that its spots were beginning to fade, a sign of maturity, but Penny could see little change. It was unquestionably growing in intelligence. Penny said that the bears had the largest brains of any of the scrub animals, and the brain of the deer came next.

Ma Baxter said, "This un's too dad-ratted smart," and Penny said, "Why, Ma, shame on you for cussin'," and winked at Jody.

Flag learned to lift the shoe-string latch on the door and come in the house at any hour of the day or night, when he was not shut up. He butted a feather pillow from Jody's bed and tossed it all over the house until it burst, so that feathers drifted for days in every nook and cranny, and appeared from nowhere in a dish of biscuit pudding. He began to romp with the dogs. Old Julia was too dignified to do much more than wag her tail slowly when he pawed at her, but Rip growled and circled and pretended to pounce, and Flag kicked up his heels and flicked his merry tail and shook his

The Yearling

head and finally, with impudence, leaped the slat fence and raced alone down the roadway. He liked best to play with Jody. They tussled and held furious butting matches and raced side by side, until Ma Baxter protested that Jody was growing as lean as a black snake.

In a late afternoon toward the end of August, Jody went with the fawn to the sink-hole for fresh water for supper. The road was bright with flowers. The sumac was in bloom, and the colic root sent up tall stalks of white or orange orchid-like flowers. The French mulberries were beginning to ripen on slim stems. They were lavender in color, close-clustered, like snails' eggs along lily stalks. Butterflies sat on the first purple buds of the fragrant deer-tongue, opening and closing their wings slowly, as though waiting for the buds to open and the nectar to be revealed. The covey call of quail sounded again from the pea-field, clear and sweet and communal. Sunset was coming a little earlier, and at the corner of the fence-row, where the old Spanish trail turned north and passed the sink-hole, the saffron light reached under the low-hanging live oaks and made of the gray pen-dulous Spanish moss a luminous curtain.

Jody stopped short with his hand on the fawn's head. A horseman with a helmet was riding through the moss. Jody took a step forward, and horse and rider vanished, as though their substance were no thicker than the moss. He stepped back and they appeared again. He drew a long breath. Here, certainly, was Fodder-wing's Spaniard. He was not sure whether he was frightened or no. He was tempted to run back home, telling himself that he had truly seen a spirit. But his father's stuff was in him, and he forced himself to walk forward slowly to the spot in which the apparition had appeared. In a moment the truth was plain. A conjunction of moss and limbs had created the illusion. He could identify the horse, the rider and the helmet. His heart thumped with relief, yet he was disappointed. It would be better not to have known; to have gone away, believing.

The Yearling

He continued on to the sink-hole. The sweet bay was still in bloom, filling the sink-hole with its fragrance. He longed for Fodder-wing. Now he should never know whether the mossy horseman in the sunset was the Spaniard, or whether Fodder-wing had seen yet another, at once more mystic and more true. He set down his buckets and went down the narrow trail that Penny had cut between banks to the floor of the sink-hole, long before he was born.

He forgot his errand and lay down under the lacy shadow of a dogwood tree at the foot of the slope. The fawn nosed about, then lay down beside him. He could see from this spot the whole deep-sunk bowl at once. The rim above caught the glow of the sunset, as though a ring of fires burned invisibly around it. Squirrels, quieted a moment by his coming, began to bark and chatter and swing across the tree-tops, frenzied with the last hour of day, as they were always frenzied with the first. The palm fronds made a loud rattling where they dashed through, but the live oaks gave almost no record of their passing. In the thick sweet gums and hickories they were almost inaudible, always unseen, until they raced up and down the tree trunks or slipped to the edge of a limb to swing into another tree. Birds made sweet sharp sounds in the branches. Far away, a red-bird sang richly, coming closer and closer, until Jody saw him drift to the Baxter drinking trough. A flock of turtle doves whirred in, to drink briefly, then flew away to their roosting places in the adjoining pine forest. Their wings whistled, as though their pointed gray and rosy feathers were thin knives to slash the air.

Jody's eye caught a motion at the edge of the slope. A mother raccoon came down to the limestone troughs, followed by two young ones. She fished the series of troughs carefully, beginning with the drinking trough at the upper level. He had the finest reason now for delaying. He would have to wait until the water had cleared and settled. The mother 'coon found nothing of interest in the troughs. One of the young clambered to the edge of the stock-trough and peered in curiously. She slapped it away, out of danger. She worked her way down the slope. Now she was lost among the tall ferns. Now her black-masked face appeared again between stalks of the Cherokee bean. The two young ones peered out after her, their small faces replicas of her own, their bushy tails ringed almost as decisively.

She reached the seepage pool at the bottom and began to fish in earnest. Her long black fingers groped under fallen twigs and branches. She lay on her side to reach into a crevice for, no doubt, a crayfish. A frog jumped and she made a quick circular pounce and waded back to the edge with it. She sat up on her hind legs and held it a moment, kicking, against her breast, then sunk her teeth in it and shook it, as a dog shakes a rat. She dropped it between her offspring. They pounced on it and snarled and growled and cracked its bones and finally shared it. She watched dispassionately a moment, then turned back into the pool. Her bushy tail was lifted just above the water level. The young ones waded out after her. Their peaked noses lifted above the water. She turned and saw them and dragged them back to land. She lifted each one in turn and spanked its small furry bottom in so human a way that Jody had to clap his hand over his mouth to keep from shouting. He watched her for a long time, fishing and feeding them. Then she ambled leisurely across the floor of the sink-hole and up the far slope and away over the rim, the young ones following, chirring and grumbling amiably together.

The sink-hole lay all in shadow. Suddenly it seemed to Jody that Fodder-wing had only now gone away with the raccoons. Something of him had been always where the wild creatures fed and played. Something of him would be always near them. Fodder-wing was like the trees. He was of the earth, as they were earthy, with his gnarled, frail roots deep in the sand. He was like the changing clouds and the setting sun and the rising moon. A part of him had been always outside his twisted body. It had come and gone like

203

the wind. It came to Jody that he need not be lonely for his friend again. He could endure his going.

He went to the drinking trough and filled the buckets with as much water as he could carry, and went home. He told at table of the 'coons, and even his mother was interested to hear about the spanking, and no one questioned his delay. After supper, he sat with his father and listened to the hoot-owls and the frogs, and a far wild-cat and still further foxes, and to the north, a wolf that howled and was answered. He tried to tell his father the thing that he had felt that day. Penny listened gravely, and nodded, but Jody could not make the words fit his feeling, and could not quite make his father understand.

Chapter XIX

THE first week in September was as parched and dry as old bones. Only the weeds grew. There was a tension in the heat. The dogs were snappish. The snakes were crawling, dog days being past, and their shedding and their blindness ended. Penny killed a rattler under the grape arbor that measured seven feet in length. He had seen the coffee-weed shaking as though an alligator were passing through and had followed. The rattler, he said, was after the quail, to fill his long belly on his way to his winter quarters. He dried the great hide on the smoke-house wall and then hung it on the front-room wall beside the fireplace.

He said, "I like to look at it. I know there's one o' the boogers'll not harm nobody."

The heat was the worst of the whole summer, yet there was a vague change, as though the vegetation sensed the passing of one season and the coming of another. The golden-rod and asters and the deer-tongue thrived on the dryness. The pokeberries ripened and the birds fed on them along the fence-rows. All the creatures, Penny said, were hard put to it for food. The spring and summer berries, the brier-berries, the huckleberries, the blueberries and choke-berries and the wild gooseberries, were long since gone. The wild plum and the mayhaw had had no fruit for bird or beast for many a month. The 'coons and foxes had stripped the wild grape-vines.

The fall fruits were not yet ripe, papaw and gallberry and persimmon. The mast of the pines, the acorns of the oaks, the berries of the palmetto, would not be ready until the first frost. The deer were feeding on the tender growth, bud of sweet bay and of myrtle, sprigs of wire-grass, tips of arrowroot in the ponds and prairies, and succulent lily stems and pads. The type of food kept them in the low, wet places, the swamps, the prairies and the bay-heads. They seldom crossed Baxter's Island. They were hard to hunt in the boggy places. In a month, Penny was able only to bring down one yearling buck. Its spike horns were still in the velvet. They felt like a coarse rough wool. Shreds hung, where the yearling had rubbed them against saplings, to ease the itch of growth and hurry their hardening. Ma Baxter ate them boiled, saying they tasted like marrow. Penny and Jody had no taste for them. They could see too plainly the big eyes under the new horns.

The bears, too, were in the low places. They were feeding for the most on palmetto buds, ripping out the hearts ruthlessly. The palm hammock around Sweetwater Spring looked as though a hurricane had swept through it. The low-growing palmettos were slashed into ribbons, the sweet cream-colored cores eaten below the level of the ground. Even some of the tall palms looked as though struck by lightning, where a less lazy bear or a hungrier one had scaled the trunk and torn out the bud. The palmettos, Penny said, would die. They were like all living things. They could not live with the heart gone. One low palm had been only shredded from the outside. The heart was intact. Penny cut out the smooth cylinder with his hunting knife to carry home to cook. The Baxters liked swamp cabbage as well as the bears.

"But when them scapers runs short o' palmeeters," Penny said, "hit's look out for the shoats. You kin look to see the bears climbin' into the lot most ary night now. And your friend Flag here, you best keep him with you faithful, especial at night. I'll stand up to your Ma, do she quarrel about it."

"Ain't Flag gittin' too big for a bear to bother?"

"A bear'll kill ary creetur cain't out-run him. Why, on the prairie one year, a bear killed my bull, was nigh as big as he was. Hit made him a meal for a week. He come back to it 'til there wasn't nothin' left o' the bull but the beller, and that was gone, too."

Ma Baxter's complaint was at lack of rain. Her rain barrels were empty. All her washing must be done at the sink-hole. The clothes were looking dingy.

She said, "Clothes washes easier, anyways, on a cloudy day. My Ma allus said, 'Soft weather, soft clothes.'"

She needed rain-water, too, to clabber the milk. The milk turned rankly sour in the heat but would not clabber. In hot weather, she always depended on a few drops of rain-water to clabber it, and at every shower would send Jody to a hickory tree to catch some, for rain-water dripped from a hickory was best for the purpose.

The Baxters watched the quartering of the September moon anxiously. Penny called his wife and son when the first quarter appeared. The silver crescent was almost perpendicular. He was jubilant.

"We'll git rain soon, shore," he told them. "If the moon was straight acrost, hit'd push the water out and we'd not git none. But look at it. Hit'll rain to where you kin hang your clothes right on the line and the Lord'll wash 'em."

He was a good prophet. Three days later every sign was of rain. Passing by Juniper Springs from a hunt, he and Jody heard the alligators bellowing. Bats flew in the daytime. Frogs caah-caah-caahed steadily at night. The Dominick rooster crowed in the middle of the day. The jay-birds bunched and flew back and forth together, screaming as one. Ground rattlers crawled across the clearing in the hot sunny afternoon. On the fourth day a flock of white sea-birds flew over. Penny shaded his eyes against the sun and watched after them uneasily.

He said to Jody, "Now them ocean jessies don't belong to be crossin' Floridy. I don't like it. Hit means bad weather, and when I say bad, I mean bad."

Jody felt a lift of spirit like the sea-birds. He loved storm. It swept in magnificently and shut the family inside in a great coziness. Work was impossible and they sat about together and the rain drummed on the hand-hewn shingles. His mother was good-natured and made him syrup candy, and Penny told tales.

He said, "I hope it's a pure hurricane."

Penny turned on him sharply.

"Don't you wish sich as that. A hurricane flattens the crops and drowns the pore sailors and takes the oranges offen the trees. And down south, why, boy, hit tears down houses and cold-out kills people."

Jody said meekly, "I won't wish it agin. But wind and rain is fine."

"All right. Wind and rain. That's another thing."

The sun set strangely that night. The sunset was not red, but green. After the sun was gone, the west turned gray. The east filled with a light the color of young corn. Penny shook his head.

"I don't like it. Hit looks mighty boogerish."

In the night, a gust of wind moved through and slammed both doors. The fawn came to Jody's bed and poked its muzzle against his face. He took it up on the bed with him. The morning, however, was clear, but the east was the color of blood. Penny spent the morning repairing the roof of the smoke-house. He brought drinking water twice from the sink-hole, filling all available buckets. In the late morning, the sky turned gray and remained so. There was no air stirring.

Jody asked, "Is it a hurricane comin'?"

"I don't think. But somethin's comin', ain't natural."

In mid-afternoon the skies turned so black that the chickens went to roost. Jody drove in Trixie and the calf and Penny milked early. He turned old Cæsar into the lot and put a forkful of the last remaining hay in his manger.

Penny said, "Git the eggs outen the nests. I'm goin' to the house. Hurry now, else you'll git ketched."

The hens were not laying and there were only three eggs in the lot nests. Jody climbed into the corn-crib where the old Barred Rock was laying. The left-over husks rustled under his feet. The dry, sweet-scented air was close and thick. He felt stifled. There were two eggs in the nest and he put all five inside his shirt and started for the house. He had not felt the hurry that had infected his father. Suddenly, in the false twilight stillness, he took alarm. A great roaring sounded in the distance. All the bears in the scrub, meeting at the river, might make such a roaring. It was wind. He heard it come closer from the northeast as plainly as though it came on vast webbed feet, brushing the tree-tops in its passing. It seemed to leap the cornfield in one gust. It struck the yard trees with a hissing, and the mulberries bent their boughs to the ground, and the chinaberry creaked in its brittleness. It passed over him with a rustle like the wings of many geese, high-flying. The pines whistled. The rain followed.

The wind had been high overhead. The rain was a solid wall, from sky to earth. Jody struck it flat, as though he had dived against it from a great height. It hurled him back and threw him off his balance. A second wind seemed now to reach long muscular fingers through the wall of rain and scoop up everything in its path. It reached down his shirt and into his mouth and eyes and ears and tried to strangle him. He dared not drop the eggs in his shirt. He kept one arm cupped under them and put the other over his face and scuttled into the yard. The fawn was waiting, quivering. Its tail hung wet and flat and its ears drooped. It ran to him and tried to find shelter behind him. He ran around the house and to the back door. The fawn bounded close behind him. The kitchen door was latched. The wind and rain blew so hard against it that he could not swing it open. He beat on the thick pine. For a moment he thought he was unheard in the tumult and that he and the fawn would be left outside to drown, like biddies. Then Penny lifted the latch from the inside and pushed the door open into the storm. Jody and the fawn darted inside. Jody stood gasping. He wiped the water from his eyes. The fawn blinked.

Penny said, "Who was it, now, wishin' for sich as this?"

Jody said, "Did I git my wish this quick allus, I'd wish mighty keerful."

Ma Baxter said, "Go change them wet clothes right away now. Couldn't you of shut up that fawn before you come in?"

"There wasn't no time, Ma. He was wet and skeert."

"Well— Long as he don't do no mischief. Now don't put on your good breeches. You got a pair there, full o' holes as a cast-net, but they'll hold together in the house."

Penny said after him, "Don't he look like a wet yearlin' crane. All he needs is tail feathers. My, ain't he growed since spring."

She said, "I think he'll be right nice-lookin', do them freckles fade and that hair ever lay flat and them bones git covered with meat."

"A few more changes," he agreed innocently, "and he'll turn out handsome as the Baxters, thank the Lord."

She looked at him belligerently.

"And mebbe, handsome as the Alverses," he added.

"That makes more sense. You better change your tune."

"I got no idee o' startin' a ruckus, sweetheart, and you and me penned up together by no storm."

She chuckled with him. Jody, overhearing from his bed-room, could not tell whether they were making fun of him, or whether there was indeed hope for his appearance.

He said to Flag, "You think I'm purty, anyways, don't you?"

Flag butted him. He took it for assurance and they ambled back to the kitchen.

Penny said, "Well, hit's a three-day nor'easter. A mite early, but I've seed change o' season this early, many a year."

"How kin you tell it'll be three days, Pa?"

"I'd not sign no papers on it, but generally the first September storm be a three-day nor'easter. The whole country changes. I reckon, one way or t'other, the world. I've heered

The Yearling

Oliver Hutto tell o' September storm as fur off as Chnia."

Ma Baxter asked, "Why ain't he come to see us this time? Grandma shocks my modesty, but I do like Oliver."

"I reckon mebbe he's had enough o' the Forresters for a whiles and jest ain't travelin' this road."

"They'll not fight without he acts quarrelsome, will they? The fiddle cain't play without the bow."

"I'm feered the Forresters, leastwise Lem, 'll romp on him ary time they come up with him. Until they git the gal business settled."

"Sich doin's! Nobody acted that-a-way when I were a gal."

"No," Penny said, "I was the only one wanted you."

She lifted the broom in pretended threat.

"But sugar," he said, "the rest jest wasn't smart as me."

There was a lull in the fierce beating wind. A pitiful whine sounded at the door. Penny went to it. Rip had found adequate shelter, but old Julia stood drenched and shivering. Or perhaps she had found shelter, too, but longed for a comfort that was more than dryness. Penny let her in.

Ma Baxter said, "Now let in Trixie and old Cæsar, and you'll have things about to suit you."

Penny said to Julia, "Jealous o' leetle ol' Flag, eh? Now you've been a Baxter longer'n Flag. You jest come dry yourself."

She wagged her slow tail and licked his hand. Jody was warmed by his father's inclusion of the fawn in the family. Flag Baxter——

Ma Baxter said, "How you men kin take on over a dumb creetur, I cain't see. Callin' a dog by your own name— And that fawn, sleepin' right in the bed with Jody."

Jody said, "He don't seem like a creetur to me, Ma. He seems jest like another boy."

"Well, it's your bed. Long as he don't bring fleas or lice or ticks or nothin' into it."

He was indignant.

The Yearling

"Look at him, Ma. Lookit that sleekity coat. Smell him, Ma."

"I don't want to smell him."

"But he smells sweet."

"Jest like a rose, I s'pose. Well, to my notion, wet fur's wet fur."

"Now I like the smell o' wet fur," Penny said. "I mind me one time, on a long hunt, I had me no coat and the weather turned cold. It was over about Salt Springs, at the head o' the run. My, it was cold. And we shot a bear, and I dressed out the skin nice, and I slept under it, with the fur side out. And in the night come a cold drizzly rain, and I poked my nose out from under, and I smelt that wet fur. Now the other fellers, Noey Ginright and Bert Harper and Milt Revells, they said I purely stunk, but I puttened my head back under the bear-skin and I was warm as a squirrel in a holler tree, and that wet bear-hide smelt better to me than yellow jessamine."

The rain drummed on the roof. The wind whistled under the eaves. Old Julia stretched out on the floor near the fawn. The storm was as cozy as Jody had hoped for. He made up his mind privately that he would wish for another in a week or two. Now and then Penny peered out of the window into the dark.

"Hit's a toad-strangler of a rain," he said.

Supper was generous. There were cowpeas and smoked venison pie and biscuit pudding. Anything that was remotely an occasion stirred Ma Baxter to extra cooking, as though her imagination could speak only by the use of flour and shortening. She fed Flag a bit of pudding with her own fingers. Jody, with a secret gratitude, helped her wash and wipe the supper dishes. Penny went to bed shortly after, for his strength did not hold out, but not to sleep. A candle burned in the bedroom and Ma Baxter brought her piecing, and Jody lay across the foot of the bed. The rain hissed against the window.

212

The Yearling

He said, "Pa, tell me a tale."

Penny said, "I've told you all the tales I know."

"No, you ain't. You allus got another."

"Well, the only one comes to me I ain't told, ain't rightly a tale. I ever tell you about the dog I had when I first come to the island? The dog could cold-out study?"

Jody wriggled closer up the counterpane.

"Tell me."

"Well, sir, the dog was part fox-hound and part blood-hound and part jest dog. He had long sorrowful ears, nigh about dragged the ground, and he was so bow-legged he couldn't walk a sweet pertater bed. He had distant kind o' eyes, lookin' off some'eres, and them distracted eyes near about caused me to trade him off. Well, I hunted him a whiles, and it begun to come to me, he didn't act like no other dog I'd ever seed. He'd leave a cat-trail or a fox-trail right in the middle, and go lay down. The first time-two he done it, I figgered I jest didn't have me no dog a-tall.

"Well sir, it begun to come to me, he knowed what he was doin'. Jody boy, go fetch me my pipe."

The interruption was exasperating. Jody tingled. He scrambled for the pipe and tobacco.

"All right now, son. You set on the floor or on a chair and keep offen the bed. Ary time I say 'trail' or 'track' you jiggle the bed to where I think the slats is busted. That's better——

"Well, sir, I was obliged to set down with that dog my ownself, to see what 'twas he was doin'. Now you know how a wild-cat or a fox'll fool most dogs? He'll double back on his own tracks. Yes sir, he'll double back on his own tracks. He'll git a good start on the dogs and he'll light out and put a heap o' distance between 'em. Then what do he do? He turns right back over his own trail. He cuts as far back as he's daresome to do, listenin' all the while for the dogs. Then he cuts off at another angle, so a picture o' his trail'd look like a big V, like the ducks makes flyin'. Well, the dogs follers the trail he made in the first place, extry strong on account

213

of him havin' been over it twicet, and then they come to a place where they jest ain't no more trail. They nose around and they nose around and they complain, and when they jest cain't figger no sense to it, they turns back agin, back-trackin'. 'Course, they picks up then the turn-off where the fox or cat cut off in another direction. But all that time is wasted, and nine to one the cat or fox has made an out of it and got plumb away. Well, what do you figger this lop-eared dog o' mine done?"

"Tell me."

"He figgered it out, that's what he done. He figgered out about when 'twas time for the creetur to double back—and he'd slip back along the trail and lay down and wait. And when Mister Fox or Mister Cat come slippin' back, there was old Dandy waitin' to pop out on him.

"Now sometimes he'd make his cut-off too fur back, and did he hang them long ears when he guessed it wrong! But mostly speakin', he studied it out right, and he ketched me more wild-cats and more foxes than ary dog I've had, before or since."

He puffed his pipe. Ma Baxter moved her rocker closer to the candle. It was depressing to have the tale end so soon.

"What else did old Dandy do, Pa?"

"Well, one day he met his match."

"A cat or a fox?"

"Neither one. A big ol' buck, was as smart a deer as he was smart a dog. He was a buck with a twisted antler. Each year it growed in twisted. Now a deer don't generally double back on his tracks. But now and agin this old buck'd do it. And that was jest to this sly ol' dog's likin'. But this is where he wasn't smart enough. The buck'd do jest the opposite to whatever the dog figgered he'd do. One time he'd double back. Next time he'd keep on runnin.' He'd change his ways ever' whip-stitch. That went on, year in, year out, the dog and the buck tryin' to out-smart each other."

"Which was the smartest, Pa? How'd it end?"

"You shore you want the answer?"

He hesitated. He wanted the droopy-eared dog to out-smart the buck, and yet he wanted the buck to get away.

"Yes. I got to know. I got to know the answer."

"Well, hit's got a answer but no endin'. Old Dandy never come up with him."

He sighed with relief. That was a proper tale. When he thought of it again, he could picture the dog trailing the buck perpetually.

He said, "Tell another tale like that un, Pa. A tale has got a answer but no endin'."

"Now boy, they ain't many tales like that in the world. You best be content with that un."

Ma Baxter said, "I ain't much for dogs, but they was a dog oncet I takened a notion to. It was a bitch and she had the purtiest coat. I said to the feller owned her, 'When she finds pups,' says I, 'I'd like one.' He said, 'You're welcome, but 'twon't do, for you got no way o' huntin' it'—I wasn't yit married to your Pa—'and a hound'll die,' he said, 'if it ain't hunted.' 'Is she a hound?' says I, and he said, 'Yessum.' And I said, 'Then I shore don't want one, for a hound'll suck eggs.'"

Jody waited eagerly for the rest of the tale, then understood that was all there was to it. It was like all his mother's tales. They were like hunts where nothing happened. He went back in his thoughts to the dog that could out-smart wild-cats and foxes, but never caught the buck.

He said, "I'll bet Flag'll be smart when he grows up."

Penny said, "What'll you do, do somebody else's dogs take out after him?"

His throat constricted.

"I'll kill ary dog or ary man comes here, huntin' him. Nobody ain't likely to come, is they?"

Penny said gently, "We'll spread the word, so folks'll be keerful. He's not likely to roam far, no-how."

Jody decided to keep his gun always loaded, against marauders. He slept that night with Flag on the bed beside him. The wind shook the windowpanes all night and he slept uneasily, dreaming of clever dogs that ran the fawn mercilessly through the rain.

In the morning he found Penny dressed as for winter, in his heavy coat and with a shawl over his head. He was preparing to go out into the storm to milk Trixie, the only chore that was entirely necessary for the time being. There was no lessening of the torrential downpour.

Ma Baxter said, "Now you be peert and git back in here or you'll die o' the pneumony."

Jody said, "Leave me go," but Penny said, "The wind'd blow you away, boy."

It seemed to him, watching the small bones of his father leaning against the tumultuous air, that there was little to choose between them in bulk and sturdiness. Penny came in again, drenched and breathless, the milk in the gourd spotted by the rain.

He said, "Hit's a mercy I toted water yestiddy."

The day continued as stormy as it had begun. The rain fell in sheets and the wind whipped it in under the eaves, so that Ma Baxter set pans and gourds to catch it. The rain barrels outside were overflowing and the rain from the roof gurgled into their fullness. Old Julia and the fawn had to be turned out by force. They were both back at the kitchen door in a brief time, wet and shivering. This time Rip was with them, whining. Ma Baxter protested, but Penny admitted the three. Jody dried them all with the crocus sack rug from in front of the hearth.

Penny said, "We're about due for a lull."

The lull did not come. Now and then there seemed to be a few moments when the wind and rain were less intense and Penny rose hopefully from his chair and peered outside. But he had no sooner decided that he would risk going out to cut wood and see to the chickens, than the deluge came again, as violent as before. In the late afternoon he went again to milk Trixie, to feed and water Cæsar, and to feed the chickens, huddled and frightened and unable to scratch for their living. Ma Baxter made him change his wet clothes immediately. They steamed and dried by the hearth with the sweet, musty smell of wet cloth.

Supper was not so ample. Penny was not inclined to tales. The dogs were allowed to sleep in the house and the family went to bed early. Darkness had come at an unseemly hour and it was impossible to tell the time. Jody awakened at what would ordinarily have been an hour before daylight. The world was dark and the rain was still falling, the wind still blowing.

Penny said, "We'll git a break this mornin'. Hit's a three-day nor'easter a'right, but sich a rain. I'll be proud to see the sun."

The sun did not appear. There was no morning break. In mid-afternoon there came the lull that Penny had expected the day before. But it was a gray lull, the roof dripping, the trees soaked, the earth sodden. The chickens came out from their huddle for a few forlorn moments and scratched half-heartedly.

Penny said, "We'll git a change o' wind now, and all be clare and fine."

The change of wind came. The gray sky turned green. The wind roared in from a distance, as before. When it came, it was not from the northeast but from the southeast, and it brought more rain.

Penny said, "I've never seed sich a thing."

The rain was more torrential than before. It poured down as though Juniper Creek and Silver Glen Run and Lake George and the St. John's River had all emptied over the scrub at once. The wind was no fiercer than before, but it was gusty. And there was no end to it. It blew and rained and blew and rained and blew and rained.

Penny said, "This must be the way the Lord made the blasted ocean."

The Yearling

Ma Baxter said, "Hush. You'll be punished."

"Cain't be no worse punished, woman. The 'taters'll be rotted and the corn flat and the hay ruint, and the cane."

The yard was afloat. Jody looked out of the window and saw two drowned biddies floating about with upturned bellies.

Penny said, "I've seed things in my time, but I've never seed a thing like this."

Jody offered to go to the sink-hole for drinking water.

Penny said, "Hit'll be nothin' but rain-water, and riled to boot."

They drank rain-water from a pan under the northwest corner of the house. It had a faintly woody taste from the cypress shingles. Jody did the evening chores. He went out of the kitchen door with the milk gourd into a strange world. It was a lost and desolate world, like the beginning of time, or the end of it. The vegetation was beaten flat. A river ran down the road, so that a flat-bottomed boat could have gone down it clear to Silver Glen. The familiar pines were like trees at the bottom of the sea, washed across not with mere rain, but with tides and currents. It seemed to him that he might swim to the top of the rain. The water was knee-deep in the lot, which lay at a lower level than the house. Trixie had broken down the bars that separated her from the calf and had taken it with her to a high corner. They stood huddled together. The calf had taken most of the milk and he was able only to draw a quart or so from the drained udders. The passage between the stalls and the corn-crib was a sluiceway. He meant to gather the dry husks for extra feed for Trixie, but the water swept through so discouragingly that he decided to let her make out until morning with the hay from the loft. It was a good thing, he thought, that the new crop of hay would soon be ready. There was little left. He did not know whether to try to separate the overgrown calf from the cow again. There was no place to put it where it would be dry. Yet the Baxters needed the milk as

THE STORM

badly. He decided to wait and ask his father, coming back again if necessary. He fought his way outside and plodded to the house. The rain blinded him. The clearing seemed alien and unfriendly. He was glad to push open the door and to be again inside the house. The kitchen seemed safe and intimate. He made his report on conditions.

Penny said, "Best leave the calf stay with its mammy, a time like this. We kin make out without milk 'til mornin'. Hit'll shorely be clare by then."

Morning brought no abatement. Penny paced up and down the kitchen.

He said, "My daddy told of a storm in the '50's was mighty bad, but I don't reckon all Floridy history has had sich a rain."

The days passed with no change. Ma Baxter usually left the weather in Penny's hands, but now she cried, and sat rocking with her hands folded. On the fifth day, Penny and Jody made a rush to the pea-field to pull enough cow-peas for a meal or two. The peas were flattened. They pulled up the whole vines with their backs to the rain and wind. They stopped at the smoke-house for a piece of pickled meat from the bear Buck Forrester had shot on his last night with them. Penny remembered that his wife was short of cooking grease. They tipped the can that held the golden bear grease and filled a stone crock. They laid the meat over the top to protect it and rushed for the house.

The cow-peas were already moulding on the outside, but the peas inside were still firm and good. Supper was again a feast. There was the wild honey to fall back on, and Ma Baxter made a pudding sweetened with its rich flavor, tasting faintly of wood and smoke.

Penny said, "Don't seem possible it'll not clare by mornin', but if so be 'tain't, Jody, you and me had best git out in it and pull as many peas as we kin manage."

Ma Baxter said, "But how'll I keep 'em?"

"Cook 'em, woman, and warm 'em ever' day, if need be."

The Yearling

The morning of the sixth day was exactly like the others. Since they would be drenched in any case, Penny and Jody stripped to their breeches and went to the field with sacks. They worked until noon in the down-pour, pulling the slippery pods from the bushes. They came in for a hurried dinner and went back again without troubling to change their clothes. They covered most of the field. The hay, Penny said, was a total loss, but they would do what they could to save the peas. Some of the pods were mature. They spent the evening and late into the night shelling the peas, sticky and mouldering. Ma Baxter built up a slow fire on the hearth and spread out the peas close to the heat to dry. Jody was awakened several times in the night by the sound of some one going out to the kitchen to replenish the fire.

The morning of the seventh day might have been the morning of the first. The gusty wind whipped around the house as though it had always blown and always would blow. The sound of the rain on the roof and in the rain-barrels was now so familiar that it was not noticed. At daylight, a limb of the chinaberry crashed to the ground. The Baxters sat silently at breakfast.

Penny said, "Well, Job takened worse punishment than this. Leastways none of us ain't got risin's."

Ma Baxter snapped, "Find the good in it, that's right."

"They ain't no good in it. Lest it is to remind a man to be humble, for there's nary thing on earth he kin call his own."

After breakfast he took Jody to the cornfield. The corn had been broken on the stalks before the storm. The stalks were beaten to the ground but the ears were unharmed. They gathered them and brought them too into the warm dry refuge of the kitchen.

Ma Baxter said, "I ain't got the peas dried yit. How'll I dry all this?"

Penny did not answer but went to the front room and kindled a fire on the hearth. Jody went outside to bring in more wood. The wood was soaked through, but when the

The Yearling

fat-wood was heated a little while it would burn. Penny strewed the ears of corn on the floor.

He said to Jody, "Now your job be to keep changin' it, so's it'll all git a mite o' the heat."

Ma Baxter said, "How's the cane?"

"Hit's flat."

"What you reckon has happened to the 'taters?"

He shook his head. In the late afternoon he went to the sweet potato field and dug enough for supper. They were beginning to rot. By trimming, some were usable. Again, supper seemed lavish, because of the sweet potatoes.

Penny said, "If they ain't no change by mornin', we jest as good to quit fightin' and lay down and die."

Jody had never heard his father speak so disconsolately. It froze him through. Flag was showing the effect of short rations. His ribs and backbone were visible. He bleated often. Penny had given up all attempt to milk the cow, for the sake of the calf.

In the middle of the night Jody awakened and thought he heard his father about. It seemed to him the rain was falling less violently. He was asleep again before he could be certain. He awakened on the morning of the eighth day. Something was different. There was silence instead of tumult. The rain had stopped. The long winds were still. A light the color of pomegranate blossoms sifted through the gray, wet atmosphere. Penny flung all the doors and windows wide open.

" 'Tain't much of a world to go out to," he said, "but let's all go out and be thankful there's a world at all."

The dogs pushed past him and bounded out side by side. Penny smiled.

"Dogged if 'tain't like goin' outen the Ark," he said. "The animals two by two— Ory, come go out with me."

Jody jumped about and leaped down the steps with the fawn.

"We're the two deer," he called.

The Yearling

Ma Baxter looked across the fields and began to cry again. But the air, Jody felt, was cool and sweet and gracious. The fawn shared his feeling and bounded over the yard-gate with swift twinkling heels. The world was devastated with the flood, but it was indeed, as Penny kept reminding his wife, the only world they had.

Chapter XX

HE second day after the storm, Buck and Mill-wheel Forrester came riding to the island to see whether all was well with the Baxters. They had come straight from their own work of caring for the stranded stock. Along the main trail the sights, they said, were new in their generation. The flood had played havoc with the small animals. It was agreed that the four of them, Buck and Mill-wheel and Penny and Jody, should make a tour of exploration for some miles around, so that they might know what to expect, in the immediate future, of the movements not only of the game, but of the predatory creatures. The Forresters had brought two dogs, and an extra horse, and asked to have Rip and Julia join them. Jody was excited that he was to be taken.

He asked, "Kin Flag foller along, too?"

Penny turned on him sharply.

"This here is serious," he said. "I'm carryin' you with us to learn you. If you figger on frolickin', you kin stay home, too."

Jody hung his head. He slipped away and shut Flag in the shed. The sand floor was still soaked and the shed smelled musty, but he made a bed of crocus sacks where the fawn might keep dry. He put out water and feed for it in case he should be long away.

"You stay quiet," he said to it, "and I'll tell you all I see when I come home agin."

The Forresters were well stocked, as always, with ammunition. Penny had spent two evenings during the storm in making low-mould shot and in loading his own shells. He had a month's supply filled and capped and ready for use. He filled his shot-bag and polished the barrels of his gun.

He said to the Forresters, "Now I worked a rabbit's-foot on you fellers about that wuthless dog I traded you. Ary time you crave to use this gun, you say so."

Buck said, "Ain't none of us but Lem mean enough to take it back, Penny. I'll swear, he got so mean, cooped up in the storm, I had to dress him down myself."

"Where's he now?"

Buck spat.

"Gone off to the river, fretted about harm comin' to that tormented gal Twink. Figgerin' on makin' it up with her, and layin' for Oliver. He kin fight it out by hisself this time."

It was decided to make a wide circle that would take in both Baxter's and Forresters' Islands, Juniper Springs, Hopkins Prairie, and the good deer territory where the live oak islands that lifted from the marshy saw-grass would certainly have provided refuge for the animals. With the exception of a rolling ridge to the west, toward the Ocklawaha River, the Baxter's Island terrain was the highest in the scrub. But it dropped down all around to low land, and the circle they had mapped out would tell the story. They would try to return to Forresters' Island to sleep, but if that was not practicable they would camp wherever night found them. Penny filled a knapsack carefully. He put in a frying pan, salt, meal, a side of bacon and a twist of tobacco. In a crocus sack he put a handful of lighter'd splinters, a bottle of thin lard, and a bottle of panther oil which he treasured for his rheumatism. The exposure during the days of storm had brought his aches on him with vicious force. He had no meat for the dogs.

Buck said, "We kin shoot somethin' for 'em."

They were ready at last. They swung into the saddles and set off briskly south-east down the road in the direction of Silver Glen and Lake George.

Penny said, "Long as we're this clost, we best go see how

ol' Doc Wilson come out. That place o' his is like to be half under water."

Buck said, "And him mebbe too drunk to know it."

The road dipped sharply between Baxter's Island and Silver Glen. The flood had washed down it with such volume and such force that the flat sand road was now a narrow ravine. Rubbish of all sorts was caught in the lower branches of the close-growing scrub pines. Farther down the road the toll of small animal life began to show. Skunks and 'possums seemed the heaviest sufferers. Their bodies lay by dozens on the ground, where the waters, receding, had deposited them, or hung with the trash in the limbs of trees. To the south and east there was a great silence. The scrub was always silent, yet Jody realized now that there had always been an undertone of cry and movement, where the creatures called and stirred, no more discernible than the wind. To the north, where high scrub land was dense with thin pines, there was an unusual rustling and distant chattering. The squirrels had evidently taken up residence here in droves, driven, if not by water, at least by hunger and fear, from the swamps and hammocks below them.

Penny said, "I'll bet that scrub there is purely alive with creeturs."

They hesitated, tempted to go in to the denseness. They agreed that it was best, as first planned, to skirt the low regions and determine the damage, and then to check on the still living creature population. Toward Silver Glen they reined in the horses.

"You see what I see?"

"If you didn't see it, too, I'd not believe it."

Silver Glen had overflowed and backed up, and the flood waters had rushed down to join it and make a greater havoc. Dead animals drifted about in the backwash.

Penny said, "I didn't know there was that many snakes in the world."

The bodies of highland reptiles were as thick as cane-stalks. There were dead rattlesnakes, king snakes, black snakes, coach whips, chicken snakes, garter snakes and coral snakes. At the thin edge of the receding water, cottonmouth moccasins and other water snakes swam about thickly.

Buck said, "I don't understand that. Ary snake kin swim. I've met a rattler in the middle o' the river."

Penny said, "Yes, but the land snakes likely got ketched in their holes."

The flood had reached everywhere, like the searching fingers of a 'coon, and had torn out all the things for whom the solid earth was their only refuge. A fawn lay dead with swelling belly. Jody's heart jumped. Flag might have perished in just this fashion, if he had not become, in time, a Baxter. As they gaped, two rattlers slithered across the ground in front of them. The rattlers ignored them, as though in the face of greater dangers man was of no concern.

Penny said, "Hit'll be all a man's life is wuth, for a while, to cross high land."

Buck said, "I mean."

They could go no farther east and turned north, skirting the low waters. Where there had been swamp, there were ponds. Where there had been hammock, there was swamp. Only the high infertile scrub had turned aside the devastation. Even here, pines were up-rooted, and those that had stood, all leaned to the west, bowed down by the week-long weight of wind and rain.

Penny said, "Hit'll be a long day before them trees stands straight agin."

They became uneasy as they approached the Branch. The water was still high here, well above the level of Lake George. Three and four days ago it must have been much higher. They stopped and stared down at the doctor's land, sloping to the lake. The thick hammock might have been a cypress slough. The giant live oaks, the hickories, the sweet gums, the magnolias, the orange trees, stood deep in a turgid wetness.

The Yearling

Penny said, "Let's try the road."

The road, like the one leading southeast from Baxter's Island, had formed a sluiceway for the waters. It was now a gully, and dry. They rode down it. Doc Wilson's house appeared ahead, dark and shadowy under the great trees.

Buck said, "I'll be blest if I see why ary man would choose a place this dark to live in, even to stay drunk."

Penny said, "If ever'body loved the same places, we'd be right over-crowded."

Water stood ankle-deep around the house. The blocks on which it rested showed that the water had at one time been over the floor. The boards of the broad veranda were warping. They waded to the front steps, eyes open warily for coiled moccasins. A white pillow-slip was tacked across the front door. A message was printed on it with ink. The ink had run but the letters were plain.

Buck said, "Us Forresters cain't read good. Read it, Penny."

Penny spelled out the liquid words.

"I have gone toward the ocean where this much water ain't so peculiar. I mean to stay drunk until the storm is over. I will be somewhere between here and the ocean. Please don't come after me unless it's a broke neck or a baby. Doc. P.S. If it's a broke neck no use anyway."

Buck and Mill-wheel and Penny shouted, and Jody laughed because they did.

Buck said, "That Doc, he'd crack him a joke right in the Lord's face."

Penny said, "That's why he's a good doctor."

"How come?"

"Well, he gits to fool the Lord now and agin."

They laughed until they were weak. It was good to be light-hearted, when the world had been gray and heavy so long. They went inside the house and found a tin of crackers and a bottle of whiskey on the table and added them to their stores. They turned back up the road and went north for a mile or so, then west again.

Penny said, "No use goin' to Hopkins Parairie. We kin figger hit's a pure lake."

Buck and Mill-wheel agreed. South of Hopkins Prairie they found the same story. The weaker animals and the ground creatures had been washed down to destruction. At the edge of a bay-head, a bear lumbered across in plain sight.

Penny said, "No use shootin' him. We may need his meat a month from now. Hit's too fur to tote him and we'll git many a shot before night-fall."

The Forresters agreed reluctantly. A shot to them was a shot, whether or no they could use the game. Penny would shoot nothing for which he could not see a use. He preferred even to kill the enemy bears at a time when their flesh was welcome and usable. They continued west. Here was a long stretch of gallberry flats that in good weather was the favorite haunt of bear and wolf and panther. The ground was always boggy, the vegetation low, and bay-heads to the north and east gave both food and a hiding place. Now the section was a swamp. Water drained off quickly from a sand soil, but where the earth was heavy, it remained as on clay. Islands of scrub oak and live oak, and a few high palm hammocks, lay between the flats and the broad stretch of the scrub itself. They skirted the new-made swamp and made for these.

At first Jody could see nothing. Then when Penny pointed to this tree and that, he was able to make out the forms of animals. They rode close. The creatures seemed unafraid. A fine buck stared at them. The shot was irresistible. Buck brought it down. They rode closer. Wild-cats and lynxes peered visibly from the branches of trees. The Forresters urged their killing.

Penny said, "Hit's a pity we should add to their troubles.

The Yearling

Seems like there'd ought to be room enough in the world for folks and creeturs, both."

Mill-wheel said, "Trouble with you, Penny, you was raised by a preacher. You look for the lion and the lamb to be layin' down together."

Penny pointed to the high earth ahead of them.

"Well," he said, "the deer and the bob-cat—there you be."

But he was forced to agree that every wild-cat on the loose, every bear, lynx, wolf or panther, meant depredations on hogs, chickens and cattle, and on the milder game, the deer, the 'coons, the squirrels and the 'possums. It seemed to make an endless circle of "Eat or be eaten. Kill or go hungry."

He joined in the attack on the great cats and six fell killed or wounded. Jody brought down a lynx. The recoil of the old muzzle-loader all but knocked him from Cæsar's rump. He dismounted to reload. The Forresters patted him on the back. The men dressed the buck. The meat was lean, showing the week of privation. They flung the carcass over the rump of Buck's horse. They went forward on foot to the oak island. Dim forms scurried at the far side. It was eery, hearing the rustling of creatures, seeing the skulking.

The hides of the wild-cats were poor and not worth saving.

Penny said, "Now them carcasses'd make a fine dinner for the dogs, and easy carried."

The dogs were already chewing on the haunches of the cats. They too had been underfed through the storm. The cat-meat was dressed out and slung over the horses. Mid-afternoon found the exploring party due north and a little west of Forresters' Island. They decided that it was best to continue, and camp out for the night. For an hour or two the sun was strong. A putrid odor began to rise from the wet earth and from the waters. Jody felt a little ill.

Buck said, "I'm proud Fodder-wing ain't here right now. He'd hate it, all these creeturs dead."

Bears began to be seen again. The wolves were not in evidence, nor the panthers. They rode through several miles of scrub. Deer and squirrels were plentiful here. Probably they had never left, feeling secure. They were all bold and plainly hungry. The Forresters, greedy, and anxious as well that both families should surely have meat, shot another buck and slung it over Mill-wheel's horse.

Toward sunset, the scrub dissolved again into live oak islands. Farther south was Juniper Prairie. That would now be flooded. A little to the east lay a stretch of land that was neither scrub nor prairie, neither island nor swamp nor hammock. It was as open as a clearing. It was agreed to camp here for the night, even though an hour or two of daylight remained. No one was of a mind to be caught in the low places, malodorous and crawling with reptiles. They made camp under two giant long-leaf pines. There was not much protection overhead, but the night would be clear, and it was better under such unnatural circumstances to be in the open.

Mill-wheel said, "When I bed with a panther, I crave for that panther to be dead."

They turned the horses loose with dropped reins to graze before tethering them for the night. Mill-wheel had disappeared into a patch of scrub oak south of the camp site. The others heard him shout. The dogs had followed him on one of the endless trails that had enchanted them all day. They were moving slowly, tired out from the abundance of scent and track. Old Julia lifted her voice.

Penny said, "That's cat."

Wild-cats had lost their zest. All four dogs were baying, their voices ranging from a high keening to the bass rumble of Rip. Mill-wheel shouted again.

Penny said, "Don't you Forresters ever git a bait o' wild-cats?"

Buck said, "Now he'd not holler that-a-way over no wild-cat."

230

The Yearling

The dogs' voices lifted into a frenzy. Penny and Jody and Buck became infected with the sound and ran into the thick growth. A scrub oak had grown to considerable size. Half-way up its gray twisted trunk they saw the quarry. It was a female panther with two cubs. She was lean and gaunt but of immense length. The cubs still wore the blue and white spots of panther infancy across their hides. Jody thought they were prettier than any kittens he had ever seen. They were the size of grown house-cats. They lifted back their delicate whiskers in imitation of their mother's snarl. Her appearance was formidable. Her teeth were bared, her long tail switched back and forth, her claws worked on the oak limb. She seemed about to drop on the first creature, man or dog, to move closer. The dogs were wild.

Jody called out, "I want the cubs! I want the cubs!"

Mill-wheel said, "Let's knock her out and leave the dogs have a go-round."

Penny said, "We'll have four tore-up dogs if you do."

Buck said, "You mighty right. We best drop her and be done with it." He shot.

The dogs were on her the instant she hit the ground. If there was a spark of life, it was at once snuffed out. Buck climbed up the low tree and shook the limb.

Jody called again, "I want the cubs."

He planned, when they dropped, to run to them and pick them up. He was sure they would be gentle. They fell finally under Buck's vigorous shaking. Jody darted in but the dogs were ahead of him. The cubs were dead, and shaken and tossed, before he could approach them. Yet in their dying, he saw that they slashed at the dogs and bit and clawed. He would have had ragged flesh, he realized, to show for his seizing of them. Yet he wished they were still alive.

Penny said, "Sorry, boy. But you'd not have had nothin' you'd of keered to keep. Them scapers learns meanness early."

Jody eyed the small fierce teeth.

"Kin I have the hides for another knapsack?"

"Why, sho'. Here, Buck, he'p me git 'em away from the dogs before they're tore up."

Jody took the limp bodies and cradled them.

"I hate things dyin'," he said.

The men were silent.

Penny said slowly, "Nothin's spared, son, if that be ary comfort to you."

" 'Tain't."

"Well, hit's a stone wall nobody's yit clumb over. You kin kick it and crack your head agin it and holler, but nobody'll listen and nobody'll answer."

Buck said, "Well, when it come my time, I shore aim to git my money's wuth hollerin'."

They called the dogs away from the dead panther. She measured nine feet from tip of nose to the end of long curled tail. She was too lean, however, to dress out for her oil.

Penny said, "I got to either ketch me a fat panther or quit havin' rheumatism."

The hide too was in poor condition. They cut away the heart and liver to roast for the dogs.

Penny said, "No use nussin' them cubs no longer, Jody. Give 'em here and go fetch wood. I'll skin 'em out for you."

He went away. The evening was clear and rosy. The sun was drawing water. Shadowy fingers reached through the luminous sky to the sodden earth. The wet leaves of the scrub oaks, the thin needles of the pines, glittered, and he forgot his distress. There was much to be done to make camp. All wood was wet, but, prowling about, he found a fallen pine whose core was rich with resin. He called, and Buck and Mill-wheel came and dragged it bodily to the camp site. It would make a burning base to dry out the other wood. They chopped it in half and laid the two long pieces side by side. Jody struggled with flint and steel from the tinder horn un-

til Penny took it away from him and kindled a fire between
the logs with fat-wood splinters. He piled on small brush
that caught fire quickly. Larger limbs and logs were added.
They smoked and smoldered but ended by bursting into
flame. Now there was a glowing bed on which the wettest
logs might dry, and then burn slowly. Jody dragged in all
available wood that was not too heavy to handle alone. He
had a high pile ready for the night's long burning. Buck and
Mill-wheel dragged in logs as big as themselves.

Penny cut out the backstraps from the fattest buck and
sliced them for frying for supper. Mill-wheel appeared from
a prowl with palmetto fronds to be used as plates, for laying
out the food, and other camp means of tidiness. He had as
well the hearts of two palms. He pulled away layer after
layer of the white cores and came at last to the hearts, crisp
and sweet.

He said, "Now I want that fryin' pan, Mr. Penny, please,
for my swamp cabbage. Then I'll leave you fry that backstrap when I'm done with the pan."

He sliced the palm-hearts thinly.

"Where's the grease, Penny?"

"In a bottle in the crocus sack."

Jody ambled about, watching the others. His job was to
feed the fire with twigs to keep the flame from dying too low.
The logs blazed brightly. There were already embers suitable for roasting. Buck whittled forked sticks on which each
could roast his meat. Mill-wheel dipped water from a nearby
pond for his pan of swamp cabbage, covered it with a section of palm-frond and set it over the coals to cook.

Penny said, "Now I forgot coffee."

Buck said, "Well, with ol' Doc Wilson's whiskey, I'll not
miss it."

He brought out the bottle and passed it. Penny was ready
for the frying pan for his venison, but the swamp cabbage
was not done. He improvised spits on which he hung the
wild-cat carcasses. He sliced the wild-cat and panther hearts

233

and livers and stuck them on sticks and propped them over the coals to roast. The smell was enticing. Jody sniffed the air and sniffed again and patted his flat stomach. Penny sliced the deer livers and placed them more carefully on Buck's forked sticks and gave each man his own toasting fork to hold, to cook his meat to his own taste. The flames licked around the dog-meat and the odor brought in the dogs. They came close and lay flat and slapped their tails back and forth and whined. Raw cat-meat was not too much to their fancy. They had gnawed a bit on it by way of proving their victory. The roasted flesh was another thing. They licked their chops.

Jody said, "I'll bet that's good."

"Well, try it." Penny withdrew a portion from the fire and held it out to him. "Look out. It's hotter'n stewed apples."

He hesitated over the strangeness, then touched his finger to the hot savory meat and put his finger in his mouth.

He said, " 'Tis good."

The men laughed, but he ate two slices.

Penny said, "Now some folks'd say hit'd make you fearless, eatin' wild-cat liver. We'll jest see."

Buck said, "Dogged if it don't smell fine. Give a mite here."

He sampled it and agreed that it was as good as any other liver. Mill-wheel ate a portion then but Penny refused.

"If I was to git any braver," he said, "I'd be rompin' on you Forresters and gittin' Hell beat out o' me agin."

They passed the bottle once more. The fire blazed, the meat dripped its juices into the flames, the fragrance eddied up with the smoke. The sun set behind the scrub oaks and Mill-wheel's swamp cabbage was done. Penny emptied it on a clean palm frond and put it over a smoldering log to keep warm. He wiped out the frying pan with a handful of moss and set it back over the coals to heat. He sliced bacon into it. When the bacon was brown and the fat sizzling hot,

234

he fried the thin slices of backstrap crisp and tender. Buck cut scoops from the palm stems and every one dipped, share and share alike, into the swamp cabbage. Penny made hush-puppies of meal and salt and water and fried them in the fat the venison had cooked in.

Buck said, "Now if I knowed they'd feed you this good in Heaven, I'd not holler when I die."

Mill-wheel said, "Rations tastes a heap better in the woods. I'd ruther eat cold bread in the woods than hot puddin' in the house."

"Now you know," Penny said, "the same dog bit me."

The cat-meat was done. They cooled it a little and threw it to the dogs. The dogs bolted it greedily, then went to the pond to drink. They prowled about for a time, excited by the varying scents, then returned to lie by the blazing camp-fire in the increasing chill of the evening. Buck and Mill-wheel and Jody had stuffed. They dropped flat on their backs and stared up into the sky.

Penny said, "Flood or no flood, this is fine. I want you fellers to promise me one thing. When I'm an old man, set me on a stump and leave me listen to the hunt. Don't go off and leave me in the bay."

Stars twinkled, the first in nine days. Penny stirred at last to clean up the debris. He tossed the dogs the left-over corn-meal patties. He put the corncob stopper back in the bottle of fat. He held it up to the firelight. He shook it.

He said, "I'll be blasted. We've et my rubbin' medicine."

He pawed in the crocus sack and brought out the other bottle and opened it. It held unmistakably the lard-oil.

"Mill-wheel, you jay-bird. You opened the panther oil for the swamp cabbage."

There was silence. Jody felt his stomach turn over.

Mill-wheel said, "How'd I know 'twas panther oil?"

Buck swore under his breath. Then he burst into a thunderous laughter.

"I ain't goin' to let my imagination quarrel with what

goes in my belly," he said. "I never et better swamp cabbage."

"Nor me," Penny said. "But when my bones gits to achin', I'll wish 'twas back where it come from."

Buck said, "Anyways, we know what to use for grease when we git ketched in the woods."

Jody's stomach quieted. After two slices of wild-cat liver, it would be poor business to be squeamish. But the panther oil did seem different, after having seen Penny rub it on his knees on winter evenings.

Mill-wheel said, "Well, I'll cut ever'body boughs for beds, long as I'm the one's in disgrace."

Penny said, "I'll come with you. If I was to go to sleep and raise up and see you in the bushes, I'd figger 'twas a bear, shore. I'll swear, I don't see how some o' you fellers growed so big."

Mill-wheel said, "Why, hell, we was raised on panther oil."

Every one went in high humor to cut his own bed. Jody broke small pine boughs with the needles on them and gathered moss for a mattress. They laid the pallets close to the fire. The Forresters lay down on their boughs with a crashing sound.

Penny said, "Now I'll bet ol' Slewfoot don't make that much fuss when he lays down."

Buck said, "And I'll bet you kin hear a June bird goin' to bed a heap further'n one o' you Baxters."

Mill-wheel said, "I wisht I had me a sack o' corn shucks now for a mattress."

Penny said, "The best bed I ever had was one made o' the fluff from cat-tail rushes. Hit were like lyin' on a cloud. But it takened a time to gather enough cat-tails."

Buck said, "The best bed in all the world is a feather bed."

Penny said, "Ary one ever tell you fellers about the time your daddy raised pure hell with a feather bed?"

"Tell it."

"Hit were before you were borned. Mebbe two-three of you was back in the house some'eres in cradles. I were jest a leetle ol' young un myself. I come over to your island with my own daddy. Reckon mebbe he come to try to give your Pa salvation. When he was young, your Pa was wilder'n you-all. He could tip a jug o' corn liquor back and drink it down like water. And he done so, in them days, right frequent. Well, we rode up to your door and here was broke dishes and rations all strowed down the walk, and chairs pitched over the gate. And all over the yard, and all along the fence row, was feathers. Looked as if chicken Heaven had done blowed up. Layin' on the stoop was the tickin' o' the feather bed where it had been split open with a knife.

"Your daddy come to the gate. Now I won't say he was drunk, but he shore had done been drunk. He'd tore up ever'thing had takened his eye. And the last thing he noticed was the feather bed. Now he wa'n't mad nor quarrelin'. He was jest havin' him a big time crackin' things open. He'd got all over it, and was peaceful and happy as could be. Now what your Ma was doin' and sayin' whilst he was at it, you'd know better'n me. But right now she was still, and cold as ice. She was settin' rockin' with her hands folded and her mouth like a steel trap. My daddy had sense, if he was a preacher, and I reckon he figgered another time'd be best for whatever 'twas he'd come to say. So he jest passed the time o' day and set out to ride on agin.

"Well, your Ma come to and remembered her manners and called out to him. 'Stay eat with us, Mr. Baxter,' she said. 'I got nothin' left to offer you but corn-pone and honey. If I kin find a whole plate for you to eat on.'

"Your Pa turned and looked at her, surprised.

" 'Honey,' he said, 'honey, is there any honey in the honey-jug?' "

The Forresters shouted and slapped each other.

Buck said, "Wait 'til I walk in and ask Ma, 'Honey, is there any honey in the honey-jug?' Oh, wait!"

The Yearling

Jody laughed to himself long after the Forresters were quiet. His father made a story so real, he could see the feathers still, blown against the split-rail fence. The dogs, roused by the laughter, stirred and changed their positions. They had edged close for the warmth of the humans and of the fire. Old Julia lay at his father's feet. He wished Flag were with him, to snuggle close with his smooth warm coat. Buck rose and pulled another log on the fire. The men began to talk of the probable movements of the scrub and swamp animals. The wolves were evidently moving in another direction from the rest of the animals. They disliked wet sections even more than the big cats and were no doubt in the heart of the high scrub. Bear had not been as plentiful as expected.

Buck said, "You know where the bears be? South in the scrub around Sellers Bear Hole and Squaw Pond Bear Hole."

Mill-wheel said, "Tollie's Hammock, I'll bet you, toward the river."

Penny said, "They'll not be south. The wind and rain the last days all come from the southeast. They'd put it behind 'em, not go into it."

Jody put his arms under his head and looked up into the sky. It was as thick with stars as a pool of silver minnows. Between the two tall pines over him, the sky was milky, as though Trixie had kicked a great bucket of milk foaming across the heavens. The pines swayed back and forth in a light cool breeze. Their needles were washed with the silver of the starlight. Smoke from the camp-fire eddied up and joined the stars. He watched it drift through the pine tops. His eyelids fluttered. He did not want to go to sleep. He wanted to listen. The hunting talk of men was the finest talk in the world. Chills went along his spine to hear it. The smoke against the stars was a veil drawn back and forth across his eyes. He closed them. For a moment the talk of the men was a deep droning against the snapping of the wet wood. Then it faded into the sound of the breeze in the pines, and was no longer sound, but the voiceless murmur of a dream.

He was awakened in the night by his father, sitting bolt upright. Buck and Mill-wheel were snoring heavily. The fire had died low. The wet wood was sizzling slowly. He sat up beside Penny.

Penny whispered, "Listen."

Far in the night an owl hooted and a panther screamed. There was a closer sound. It sounded like the air dying from a bellows.

"Whoo—oo—. Whoo—oo—oo. Whoo—oo—oo."

It seemed almost at their feet. Jody's flesh crept. It might be Fodder-wing's Spaniard. Were ha'nts susceptible, like mortals, he wondered, to flood and rain? Did they yearn to warm their thin transparent hands at a hunter's camp-fire? Penny eased himself to his feet and fumbled for a pine knot for a torch. He lit it at the fire and started forward cautiously. The sighing sound had ceased. Jody followed close behind him. There was a rustling. Penny swung the torch. A pair of eyes, red as a bull-bat's, caught the light. He shifted the light. He laughed. The visitor was an alligator from the pond.

He said, "He smelt the fresh meat. Now wouldn't I love to drop him on top o' them Forresters."

Jody said, "Was it him, makin' that sighin'?"

"It were him, breathin' and blowin' and raisin' hisself up and down."

"Let's torment Buck and Mill-wheel with him."

Penny hesitated.

"He's a mite big for funnin'. He'll go six feet. If he was to take a chunk outen one of 'em, hit'd be a sorry joke."

"Will we kill him?"

"No use. We'll be gittin' meat for the dogs and to spare. 'Gators is harmless things."

"You goin' to leave him blow around all night?"

"No, for he'd quit blowin' and go to huntin' that meat he smells."

The Yearling

Penny made a rush at the alligator. It lifted its body on its short legs and turned back toward the pond. Penny ran after it, stopping to pick up sand or whatever came under his hand to throw after it. It ran with amazing speed. Penny followed, and Jody behind him, until a splash sounded at some distance.

"There. He's back with his kin folks. Now do he be polite enough to stay there, we'll not bother him."

They turned back to the camp-fire. It glowed comfortingly in the darkness. The midnight was still. The stars were so bright that when they looked away from the fire, they could see the water shining in the ponds. The air was cool. Jody wished that he could camp always like this, with his father. All that he lacked was Flag beside him. Penny moved the torch across the Forresters. Buck threw his arm across his face, but slept on. Mill-wheel was flat on his back. His black beard lifted and fell with his heavy breathing.

"He blows near about as deep as a 'gator," Penny said.

They piled more wood on the fire and returned to their pallets. They did not seem as comfortable as when they had first lain down on them. They shook up the moss and tried to flatten the pine boughs. Jody made a nest for himself in the middle and curled up kitten-wise. He lay a few luxurious moments watching the fresh blaze, then fell into a sleep as deep as the first.

The dogs were the first to awaken at daybreak. A fox had crossed under their noses, leaving its rank taint fresh on the air. Penny jumped up and caught them and tied them.

"We got bigger business today than fox," he told them.

From where he lay, Jody could look straight across into the sunrise. It was strange to see it on a level with his face. At home the thick scrub growth beyond the cleared fields obscured it. Now there was only a morning fog between. The sun did not seem to rise, but to sweep forward through a gray curtain. The curtain began to part its folds for the passing. The light was the thin pale gold of his mother's

240

wedding ring. It grew brighter and brighter until he found himself blinking into the very face of the sun. The light September fog clung tenaciously a little while to the tops of the trees, as though resisting the tearing and destructive fingers of the sun. Then it too was gone and the whole east was the color of ripe guavas.

Penny called, "I need somebody to he'p find the panther oil so I kin cook breakfast."

Buck and Mill-wheel sat up. They were stiff from their heavy sleep.

Penny said, "The 'gators and the foxes has been runnin' right acrost you fellers."

He told of the night's encounter.

Buck said, "You shore 'twasn't one o' them swamp skeeters you seed, after Doc Wilson's liquor?"

"A foot less, and I'd say mebbe. But not scarcely six feet."

"Oh, yes. Why, I went to sleep on a camp like this oncet, and I dreamed I heered a skeeter buzzin', and when I waked up, here was me and my bed both, hangin' up on a snag in a cypress swamp."

Penny called Jody to wash his face and hands at the pond's edge. When they reached the water, the stench turned them back.

Penny said comfortably, "Well, our dirt is nothin' but wood-smoke. Even your Ma wouldn't make you wash in that kind o' water."

Breakfast was the same as supper, except that there was no more swamp cabbage with panther oil. Again the Forresters substituted a draught of whiskey for the missing coffee. Penny refused it. The pond water was not fit to drink and Jody was thirsty. In a world so full of water, it had occurred to no one to carry it.

Penny said, "You watch for a holler log is well off the ground, and has rain water in it. Rain water's allus fitten."

The fried and roasted venison and the hush-puppies did not taste as good as the night before. Penny cleaned up after breakfast. Grazing for the horses had been poor because the grasses were beaten flat. Jody gathered armfuls of moss for them and they ate it with relish. Breaking camp, mounting, turning the heads of the horses south, was the beginning of a fresh journey. Jody looked over his shoulder. The camp site was desolate. The charred logs, the gray ashes, were forlorn. The magic had died out with the flames of the camp-fire. The morning had been cool but the climbing sun began to heat the day. The earth steamed. The stench of the polluted waters was often overpowering.

Penny, in the lead, called back, "I wonder, kin the creeturs' bellies stand this rotten water?"

Buck and Mill-wheel shook their heads. The flood was unprecedented in the scrub. No man could tell what would come of it. The cavalcade continued steadily south.

Penny called to Jody, "Remember where we seed the whoopin' cranes dancin' so purty?"

Jody would not have recognized the prairie. It was a flat body of water, where even a crane might hesitate to wade and wander. Farther south was scrub again, then gallberry flats and bay-heads. But where marsh should be, was a lake. They reined in the horses. It was as though they had camped overnight on some strange borderland and had now come into another country. Fish were leaping in the air from water that a week ago had been land. And here, after all the miles, were the bears— They were fishing with an abandon that made them unaware of, or indifferent to, the approach of horses and riders. Two or three dozen black forms moved through the waters, belly-deep. Fish jumped ahead of them.

Penny called, "Hit's mullet!"

But mullet, Jody thought, lived in the ocean. They lived in Lake George, with its touch of salt, its faint surge of tide. They lived in the tidal rivers, and in a few fresh-water rivers where flowing springs and swift currents pleased them as well as the ocean, and from which they might leap, as they were doing now, in tensile silver arcs.

The Yearling

Penny said, "Hit's plain as day. Lake George backed up Juniper Creek, and the creek backed up, and the spring overflowed onto the parairie. And here's mullet."

Buck said, "We got a new parairie then. Mullet Parairie. And look at them bears——"

Mill-wheel said, "Hit's bear Heaven. Well, men, how many do we want?"

He sighted his rifle experimentally. Jody blinked his eyes. He had never seen so many bears at once in his life, except in dreams.

Penny said, "Don't let's be hogs about it, even if 'tis bears."

Buck said, "Four'll do us for a while."

"One'll do the Baxters. Jody, you want to kill a bear?"

"Yes, sir."

"Well— Now men, if it's agreeable, we'll pick our shots here and spread out a leetle. Somebody'll be obliged to git a second shot. Mebbe three, do Jody miss."

He assigned Jody the closest shot. It was a large fellow, probably a male.

Penny said, "Now Jody, you ride to the left a mite, 'til you git a bead on his cheek. When I give the word, ever'-body'll fire. If he's moved by that time, take the best head shot you kin git. And if his head's down, and hid from you, aim for his middle and one of us'll finish him after."

Buck and Mill-wheel indicated their choices and the group spread cautiously in both directions. Penny lifted his hand. They halted. Jody was trembling so violently that when he lifted his gun he could see nothing in front of him but a blur of water. He forced himself to steady his aim. His bear was quartering from him, but he was able to draw a bead on the left cheek from the rear. Penny dropped his hand. Guns barked. There was a second bombardment from Buck and Mill-wheel. The horses reared a little. Jody could not remember having pulled the trigger. But fifty yards in front of him a black body, that had been upright, lay half-sunk in the water.

243

The Yearling

Penny shouted, "Nice shootin', boy!" and rode forward.

The remaining bears were scrambling across the swamp like paddle boats, churning the water behind them. It would take a long shot now to bring one down. Again Jody was amazed at the speed of the bulky bodies. The first shot of each man had been accurate and deadly. Buck and Mill-wheel had only wounded on their second shots. The dogs, kept at heel, broke into bedlam. They barked in a frenzy and dashed into the water. It was too deep for wading and too thick with growth for swimming. They were forced to retreat, shrill with frustration. The men rode in close on the two wounded animals. They fired again and the game lay still. The unharmed bears were vanishing before their eyes. No game was quicker or cleverer.

Buck said, "Now we never figgered on gittin' these scapers outen the water."

Jody had eyes only for his own kill. He could not believe that he had done it. Here lay food for the Baxter table for a fortnight, and it was of his providing.

Mill-wheel said, "We best go back home and git a yoke o' oxen."

Penny said, "Tell you. You got five to haul and we ain't got but the one. Now I'm satisfied with the hunt, and I'm satisfied we all know for a while where to look for the game. Do it suit you, you he'p me and Jody with this un o' his, and leave me keep this horse a day-two, and we'll jest go on our way and you go yours."

"Suits us."

Penny said, "You'd think men our age would of thought to of throwed in a rope."

"Who'd of guessed the hull blasted scrub was under water?"

Buck called, "Our legs is longer'n you Baxters'. You stay in the saddle."

Penny was already on his feet. The water was over his knees. Jody was ashamed to stay on his horse as though he were a child. He too slid off into the water. The bottom was firm. He helped drag his bear to high ground. The Forresters seemed unaware that it was important that he had shot it, for it was his first. Penny touched his shoulder, and that was praise enough. The bear would weigh better than three hundred pounds. They agreed that it was best to halve it lengthwise so that the portions might easily be thrown over the rumps of the two horses. They skinned it and were surprised at its fatness, when deer and panther were so lean. The bears must have fed here through the latter days of the storm.

Old Cæsar jumped and shied when the half of the long frame was thrown across him. The taint of the hide was not to his liking. He had smelled the rank odor too often through alarmed nights at the clearing. Once a bear had climbed into the lot and was in the stall with him before Penny, awakened by his whinnying, had come to him. The Forrester horse was better able to carry the extra load in any case and the bear hide was added to Penny's portion. Buck and Mill-wheel turned their horses' heads toward home.

Penny called, "Turn your hames backward and the oxen kin haul all the load to oncet. Come see us."

"You come."

They lifted their hands and were gone. Penny and Jody jogged after them. They would all use the same trail for some miles, but the Forresters, unburdened, on their fast horses, were already far ahead. To the east, they came out on the trail toward home. The going was slow and troublesome. Old Cæsar would not follow behind the bear hide. But when Penny had Jody rode ahead, the Forrester horse insisted on taking the lead. There was a constant struggle. At last, through Juniper Prairie, Penny touched his heels to the horse and took a long lead. With the bear hide out of sight and smelling, old Cæsar was content to trot along reasonably. At first Jody was uneasy, alone in the new wilderness of water. Then, with his bear meat behind him, he felt bold again, and mature.

He had thought that he wanted to hunt forever. But when the tall trees of Baxter's Island drew in sight, and he passed the path to the sink-hole and came to the split-rail fences of his father's fields, he was glad to be coming home. The fields were desolate from the waste of waters. The yard was swept barren. But he was coming in with meat that he had killed for the family, and Flag was waiting.

Chapter XXI

FOR two weeks Penny concerned himself with the salvaging of crops. The sweet potatoes were not ready, by two months, for digging. But they were rotting and would be a total loss if they were not dug. Jody worked long hours at them. He must be careful to go deeply enough with the potato fork and not go too close to the middle of the beds. Then, by lifting carefully, he brought up a forkful of potatoes unharmed. When they were all dug, Ma Baxter spread them out to dry and cure as best they could on the back porch. They all had to be gone over and more than half discarded. Rotting ends were cut off and with the nubbins set aside for the hogs.

The sugar cane was flattened to the ground. There was nothing to do for the present but leave it, for it was immature. It was already putting out roots along the stalks, but it could be trimmed and salvaged later.

The cow-pea hay was ruined. It had been near maturity and the week's soaking left it on the ground, a mouldy mass. The peas that the Baxters had shelled were the only salvage. Three weeks after the flood, after good days of sun, Penny took his scythe to Mullet Prairie, as he now called it, and cut marsh grass and left it to cure.

"Good fodder in bad times," he said.

The prairie waters had receded and left no trace of the fish except their stench. Even Jody, whom few odors offended, was sickened. The smell of death lay everywhere.

Penny said uneasily, "Somethin's wrong. That stink's due to be done with. Things is yit dyin'."

A month after the flood, in October, he returned with Jody in the wagon beside him to Mullet Prairie to gather the cut and cured hay. Rip and Julia trotted along behind the wagon. Penny allowed Flag, too, to follow, for he had begun to make a great commotion whenever he was shut up and left behind in the shed. He ran, sometimes ahead of old Cæsar, sometimes, when the road was wide enough, beside him. Now and then he dropped back and frolicked with the dogs. He had learned to eat green stuff and he stopped occasionally to nibble a tender bud or sprout.

Jody said, "Look back at him, Pa, pullin' buds like he was growed."

Penny smiled and said, "I tell you, never were sich a fawn."

Suddenly old Julia gave tongue and tore to the right into the bushes. Rip followed and Penny halted the wagon.

"Go see what them fools is after, Jody."

Jody jumped down and went after them. A few yards beyond he was able to identify the trail.

He called back, "Nothin' but cat."

Penny lifted his horn to blow the dogs in when he heard Julia bay. He dismounted and pushed into the thick growth. The dogs had the cat at bay, but there was no fight. He went to them. Jody stood, puzzled. The wild-cat lay on its side, untouched. Julia and Rip circled, nipping, but with no responding attack. The cat bared its teeth and lashed its tail but did not stir. It was gaunt and weak.

Penny said, "The creetur's dyin'. Leave it be."

He called off the dogs and returned to the wagon.

Jody asked, "What's it dyin' of, Pa?"

"Why, the creeturs dies the same as us. Them as ain't kilt by their enemies. He's likely old and couldn't ketch hisself nothin' to feed on."

"His teeth wasn't wore down, like a old creetur."

Penny looked at him.

"Boy, you gittin' real observin'. Now I like to see that."

There was still no explanation of the wild-cat's feebleness. They reached the prairie and loaded the wagon with hay.

The Yearling

Penny estimated that three more trips would be necessary. The marsh hay was coarse and stringy, but when frost had come and the wire grass was dry and harsh, Cæsar and Trixie and the heifer calf would be glad to have it. They drove toward home leisurely. Old Cæsar quickened his gait and even Julia ran on ahead, eager, as all domestic animals, for home. Past the trail to the sink-hole, at the corner of the first fence-row, Julia lifted her nose and bayed.

Penny said, "Now there'd be nothin' there in broad daylight."

Julia was insistent and jumped the fence and stopped, her bay turned to a shrill barking. Rip, clumsy in bull-dog fashion, clambered over the fence that the hound had cleared lightly. He too barked fiercely.

Penny said, "Well, I know better than to question a good dog's sense."

He stopped the wagon and took up his gun and went with Jody over the fence to the dogs. A buck deer lay in the corner. It shook its head, making a menacing motion with its horns. Penny lifted his gun, then lowered it.

"Now that buck's sick, too."

He approached close and the deer did not move. Its tongue lolled. Julia and Rip were in a frenzy. They could not understand the refusal of live game either to run or to fight.

"No use to waste shot."

He took his knife from its scabbard and went to the deer and slit its throat. It died with the quiet of a thing to whom death is only one short step beyond a present misery. He drove off the dogs and examined it carefully. Its tongue was black and swollen. Its eyes were red and watery. It was as thin as the dying wild-cat.

He said, "This is worse'n I figgered. A plague has hit the wild creeturs. Hit's the black tongue."

Jody had heard of human plagues. The wild animals had always seemed to him to be charmed, and beyond all human ills. A creature died in the chase, or when another creature, more powerful, pounced and destroyed. Death in the scrub was clean and violent, never a slow sickness and lingering. He stared down at the dead deer.

He said, "We'll not eat it, will we?"

Penny shook his head.

" 'Tain't fitten."

The dogs were sniffing farther down the fence-row. Julia barked again. Penny looked after her. A pile of carcasses lay in a heap. Two old bucks and a yearling had died together. Jody had seldom seen his father's face so grave. Penny examined the plague-killed deer and turned away without speaking. Death seemed to have appeared wholesale out of the air.

"What done it, Pa? What kilt 'em?"

Again Penny shook his head.

"I've never knowed what give the black tongue. Mebbe hit's the flood water, full o' dead things, has got pizenous."

A fear shot through Jody like a hot knife.

"Pa—Flag. He'll not git it, will he?"

"Son, I've told you all I know."

They returned to the wagon and drove on and into the lot and unloaded the hay. Jody felt weak and sick. Flag bleated. He went to him and clutched him around the neck and held him tightly, until the fawn pulled away for breath.

Jody whispered, "Don't git it. Please don't git it."

At the house, Ma Baxter received the news stolidly. She had shed her tears and wailed her laments when the crops were ruined. As the going of too many of her children had wrung her dry of feeling, now the passing of the game was only another unprotested incident.

She said only, "Best water the stock from the high trough and not let 'em git to the seepage pool."

Jody felt a hope for Flag. He would feed him only what he ate himself, keep him away from the tainted grass, water him from the Baxters' own drinking water. If Flag died, he thought with a mournful satisfaction, they would die together.

He asked, "Do folkses git the black tongue?"

"Only the creeturs."

He tied Flag stoutly in the shed when he made the next trip in the wagon for hay. Penny tied up the dogs as well. Jody asked countless questions. Would the hay be tainted? Would the plague last forever? Would there be any game left? To all, Penny, who knew, he had thought, almost everything, shook his head in ignorance.

"Keep still, boy, for the Lord's sake. A thing's happened has never happened before. How would ary man know the answers?"

His father left him alone to take hay and load the wagon while he unhitched Cæsar and rode on to the Forresters for information. Jody felt uneasy and miserable, alone at the edge of the marsh. The world seemed empty. Only over the scrub the buzzards wheeled, profiting. He hurried at his work and had finished it long before his father returned. He climbed to the top of the load of hay and lay flat on his back, staring at the sky. He decided that the world was a very peculiar place to live in. Things happened that had no reason and made no sense and did harm, like the bears and panthers, but without their excuse of hunger. He did not approve.

Against the uncomfortable and alarming things that happened, he balanced Flag. His father, too, of course. But Flag lived in a secret place in his heart that had been long aching and vacant. If Flag were not stricken with the plague, the flood, he decided, would be interesting. If he lived to be as old as Penny, as old as Grandma Hutto and Ma Forrester, he would never forget, he knew, the fright and enchantment of the endless days and nights of storm. He wondered if the quail would die of the black tongue. In another month, his father had told him, he might make a trap of crossed twigs and catch a few for eating. Shot was too valuable to be wasted on such small mouthfuls. But Penny would not allow them to be trapped until the covey was full-grown, and he insisted each year that two or three pairs of cocks and hens be left for seed. And would the turkeys die, and the squirrels, and the wolves and bears and panthers? Speculation absorbed him.

When a muffled sound in the distance became the recognizable beat of old Cæsar's hooves, he had forgotten his discomfort. Penny was as grave as before, but he was relieved and stimulated by his talk with the Forresters. On the trail of game for food, they had discovered the condition two days before. No breed of animals, they said, had been spared. They had found the predatory creatures dead or dying beside their quarry, on an equal footing at last, the weak and the strong brought together to earth, the sharp-toothed and the dull, the clawless and the clawed.

Jody asked, "Will ever'thing die?"

Penny spoke sharply.

"I've told you the last time, don't ask me them questions. Wait like me and see."

Chapter XXII

B Y NOVEMBER, the Baxters and the Forresters knew the extent of the plague and what to expect, both of the game and the predatory animals, during the winter. The deer had been cut down to a fraction of their usual numbers. Where a herd of a dozen had fed across the edge of the clearing, a lone buck or doe leaped the fence into the cow-pea field in search of food that was not there. The deer became bold, nosing in the old sweet potato beds for undiscovered nubbins. The quail appeared in almost their usual numbers, but the wild turkeys were decimated. From that fact, Penny concluded that the damage indeed lay somehow in the polluted swamp waters, for the turkeys fed there and the quail did not.

All the food animals, deer and turkey, squirrel and 'possum, were so scarce that a day's hunt might produce nothing. The unfriendly animals had suffered as heavy losses. At first Penny thought that this would be of advantage. It became plain almost at once that the result was to make the remaining killers hungrier and more desperate because of their own shortened food supply. He became alarmed for the Baxter hogs and built a pen for them inside the lot. All the family went together to the woods and gathered acorns and scrub palmetto berries for the hogs. Penny set aside a measure of the new corn for fattening them. A few days later a stamping and squealing sounded in the lot at midnight. The dogs, aroused, ran barking and Penny and Jody pulled on their breeches and followed with a torch. The fattest barrow was missing. The kill had been made so neatly that there was no sign of struggle. A small trail of blood led across the lot

253

and over the fence. It had required a large animal to kill and carry a heavy hog so handily. Penny took a hasty look at the tracks.

"Bear," he said. "A big un."

Old Julia begged to take the trail and Penny himself was tempted, for the killer might be easily and quickly come up on, gorging. But the night was dark and the risk of an encounter if the bear should be shot and only wounded was, he decided, too great. The trail would still be fresh enough in the morning. They went back to bed, to sleep lightly. At daylight they called the dogs and set out. The track was that of old Slewfoot.

Penny said, "I'd as good to of knowed, him, of all the bears in the scrub, 'd live through a plague."

Slewfoot had fed a short distance away. He had eaten heartily and scratched a covering of trash across the carcass. Then he had gone south and crossed Juniper Creek.

Penny said, "He'll be back agin to feed. A bear'll stay a week with his kill. I've seed 'em fight off the buzzards even when they didn't want to eat, theirselves. If 'twas ary bear but this un, we could set us a trap. But no trap was made will fool him since he lost his toe in one."

"Cain't we come wait for him and ketch him at his feedin'?"

"We'll try."

"Tomorrer?"

"Tomorrer."

They turned back toward home. A light galloping sound came close and closer. Flag had broken loose and joined the hunt. He kicked up his heels and held his small tail erect.

"Ain't he a sight, Pa?"

"He's a sight, son, a'right."

The next day, Penny was down with chills and fever. He was in bed for three days. There was no use in trying to catch old Slewfoot now. Jody begged to go alone and watch for him in ambush, but Penny refused permission. The great bear was too wise and too dangerous, he said, and Jody was too rattle-headed.

Ma Baxter said, "Now I don't crave to feed them shoats to no bear, even if they ain't plumb fat."

When Penny was able to leave the bed, they agreed that it was best to kill the hogs without waiting either for the full moon, or for the animals to be properly fattened. Jody split fat-wood and built a fire under the syrup kettle and brought water from the sink-hole to heat in it. He tilted a barrel on its side and propped it with sand. When the water was exactly right, Ma Baxter ladled it into the barrel. Penny killed the hogs and scalded them one after the other in the barrel, twirling them by the legs with his quick deftness. Ma and Jody had to help him lift them to the cross-trees, for his strength suddenly failed him. All three worked furiously at the scraping, for the hair must come off before it set.

Again Jody marveled at the metamorphosis of live creatures in whom he had felt interest and sympathy, into cold flesh that made acceptable food. He was glad when the killing was over. Now, scraping away on the smooth firm hides, he enjoyed seeing the skin become clean and white. He began to anticipate the smell of sausage frying and of cracklings browning in the fat. Nothing was wasted, not even the entrails. The meat itself was dressed out into hams and shoulders, side-meat and belly-bacon, which would be cured with salt and pepper and brown sugar made from their own cane juice, and then smoked slowly over hickory coals in the smoke-house. There remained the hocks and feet, which would be pickled in brine; the ribs and backbones which would be fried and put down in crocks under a protective layer of lard; the heads and livers and kidneys and hearts which would be made into head-cheese and put down the same way. The trimmings of lean meat would be ground into sausage. The fat would be tried out in the wash-pot and the lard put down in crocks and cans and the brown cracklings laid away for shortening in cornbread. The stomachs and intestines would be scraped and turned and soaked, and then used for casings in which the sausage meat would be stuffed, and the sausages hung in festoons and smoked along with the hams and bacons. Odds and ends would be cooked with cornmeal for the dogs and chickens. Even the tails were dressed. Only one part, like a windpipe, seemed without use and was tossed away.

Jody asked, "What's that, Ma?"

"Why, that's his goozle. What's a goozle? Well, if he didn't have no goozle, he couldn't squeal."

Eight hogs in all were dressed. Only the old boar hog, two young sows, and the brood-sow, peace offering from the Forresters, were left to begin the cycle over again. These must take their chances in the woods. They would be fed the slops, and a little corn at evening, to toll them into their pen to be shut up at night for approximate safety. For the rest, they must root for a living, maintaining life if they could, dying if they must.

Supper that night was a feast, and the table seemed lavish long afterward. There would soon be collards in the garden behind the house, and wild mustard greens all about the clearing. There would be bacon to cook with them, and with the dried shelled cow-peas. Cracklings would hold out for crackling bread for months. The Baxters were in fair shape for the winter. The season was the most abundant of the year. The scarceness of game would not be so serious with the smoke-house full.

The flattened sugar-cane had sent out whiskered roots along the stalks and had to be torn free of the clutching earth. The stalks were like ragged mops. The extraneous roots had to be cut off before the cane could be ground. Jody drove old Cæsar around and around the small cane-mill and Penny fed the thin, fibrous stalks into the revolving gears. The yield was low, and the syrup was thin and acid, but there was again sweetening in the house. Ma Baxter dropped oranges into the last boiling of syrup and the result made a rich preserve.

The corn was not much damaged, even the ears that had stood in the field through the rains. Jody spent hours every day at the millstone. The lower stone had small grooves that waved out from the center like the spirals on a snail shell. The upper stone rested on it, and the pair sat in a wooden frame with four legs. The shelled corn was fed into a hole in the center of the upper millstone, and when the ground meal reached a certain fineness, it sifted out through the waste hole and was collected in a bucket. Swinging the overhead lever in a circle hour after hour was monotonous but not unpleasant. Jody dragged up a high stump and when his back was tired, sat on it by way of rest and variety.

He said to his father, "I do most o' my figgerin' here."

Penny said, "I hope you do a heap of it, for the flood's done you outen a teacher. The Forresters and me had it settled to board a teacher between us for you and Fodder-wing this winter. When Fodder-wing died, I still figgered I'd do some trappin' and git cash money that-a-way. But the creeturs is so scarcet now and the hides so pore, hit's no use."

Jody said comfortingly, "That's all right. I know a heap now."

"That jest proves your ignorance, young feller. I do hate for you to grow up and not know nothin'. You'll jest have to make out this year with what leetle I kin learn you."

The prospect was more than acceptable. Penny would start him on his reading lesson or his sums, and then, before either of them knew it, would be off on a tale. Jody went on with his grinding with a light heart. Flag came up and he stopped to let the fawn lick the meal at the waste-hole. He often took a taste himself. The stones became hot from friction and the meal smelled like popcorn or cornpone. When he was hungry enough, a mouthful was palatable, but it never tasted as good as it smelled. Flag was bored with the inactivity and wandered away. He was becoming bolder and was sometimes gone in the scrub for an hour or so. There was no holding him in the shed. He had learned to kick down the loose board walls. Ma Baxter expressed the belief, only because it was her hope, that the fawn was going wild and would eventually disappear. Jody was no longer even troubled by the remark. He knew that the same restlessness came to the fawn that came to him. Flag merely felt the need of stretching his legs and exploring the world about him. They understood each other perfectly. He knew, too, that when Flag wandered away, he moved in a circle, and was never out of hearing of Jody's call.

That evening Flag got himself in serious disgrace. The sweet potatoes had been cured and heaped in a pile on the back porch. Flag roamed there while every one was occupied and found that by butting the pile, the potatoes would roll. The sound and motion charmed him. He butted the pile until it was strewn over most of the yard. He tramped on the potatoes with his sharp hooves. The odor enticed him and he nibbled one. The taste pleased him and he went from one to another, nibbling. Ma Baxter discovered him too late. Grave damage had been done. She drove him furiously with a palmetto broom. The game was much the one of chase that Jody played with him. When she turned away, he turned as well, and, following, butted her in her ample rear. Jody came in from his grinding to a hullabaloo and a crisis. Even Penny upheld Ma Baxter in the gravity of the matter. Jody could not endure the expression on his father's face. He could not keep back the tears.

He said, "He didn't know what he was doin'."

"I know, Jody, but the harm's as bad to the 'taters as if he done it for meanness. We got scarcely enough rations now to do the year."

"Then I'll not eat no 'taters, and make it up."

"Nobody wants you should do without 'taters. You jest got to keep track o' that scaper. If you keep him, it's your place to see he don't do no damage."

PENNY TEACHES JODY HIS SUMS

"I couldn't watch him and grind corn, all two."

"Then keep him tied good in the shed when you cain't watch him."

"He hates that ol' dark shed."

"Then pen him."

Jody rose before day the next morning and began work on a pen in the corner of the yard. He studied its position with an eye to using the fence for two corners of the pen, and to having it where he could see Flag from most of his own work-spots, the millstone, the wood-pile and the barn lot in particular. Flag would be content, he knew, if he was in sight of him. He finished the pen in the evening, when his chores were done. The next day he untied Flag from the shed and lifted him into the pen, kicking and struggling. Flag was over the bars and out and at his heels again before he reached the house. Penny found him again in tears.

"Don't git in a swivet, boy. We'll work this out, one way or t'other. Now the 'taters is near about the only thing he'll bother, do you keep him outen the house. They'd ought to be under kiver, anyway. Now you take down that tipply-tumbly pen, and build a coop to kiver the 'taters. Like a chicken coop, with two sides comin' to a peak. I'll start you on it."

Jody wiped his nose on his sleeve.

"I shore am obliged, Pa."

With the potatoes bedded and covered, there was no more serious trouble. Flag had to be kept out of the smoke-house as well as the house, for he had grown so large that by rearing on his hind legs he could reach the hanging sides of bacon and lick the salt.

Ma Baxter said, "I don't want nobody but me lickin' the meat I eat, let alone a nasty creetur."

Flag was annoyingly curious, as well, and butted over a can of lard in the smoke-house to hear the cover fall and see what was inside. The day was cool and the thin loose lard was discovered before it had run out. But such intrusions could be taken care of simply by keeping the doors shut, as was desirable in any case. Jody developed a good memory for such details.

Penny said, "Hit'll do you no harm to learn to be keerful. You got to learn takin' keer o' rations comes first of all—first after gittin' 'em."

Chapter XXIII

HE first heavy frost came at the end of November. The leaves of the big hickory at the north end of the clearing turned as yellow as butter. The sweet gums were yellow and red and the black-jack thicket across the road from the house flamed with a red as bright as a camp-fire. The grapevines were golden and the sumac was like oak embers. The October blooming of dog-fennel and sea-myrtle had turned to a feathery fluff. The days came in, cool and crisp, warmed to a pleasant slowness, and chilled again. The Baxters sat in the evening in the front room before the first hearth-fire.

Ma Baxter said, "Don't seem possible fire-time's here agin."

Jody lay flat on his belly, staring into the flames. It was here that he was often able to see Fodder-wing's Spaniard. By squinting his eyes and waiting for the blaze to shift just-so up a crotched log, he could picture, with no trouble at all, a horseman in a red cape, wearing a shining helmet. The picture never lasted long, for the wood stirred and the logs fell, and the Spaniard rode away again.

He asked, "Did the Spaniards have red capes?"

Penny said, "I don't know, son. Now you see how handy a teacher'd be."

Ma Baxter said wonderingly, "Now what put sich a idee as that in his head?"

He rolled over on his side and stretched one arm across Flag. The fawn lay asleep, his legs tucked under his stomach, like a calf. His white tail twitched in his sleep. Ma Baxter did not mind his being in the house in the evening, after supper. She even turned an unseeing eye on his sleeping in

The Yearling

Jody's bedroom, for at least then he was into no mischief. She took him for granted with the critical disinterest she showed the dogs. They were outside, sleeping under the house. On bitter nights Penny brought them in too, not that it was necessary, but because he enjoyed sharing his comfort.

Ma Baxter said, "Throw a stick on the fire. I cain't quite see to foller my seams."

She had cut down a pair of Penny's winter breeches for Jody.

She said, "Now you take another notion to grow like you done this spring, and I'll be cuttin' down your breeches to fit your daddy."

Jody laughed out loud and Penny pretended to be offended. Then his eyes twinkled in the firelight and his thin shoulders shook. Ma Baxter rocked complacently. They were all pleased whenever she made a joke. Her good nature made the same difference in the house as the hearth-fire had made in the chill of the evening.

Penny said, "You and me had ought to be gittin' out that speller, boy."

"Mebbe the roaches has ate it."

Ma Baxter poised her needle in the air. She pointed it at him.

"You best study your grammar, too," she said. "You'd ought to say, 'The roaches has eat it.'"

She rocked again, placidly.

Penny said, "You know, I got a idee we'll not have no great cold this winter."

Jody said, "I like it cold, if 'twa'n't for totin' in wood."

"Yes, sir, hit look like a good winter. We come out a heap better'n I figgered on the crops and meat. Mebbe a feller kin git his breath now."

Ma Baxter said, "About time."

"Yes, sir, ol' Starvation's doin' his huntin' another place."

The evening wore on without further speech. There was

no sound but the hearth-fire simmering, the puff of Penny's pipe, and the *creak-pat, creak-pat* of Ma Baxter's rocker on the board floor. Once a great whistling passed over the house, like a sudden wind in the pine trees. Ducks were flying south. Jody looked up at his father. Penny pointed the stem of his pipe upward and nodded. If he were not so comfortable, Jody would have liked to ask what kind they were and where they were going. If he could know such things as his father knew them, he could manage, he thought, without the sums and the spelling. He liked the reading. Most of it was tales, not as good as Penny's—none was—but still, tales.

Penny said, "Well, it's go to sleep here, or find the bed."

He rose and knocked out his pipe on the hearth. As he bent, the dogs began to bark and dashed from under the house. It seemed as though his stirring had awakened them from sleep, and they had plunged after an imaginary enemy. Penny opened the front door and cupped his hand to his ear.

"Now I don't hear a thing but them dogs."

The calf bleated. The cry was at once of terror and pain. There was another that lifted to a scream, then was abruptly muffled. Penny ran to the kitchen for his gun.

"Fetch a light!"

Jody chose to believe that his mother was indicated. He ran after his father with his own gun, which since old Slewfoot's last visit he was allowed to keep loaded. Ma Baxter followed unwillingly with a lighted splinter, feeling her way with slow feet. Jody climbed the lot fence. He was sorry now that he had not brought the torch himself. He could see nothing. He could hear only a tumult of fighting and snarling, a snapping of many teeth, the voices of Rip and old Julia silenced. Above it came the desperate voice of his father.

"Git 'em, Julia! Hold 'em, Rip! My Lord, the light!"

Jody turned back over the fence and ran to his mother and took the torch from her. The thing that was happening was for Penny to handle. He ran back again. He lifted the torch high in his hand. The wolves had invaded the lot and killed the heifer calf. A band of them, three dozen or more, milled about the enclosure. Their eyes caught the light in pairs, like corrupt pools of shining water. They were emaciated and rough-coated. Their fangs glistened as white as gar-fish bones. He heard his mother screaming beyond the fence and became aware that he was screaming, too.

Penny shouted, "Hold that light still!"

He tried to steady it. He saw Penny lift his gun and shoot once, then again. The wolves turned and flowed over the fence in a gray wave. Rip snapped at their heels. Penny ran shouting after them. Jody ran behind him, trying to keep the light on the swift forms. He remembered that he had his own gun in the other hand. He pushed it at his father and Penny took it and shot again. The wolves were gone like a thunderstorm. Rip hesitated, his light hide plain in the darkness, then turned and limped back to his master. Penny stooped and petted him. He, too, turned, and walked back slowly into the lot. The cow was bellowing.

Penny said quietly, "I'll take the light."

He lifted it and swung it about the enclosure. The shredded body of the calf lay in the middle. Near it lay old Julia, her teeth in the throat of a gaunt wolf. The wolf was taking its last breaths. Its eyes glazed. It was tick-ridden and mangy.

Penny said, "All right, gal. Leave go."

Julia released her hold and stood back. Her teeth, worn by age to the flatness of corn kernels, had accounted for the only casualty. Penny looked at the mangled calf, and at the dead wolf. Then, as though he stared into the green eyes of an invisible enemy, he looked off into the night. He seemed small and shrunken.

He said, "Well——"

He handed Jody his gun and retrieved his own from the side of the fence. He leaned and picked up a hoof of the calf and walked decisively toward the house, dragging the carcass. Jody understood, shivering, that his father meant to have it handy if the marauders returned. He was still frightened. A panther or a bear at bay always terrified him. But there the men had always stood with leveled guns. There the dogs had room to dart in and get away. The fierce pack in the lot had made a sight he wanted never to see again. He wished his father had dragged the carcass into the woods. Ma Baxter came to the door and called quaveringly.

"I had to come to the house in the dark. I never been so scairt. Were it bears agin?"

They went into the house and Penny brushed past her to go to the hearth to the swinging kettle for hot water for the dogs' wounds.

"Wolves."

"Oh dear Heaven! Did they kill the calf?"

"They kilt it."

"Oh dear Heaven! And hit a heifer!"

She followed him about while he poured hot water in a basin and bathed the dogs' wounds. They were not serious.

"I wisht I could git the dogs on them beasts one at a time," he said grimly.

In the warm safety of the house, bold now because his mother was afraid, Jody could speak at last.

"Will they be back tonight, Pa? Will we go hunt 'em?"

Penny rubbed boiled pine gum into Rip's one deep wound, a jagged tear on one flank. He was in no mood for answers or talk of any kind. He did not speak until he was done with the dogs and had made them a good bed under the house near his bedroom window. He did not mean to be taken by surprise again. He came in and washed his hands and warmed them by the fire.

"Now this be the kind o' time a man needs a snort," he said. "I shore aim to beg a quart offen the Forresters tomorrer."

"You goin' there tomorrer?"

"I got to have he'p. My dogs is all right, but a big woman

and a leetle man and a yearlin' boy is no match for that many hongry wolves huntin' in a pack."

It gave Jody a strange feeling to have his father admit that he could not handle anything alone. But the wolves had never before descended on the clearing in a band. Deer and small animals had been plentiful to feed them. Only a few had come, singly or in pairs, skulking about timorously, running at the first alarm. They had never before been a major menace. Penny took off his breeches and turned his back to the fire.

"Now I was scairt," he said. "My very bottom's cold."

The Baxters went to bed. Jody made sure his window was tight shut. He tried to make Flag lie under the covers with him, but the fawn kicked off the quilt as often as he drew it over him. He was content to sleep on the foot of the bed, and Jody awakened twice in the night and felt down to make sure he was still there. Flag was not as large as the nearly grown calf— His heart thumped in the darkness. The fortress that was the clearing was vulnerable. He drew the quilt over his head and was afraid to go to sleep again. But bed was a comfortable and a sleepy place on the first cold night in autumn——

Penny got an early start for the Forresters' in the morning. The pack had not returned in the night. He hoped that perhaps one or two were wounded. Jody begged to go with him, but his mother refused outright to stay alone.

"Hit's all fun to you," she complained. " 'Kin I go? Kin I go?' No thought o' bein' a man and lookin' out for your Ma."

His pride was touched. He patted her arm.

"Don't fret, Ma. I'll stay and keep off the wolves."

"About time. I git the weak jerks, thinkin' about 'em."

He felt bold after his father's assurance that the pack would not be seen in the daytime, but when Penny rode off on old Cæsar he was uneasy in spite of himself. He tied Flag in his room to a post of the bed and went to the sink-hole for water. On the way back, he was certain he heard sounds that he had never heard before. He looked back frequently, and broke into a trot past the fence-corner. He was not afraid, he told himself, but his mother might be. He chopped wood hurriedly and filled the kitchen wood-box to overflowing and stacked a pile by the hearth, in case his mother thought of it later. He asked if she needed meat from the smoke-house. She did not, but called for a can of cracklings and a bowl of lard.

She said, "Now your Pa went off and never said what to do with the pore calf, bury it or cook it for the dogs or save it for bait. Well, best wait 'til he says."

No further outside work was necessary. He bolted the kitchen door behind him.

"You put that fawn out," she said.

"Ma, don't make me put him out. Why, the smell of him'd jest toll the wolves from all over."

"All right, but you got to clean up after him if he don't mind his manners."

"I will."

He decided to study his speller. His mother fished it out from the trunk that held extra quilts and winter clothes and the deed to the Baxter land. He occupied himself with it all morning.

"I never seed you so content with that book," she said suspiciously.

He scarcely saw the words on the page. He was not afraid, he told himself again. But his ears were strained with listening. He listened all morning for a swift rush of padded feet. He listened for the sweet sound of old Cæsar's hooves in the sand, and his father's voice at the gate.

Penny was back in time for dinner. He had eaten little breakfast and was hungry. He would not talk until he had eaten his fill. He lit his pipe and tilted back his chair. Ma Baxter washed the dishes and brushed out the floor with the palmetto sweep.

"All right," Penny said, "I'll tell you jest how it stand.

The Yearling

Hit's like I figgered, the wolves was about the worst destroyed by the plague of ary o' the creeturs. This pack was here last night is all there is left. Buck and Lem has been to Fort Butler and Volusia and no wolves has been seed nor heered since the plague but these uns. Allus in a bunch. They worked over here from near Fort Gates and has been cleanin' out stock all the way acrost. They ain't got to feed much, for they've been caught at it before they fed, and drove off. They're purely starvin', and night before last they got a heifer and a yearlin' bull o' the Forresters. Toward daylight this mornin' they heered 'em howlin'. After they was here."

Jody now was eager.

"Will we git to hunt with the Forresters?"

"That's it. I had me a good go-round with them jessies. We cain't see it the same way about killin' 'em. I want a couple o' good hunts, and traps around our lot and their corral. But the Forresters is bent on pizenin' 'em. Now I ain't never pizened a creetur and I don't aim to."

Ma Baxter flung her dishcloth at the wall.

"Ezra Baxter, if your heart was to be cut out, hit'd not be meat. Hit'd be purely butter. You're a plague-taked ninny, that's what you be. Leave them wild things kill our stock cold-blooded, and us starve to death. But no, you're too tender to give 'em a belly-ache."

He sighed.

"Do seem foolish, don't it? I jest cain't he'p it. Anyways, innocent things is likely to git the pizen. Dogs and sich."

"Better that, than the wolves clean us out."

"Oh now Ory, they ain't goin' to clean us out. They ain't like to bother Trixie nor Cæsar. I mis-doubt could they git their teeth through their old hides. They shore ain't goin' to mess up with dogs that fights as good as mine. They ain't goin' to climb trees and ketch the chickens. They's nary other thing here to bother, now the calf's gone."

"There's Flag, Pa."

The Yearling

It seemed to Jody that for once his father was wrong.

"Pizen's no worse'n them tearin' up the calf, Pa."

"Tearin' up the calf was nature. They was hongry. Pizen jest someway ain't natural. Tain't fair fightin'."

Ma Baxter said, "Hit takes you to want to fight fair with a wolf, you——"

"Go ahead, Ory. Ease yourself and say it."

"If I was to say it, hit'd take words I don't scarcely know to think, let alone speak."

"Then bust with it, wife. Pizenin's a thing I jest won't be a party to."

He puffed on his pipe.

"If it'll make you feel better," he said, "the Forresters said worse'n you. I knowed they'd mock me in the head when I takened my stand, and they done so. And they're fixin' to go right ahead and set out the pizen."

"I'm proud there's men some'eres around."

Jody glowered at both of them. His father was wrong, he thought, but his mother was unfair. Something in his father towered over the Forresters. The fact that this time the Forresters would not listen to him, must mean, not that he was not a man, but that he was mistaken. Perhaps, even, he was not wrong.

"You leave my Pa alone. I reckon he's got more sense than the Forresters."

She wheeled on him.

"Now mister impudent big-mouth, you'll git yourself frammed good with a bresh."

Penny rapped on the table with his pipe.

"Leave off! Ain't it enough to have trouble with the animals, without the family quarrelin'? Has a man got to die to find peace?"

Ma Baxter turned back to her work. Jody skulked away to the bedroom and untied Flag and took him outdoors for a run. He was uneasy in the woods and did not go far. He called the fawn in and went and sat with him under the hickory tree and watched the squirrels. He decided to gather hickory nuts before the squirrels finished the crop. Mast was plentiful and the squirrels, because of the plague, were not, but he wished, crossly, not to divide the nuts on his own land. He climbed the tree and shook the limbs. The nuts fell in a shower and he climbed down and gathered a pile. He took off his shirt and made a sack of it and filled it with nuts and took them to the house. He emptied the pile on the ground in the shed and spread them out to dry. When he put on his shirt, he realized that he had stained it past all washing with the juice from the hulls. It was a quite good shirt, with only one small patch on it where he had snagged the sleeve sliding down the roof of the corn-crib. He grunted to himself. It was peculiarly difficult to know ahead of time what would get him into trouble and what would keep him out. However, when his mother was angry at Penny, she seldom noticed anything he did.

She smoothed down through the afternoon. After all, the Forresters would get the job done. Three of them rode in toward sunset. They had come to notify Penny of the exact location of the poison, so that he might keep his dogs away from the trail. They had set it out ingeniously. They had done it entirely from horseback, so that the wolves should not scent the hated taint of man. They had prepared chunks of raw meat from their killed heifer and yearling, handling it with pieces of buckskin over their hands while they inserted the poison. The three had separated and ridden over the trails the pack might be expected to follow. They had dug holes with pointed palmetto stems, leaning from the saddle, and dropped in the poisoned bait, raking leaves over it again with their sticks. They had brought the last trail back toward Penny's lot, in a line from the sink-hole, where the wolves might water or wait for other game. Penny accepted the situation philosophically.

"All right. I'll keep my dogs tied for a week."

They accepted a drink of water and a twist of Penny's

tobacco, but refused supper with thanks. They wanted to be home again before night when the pack might return to the corral. They visited with Penny a few minutes and rode away again. The evening passed peacefully. Penny filled more shell-cases, capped them and loaded his gun. He loaded Jody's muzzle-loader as well. Jody took it and propped it carefully by his bed. He was grateful to his father for including him in such preparations. He lay thinking after they were all in bed. He could hear his father talking with his mother.

He heard him say, "I got news for you. Buck told me Oliver Hutto takened a boat from Jacksonville to Boston and figgered on bein' there a while before he shipped agin. He give Twink Weatherby money and she slipped off to Jacksonville and got on a boat and follered him. Lem's rarin'. He says do he meet Twink and Oliver, he'll kill 'em all two."

Jody heard his mother's bulk, turning, creak the bed.

She said, "Now if the gal's honest, why don't Oliver marry her and be done with it? If she's nothin' but one o' them leetle ol' chipperdales, why do he mess up with her?"

"I couldn't rightly say. Been so long sincet I was a young buck, studyin' on courtin', I dis-remember how Oliver mought figger."

"Anyways, he hadn't ought to of let her foller him that-a-way."

Jody agreed with her. He threshed his legs under the covers in fury. He was finished with Oliver. If he ever saw him again, he would tell him what he thought of him. He hoped most to see Twink Weatherby and pull her yellow hair or throw something at her. Because of her, Oliver had gone away without coming to visit them. He had lost him. He was so angry at him that he did not care. He dropped asleep, painting enjoyable pictures of Twink wandering in the scrub and eating the wolf-poison and falling dead in deserved agonies.

Chapter XXIV

THE Forrester poisoning killed thirty wolves in one week. There was a pack left of a dozen or two that was wary and avoided the poison. Penny agreed to help with their extermination by the legitimate means of trap and gun. The pack ranged wide and never killed twice in the same place. It invaded the Forrester corral one night. The calves bleated and the Forresters poured out. They found the cows holding the wolves at bay. They had formed a ring, with the calves in the center, and were on the defensive with lowered horns. One calf was dying with a torn throat and two had their tails bitten off neatly at the rump. The Forresters brought down six of the pack. The next day they set poison again, but the wolves did not return. Two of their own dogs found the bait and died horribly. The Forresters were willing to track down the rest of the pack in slower fashion.

Buck came one evening at dusk to invite Penny to join them in a hunt the next morning at dawn. The wolves had been heard howling early that day at a water-hole west of Forresters' Island. A long dry spell had followed the flood and the high waters had shrunk away. The swamps, the marshes, the ponds, the creeks, were at nearly their usual level. What game was left could be counted on to visit various known water-holes. The wolves had made the same discovery. The hunt would serve two purposes. With luck, all the remaining wolves might be killed. Game also could easily be taken. The plague seemed to have run its course. Venison and bear-meat again tempted the imagination. Penny accepted the invitation gratefully. There were enough Forresters to make any hunt without outside help. It was generosity that had sent Buck to Baxter's Island. Jody knew it. He knew, too, that his father's knowledge of the ways of the game was always welcome.

Penny said, "Spend the night, Buck, and we'll git off soon before day."

"No, for do I come up missin' at bed-time, they'll figger they's no hunt and not be ready."

It was agreed that Penny should meet them an hour or so before day, at the intersection of the main trail with their own. Jody tugged at his father's sleeve.

Penny said, "Kin I carry my boy and my dogs?"

"The dogs, we counted on, since Nell and Big Un was pizened. The boy we hadn't figgered on, but if you'll speak for him not to mess up the hunt——"

"I'll speak for him."

Buck rode away. Penny prepared ammunition and oiled the guns. The Baxters went to bed early.

It seemed to Jody that Penny was leaning over him, shaking him awake, before he had even had time to go to sleep. It was still night. Rising was always early, but there was usually at least a thin streak of light across the east. Now the world was as black as tar, and the trees still rustled with the night winds. There was no other sound quite like it. For a moment he regretted his anxiety of the evening before. Then he thought ahead to the hunt and excitement warmed him and he jumped from bed in the cold air. He slid his feet along the snug softness of his deerskin rug as he pulled on his shirt and breeches. He hurried to the kitchen.

A fire was crackling on the kitchen hearth. His mother was placing a pan of biscuits in the Dutch oven. She had an old hunting coat of Penny's over her long flannel nightgown. Her gray hair hung in braids over her shoulders. He went to her and smelled of her and rubbed his nose against her flannel breast. She felt big and warm and soft and he slipped his hands under the back of the coat to warm them. She tolerated him a moment, then pushed him away.

"I never had no hunter act like sich a baby," she said. "You'll be late for the meetin' if breakfast's late."

But her tone was friendly.

Jody sliced bacon for her. She freshened it in hot water, then dipped it in flour and put it in an iron skillet to fry to a crisp brown. He had not thought he was hungry, but the sweet nut-like fragrance of it was overwhelming. Flag came from the bedroom and sniffed too.

She said, "You feed that fawn and tie him in the shed before you forgit it. I'll not be tormented with him while you're gone."

He led Flag outside. The fawn was frisky and bolted away. He had trouble in following him and catching him in the blackness. He tied him first, then gave him a mash of meal and water.

He said, "You be good and I'll tell you about the wolves when I git home."

Flag bleated after him. If it were only an ordinary hunt, he would almost rather stay home with him. But Penny had said that they meant to kill off the last wolf in the scrub, and he might never see another again as long as he lived. When he went to the house, Penny had come in from milking. The quantity was short because of the early hour. Breakfast was ready. They ate hurriedly. Ma Baxter did not eat but put up a lunch for them. Penny insisted that they would be home again for dinner.

She said, "You've said that before, and then come in after dark with your belly pinchin' you."

Jody said, "Ma, you're shore good."

"Oh, yes. When it's rations."

"Well, I'd a heap ruther you was good about rations and mean about other things."

"Oh, I be mean, be I?"

"Only about jest a very few things," he soothed her.

Penny had saddled Cæsar when he was at the barn. The horse stamped now, hitched at the gate. He knew a hunt as well as the dogs. They came with waving tails, gulped a pan of grits and gravy, and followed after. Penny slung a coil of rope and the saddle-bags over Cæsar's back, mounted into the saddle, and pulled Jody up after him. Ma Baxter handed their guns up to them.

Penny said to Jody, "Now take keer how you swing that thing around. You kill your Pa, and you'll r'aly have to hunt for a livin'."

It seemed surely that day must break. The horse's hooves thumped in the sand. The road gave back the sound, then dropped behind them, as it stretched before, in silence. Strange, he thought, that the night should feel more silent than the day, when most of the creatures stirred then, and did their sleeping when the sun rose. Only a hoot-owl cried, and when its crying ended, they rode forward into a dark emptiness. It was natural to speak in whispers. The air was chill. In his excitement, he had forgotten to put on his ragged jacket. He leaned close against his father's back.

"Boy, you ain't got on your coat. You want mine?"

He was tempted but refused.

"I ain't cold," he said.

Penny's back was thinner than his own. It was his own fault that he had no coat.

"You reckon we'll be too late, Pa?"

"Reckon not. Mebbe day'll hold off 'til we git there."

They were ahead of the Forresters. Jody climbed down and tussled with Rip to warm himself, and because the waiting was intolerable. He began to fear they had missed them. Then a clop-clop of hoofs sounded at what seemed some distance and the Forresters were there. All six had come. They greeted the Baxters briefly. The light wind was favorable, blowing from the southwest. If they did not stumble on a wolf sentry, they might take the pack unawares. It would be long-range shooting at best. Buck and Penny took the lead, side by side. The rest followed in single file.

A grayness that was scarcely light crept through the forest.

The Yearling

There was an interval between daylight and sunrise that was an unreal hour. It seemed to Jody that he moved in a dream between night and day, and when the sun rose, he would awaken. The morning would be foggy. The grayness lingered in the fog and seemed unwilling to rise through it. The two merged, joined against the sun that would tear them to tatters. The file of riders came out of the scrub and into an open area of grass and live oak islands. A favorite water-hole of the game lay beyond. It was a clear deep pool and something about the water was to the taste of the creatures. It was protected as well with marsh on two sides, from which danger might be seen approaching, and forest on the other two, into which they might quickly retreat.

The wolves had not yet come, if they were coming. Buck and Lem and Penny dismounted and tied the dogs to trees. A thin strip of color like a yellow ribbon lay low across the east. The autumn mist hung above it. Figures were visible only a few feet above the ground. At first the water-hole seemed deserted. Then bodies took shape here and there about it, as though the fog itself had solidified, still gray and tenuous. The antlers of a buck deer formed in the distance. Lem lifted his gun instinctively, then lowered it. The wolves were more important for the moment.

Mill-wheel murmured, "I don't remember no stumps around that pond."

As he spoke, the stumps moved. Jody blinked his eyes. The stumps were young bears. There were a good dozen of them. Two larger bears ambled slowly beyond them. They had not seen or winded the buck, or chose to ignore him. The curtain of mist lifted higher. The band of color broadened in the east. Penny pointed. There was movement in the north-west. The forms of the wolves were barely visible, slipping down in single file as the humans had done. The keen nose of old Julia caught a faint taint and she lifted it high and wailed. Penny struck at her to hush her. She dropped flat to the ground.

The Yearling

Penny whispered, "We ain't got a chancet in the world o' gittin' a shot this way. We cain't git clost enough."

Buck's whisper was a growl.

"How about a shot at the buck and mebbe the old bears?"

"Listen to me. One of us kin slip around to the east and south and make a quick dash acrost the south marsh. The wolves'll be too fur down to turn back. They won't go to the marsh. They're obliged to come out to the woods right past where we be now."

Acceptance of the idea was immediate.

"Go ahead."

"Jody kin do it as good as a man. And he's no shot. We'll need all our shots here."

"All right."

"Jody, you ride down jest inside the edge o' the woods yonder. When you git opposite that tallest pine, you cut right back acrost the marsh towards us here. Jest as you turn, take a pot-shot at the pack. Ne' mind tryin' to hit 'em. Git goin'. Go fast but quiet."

Jody touched Cæsar's rump and trotted away. His heart had jumped from its normal position and was beating somewhere high in his throat. His vision blurred. He was afraid he would never see the tall pine, and cut in too soon or too late and bungle the whole business. He rode unseeing. He straightened his back and slid one hand along the barrel of his gun. A blessed stiffening and clarity came to him. He picked out the pine before he reached it. He swung Cæsar's head sharply to the right, dug his heels into him, slapped his neck with the reins and shot into the open. The marsh water flew under him. He saw the young bears scatter. He was afraid he had not come in far enough behind the wolves. The creeping pack ahead of him hesitated, on the verge of turning back the way they had come. He lifted his gun and shot behind them. They bolted in a mass. He held his breath. He saw them stream toward the scrub. He heard the barking of guns and the sound was music. He had done his part and it was out of his hands. He galloped around the south side of the pond toward the men. The tethered dogs lifted their voices. A single gun spoke now and again. His mind was clear. He wished that he had another shot. He was sure he could take it coolly and accurately.

Penny's ruse had worked to perfection. A dozen of the gray bodies lay about on the earth. An argument was in progress. Lem wanted the dogs turned loose after the rest of the pack. Buck and Penny were opposed.

Penny said, "Lem, you know we ain't got a dog kin run down one o' them streaks o' lightnin'. They won't tree like a cat, they won't turn at bay like a bear. They'll run forever."

Buck said, "He's right, Lem."

Penny turned excitedly.

"Look at what them young bears has done. They've treed. What say we have a go at ketchin' 'em alive? Ain't there a good price on the east coast for live creeturs?"

"That's what they say."

Penny swung up in the saddle and Jody eased back behind him.

"Take it easy, men, slower you work on this, better we'll do."

Three of the spring cubs, motherless, perhaps, long enough to have forgotten discipline, had not even treed. They sat on their haunches, crying like babies. They made no effort to escape. Penny tied the three together and looped the end of the rope around a large pine. Some of the cubs had only climbed saplings. It was a simple matter to shake them out and tie them too. Two others were high in a larger tree. Jody, as the lightest and nimblest, climbed after them. They climbed higher above him, then scrambled out on a limb. He edged along the limb. It was ticklish work to shake it without falling off himself. The limb cracked faintly. Penny shouted to him to wait. An oak limb was cut and trimmed and handed up. Jody slid down the tree until he could reach it and climbed back. He poked it at the cubs. They clung as though they had grown to the limb. At last they dropped. He climbed down.

The old bears and the buck had vanished with the first shot. Two yearling bears showed too much fight to be taken alive. They were sleek and plump and since both houses were in need of fresh meat, they were shot down for food. The take of cubs was ten.

Buck said, "Now wouldn't Fodder-wing of loved to of seed this? Now I wisht he was alive to see it."

Jody said, "If I didn't have me Flag a'ready, I shore would carry one home."

Penny said, "And you and hit both git barred out together."

Jody went close and talked to the cubs. They lifted their sharp snouts, scenting him, and stood up on their hind legs.

He said, "Now ain't you-all proud you goin' to git to live?"

He moved closer and reached out a tentative hand to touch one. It raked its sharp claws across his sleeve. He jumped back.

He said, "They ain't grateful, Pa. They ain't a mite grateful we saved 'em from the wolves."

Penny said, "You didn't look at his eyes good. You picked a mean un to pet. I've done told you, where there's twin cubs, one'll be friendly and t'other'll be mean. Now see kin you find one has got a friendly eye."

"I mought not pick good. I'll leave 'em be."

The Forresters laughed. Lem picked up a stick and began to tease one of the cubs. He poked it in the ribs to make it bite the stick. He knocked it over and it squealed in pain.

Penny said, "Now kill the thing, Lem, if you're goin' to torment it."

Lem turned angrily.

"You save your say-so for your young un. I'll do what I please."

"You'll not torment nothin' long as I got breath to interfere."

"You want the breath knocked outen you then, eh?"

Buck said, "Leave off your meanness a little while, Lem."

"You want a fight, too?"

The Forresters took sides among themselves without rhyme or reason, but this time they all sided with Buck and Penny. They were good-natured from the kill and the catch. Lem glowered but put down his fists. It was agreed that Gabby and Mill-wheel should stay and keep an eye on the cubs in case they chewed loose from their bindings, which ranged from Penny's rope to Buck's deer-hide boot laces. The rest would return to Forresters' Island for the wagon to fetch the cubs.

"Now kin we agree on where to carry 'em," Penny said, "me and Jody jest as good to go on home. I got a leetle huntin' business o' my own on the way."

"You fixin' to go run down that buck?" Lem asked suspiciously.

"If you got to know my business, I'm fixin' to go on to Juniper Spring and shoot me a 'gator. I need grease for my boots and I want to smoke me the tail for meat for my dogs. Now you satisfied?"

Lem did not answer. Penny turned to Buck.

"Don't you reckon St. Augustine's the best place to sell them cubs?"

"Well, if the price ain't right, hit'd be wuth a try to go on to Jacksonville."

"Jacksonville," Lem said. "I got some business there myself."

"I got a gal in Jacksonville," Mill-wheel said, "but I got no business there."

"If she's the one got married," Buck said, "you shore as the devil got no business there."

Penny said patiently, "Hit's Jacksonville, then. Now who's goin'?"

The Forresters looked at one another.

Penny said, "Buck's the only one o' you kin trade without quarrelin'."

Lem said, "The wagon don't go without me."

"That's Buck and Lem, then. Now you want I should go? Ain't room for but three on the seat."

They were silent.

Mill-wheel said at last, "You got high shares in the cubs, Penny, but I shore do crave to go. Come to think on it, I got a barrel o' somethin' else I'd love to carry and trade."

Penny said, "Well, I got no cravin' a-tall to go. Buck, I'll be beholden to you to look out for my share and do my tradin' for me. When'll you go? Tomorrer? All right, if you'll stop by tomorrer, me and Ma'll have it figgered what-all we want you to trade for."

"I'll not fail you, you know that."

"I know."

The party separated. The Forresters went north and the Baxters south.

Penny said, "Love nor money wouldn't git me to the east coast with them jay-birds. There'll be broke jugs and broke heads all the way along their track."

"You reckon Buck'll do us right?"

"He'll do right. Buck's the only one o' the litter was wuth raisin'. Him and pore Fodder-wing."

Jody said, "Pa, I feel peculiar."

Penny halted Cæsar and looked around. Jody was white.

"Why, boy, you jest had too much excitement. Now it's over, you've give out."

He got down and lifted Jody in his arms. He was limp. Penny propped him against a sapling.

"You've done a growed man's work today. Now set easy and I'll fetch you a bite to eat."

He fumbled in the saddle-bags and brought out a cold baked sweet potato and peeled it.

"This'll freshen you up. When we git to the spring, you take a good drink o' water."

The Yearling

At first Jody could not swallow. Then the taste of the sweet potato touched his palate. He sat up and ate it in small mouthfuls. He felt better immediately.

"You're jest like I was when I were a boy," Penny said. "You take ever'thing hard and hit leaves you faintified."

Jody grinned. With any one but his father, he would have been ashamed. He clambered to his feet. Penny laid a hand on his shoulder.

"I didn't keer to praise you in front o' the men, but you done noble."

The words were as strengthening as the sweet potato.

"I'm all right now, Pa."

They mounted and rode on. The morning haze had thinned and vanished. The November air was crisp. The sun was a warm arm across their shoulders. The black-jacks flamed, the scrub oaks glistened. The fragrance of the purple deer-tongue filled the road. Scrub jays flew across the road. Their solid blue feathered coats, Jody thought, were prettier than the bluebirds', because there was more of it. The strong smell of the yearling bear over old Cæsar's rump behind him blended not unpleasantly with the sweat of the horse, the rich smell of the saddle, the deer-tongue and the lingering odor of the sweet potato. He would have a great deal, he thought, to tell Flag when he got home. The finest part about talking to Flag was that he could think most of the talk and not have to try to say it. He preferred talking to his father, but he could never find the words in which to make things clear. When he tried to say a thing that he had thought, the idea vanished while he was still floundering. It was like his efforts to shoot doves in a tree. He saw them, he cocked his gun, he crept close. Then they were gone before he could pull the trigger.

With Flag, he could say, "There come the wolves, slippin' in to the pond," and he could sit and see the whole thing, and feel the feelings again, the fears and the sharp ecstasies.

Flag would nuzzle him and look at him with his soft liquid eyes, and he could feel that he was understood.

He came to himself with a start. They had picked up the old Spanish trail through the hammock to Juniper Spring. The spring was at its normal level. Debris from the flood was thick about its banks. The spring itself bubbled clear and blue from a bottomless cavern. A fallen tree lay across it. They hitched Cæsar to a magnolia and skirted the spring for 'gator sign. There was none. An old female alligator who was almost tame inhabited the spring. She raised a swarm of young every second year, and she would swim to the bank when called and take meat thrown to her. She was perhaps down in her cave with the year's young. Because she was so tame and had been there so long, no one ever disturbed her. Penny was afraid that some day a stranger would come and kill her, finding her easy prey. They worked down the bank of the run. A shipoke flew.

Penny put out a hand behind him to halt Jody. On the opposite bank was a fresh 'gator wallow. The mud had been packed smooth where they turned and rolled their hard bodies. Penny dropped to his haunches behind a buttonwood bush. Jody dropped behind him. Penny had reloaded his gun. There was shortly a commotion in the waters of the swift-running creek. What seemed a log lifted not quite to the surface. There were two bumps at one end. The log was an eight-foot alligator. The bumps were its heavy-lidded eyes. It submerged again, then raised clear and lifted its fore-quarters to the bank. It crawled slowly to the wallow, heaved its bulk up and down on its short legs, flipped its tail and lay quietly. Penny drew a bead more carefully than Jody had ever seen him do on bear or deer. He fired. The long tail thrashed wildly, but the body sank instantly to the mud. Penny ran up-stream, around the head of the spring with Jody at his heels, and down-stream on the other side of the wallow. The broad flat jaws were opening and closing automatically. Penny held them shut with one hand

and gripped a fore-leg with the other. The dogs barked excitedly. Jody took hold and they dragged the body to firm ground. Penny stood up and wiped his forehead with his sleeve.

"That's light totin' for a leetle bit," he said.

They rested, then bent to the work of slicing out the tail meat, which, smoked, would make convenient hunting rations for the dogs. Penny turned back the hide and sliced out the layers of fat.

"The 'gators is one thing got fat on the flood," he said.

Jody sat back on his heels with his knife in his hand.

"And likely the moccasins and the turtles," he said.

"And the birds now," Penny said. "All excusin' the turkeys, the birds ain't suffered pertickler."

Jody pondered the strangeness of it. The creatures of the water and the creatures of the air had survived. Only the things whose home was the solid land itself had perished, trapped between the alien elements of wind and water. The thought was one of those that stirred him, and that he could never bring to earth to share with his father. It moved now across his mind like a remnant of the morning's haze. He returned to the fat of the alligator.

The dogs were not tempted by the 'gator flesh, just as frogs were not to their taste, or coots, or ducks that fed on fishy matters. But when the tail meat, pink as veal, was smoked, the foreign taste and odor would disappear and they would eat it when no better meat was at hand. Penny emptied the lunch from the saddle-bags and filled them with the strips of meat and of fat. He looked at the package of food.

"Kin you eat now, boy?"

"I kin near about eat ary time."

"Then we'll eat it jest to be done with it."

They washed their hands in the running creek and went to the head of the spring for drinking water. They lay flat on their bellies and drank deeply. They opened the lunch and divided it evenly into two portions. Penny left a biscuit filled with mayhaw jelly and a square of cassava pudding. Jody accepted them gratefully. Penny looked at the small protruding belly.

"Where you put it all, I cain't see. But I'm proud I got it to give to you. There was times when I were a boy, they was sich a passel of us, my own belly lay mighty flat."

They lay comfortably on their backs. Jody stared up into the magnolia tree over him. The under-sides of the thick leaves were like the copper of the pot that had belonged to his mother's grandmother. The red cones of the magnolia were beginning to spill their seeds. Jody gathered a handful and dropped them idly on his chest. Penny rose lazily and fed the dogs the scraps. He led Cæsar to the spring to drink. They mounted and turned north toward Baxter's Island.

West of Sweetwater Spring, Julia began to work a trail. Penny leaned down to look at it.

"Now that's a mighty fresh buck track she's got there," he said. "I've a notion to leave her foller it."

Her tail was in constant motion. Her nose was glued to the ground. She moved ahead rapidly. She lifted her nose high and began to trot with a gaited motion, scenting only by the wind.

"He must o' cut in right ahead of us here," Penny said.

The trail kept to the road for several hundred yards, then turned to the right. Julia gave a high thin cry.

Penny said, "Now he's clost. I'll bet he's layin' up right in the thick."

He rode into the thicket after the dog. She bayed and a buck swayed to its knees and leaped to its feet. The buck was in full antlers. Instead of rushing away in flight, he charged headlong at the dog. The reason was instantly plain. A doe lifted her smooth unhorned head beyond him. Because of the interruption of the flood, the deer were late with their mating. The buck was courting and ready for fight. Penny held his fire, as he did often when a thing was strange. Old

The Yearling

Julia and Rip were as amazed as he. They were fearless with bear and panther and wild-cat, but here, they had expected the game to run. They retreated. The buck pawed the earth like a bull and shook his antlers. Julia gathered her wits and jumped for his throat. He caught her on his horns and tossed her into the bushes. Jody saw the doe wheel and bolt away. Julia was unhurt and came back for action. Rip was at the buck's heels. The buck charged again, then stood at bay with lowered antlers.

Penny said, "I'm shore sorry, ol' feller," and fired.

The buck dropped, kicked a moment and lay still. Julia lifted her hound's voice in a howl of triumph.

Penny said, "Now I hated to do that."

The buck was large and fine, well fattened on acorn mast and palmetto berries. His red coat of summer, however, was already shabby. It had turned to the winter's grayness, the color of the Spanish moss, or the lichens that grew on the north side of the pine trees.

"A month from now," Penny said, "what with runnin' all over the scrub courtin', he'd of been pore and his meat stringy."

He stood beaming.

"Now ain't this our day, boy? Ain't this jest our day?"

They dressed the buck.

Penny said, "I mistrust kin old Cæsar tote all we got."

"I'll walk, Pa. Do the buck weigh more'n me?"

"As many stone agin. We'd both best walk."

Cæsar accepted his load patiently. He seemed to have no fear of the yearling bear, as he had had of the large one. Penny walked ahead, leading him. Jody felt as fresh as though the day were only beginning. He ran in front. The dogs trailed behind. It was not much after noon when they reached the clearing. Ma Baxter was not expecting them so soon. She heard them and came to the gate to meet them. She shaded her eyes against the sun. Her heavy face lightened at sight of the game.

286

The Yearling

"I don't mind stayin' alone when you-all come home with sich as that," she called.

Jody broke into a babble of talk. His mother only half-listened, concerned with the quality of the meat of buck and bear. He left her and slipped into the shed to Flag. There was not time to sit and talk. He let Flag smell his hands and shirt and breeches.

"That's bear smell," he told him. "You run like lightnin' do you ever smell it clost. And that's wolf. Since the flood, they're wusser'n the bear, but we shore cleaned 'em out this mornin'. There's three-four left, and you run from them. Now t'other smell is your kin-folks." He added with a horrified fascination, "Mebbe your daddy. No need to run from them. Yes, they is, too. A ol' buck'll kill a fawn or a yearlin', Pa says, times, in ruttin' season. You jest run from ever'-thing."

Flag switched his white tail and stamped his feet and tossed his head.

"Don't you say 'No' to me. You listen to what I tell you."

He untied him and took him outside. Penny was calling him to help with the carrying of the game to the back of the house. Flag bolted at scent of the bear, then returned to sniff cautiously from a distance, craning his slim neck. The skinning and cutting up of the meat took the rest of the afternoon. Dinner had not been cooked. They were not hungry and Ma Baxter waited and cooked the big hot meal an hour ahead of the usual supper time. Penny and Jody ate ravenously at first, but were suddenly so tired that appetite left them when they were half through. Jody left the table to go to Flag. The sun was only now setting. His back ached and his eyes grew heavy. He whistled Flag in. He had wanted to listen to his mother's and father's talk about the trading, and to decide what he wanted from Jacksonville for his special portion. But his eyes would not stay open. He stumbled into bed and was instantly asleep.

Penny and Ma Baxter spent the evening discussing their

most urgent needs for the winter. Ma Baxter drew up at last a list, carefully written in pencil on ruled paper.

A bolt good wool for huntin jeans for Mr. B & Jody
A haf bolt perty blue and wite check gingham for Mrs.
  B now a real perty blue
A bolt domestick
A sack cofee beans
A barrl flowr
A ax hed
Sack salt 2 lb sody
2 stiks lead for shot
Buckshot 4 lb
Some more shel casis Mr. B's gun
1 lb powder for shels
Homespun 6 yd
Hickory shirtin 4 yd
Osnaburg 6 yd
Brogan shoes, Jody
½ quire paper
1 box buttons, pantaloon
1 paper shirt buttons
1 bottle caster oil 50¢
1 box worm candy
1 box liver pills
1 pain curer
1 vial laudnum
1 do camphire
1 do Paragorick
1 do lemon
1 do pepermint
Now if enuf money left 2 yd black alpacy

The Forresters stopped the next morning on their way. Jody ran out to meet them and Penny and Ma Baxter followed. Buck and Mill-wheel and Lem were crowded to-

THE FORRESTERS GO TO TOWN

gether on the wagon seat. The wagon body behind them was filled with a quarreling, wrestling, whining tangle of shiny black fur, shot through with flashes of small teeth and claws and pairs of bright beady black eyes. Their individual ropes and chains were hopelessly tangled. A barrel of moonshine whiskey stood in the middle. One cub with a longer chain had climbed to its top and sat loftily above the tumult. Jody jumped up on a wagon wheel to peer in. A clawed paw went past his face and he dropped back to the ground. The wagon-load was bedlam.

Penny called, "Don't be surprised do all Jacksonville take out and foller you."

Mill-wheel said, "Mebbe hit'd raise the price."

Buck said to Jody, "I cain't git over how Fodder-wing would of loved to of seed 'em."

If Fodder-wing had been alive, Jody thought wistfully, the two of them might have been taken along to Jacksonville. He looked longingly at the cramped space on the floor-boards under the men's feet. He and Fodder-wing could have sat there comfortably, and so have seen the world.

Buck took the Baxters' list.

He said, "This look like a heap o' things wrote out here. If we don't git a good price and the money don't hold out, what must I skip?"

"The gingham and the domestick," Ma Baxter said.

Penny said, "No, Buck, you git Ma's gingham, whatever come. Git the gingham and the ax head and the shell cases and lead. And the hickory shirtin', that's Jody's portion."

"Blue and white," Jody called. "All mingledy, Buck, like a joint snake."

Buck shouted, "Well, if they ain't money enough, we'll stop and ketch some more bears."

He slapped the reins over the backs of the horses.

Ma Baxter shrilled after him, "The wool cloth's the worst needed."

Lem said, "Stop this wagon. You see what I see?"

He jerked his thumb at the deer-hide stretched on the smoke-house wall. He jumped down from the wagon-seat and opened the gate and walked with long rangy strides to the smoke-house. He turned aside, searching. He discovered the antlers, drying on a nail. He walked deliberately to Penny and knocked him against the smoke-house wall. Penny went white. Buck and Mill-wheel came hurrying. Ma Baxter turned and ran into the house for Penny's gun.

Lem said, "That'll learn you to lie to me and slip off that-a-way. Wasn't goin' after the buck, eh?"

Penny said, "I'd ought to kill you for that, Lem, but you're too sorry to kill. Gittin' that buck was pure happen-so."

"You're lyin'."

Penny turned to Buck, ignoring Lem.

He said, "Buck, no man's never knowed me to lie. If you-all had remembered that, you'd not of got beat in the dog-trade."

Buck said, "That's right. Don't pay him no mind, Penny."

Lem turned and stalked back to the wagon and climbed into the seat.

Buck said in a low voice, "I'm powerful sorry, Penny. He's mean, at best. He's been this-a-way ever since Oliver takened his gal away from him. He's got ugly as a buck-deer that cain't find his doe."

Penny said, "I was aimin' to give you-all a quarter o' the venison on your way back. I'll swear, Buck, this be hard to forgive."

"I'd not blame you. Well, don't fret about your share in the cubs, or the tradin'. Me and Mill-wheel kin tie Lem in knots ary time he need it."

They returned to the wagon. Buck lifted the reins and turned the horses around. He would pick up the north road past the sink-hole. It would take them through Hopkins Prairie, past Salt Springs, and so north to Palatka, where they would cross the river and perhaps spend the night before proceeding. Jody and Penny watched after the wagon and Ma Baxter, peering from the door, set down the gun. Penny went into the house and sat down.

Ma Baxter said, "Why'd you take it from him?"

"When one man's on-reasonable, t'other has got to keep his head. I ain't big enough to fight him jest-so. All I could of done was to of takened the gun and shot him. When I kill a man, hit'll be for somethin' more serious than a ignorant man's meanness."

He was plainly unhappy.

"Now I would love to live peaceable," he said.

To Jody's surprise, his mother said, "I reckon you done the right thing. Don't set studyin' about it no more."

He could not quite understand either of them. He was filled with resentment at Lem, and with disappointment that his father had let him go unpunished. He was confused by his own feelings. Just as he had changed his allegiance from Oliver to the Forresters, Lem betrayed his father. He finally solved it in his mind by deciding to hate Lem, but to continue to like the others, especially Buck. The hate and the friendliness were of equal satisfaction.

There was nothing in particular to be done in the way of work, and he spent the morning helping his mother peel pomegranates and string the peelings to dry. They were the best remedy, she said, for dysentery. He ate so many pomegranates that she was afraid he would need the remedy before it was ready. He liked to bite the transparent crispness from around the seeds.

Chapter XXV

NOVEMBER slid into December with no more sign than the high, sad cry of the wood ducks flying. They left their hammock nests and moved from lake to pond and back again. Jody wondered why some birds cried in flight while others were silent. The whooping cranes gave their rusty call only in motion. Hawks screamed from the air but sat still and frozen in the tree. Sapsuckers were noisy on the wing but gave themselves to the bark of trees with no further sound than the tat-tat of their pecking. Quail spoke only from the ground, and soldier blackbirds shrilled from the rushes. Mocking birds sang and chattered day or night, on the wing, or perched along the fences or in the poke-berry bushes.

The curlews were coming south. They came every winter from Georgia. The old ones were white with long curved bills. The young ones, from the spring hatching, were gray-brown in color. The young curlews made fine eating. When fresh meat was scarce, or the Baxters were tired of squirrel, Penny and Jody rode old Cæsar to Mullet Prairie and shot half a dozen. Ma Baxter roasted them like turkey and Penny swore the flavor was even sweeter.

Buck Forrester had traded the bear cubs in Jacksonville for a good price. He had brought the Baxters all the articles on Ma's list and a small sack of silver and copper in change, to boot. Relations between the Forresters and the Baxters were strained since Lem's attack on Penny and after the settlement the big dark men rode by without stopping.

Penny said, "Likely Lem persuaded the rest I raly meant to cheat about the deer. We'll git it all straight one day."

292

The Yearling

Ma Baxter said, "Hit suits me jest as good to have nothin' to do with 'em."

"Now Ma, don't fergit how Buck lit in when I was snake-bit."

"I ain't fergot. But that Lem's like a snake hisself. Turn and strike at you jest 'cause he hears the leaves rustle."

Buck stopped one day, however, to announce that he believed they had accounted for all the wolves. They had shot one at the corral, had trapped three more and had seen no sign of one since. The bears were giving them constant trouble. The most troublesome was old Slewfoot, whose maraudings were taking him, Buck said, from the river on the east to Lake Jumper on the west. His favorite stopping place was the Forrester corral. He watched the wind and eluded both dogs and traps, slipped into the corral and made off with a calf whenever it pleased him to do so. The nights the Forresters sat up and waited for him, he did not appear.

Buck said, "Hit'll not do you much good to look out for him, but I thought I'd pass the word."

Penny said, "My lot lays so clost to the house, mebbe I kin ketch him at his tricks. I thank you. Buck, I been wantin' to say somethin'. I hope you ain't mixed up in your mind about that buck Lem got so ornery about."

Buck said evasively, "That's all right. What's one deer? Well, so long."

Penny shook his head and went back to his work. It disturbed him not to be on friendly terms with his only neighbors in his small scrub-world.

Work was light and Jody spent long hours with Flag. The fawn was growing fast. His legs were long and spindling. Jody discovered one day that his light spots, the emblem of deer infancy, had disappeared. He examined the smooth hard head at once for signs of horns. Penny saw him at it and was obliged to laugh at him.

"You shore expect wonders, boy. He'll be butt-headed 'til summer. He'll not have no horns 'til he's a yearlin'. Then they'll be leetle ol' spiky ones."

The Yearling

Jody knew a content that filled him with a warm and lazy wonder. Even Oliver Hutto's desertion and the Forresters' withdrawal were distant ills that scarcely concerned him. Almost every day he took his gun and shot-bag and went to the woods with Flag. The black-jack oaks were no longer red but a rich brown. There was frost every morning. It made the scrub glitter like a forest full of Christmas trees. It reminded him that Christmas was not far away.

Penny said, "We'll flunk around 'til Christmas, and we'll go to the Christmas doin's at Volusia. Then after that we'll git down to work agin."

Jody found a patch of Cherokee beans in the pine woods beyond the sink-hole. He gathered his pockets full of the bright red seeds. They were as hard as flint. He stole a large needle and a length of stout cotton thread from his mother's sewing basket and took them with him when he went prowling. He sat down in the warmth of the sun with his back against a tree and strung them laboriously, a few each day, to make a necklace for his mother. The seeds were strung unevenly but the effect pleased him. He carried the completed necklace in his pocket so that he might look at it often, until it began to have a sticky appearance from crumbled biscuits and squirrel tails and other such articles. He washed the necklace at the sink-hole and hid it on a rafter of his bedroom.

There had been nothing special for Christmas the year before except a wild turkey for dinner because there had been no money. This year there was the money left from the sale of the bear cubs. Penny set aside a portion for cotton-seed and said the rest might be spent for Christmas.

Ma Baxter said, "Now if we goin' to the doin's, I want to go tradin' to Volusia 'fore then. I want me four yards o' alpacy so I kin have Christmas decent."

Penny said, "Wife, your figger's no secret. I ain't quarrel-in', for you're plumb welcome to all I got. But seems to me four yards won't no more'n make you a pair o' drawers."

294

The Yearling

"If you got to know, I aim to fix over my weddin' dress. Hit's long enough, for I ain't growed up nor down. I done my growin' sideways, and I aim to set in a piece down the front so's it'll meet around me."

Penny patted her broad back.

"Now don't take on. A good wife like you deserves a piece o' goods to set down the front of her weddin' dress."

She said, mollified, "You jest tootlin' me. I don't never ask for nothin' and you git so you don't expect me to ask for nothin'."

"I know. Hit frets me, you makin' out with so leetle. I'd love to fetch you a bolt o' silk, and do the Lord spare me, one day you'll have a well o' water at the house, and not have to wash no more at the sink-hole."

She said, "I want to go to Volusia tomorrer."

He said, "Now give Jody and me a day-two to hunt some, and mebbe we kin carry some meat and hides to the store and you kin trade to your heart's content."

The first day's hunt brought nothing.

"When you ain't lookin' for deer," Penny said, "they're all over the place. When you hunt 'em, you'd think you was in a tormented city."

A puzzling incident occurred. South of the island Penny tried to put the dogs on the track of what appeared to be a small yearling or a well-grown fawn. The dogs refused to take the trail. Penny did a thing he had not done in years. He broke a switch and thrashed old Julia for her stubbornness. She yelped and whined, but still refused. The mystery became clear at the end of the day. Flag showed up, as he had made a habit of doing, in the middle of the hunt. Penny exclaimed sharply, then knelt to the ground to compare his tracks with those the dogs had refused to follow. They were the same. Old Julia, wiser than he, had recognized either the track or the scent of the newest Baxter.

He said, "That makes me feel right humble. A dog know-in' what you mought call kin-folks."

The Yearling

Jody was elated. He felt a deep gratitude to the old hound. He should have hated having Flag frightened by their pursuit.

The second day's hunt was more profitable. They found deer feeding in the swamp. Penny shot a large buck. He trailed still another, a smaller, and jumped it in a bay-head. He gave Jody a shot, and as he missed, shot it down. They had come on foot, for slow-trailing was the only chance these days of getting game, except by accident. Jody tried to carry the smaller deer, but its weight knocked him almost to the earth. He stayed with the kill while Penny went back for the horse and wagon. Flag was with them when they returned.

Penny called, "This pet o' yours loves a hunt as good as the dogs."

On the way home, Penny pointed out where the bears were feeding. They were eating the berries of the saw palmetto.

"Hit cleans 'em out and tonics 'em. They go into their winter beds fat as butter. The bears is like to be our salvation for fresh this year."

"What else eats the berries, Pa?"

"The deer loves 'em. And leave me tell you, do you fill a demi-john with 'em and pour Cuby rum over 'em and leave 'em stand five months, you've got a drink would make even your Ma shout Hallelujah, could you oncet git it down her."

Where the palmettos began to grow on higher land and merge into black-jack, Penny pointed out narrow trails leading into the gopher holes. The rattlesnakes had denned up for the winter but on warm bright days they came out for a few hours and sunned themselves near the holes. It seemed to Jody that all the invisible creatures of the scrub walked in plain sight before Penny's eyes.

At the house, Jody helped him skin the deer and dress out the hides and the hindquarters, which would be the only

salable portions. Ma Baxter fried the meat from the fore-
quarters and put it down for keeping in its own fat. The
bones and scraps were boiled in the wash-pot for the dogs.
The family feasted that night on the hearts and livers. There
was not much wasted on Baxter's Island.

In the morning, Penny said, "We got to agree now, will
we stay with Grandma Hutto tonight or come home. Do we
spend the night, Jody's got to stay here to milk and feed the
dogs and chickens."

Jody said, "Trixie's near about dry, Pa. And we kin leave
feed. Leave me go, but please let's stay with Grandma
Hutto."

Penny said to his wife, "You want to stay there tonight?"

"No, I don't. Her and me don't never swop much honey."

"Then we'll not stay. Jody, you kin go, but no teasin' to
stay after we git there."

"What must I do with Flag? Cain't he foller along so
Grandma kin see him?"

Ma Baxter burst out, "That blasted fawn! They ain't
never been such a nuisance on the place, even countin' you."

He said with hurt pride, "I reckon I'll jest stay here with
him."

Penny said, "Now boy, tie up the creetur and fergit him.
He ain't a dog, he ain't a young un, though you've near
about made one outen him. You cain't carry him places like
a gal would a play-dolly."

He tied Flag reluctantly in the shed and changed into
clean clothes to go to Volusia. Penny was dressed in his
broadcloth suit with the shrunken sleeves, with his black
felt hat on top of his head. The roaches had eaten a hole in
the brim, but it was after all a hat. He had no other except
his wool hunting cap and his palmetto field hat. Jody was
in his best, brogan shoes, homespun breeches, big wire-grass
hat and a new black alpaca coat bound with red tape. Ma
Baxter was clean and crisp in a new dress made of the blue
and white checked gingham from Jacksonville. It was a

darker blue than she wanted, but the check was pretty. She wore her blue sun-bonnet but carried her black frilled bonnet to put on when she should approach the village.

It was pleasant, jogging down the sand road in the wagon. Jody sat on the floor of the wagon body with his back against the seat. It was interesting to see the scrub drop away behind him as he watched it. The sense of progressing was more acute than when he faced forward. The wagon jolted and his thin rump felt bruised by the time they reached the river. He had nothing much to think about and he gave himself over to thoughts of Grandma Hutto. She would be surprised to know that he was angry with Oliver. He pictured her face with satisfaction. Then he felt uncomfortable. He felt toward her exactly as he had always felt, except that through the summer he had actually forgotten her. Perhaps he would not tell her that he was through with Oliver. He saw himself being kind to her and maintaining a noble silence. The imagined scene pleased him. He made up his mind definitely to inquire politely after Oliver's health.

Penny had the deer meat in two pokes. The hides were in crocus sacks. Ma Baxter had a basket of eggs and a small pat of butter to trade at the store, and another basket containing gifts for Grandma Hutto: a quart of new syrup, a peck of sweet potatoes, and a shoulder of the Baxters' sugar-cured ham. She would not have gone empty-handed even to the house of an enemy.

Penny hallooed on the west side of the river to call the ferry from the east. The sound echoed down the river. A boy appeared on the opposite bank. He came leisurely. For an instant it seemed to Jody that the boy had an enviable life, pulling the ferry back and forth across the river. Then it occurred to him that such a life was quite without freedom. There would be for such a boy no hunts, no jaunts into the scrub, no Flag. He was glad he was not the ferry-man's son. He said "Hey" to him with condescension. The boy was ugly and bashful. He helped lead the Baxters' horse on the ferry with lowered head. Jody was filled with curiosity about his life.

He asked, "You got a gun?"

The boy jerked his head sideways in a negative and fastened his eyes on the east shore of the river. Jody recalled Fodder-wing longingly. From the minute he used to come in sight, Fodder-wing had talked to him. He gave up the new boy as a bad job. Ma Baxter was anxious to do her trading before she went visiting. They drove the wagon the short distance to the store and laid their articles of exchange on the counter. Storekeeper Boyles was in no hurry to trade. He wanted news of the scrub. The Forresters had given an incredible account of conditions after the flood. A few hunters from the Volusia territory had been there and had reported game almost impossible to find. The bears were troubling stock along the river, which they had not done in years. He wanted Penny's verification of the tales.

"Hit's ever' word true," Penny said.

He leaned over the counter and settled himself for talk.

Ma Baxter said, "You know I cain't stand on my feet too long. If you men'll agree on your trade, I'll do my buyin' and go on to Mis' Hutto's. Then you kin talk here all day."

Boyles weighed out the meat promptly. With venison scarce, he could find a ready sale for it at a good price. The river steamer would take a haunch or two by way of novelty to the English and Yankee travelers. He examined the hides carefully, and at last expressed his satisfaction with their condition. He had an order and could pay five dollars each. The rate was higher than the Baxters had hoped for. Ma turned to the dry goods counter with a complacent air. She was high-handed and would have only the best. He was out of brown alpaca. He could send for it by the next boat, he said. She shook her head. It was too far to send back for it from the Island.

He said, "Now why don't you take a dress length of this black alpaca and start new?"

She fingered it.

"Shore is purty. How much did you say? Oh——"

She turned away. She retreated into her pride.

"I said 'brown' and I meant 'brown,' " she said coldly.

She bought spices and raisins for a Christmas cake.

She said, "Jody, go look and see has old Cæsar broke loose."

The request was so absurd that he gaped at her. Penny winked at him. He wheeled quickly so that she could not see him smile. She meant to buy something to surprise him for Christmas. Penny would have thought of a better excuse to get him out of the way. He went outside and stared at the boy who tended the ferry. The boy sat and studied his own knees. Jody picked up bits of limestone and aimed them at the trunk of a live oak up the road. The boy watched him furtively, then came behind him without speaking and picked up bits, too, and hurled them at the tree. The contest continued wordlessly. After a time Jody thought his mother would have finished and he ran back into the store.

His mother said, "You comin' with me or stayin' with your Pa?"

He stood hesitant. Grandma Hutto would bring out cake or cookies the moment he was in her house. On the other hand, he could never get enough of hearing his father talk with other men. The matter was settled for him by the store-keeper's handing him a licorice stick for himself. It would keep body and soul together for the time being.

He said loftily, "Me and Pa'll foller."

She went out. Penny watched after her. He frowned. Boyles was stroking the fur of the deer hides with approval.

Penny said, "I'd figgered on takin' cash for them hides. But if you'd as soon trade me a dress length o' that black alpacy, why, I don't much keer."

Boyles said reluctantly, "I'd not do it for anybody else. But you've traded here a long time. All right."

"Best cut it up and wrap it before I change my mind."

300

Boyles said wryly, "You mean before I change mine."

The scissors snipped crisply across the alpaca.

"Now gimme silk thread to match and a card o' them glass buttons."

"That's not in the bargain."

"I got money for it. And put the alpacy in a box, do it rain this evenin'."

Boyles said good-naturedly, "Now you've cheated me, tell me where a man can go to shoot him a wild turkey for Christmas dinner."

"I cain't no more'n tell you where I'm fixin' to hunt one myself. They're mighty scarce. The plague got 'em bad. But you cross the river about where Seven-Mile Branch flows into it. You know that cypress swamp with two-three good big cedars in it, jest southwest o' the run? You work through there——"

The good male talk was beginning. Jody sat down on a cracker box to listen. There were no other customers and Boyles came out from behind the counter and pulled up a straight chair and an old cowhide rocker beside the thumper stove for himself and Penny. They got out their pipes and Penny shaved Boyles a pipeful of his own tobacco.

"Nothing like home-raised tobacky for satisfaction," Boyles said. "You plant a patch for me this spring. I'll pay as high as anybody. Now go on— Southwest o' the run——?"

Jody chewed on his licorice stick. The rich black juice filled his mouth and the talk filled another hunger, back of his palate, that was seldom satisfied. Penny told of the flood in the scrub. It had been bad along the river, too, Boyles interrupted to say, but the river had carried most of the water away as fast as it fell. The banks had been flooded, and Easy Ozell's shack had swayed back and forth in the wind and finally capsized.

"He's living in Grandma's shed," Boyles said, "and happy as a pine borer in a fresh log."

Penny recounted the wolf hunt and the bear hunt; told of

the rattler's strike, which the Forresters had not thought to mention. Jody lived the summer over again, and it was better than when it happened, the way Penny told it. Boyles was as fascinated, and sat leaning forward, forgetting to smoke. A customer came in and he left the stove grudgingly.

Penny said, "Your Ma's been gone a hour-two, boy. You best run on to Grandma's. Tell 'em I'll be along directly."

The licorice had long been swallowed. It was getting on toward noon and he was famished.

"Will we eat dinner at Grandma's?"

"Why, yes. If we wasn't invited, your Ma'd of been back by now. You go on now. And carry that forequarter to her yourself."

He went, a little drugged with Penny's tale-telling.

Grandma's tidy yard was recovering from the effect of the high water. The river had been over its bank here and her fall flower garden had been washed away. There was unaccustomed debris here and there. The second planting was thriving, but there was no bloom, except of shrubs close beside the house. The blooms of the indigo had fruited into small black seed-pods, curved like scythe blades. Grandma was inside the house with his mother. He heard their voices and as he stepped up on the porch and looked through the window, he saw the flickering of flames on the hearth. She saw him and came to the door.

Her embrace was friendly, but it lacked something of enthusiasm. The two Baxter men were more welcome without Ma. There was no plate of cookies anywhere in sight. The smell of cooking, however, came from the kitchen. Otherwise he could scarcely have endured his disappointment. Grandma Hutto sat down again to talk with his mother with a tight-lipped patience. His mother was behaving no better. She looked critically at Grandma's frilled white apron.

She said, "No matter where I be, I like to dress plain in the mornin'."

Grandma Hutto said tartly, "I wouldn't be caught dead

without a frill on me. Men-folks like a woman dressed pretty."

"I was raised to call it indecent, to dress to please the men. Well, some of us plain folks has had to go pore on this earth, 'll git our frills in Heaven."

Grandma Hutto rocked rapidly.

"Now I don't want to go to Heaven," she announced.

Ma Baxter said, "Reckon there's no danger."

Grandma's black eyes snapped.

"Why wouldn't you want to go, Grandma?" Jody asked.

"One thing, the company I'd have to keep."

Ma Baxter ignored this.

"Another thing's the music. There's nothin' played there, they claim, but harps. Now the only music I like is a flute and a bass viol and an octave harp. Unless one o' your preachers'll guarantee that, I'll jest refuse the trip with thanks."

Ma Baxter's face was stormy.

"Another thing's the food. Even the Lord likes the incense of roasted meat before him. But accordin' to the preachers, folks in Heaven live on milk and honey. I despise milk and honey makes me sick to my stummick." She smoothed her apron complacently. "I figger Heaven's only folks' longin' for what they ain't had on earth. Well, I've had near about ever'thing a woman could want. Mebbe that's why I've got no interest."

Ma Baxter said, "Includin' Oliver runnin' off with a yaller-headed chipperdale, I reckon."

Grandma's rocker beat a tune on the floor.

"Oliver's up-standin' and fine-lookin' and women has allus follered him and allus will. Take Twink, now. She's not to blame. She'd never had a fine thing in her life and then Oliver takened a notion to her. Why wouldn't she foller him? The pore child's an orphan." She shook out her frills. "Left an orphan at the mercy of the Christians."

Jody fidgeted in his chair. The coziness of Grandma's

house was chilled, as though the doors were open. It was more woman-business, he decided. Women were all right when they cooked good things to eat. The rest of the time they did nothing but make trouble. Penny's step sounded on the porch. Jody was relieved. Perhaps his father could straighten them out. Penny came into the room. He rubbed his hands together by the open fire.

He said, "Now ain't this fine? The two women I love the most in all the world, waitin' for me by the hearth-fire."

Grandma said, "If the two women loved each other as good, Ezra, all'd be well."

"I know you two don't git on," he said. "You want to know the reason? You're jealous, Grandma, 'cause I'm livin' with Ory. And Ory, you're jealous 'cause you ain't as handsome as Grandma. Now hit takes a bit of age to make a woman handsome—I don't say purty—and time Ory's got a bit of age on her, mebbe she'll be handsome, too."

It was impossible to quarrel around his good-nature. The two women laughed and bridled.

Penny said, "What I want to know, is the Baxters invited to eat o' the fat o' the land, or be they obliged to turn around and go home to cold cornpone?"

"Now you know you're welcome, day or night. And I do thank you for the deer meat. I only wish Oliver was here to eat it with us."

"What's the news from him? We was right hurt he didn't come to visit us before he put to sea."

"It was a long time before he got over his beatin'. Then he had word there was a boat in Boston wanted him for mate."

"I reckon there was a gal in Floridy wanted him for the same thing, eh?"

They laughed together and Jody laughed with them for relief. Grandma's house was warm again.

She said, "Dinner's ready, and if you scrub creeturs don't eat hearty, my feelin's'll be mighty hurt."

The Yearling

Dinner was not as lavish as when Penny and Jody came alone. Yet there were furbelows to impress Ma Baxter that were very tasty. The meal was friendly.

Ma Baxter said, "Well, we made up our minds to come to the Christmas doin's. We couldn't come last year for we'd not come empty-handed. You figger a fruit cake and a bait o' syrup candy'll be welcome for my share?"

"Nothin' better. How about you-all spendin' the night and havin' Christmas with me?"

Penny said, "That'll be fine. And you kin depend on me for meat. I'll git a turkey if I have to hatch one."

Ma Baxter said, "What about the cow and dogs and chickens? We cain't all come off and leave 'em, Christmas or no Christmas."

"We kin leave enough for the dogs and chickens. They'll not starve in a day. And I got a idee Trixie'll be fresh and we kin leave the calf to nuss her."

"And lose the calf to a blasted bear or panther."

"I kin fix a corral inside the barn where nothin' won't bother 'em. Now if you want to stay home and keep off the creeturs, you stay, but I mean to have Christmas."

"And me," Jody said.

Ma Baxter said to Grandma, "I got no more chancet agin 'em than a rabbit agin a pair o' wild-cats."

Penny said, "Now allus seemed to me 'twas Jody and me was two rabbits agin one wild-cat."

"You make a mighty good race of it," she said, but she had to laugh.

It was settled that they would come for Grandma to go to the doings, returning to her house to spend the night and the next day. Jody was elated. Then the thought of Flag came over him like a dark cloud in a sunny sky.

He burst out, "Now I jest cain't come. I got to stay home."

Penny said, "Why, what ails you, boy?"

Ma Baxter turned to Grandma Hutto.

"Hit's that tormented fawn o' hissen. He cain't bear it out of his sight. I never knowed a young un so crazy for a live thing to mess with. He'll go hongry to feed it, he sleeps with it, he talks to it like it was a person—oh, I've heered you, out in that shed—he don't think of nary thing else but that troublesome fawn."

Penny said gently, "Don't make the boy feel like he has the small-pox, Ory."

Grandma said, "Why can't he bring it along?"

He threw his arms around her.

"You'll love Flag, Grandma. He's so smart, you kin learn him like a dog."

" 'Course I'll love him. Will he git along with Fluff?"

"He likes dogs. He plays with ourn. When they go on a hunt, he slips off another way and meets up with 'em. He loves a bear hunt good as the dogs."

Praise of the fawn tumbled from him. Penny stopped him, laughing.

"You tell her all them things, you'll leave nothin' good for her to find out about him. Then she mought find out some o' the bad."

"They's nothin' bad about him," he said passionately.

"Only jumpin' on the table and knockin' the tops off the lard cans and buttin' over the 'taters, and into ever'thing worse'n ten young uns," Ma Baxter said.

She went into the garden to look at the flowers. Penny took Grandma aside.

"I been worryin' about Oliver," he said. "Them big bullies ain't drove him off 'fore he was ready to go, have they?"

"It was me drove him off. I got tired o' him traipsin' off on the sly to see that gal. I said to him, 'Oliver,' I said, 'you jest as good go on back to sea, for you ain't a mite o' good to me nor a mite o' comfort.' He said, 'I ain't a mite o' good to myself. The sea's the place for me.' I never figgered the gal'd foller him."

"You know Lem Forrester's rarin', don't you? Do he ever

come here drunk, remember he ain't human when he gits to sulkin'. Ease him off the best you kin."

"Now I shore as the devil won't waste no time tootlin' him. You know me better'n that. You know I'm made outen whalebone and hell."

"Ain't the whalebone gittin' a mite limber?"

" 'Tis, but the hell's hot as ever."

"I'd depend on you to back most men down, but Lem's different."

Jody was all ears. Now that he was at Grandma's again, Oliver seemed real once more. It was satisfying, however, to find that she had lost patience with Oliver, too. He would show his displeasure when he saw him again, but he would forgive him. He would never forgive Twink.

The Baxters gathered up their baskets and bags and purchases. Jody tried to guess which sack contained his Christmas surprise, but they all looked alike. The distressing thought came to him that perhaps his mother had really wanted him to see if old Cæsar had broken loose and had bought nothing for him at all. All the way home he sounded her out on the subject.

"You jest as good ask questions o' that wagon-wheel," she said.

He took her evasion as a sure sign that she did have something for him.

Chapter XXVI

HE cow freshened the week before Christmas. The calf was a heifer and there was rejoicing on Baxter's Island. It would take the place of the one the wolves had killed. Trixie was no longer young and it was necessary to raise a heifer soon to replace her. There was little talk at the house except of the coming Christmas. Now that the calf was born, the whole family would be able to be away for over-night on Christmas Eve, for the nursling would take care of the milking.

Ma Baxter baked a fruit-cake in the largest Dutch oven. Jody helped her pick out hickory nut meats for it. It took all day to bake it. For three days, the cake was all there was of life; a day for preparing it, a day for baking it, and the day after for admiring it. Jody had never seen a cake so huge. His mother bulged with her pride.

She said, "I don't go to the doin's often, and when I do go, I aim not to go scarce."

Penny presented her with the black alpaca the evening the cake was done. She looked at him and at the material. She burst into tears. She dropped into a chair and threw her apron over her head and swayed back and forth with every appearance of grief. Jody was alarmed. She must be disappointed. Penny went to her and laid his hand on her hair.

He said, " 'Tain't the lack o' will I don't do sich as that for you all the time."

Jody understood then that she was pleased. She wiped her eyes and gathered the alpaca in her lap and sat holding it for a long time, now and then stroking it lengthwise.

She said, "Now I got to move quick as a black snake to git this made in time."

The Yearling

She worked day and night for three days, her eyes bright and contented. She was forced to call on Penny for help in the fitting. He knelt humbly, his mouth full of pins, and took up and let out as she directed. Jody and Flag watched, fascinated. The dress was done and hung under a sheet for clean keeping.

Four days before Christmas, Buck Forrester stopped by. He was good-humored and Penny decided that he had imagined any mistrust. Old Slewfoot had visited Forresters' Island again and had killed a two hundred and fifty pound blue male hog in the nearby hammock. The kill had been in battle and not for food. The hog had put up a mighty fight, he reported. The ground was torn up for yards around. One of the boar's tusks was broken off and the other was wrapped with old Slewfoot's black fur.

"Hit's a good time to come up with him," Buck said, "for he belongs to be hurt."

They themselves had not discovered the kill until the day after it had happened. It had been too late to follow. Penny thanked him for the information.

"I reckon I'll set a trap inside the lot, jest to scare him," he said. "We-all are fixin' to go to the river for the doin's." He hesitated. "You fellers comin'?"

Buck too hesitated.

"I reckon not. We don't fool much with them Volusia jessies. No fun goin' if we wasn't drunk, and Lem'd likely pick a fight with some of Oliver's friends. No, reckon we'll git Christmas-drunk to home. Or mebbe Fort Gates."

Penny was relieved. He could imagine the distress of the river folk if the Forresters had rolled into the prim and Christian gathering.

He oiled his largest bear-trap. It was six feet in width and weighed, he said, nearly six stone. The chain alone weighed two. He planned to shut the cow and calf together inside the stable, barricade the door and set the trap just outside. If old Slewfoot came to make Christmas dinner of the new heifer while they were all away, he would have to take the trap first. The day passed busily. Jody polished again the necklace of Cherokee beans. He hoped his mother would wear them with the black alpaca. He had nothing for a gift for Penny. He worried and puzzled and in the afternoon went to a low place where pipe-elders grew. He cut a reed and made a pipe stem, and cut a bowl from a corn-cob and fitted it. The Indians who had once been here had made pipe-stems of the reeds, Penny had told him, and he had always meant to make one for himself. He could think of nothing for Flag. He admitted to himself that the fawn would be satisfied with an extra piece of cornbread. He would make him a halter of mistletoe and holly.

That night Penny stayed up after Jody had gone to bed. He occupied himself with a mysterious pounding and slapping and scraping that had something to do, no doubt, with Christmas. The three days left seemed like a month.

No one, not even the dogs, heard any sound in the night. When Penny went to the lot in the morning to milk Trixie, and then to the calf's stall to turn it in to the mother to nurse, the calf was gone. He thought it had broken down its bars. They were intact. He went into the soft sand of the lot and studied it for tracks. In a straight line across the criss-cross of cow and horse and human trails, the track of old Slewfoot stretched inexorably. Penny came to the house with the news. He was white with anger and frustration.

"I've had a bait of it," he said. "I mean to track that creetur down if I foller him clare to Jacksonville. This time, hit's me or him."

He went immediately at the business of oiling his gun and preparing shells. He worked rapidly, his manner grim.

"Put me some bread and 'taters in a bag, Ory."

Jody asked timidly, "Kin I go, Pa?"

"If you kin keep the pace with me and not holler quits. If you give out, you got to lay where you fall or come on back alone. I ain't stoppin' before night-fall."

The Yearling

"Must I shut up Flag or leave him foller?"

"I don't give a blasted rap who follers. Jest don't nobody look for me for mercy do the goin' git rough."

He went to the smoke-house and cut strips of 'gator tail for the dogs. He was ready. He trudged through the yard to the lot to take up the trail. He whistled for the dogs and put Julia on the track. She bayed and was off. Jody looked after him in a panic. His gun was not loaded, he had on no shoes, and he could not remember where he had left his jacket. He knew from the set of Penny's back that it was useless to beg him to wait. He scrambled about, gathering up his belongings. He shouted to his mother to put bread and potatoes in his shot-bag, too.

She said, "You're like to be in for it. Your Pa's locked horns with that bear. I know him."

He called to Flag and tore madly after his father and the dogs. Their pace was swift. He was out of breath by the time he caught up to them. Old Julia was jubilant on the fresh trail. Her voice, her merry tail, her easy lope, showed plainly that this was the thing above all others she wished to be doing. Flag kicked up his heels and ran beside her.

"He'll not be so frisky," Penny said ominously, "do old Slewfoot raise up in front of him."

A mile to the west they found the remains of the calf. The old bear, kept perhaps by his injuries inflicted by the Forresters' boar, from recent hunting, had eaten heavily. The carcass was well covered with trash.

Penny said, "He's due to lay up not too fur away, figgerin' on comin' back."

But the animal followed no rules. The trail continued. It led nearly to Forresters' Island, swung north and west and skirted Hopkins Prairie to the north. The wind was strong from the southwest and Penny said that it was almost certain old Slewfoot was not far ahead of them, but had winded them.

The pace was so rapid and the distance so long that in the

late morning even Penny was obliged to stop for a rest. The dogs were willing to continue, but their heaving sides and hanging tongues showed that they too were weary. Penny stopped on a high live oak island by a clear pond on the prairie for the dogs to drink. He threw himself on the ground in the sunlight. He lay on his back without speaking. His eyes were closed. Jody lay down beside him. The dogs dropped flat on their bellies. Flag was unwearied and pranced about the island. Jody watched his father. They had never come so hard and so fast. Here was not the joy of the chase, the careless pitting of man's brain against creature speed and cunning. This was hate and revenge and there was no happiness in it.

Penny opened his eyes and rolled over on his side and opened his shot-bag and took out his lunch. Jody took out his own. They ate without speaking. The biscuits and cold baked sweet potato seemed almost savorless. Penny threw a few strips of the 'gator meat to the dogs. They gnawed contentedly. It was all one to them whether Penny hunted casually or with a desperate intent. The game was the same, the strong sweet trail, and the good fight at the end. Penny sat upright and swung to his feet.

"All right. Time to git goin'."

The siesta had been brief. Jody's shoes were heavy on his feet. The trail led into scrub, then out again, back to Hopkins Prairie. Old Slewfoot was trying to shake the dogs. Their scent still came to him. Penny was obliged to stop twice in the afternoon to rest. He was furious.

"Dog take it, time was I didn't have to stop," he said.

Yet each time that he set out again his walk was so fast that Jody was tired out from following him. He dared not say so. Only Flag frisked and frolicked. The long trek was a casual jaunt for his long legs. The trail led almost to Lake George, cut back sharply south, and again, to the east, lost itself in the dusk of the swamp. The sun was setting and visibility was low in the shadows.

Penny said, "Uh-huh. He's fixin' to come back and feed on that calf agin. We'll go home and fool him."

The distance back to Baxter's Island was not great, but it seemed to Jody that he could never make it. On any other hunt, he could have said so and Penny would have waited for him patiently. His father moved toward home as doggedly and relentlessly as he had left it. It was dark when they reached it, but Penny at once loaded the great bear trap on the slide, hitched Cæsar to it and dragged it to the site of the kill. He allowed Jody to ride on the slide. He himself walked beside Cæsar, leading him. Jody stretched out his aching legs with relief. Flag had lost interest and hung around the kitchen door.

Jody called, "Ain't you tired, Pa?"

"I don't git tired when I be this mad."

Jody held a fatwood torch for him while he lifted the ragged carcass with sticks, in order to leave no human taint, baited the trap and set it, and scratched leaves and rubbish over it with a pine bough. Penny squatted on the slide for the ride home, dropping the reins and allowing old Cæsar to pick his own way. He put up the horse and found gratefully that Ma Baxter had done the milking. They went to the house. Hot supper was on the table and he ate quickly and lightly, then went directly to his bed.

"Ory, what'd you take to rub my back with panther oil?"

She came and worked on him with big strong hands. He groaned with the comfort of it. Jody stood watching. Penny rolled over and dropped his head on the pillow with a sigh.

"How you makin' it, boy? Had enough?"

"I feel good sincet I ate."

"Uh. A boy's strength rise and fall on his belly. Ory."

"What?"

"I want breakfast before crack o' day."

He closed his eyes and was asleep. Jody went to bed and lay a moment aching, then he too passed beyond hearing of

The Yearling

Ma Baxter clattering in the kitchen, laying out materials for the early breakfast.

He slept through the first sounds in the morning. He awakened, still drowsy. He stretched. He was stiff. He heard his father's voice in the kitchen. Evidently Penny was in the same grim mood as yesterday and had not even thought to call him. He got out of bed and pulled on his shirt and breeches and went sleepily to the kitchen with his shoes in his hand. His hair was shaggy in his eyes.

Penny said, "Mornin', feller. You ready for more?"

He nodded.

"That's the spirit."

He was too sleepy to eat much. He rubbed his eyes and dallied with his food.

He said, "Ain't it too soon to see?"

"Time we git there it'll jest be soon enough. I aim to creep up on him, do he be suspicious and jest sniffin' around."

Penny rose and leaned a moment on the table. He grinned wryly.

"I'd feel right good," he said, "if my back wasn't broke smack in two."

The black morning was bitter cold. Ma Baxter had made up the wool from Jacksonville into hunting jackets and jeans for both of them. They seemed too fine to wear, but walking slowly through the pine woods they wished they had put them on. The dogs were still sleepy and tired and were willing to follow silently at heel. Penny put his finger in his mouth and lifted it to test any imperceptible stirring of air. There seemed to be none and he went in a direct line toward the baited trap. It was in a place that was comparatively open and he halted a hundred yards away. Day was breaking in the east behind them. He slapped the dogs lightly and they dropped to the ground. Jody grew numb with the cold. Penny was shivering in his thin clothes and ragged jacket. Jody saw old Slewfoot in every stump and behind every tree. Interminably slow, the sun rose.

Penny whispered, "If he's ketched, he's dead, for I've heered nothin'."

They crept forward with lifted guns. The trap was exactly as they had left it the night before. There was not light enough to make certain of the tracks, to determine whether the wary creature had come and been suspicious and gone away. They rested their guns against a tree and swung their arms and stamped their feet to warm themselves.

"If he's been here," Penny said, "he ain't fur away. Ol' Julia'll jump him right quick."

The light was without warmth but it spread through the forest. Penny walked forward, bent low to the ground. Julia was snuffing, silently.

Penny said, "I be dogged. I jest be dogged."

Even Jody could see that the only tracks were the day-old ones.

"He ain't been anywhere near," Penny said. "He wouldn't foller a rule to save him."

He straightened and called in the dogs and turned back for home.

"Anyways," he said, "we know where he left off yes-tiddy."

He did not speak again until they reached the house. He went to his room and pulled on his new wool hunting clothes over the old thin ones.

He called to the kitchen, "Ma, put me up meal and bacon and salt and coffee and all the cooked rations you got. Put 'em in the knapsack. And scorch me some more rags for my tinderhorn."

Jody tagged after him.

"Must I put on my new things, too?"

Ma Baxter came to the door of the room with the knapsack. Penny paused in his dressing.

"Now boy, you're plumb welcome to go. But git this in your head and git it good. This is nary pleasure hunt. Hit's cold weather and hit'll mebbe be hard goin' and cold camp-in'. I jest ain't comin' home agin 'til I git that bear. Now you still want to go?"

"Yes."

"Then git ready."

Ma Baxter glanced at the sheet over the black alpaca dress.

"You'll be gone tonight?"

"More'n likely. He's got a night's start on me. Mebbe to-morrer night, too. Mebbe a week."

She swallowed.

She said weakly, "Ezra—tomorrer's Christmas Eve."

"Cain't he'p it. I got a right fresh trail to foller and I'm takin' it."

He stood up and fastened his braces. His eye caught the look of misery on his wife's face. He pursed his mouth.

"Tomorrer's Christmas Eve, eh? Ma, you'd not be afeered to drive the horse and wagon to the river in daylight, would you?"

"No, not in daylight."

"Then if we ain't back tomorrer by time to make it, you hitch up and go on. And if they's a chancet in the world, we'll come on to the doin's. You milk before you go, and if we don't make it in, you'll be obliged to come on back next mornin' and milk. Now that's the best I kin do."

Her eyes were moist but she went without comment and filled the knapsack. Jody waited his chance when she went to the smoke-house for meat for Penny. He pilfered a quart of meal from the barrel and hid it, for Flag, in his own new knapsack made of the hides of the panther kittens. It was the first time he had carried it. He stroked it. It was not as soft as the albino, coonskin knapsack he had given Doc Wilson, but the blue and white spots were almost as pretty. Ma Baxter returned with Penny's meat and finished the packing. Jody stood hesitant. He had anticipated eagerly the Christmas doings at the river. Now he would miss them.

The Yearling

His mother would be glad to have him stay with her, and he would be considered honorable and even unselfish for doing so. Penny slung his knapsack over his shoulder and picked up his gun. Suddenly Jody would not be left behind for all the festivities in the world. They were out to kill old Slew-foot. He swung his little knapsack over his own warm wool shoulder and picked up his gun and followed his father with a light heart.

They cut directly north to pick up the trail where it had ended the evening before. Flag made a sortie into the brush. Jody whistled shrilly.

"Huntin's a man's business, ain't it, Pa, even on a Christmas?"

"Hit's a man's business."

The track was still fresh enough for old Julia to keep it without pause or difficulty. It led east only a short distance beyond the point where they had left it, then turned sharply north.

"Jest as good we didn't foller it last night," Penny said. "He was makin' for other counties."

The trail swung west again toward Hopkins Prairie and ran into wet marsh. It was difficult to follow. Old Julia splashed through the water. Now and then she lapped it, tasting, it seemed, the very scent of it. Again she laid her long nose against the rushes and stared vacantly, deciding for herself on which side the rank fur had brushed them. Then she was off again. She lost the scent entirely at times. Then Penny cut back to firm land and followed the line of the marsh to watch for the great nubbed track where it came out. If he found it before she struck, he called her with the hunting horn and put her on it.

"Here he goes, gal! Here he goes! Git him!"

Rip with his short legs followed Penny. Flag was everywhere.

Jody asked anxiously, "Flag ain't no hindrance, is he, Pa?"

The Yearling

"Not a bit in the world. Did a bear wind him, he'd pay him no mind, lessen it was to turn around and come to him."

In spite of Penny's grimness the hunt began to take on the old delight. The day was crisp and bright. Penny slapped Jody on the back.

"This is better'n Christmas play-dollies, ain't it?"

"I mean."

The cold food at noon tasted better than most hot dinners. They sat and ate and rested under the good strong sun. They loosened their jackets. When they rose to go on, the knapsacks seemed heavy for a time, then they became once more accustomed to them. It seemed for a time that old Slewfoot meant either to make a wide circle back to Forresters' or Baxter's Island, or to continue straight across the scrub to new feeding grounds on the Ocklawaha.

"If Forresters' hog hurt him," Penny said, "he shore don't give a tinker's damn."

Irrationally, in mid-afternoon, the great tracks turned back into the swamp toward the east. The going was rough.

"Minds me o' the time last spring you and me tracked him through Juniper swamp," Penny said.

In the late afternoon they were not far, he said, from the lower reaches of Salt Springs Run. Suddenly old Julia gave tongue.

"He would bed up in sich a place!"

Julia dashed forward. Penny began to run.

"She's jumped him!"

There was a crashing ahead as though a storm broke through the denseness.

"Git him, gal! Hold him! Yippee! Git him! Yippee!"

The bear moved with incredible speed. He crashed through thickets that slowed the dogs. He was like a steamboat on the river, and the dense tangle of briers and thorny vines and fallen logs was no more than a fluid current under him. Penny and Jody were sweating. Julia gave tongue with a new note of desperation. She could not gain. The swamp became so wet and so dense that they sank in muck to their boot-tops and must pull out inch by inch, with no more support perhaps than a bull-brier vine. Cypress grew here, and the sharp knees were slippery and treacherous. Jody bogged down to his hips. Penny turned back to give him a hand. Flag had made a circle to the left, seeking higher ground. Penny stopped to get his wind. He was breathing heavily.

He panted, "He's like to give us the slip."

When his breath came more easily, he set out again. Jody dropped behind, but across a patch of low hammock found better going and was able to catch up. The growth was of bay and ash and palmetto. Hummocks of land could be used for stepping stones. The water between was clear and brown. Ahead, Julia bayed on a high long note.

"Hold him, gal! Hold him!"

The growth dissolved ahead into grasses. Through the opening old Slewfoot loomed into sight. He was going like a black whirlwind. Julia flashed into sight, a yard behind him. The bright swift waters of Salt Springs Run shone beyond. The bear splashed into the current and struck out for the far bank. Penny lifted his gun and shot twice. Julia slid to a stop. She sat on her haunches and lifted her nose high in the air. She wailed dismally, in misery and frustration. Slewfoot was clambering out on the opposite shore. Penny and Jody broke through to the low wet bank. The black rounded rump was all that was visible. Penny seized Jody's muzzle-loader and fired after it. The bear gave a leap.

Penny shouted, "I tetched him!"

Slewfoot continued on his way. There was a moment's crashing as he broke a path through the thicket, then even the sound of him was gone. Penny urged the dogs desperately. They refused flatly to cross the wide creek. He threw up his hands in despair and dropped down on his haunches in the wetness and shook his head. Old Julia rose and snuffed the foot-prints at the edge of the bank, then sat down and took up her lament where she had left it. Jody's flesh quivered. He supposed the hunt was done with. Old Slewfoot had given them the slip again.

He was astonished when Penny rose, wiped the sweat from his face, reloaded both guns and set off northwest along the open edge of the run. He decided that his father knew a less tangled way of returning home. Yet Penny kept to the creek even when open pine woods showed to their left. He dared not question him. Flag had disappeared and he was in a panic for him. It was part of his bargain not to whimper, either for himself or the fawn. Penny's narrow back was stooped with weariness and discouragement, but it was a back of stone. Jody could only follow with sore feet and aching legs. The old muzzle-loader was heavy across his shoulder. Penny spoke, but rather to himself than to his son.

"Now I seem to remember her house yonder——"

The edge of the creek began to lift to high ground. Oaks and pines towered against the sunset. They came to a tall bluff overlooking the run. There was a cabin at the top of it and a cleared field below. Penny climbed the winding path and walked up on the stoop. The door was shut and no smoke came from the chimney. The cabin had no windows. Wooden shutters over square openings served the purpose. These were drawn closed. Penny walked around to the back of the cabin. A shutter here was ajar. He looked in.

"She ain't here, but we'll go in all the same."

Jody asked hopefully, "Will we go home from here tonight?"

Penny turned and eyed him.

"Go home? Tonight? I tol' you, I'm goin' to git that bear. You kin go home——"

He had never seen his father so cold and implacable. He followed after him meekly. The dogs had lain down in the sand by the house, panting. Penny went to the wood-pile and chopped wood. He gathered an armful and dropped it through the shutter opening. He climbed through after it and unbarred the kitchen door from the inside. Jody went back to the woodpile and split off a handful of fatwood splinters and brought them in and laid them on the floor. A Dutch oven and iron kettles stood or hung on cranes at an open hearth.

Penny kindled a fire and hung a shallow kettle over it. He opened his knapsack on the floor and took out the slab of bacon and cut slices of it into the kettle. It began to sizzle slowly. He went outside to an open well and drew up a bucket of water on the windlass. He took a stained coffee-pot from a shelf in the kitchen and made coffee and set it close to the growing blaze. He stirred up a cornpone in a borrowed pan. He laid two cold baked sweet potatoes near the fire to warm through. When the bacon had fried, he scraped the cornmeal batter into the grease, turned it in a solid cake when it was brown and turned the crane away from the blaze to finish the baking. The coffee boiled. He set it aside. He took cups and plates from the rickety safe and set them on the bare deal table.

"Draw up," he said. "Hit's ready."

He ate quickly and hungrily and took what cornpone seemed likely to be left and gave it to the dogs outside, with two more strips each of 'gator meat. Jody was cold with more than the evening's bitterness. He hated having his father so silent. It was like eating with a stranger. Penny heated water in the kettle he had cooked in and washed the cups and plates and put them back in the safe. There was coffee left and he set the pot aside on the hearth. He swept the floor. He went outside and gathered armfuls of moss from a live oak and made a bed under a sheltered corner of the house for the dogs. The night was settling down, very still and bitter cold. He brought in logs from the woods and pushed the ends of two of them into the fire, to be pushed forward from time to time, nigger-fashion. He filled his pipe and lit it and lay down on the floor by the fire with his rolled knapsack for a pillow.

He said kindly, "You best do the same, boy. We'll be set-tin' out soon in the mornin'."

He seemed more himself and Jody dared now to question him.

"You figger ol' Slewfoot'll come back by here, Pa?"

"Not him. Not for longer'n I keer to wait. I'm right cer-tain he's wounded. I'm goin' up to Salt Springs and cross over above the head o' the run. Then down t'other side to where he lit into the thicket this evenin'."

"That's a heap o' distance, ain't it?"

"Hit's a fur piece."

"Pa——"

"Well?"

"You reckon Flag ain't come to no harm?"

"You ain't forgot what I tol' you, about lettin' him foller?"

"I ain't forgot. I——"

Penny relented.

"He ain't lost, if that's frettin' you. You couldn't lose no deer in the woods. He'll turn up, if he ain't takened the no-tion to go wild."

"He'll not go wild, Pa. Never."

"Not so young, anyways. He's likely tormentin' your Ma this minute. Go to sleep."

"Whose house is this, Pa?"

"Used to belong to a widder woman. I ain't been here in a long whiles."

"Will she keer, us comin' in?"

"If it's the woman used to be here, she'll not keer. I come all around courtin' her, 'fore I married your Ma. Go to sleep."

"Pa——"

"Now you got one more question comin' to you 'fore I take a bresh to you. And if 'tain't a question with sense to it, I will anyway."

He hesitated. The question was whether Penny thought

they could possibly reach the Christmas doings the next night. He decided that the query was not sensible. Following old Slewfoot was probably a life-time job. He brought his thoughts back to Flag. He pictured him lost and hungry and followed by a panther. He was lonely without him. He wondered if his mother had ever been so concerned about him, her only son, and doubted it. He went with some mournfulness to sleep.

He was awakened in the morning by the sound of wagon wheels in the yard. He heard the dogs bark and a strange dog answer. He sat up. Penny was on his feet, shaking his head to clear it. They had overslept. The sunrise lay rosy about the cabin. The fire had burned to embers and the charred ends of two logs still extended over the hearth. The air was like ice. Their breaths hung in frosty clouds. They were chilled to the bone. Penny went to the kitchen door and pulled it open. A step sounded and a middle-aged woman came into the room, followed by a youth.

She said, "For the Lord's sake."

Penny said, "Well, Nellie. Looks like you cain't git rid o' me."

"Ezra Baxter. Now you could wait to be invited."

He grinned at her.

"Meet my boy, Jody."

She glanced at Jody quickly. She was a pretty woman, plump and rosy.

"He favors you a mite. This here's my nephew, Asa Revells."

"Not Matt Revells' boy? I'll swear. Why, boy, I knowed you when you was no bigger'n a dirt-dauber."

They shook hands. The youth looked sheepish.

The woman said, "Now you're so mannerly and all, Mr. Baxter, you could tell me how come you're makin' free o' my house."

Her tone was jovial. Jody liked her. Women ran in breeds, like dogs, he thought. She was of Grandma Hutto's breed, that made men easy. And two women could say the same words and the meaning would not be the same, as the bark of two dogs, one menacing and the other friendly.

Penny said, "Lemme git us a fire goin'. My breath's too froze to talk."

He knelt by the hearth and Asa went outside for wood. Jody followed to help. Julia and Rip were moving with stiff tails around the strange dog.

Asa said, "Your dogs like to scared Aunt Nellie and me to death."

Jody could think of no suitable response and hurried into the house with wood.

Penny was saying, "If you never been a angel from Heaven, Nellie, you was one last night. Jody and me and the dogs has been trailin' a big nub-footed bear two days steady. He'd kilt my stock one time too many."

She interrupted, "A bear with one toe gone off his front foot? Why, he's cleaned me out o' hogs, the past year."

"Well, we trailed him clear from home and jumped him in the swamp south o' the lower end o' the run. Iffen I'd had ten more yards on him, I'd o' had him. I shot after him three times, but he was too fur. The last time I stung him. He swum the creek and the dogs wouldn't take the water. Well, Nellie, I never been so near give out since the time you told me Fred wanted to keep steady comp'ny with you."

She laughed, "Oh, go on with you. You never wanted me."

"Hit's too late to commit myself— Well, I knowed if you hadn't married agin and moved off, your place was up here some'eres. And I knowed you'd not begrudge me your floor and hearth. And when I laid down to sleep last night, I said, 'God bless leetle Nellie Ginright.' "

She laughed out loud.

"Well, I don't know nobody is more welcome. But next time, I'd not have sich a start did I know ahead o' time. A

324

widder woman ain't used to strange dogs in the yard and a man by the hearth. What you fixin' to do now?"

"Soon as I eat a bite o' breakfast, I'm fixin' to cross the run above the head o' the spring and take up the trail on t'other side where we last seed him."

She knitted her forehead.

"Now Ezra, no need to do that. I got a old dug-out right above here, is mighty sorry and season-cracked, but hit'd carry you acrost the creek. Take it and welcome and save the miles."

"Hi-yippee! You hear that, Jody? Now I got to say agin, 'God bless leetle Nellie Ginright.' "

"Not so leetle as when you knowed me."

"No, but you're a heap better lookin' now. You was allus purty, but you was too thin. You had legs like a buck-rubbed saplin'."

They laughed together. She took off her bonnet and bustled about the kitchen. Penny seemed now in no great hurry. The distance saved by the use of the dug-out to cross the creek gave them time for a leisurely breakfast. He donated the rest of the bacon. She cooked grits and made fresh coffee and biscuits. There was syrup for the biscuits, but no butter or milk.

"I cain't keep stock here," she said. "The 'gators gits what the bears and panthers don't." She sighed. "A widder woman's hard put to it, times."

"Asa, here, don't live with you?"

"No. He jest come back with me from Fort Gates, and he's goin' to the doin's at the river with me tonight."

"We was aimin' to go, too, but I reckon we jest as good fergit it." A thought struck him. "But now my wife'll be there. You tell her you met up with us, so she'll not be fretted."

"You're jest the kind, Ezra, would worry was his wife fretted. You never asked me, but I often figger I made a sorry out of it, not encouragin' you."

"And I reckon my wife figgers she made a sorry out of it, doin' so."

"None of us don't never know what we want 'til it's mebbe too late to git it."

Penny was judiciously silent.

Breakfast was a feast. Nellie Ginright fed the dogs generously and insisted on putting up a lunch for the Baxters. They left reluctantly, warmed in body and spirit.

"The dug-out's less'n a quarter up the run," she called after them.

There was ice everywhere. The switch grass was coated with it. The old canoe was embedded in it. They broke it loose and launched it. It had been out of water a long time. It leaked so fast behind their efforts that they gave up bailing and got in to make a dash for it. The dogs were suspicious of the boat and as fast as Penny lifted them into it, they jumped out. In the wasted minutes, the canoe accuqired several inches of icy water. They bailed again. Jody climbed into the middle and squatted. Penny handed him the two dogs by the scruff of their necks. He clasped them tightly around their middles and held on desperately against their struggles. Penny poled out from shore with an oak limb. Once out from the fringes of ice, the current ran swiftly. It caught the dug-out and swung it down-stream. The water seeped in to Jody's ankles. Penny sculled madly. The water gushed in from a crack at the bow. The dogs stood quiet now, trembling with fear at the strangeness. Jody crouched and paddled with his hands.

The creeks all seemed friendly in summer. When he was dressed in a thin ragged shirt and as ragged breeches, a spill meant only a quick cool swim to either shore. The heavy wool jeans and jackets would be poor friends in the freezing water. The canoe was sluggish and unmanageable with its weight of water. Penny made the far bank just as it settled obstinately to the creek bottom. The water sloshed over their boot tops and numbed their feet. But they were on land, on the same side of the run as old Slewfoot, and they had saved hours of heavy going. The dogs shivered with the cold and looked to Penny for orders. He gave none, but set out immediately southwest along the creek bank. In places it was so low and marshy that they were forced to cut back into the swamp or even higher into the woods. The area lay between an arm of Lake George and the continued northward reach of the St. John's River. It was boggy and treacherous going.

Penny halted to take his bearings. He could depend on old Julia to pick up the trail when they crossed it, but he dared not push her too rapidly. He had an uncanny feeling for distance. He identified a dead cypress across the run as one they had passed shortly after losing the bear. He slowed his pace to a walk and went cautiously, studying the frozen earth. He pretended to find a track.

He said to Julia, "Here he goes. Git him. Here he goes——"

She stirred from her cold lethargy, swayed her long tail and began to snuff noisily. After a few yards she gave a small thin cry.

"There 'tis. She's got it."

The great tracks were imprinted solidly in the muck. They could be followed easily with the eye. Bushes were broken in the thicket where Slewfoot had crashed through. Penny was close behind the dogs. The bear had bedded as soon as he was certain he was no longer followed. A scant four hundred yards beyond the creek bank, Julia jumped him. He was invisible in the thicket. His ponderous leap sounded. Penny could not shoot without a sight, for the dogs were close on the leathery heels. Jody expected his father to break into as much of a run as was possible in the dense swamp growth.

Penny said, "We cain't ketch him ourselves, no-way. Leave him to the dogs. I got a idee slow time'll prove the fastest."

They pushed through steadily.

Penny said, "We got this much satisfaction, he's wore out, too."

He underestimated his enemy. The chase continued.

Penny said, "Looks like he's got a ticket to Jacksonville."

Bear and dogs were out of sight and hearing. The trail was still plain to Penny's eyes. A broken bough, a bent clump of grasses, unrolled a map before him even where the ground was hard and showed no foot-prints. In late morning they were winded and had to stop to rest. Penny cupped his ear into the light icy wind that had risen.

"Now I think I hear old Julia," he said. "At the bay."

The impetus sent them forward again. At high noon they came up with the quarry. He had decided, at long last, to stop and fight it out. The dogs had him at bay. He swayed sideways on his thick short legs, growling and baring his teeth. His ears were laid flat in his fury. When he turned his back for further retreat, Julia nipped at his flanks and Rip rounded him to spring for his shaggy throat. He slashed at them with great curved claws. He backed away. Rip swung behind him and sunk his teeth in a leg. Slewfoot squealed shrilly. He wheeled with the swiftness of a hawk and raked the bulldog to him. He caught him up in his fore-paws. Rip yelped in pain, then fought gamely to keep the jaws above him from closing on his backbone. The two heads tossed back and forth, snarling and snapping, each trying for the other's throat while protecting his own. Penny lifted his gun. He took steady aim and fired. With Rip hugged to his breast, old Slewfoot dropped. His killing days were done.

It seemed so easy now that it was over. They had followed him. Penny had shot him. There he lay——

They looked wonderingly at each other. They approached the prone carcass. Jody was weak in the knees. Penny's walk was unsteady. Jody felt a clear lightness fill him, as though he were a balloon.

Penny said, "I declare, I believe I'm surprised."

He slapped Jody on the back and cut a buck-and-wing.

He screeched, "Yippee!"

The sound echoed through the swamp. A jay-bird screeched after him and flew away. Jody took up his excitement and shrilled "Yippee!" Old Julia crouched and barked with them. Rip, licking his wounds, wagged his stumpy tail.

Penny shouted tunelessly,

> "My name is Sam.
> I don't give a damn.
> I'd ruther be a nigger
> Than a pore white man."

He pounded Jody again.

"Who's a poor white man?"

Jody shouted, "We ain't pore. We got ol' Slewfoot."

They capered together and shouted and yipped until their throats were hoarse and the squirrels were chattering all about them. They were at last relieved. Penny laughed breathlessly.

"I ain't whooped and hollered that-a-way, I don't know when. I'll swear, it done me good."

Jody's exuberance was still on him and he whooped again. Penny sobered and leaned to examine the bear. He would weigh five hundred pounds. His hide was magnificent. Penny lifted up the huge front paw with its missing toe.

He said, "Well, old fellow, you was a mighty mean enemy, but you got my respect."

He sat down victoriously on the stout ribs. Jody touched the thick fur.

Penny said, "Now we got to do a piece o' studyin'. Here we be in the middle o' nowhere, with a thing bigger'n you and me and your Ma put together, and the cow throwed in."

He took out his pipe and filled and lighted it leisurely.

"Jest as good to study comfortable," he said.

The Yearling

He was in such high spirits that the problem, which seemed insoluble to Jody, was no more to him than a pleasant challenge. He began to figure, half to himself.

"Let's see, now. We'd ought to be jest about between Bear Spring and the river. The Fort Gates road to the west—the river to the east. Now kin we git the black gentleman here to Horse Landin'—there's boats passin' all the time—Well, we'll git him gutted and figger some more."

It was like turning a wagon-load of sacks of meal all at once, to turn him over on his back. The thick layers of fat under the hide made him roly-poly and flabby. He would not stay firmly when held.

"Jest as ornery dead as alive," Penny said.

He disemboweled the carcass neatly. Old Slewfoot was as trim and harmless as a whole beef hanging in a butcher shop. Jody tingled, holding out the heavy legs so that Penny could get at his work. He had never thought to see the day when he would hold the huge paws in his small ones. He had had no share in the hunt except to follow his father's small inexorable back, but now he felt strong and mighty.

Penny said, "Now we'll see be we men enough to budge him."

Each took a fore-paw and strained ahead. The effort needed to move the dead weight was prodigious. By heaving and jerking it was possible to pull it a foot at a time.

"We'll not git to the river by spring, this-a-way," Penny said, "and starve to death on the way to boot."

The inability to keep a firm grip on the smooth-haired paws was the greatest bar to their progress. Penny sat on his heels and pondered.

He said at last, "We kin walk on to Fort Gates and git he'p. That'll cost us a good share o' the meat but hit'll spare our own gizzards. Or else we kin rig up a kind of a pullin' harness and fight it out to the river. And mebbe tear our very hearts out. Or we kin make it on in home and git the wagon."

330

THE DEATH OF OLD SLEWFOOT

The Yearling

"But the wagon'll not be there, Pa. Ma'll be done gone to the doin's."

"Now you know I plumb forgot 'twas Christmas Eve day." Penny pushed back his cap and scratched his head.

"Well, come on, boy."

"Where we goin'?"

"Fort Gates."

The road leading to the small settlement on the river was a scant two miles to the west, as Penny had been certain. It was good to turn from the swamp and the scrub to the open sandy road. A cold wind blew down it but the sun was beneficent. Penny found a patch of cancer-weed by the road-side and broke the stems and let the healing sap drip on Rip's wounds. He was talkative, and as they walked on he brought out from his half-forgotten lore tales of other bear hunts, long ago.

Penny said, "When I were about your size, my uncle Miles come visitin' from Georgia. And a cold day about like this he takened me in the very swamp we come through today. We was moseyin' along, not lookin' for nothin' in per-tickler, and on beyond us we seed what looked like a buzzard settin' on a stump, peckin' at somethin'. Well, we got there and what do you suppose 'twas?"

" 'Twasn't no buzzard?"

" 'Twasn't no buzzard a-tall. 'Twas a bear cub cuffin' playful-like at his twin on the ground below him.

"My uncle Miles said, 'Now we'll jest ketch us a bear cub.' They was right gentle and he goes up to the one on the stump and ketched it. Well, when he'd ketched it, he didn't have nary thing to tote it in. And them scaper's'll gnaw on you if they ain't in a sack. Well, them up-country folks wears underwear in the winter. He takened off his breeches and he takened off his long drawers and he tied knots in the legs of 'em and he made him a sack. He put-tened the cub in it and about the time he reached for his breeches to put 'em back on agin, here come a crashin' and a woofin' and a stompin' in the bresh, and the old she-bear come outen the thick right at him. Well, he takened out through the swamp and dropped the cub and the mammy gathered it up, drawers and all. But she were so clost behind him she stepped on a vine and it tripped him and throwed him flat amongst the thorns and brambles. And aunt Moll was a muddle-minded kind o' woman and she couldn't never make it out how he come home without his drawers on a cold day, and his bottom scratched. But uncle Miles allus said that wasn't nothin' to the puzzlin' the mammy bear must o' done over them drawers on her young un."

Jody laughed until he could laugh no more.

He complained, "Pa, you got all them tales in your mind and you don't tell 'em."

"Well, it takes a thing like bein' in the swamp where it happened, to call it back to me. Now in that same swamp, one very cold March, I remember comin' on another pair o' bear cubs. They was whimperin' with the cold. New-borned cubs is no bigger'n rats and plumb naked, and these uns hadn't yit growed much fur. They was huddled up in a red bay thicket and cryin' like human babies. Listen!"

The sound of hoof beats was unmistakable along the road behind them.

"Now wouldn't it be fine not to have to go clare to Fort Gates for he'p?"

The sounds came closer. They stepped to the side of the road. The riders were the Forresters.

Penny said, "Looks like I mis-called myself."

Buck led the cavalcade. They streamed down the road. They were drunk as lords. They reined in.

"Now look at this! Ol' Penny Baxter and his he-cub! Hey, Penny! What the devil you doin' up here?"

Penny said, "I been on a hunt. And this un was deliberate. Me and Jody takened out after ol' Slewfoot."

"Whoops! On foot? Listen to that, boys! That's better'n a pair o' biddies rompin' on a hawk."

"And we got him," Penny said.

Buck shook himself. The whole array seemed to sober.

"Don't tell me none o' them tales. Where's he at?"

" 'Bout two mile to the east, between Bear Spring and the river."

"Reckon he is. He fools around there a good bit."

"He's dead. How I know he's dead, I gutted him. Me and Jody's walkin' to Fort Gates for he'p in totin' him outen the swamp."

Buck stiffened in a drunken dignity.

"You goin' to Fort Gates for he'p gittin' out ol' Slew-foot? And the best slew-footers in the county right here beside you?"

Lem called, "What'll you give us, do we go tote him out?"

"Half the meat. I figgered on givin' it to you anyways, account of him tormentin' you so, and Buck comin' to warn me."

Buck said, "You and me's friends, Penny Baxter. I warn you and you warn me. Git up here behind me and point the way."

Mill-wheel said, "I don't know as I crave goin' into no swamp today, and clare back to Baxter's Island. I got my mind set on a frolic."

Buck said, "You ain't got no mind. Penny Baxter!"

"What you want?"

"You still figgerin' on goin' to them doin's at Volusia?"

"Could we git the bear out in time to make it, we figgered on it. We're runnin' mighty late."

"Git up here behind me and point the way. Boys, we'll git out the bear and we'll go to the doin's at Volusia. If they don't want us, they kin throw us out—if they kin."

Penny hesitated. Help of any sort from Fort Gates, especially Christmas Eve day, would be hard to obtain. But the Forresters at the respectable gathering would scarcely be welcome. He decided to let them help him with the big carcass and then trust to luck to send them on their way again. He swung up behind Buck. Mill-wheel held down a hand for Jody to clamber up behind him.

Penny said, "Who's big-hearted enough to tote my bull-dog? He's not bad hurt, but he's done a heap o' runnin' and fightin'."

Gabby picked up Rip and carried him in the saddle in front of him.

Penny said, "Likely the way we come out is as good as any. You kin about see where we come."

The walk that had seemed so long was as nothing on the Forresters' horses. The Baxters remembered that they had not eaten since breakfast. They fished in their knapsacks and munched on Nellie Ginright's bread and meat. Penny in his light-heartedness fell into the spirit of the Forresters' drunkenness.

He shouted back, "Spent the night with an old gal o' mine."

They whooped noisily in applause.

"Only she wasn't there!"

They whooped again.

Jody, at leisure, remembered the jovial air of Nellie Ginright.

He said to Mill-wheel's back, "Mill-wheel, if my Ma had been somebody else, would I be me, or would I be somebody else, too?"

Mill-wheel shouted ahead, "Hey! Jody wants a new Ma!"

He thumped on Mill-wheel's back.

"I do not either. I jest want to know."

The question was beyond Mill-wheel, sober. It was only a source of ribald comment, drunk.

Penny said, "Now jest past that stretch o' low hammock, there's our bear."

They dismounted. Lem spat in disgust.

"You lucky son of a preacher——"

334

The Yearling

"Ary man could of come up with him that was willin' to stay with him," Penny said. "Or got mad enough, the way I done, to foller."

There was disagreement as to how to cut up the meat. Buck wanted to take it in whole for effect. Penny struggled to convince him of the impossibility. They talked him at last into agreeing to quarter it as was usually done with a bear of so great a size. Each dressed quarter would weigh a hundred pounds. They skinned and quartered it. The hide was left intact, with the great head and clawed feet.

Buck said, "I got to have it that-a-way. I got a idee for some fun."

They had a round of drinks from their bottles. They set back for the road with a bear quarter over each of four horses and the hide over a fifth. It needed a family as big as the Forresters' to provide transportation for old Slewfoot and both Baxters too. The procession was boisterous. They shouted back and forth to one another.

They reached Baxter's Island after dark. The house was barred and shuttered. There was no light, no curl of smoke from the chimney. Ma Baxter had gone on to the river with the horse and wagon. Flag was not about. The Forresters dismounted and drank again and called for water. Penny suggested cooking supper, but their minds were fixed on Volusia. They hung the bear-meat in the smoke-house. Buck clung stubbornly to the hide.

Jody found it strange to go around his own closed house in the dark, as though other people lived there and not the Baxters. He went to the back and called, "Flag! Here, feller!" There was no answering thump of small sharp hooves. He called again, fearfully. He turned back to the road. Flag came galloping to him from the forest. Jody clutched him so hard that he broke loose in impatience. The Forresters were shouting to him to hurry. He longed to have Flag follow along with them, but he could not endure it if he should run away again. He led him into the shed and tied him safely and barred the door against marauders. He ran back and opened it and spread out the meal he had been carrying for him in his knapsack. The Forresters thundered at him. He barred the door again and ran and climbed up behind Mill-wheel with a full heart. He could depend on Flag to come home to him.

When the Forresters burst into harsh-voiced song, like a flock of crows strung out along a fence-row, he sang with them.

Buck sang:

> "I went to see my Susan.
> She met me at the door.
> She told me that I needn't to come
> To see her any more."

Mill-wheel called, "Whoopee! How 'bout it, Lem?"
Buck went on:

> "She'd fallen in love with Rufus
> Of Andrew Jackson fame.
> I looked her in the face and said,
> 'Good-bye, Miss Susan Jane!'"

"Whoopee!"
Gabby sang a plaintive lament of matrimony, each stanza ending with the refrain:

> "I married another,
> The devil's grandmother.
> I wish I was single again."

The scrub echoed with their shouting.

They reached the river at nine o'clock and bellowed for the ferry. Across the river, they rode on to the church. It was lighted. Horses and wagons and oxen and carts were tethered to the trees in the yard.

Penny said, "Now we're all right rough-lookin' for church doin's. How about Jody goin' in and fetchin' us out rations?"

But the Forresters had passed beyond persuasion or interference.

Buck said, "Now you-all he'p me git fixed. I'm aimin' to scare the devil right outen that church buildin'."

Lem and Mill-wheel draped the bear-skin over him. He got down on all fours. He could not get an effect realistic enough to suit him, for the hide, split down the belly, allowed the great heavy head to slide forward. Penny was impatient to be inside and to reassure Ma Baxter, but the Forresters were in no hurry. They donated two or three pairs of boot laces and laced the hide together across Buck's chest. The result was all he could ask for. His bulky back and shoulders filled out the hide almost as completely as the original owner. He gave a trial growl. They crept up the steps of the church. Lem swung the door open to let Buck pass inside, then pulled it back, leaving a crack wide enough for the rest to watch through. It was a moment or two before the visitor was noticed. Buck swayed forward with so true an imitation of a bear's rolling gait that Jody felt the hair crawl on the back of his neck. Buck growled. The assembled company turned. Buck halted. There was an instant of paralysis, then the church emptied through the windows as though a gale of wind had blown a pile of oak leaves.

The Forresters entered through the door, bellowing with laughter. Penny and Jody followed. Suddenly Penny leaped for Buck and pulled the bear's head away so that the human face was exposed.

"Git outen that thing, Buck. You want to git kilt?"

His eye had caught the glint of a gun-barrel at one of the windows. Buck stood up and the hide slipped to the floor. The frolickers crowded in again. Outside, a woman screaming could not be quieted and two or three children wailed in fear. The first reaction of the gathering was one of anger.

The Yearling

One man called, "This be a purty way to come celebratin'
Christmas Eve. Scarin' young uns outen their wits."

But the holiday spirit was strong, and the drunken jovi-
ality of the Forresters was infectious. Interest centered in
the great bear hide. Here and there a man guffawed and at
last the crowd was laughing, and agreeing that Buck had
looked more like a bear than old Slewfoot himself. The big
bear had done damage for several years. His reputation was
known to all.

Penny was surrounded by most of the men and boys. His
wife greeted him and bustled away to bring him a plate of
food. He sat on the edge of one of the church benches,
pushed back against the plain bare walls, and tried to eat.
He swallowed a few mouthfuls. Then the men's eager questions enmeshed him and he was away on the flowing stream
of his tale of the hunt. The food sat in his lap, uneaten.

Jody looked shyly about in the unaccustomed color and
brightness. The small church was decorated with holly and
mistletoe and donations of house plants; sultanas and gerani-
ums, aspidistras and coleas. Kerosene lamps shone from
brackets along the walls. The ceiling was half hidden with
suspended ropes of colored paper, green and red and yellow.
At the front, where the rostrum stood for services, a Christmas tree was hung with tinsel and strings of popcorn, figures
cut from paper, and a few shining balls that had been a
present from the captain of the *Mary Draper*. Gifts had been
exchanged and the wrappings were strewn under the tree.
Little girls moved trance-like with new rag dolls clutched to
their flat gingham breasts. The boys too young to be en-
grossed with Penny, played on the floor.

The food was on long plank tables near the Christmas tree.
Grandma Hutto and his mother bore down on him to lead
him to it. He found that glory hung about him, too, in a
sweet aroma. Women crowded around him and pressed food
on him. They too asked questions about the hunt. At first he
was struck dumb and could not answer. He felt hot and cold

338

and spilled salad from the plate in one hand. The other hand held three varieties of cake.

Grandma Hutto said, "Now leave him be."

He was suddenly afraid he would not have a chance to answer the questions and would miss the shining triumph of the hour.

He said quickly, "We follered him near about three days. We jumped him twice. We got into mud Pa said would bog a buzzard's shadow, and we wrangled out of it——"

They listened with flattering attention. He was filled with enthusiasm. He began at the beginning and tried to tell it as he thought Penny would do. Half-way through, he looked down at the cake. He lost interest in the account.

"Then Pa shot him," he ended abruptly.

He crammed a chunk of pound cake in his mouth. The clustered women turned to bring him more sweets.

Ma Baxter said, "Now you begin on cake, you'll not be able to hold nothin' else."

"I don't want nothin' else."

Grandma Hutto said, "Leave him be, Ory. He kin eat cornbread the rest o' the year."

"I'll eat it tomorrer," he promised. "I know you got to have cornbread to grow on."

He went from one kind of cake to another and back again.

He asked, "Ma, did Flag come in 'fore you left?"

"He come in yestiddy at dark. I declare, hit worried me, him comin' in without you. Then Nellie Ginright was here a while tonight and reported you."

He looked at her with approval. She was really handsome, he thought, in the black alpaca. Her gray hair was combed smoothly and her cheeks were flushed with her contentment and her pride. The other women addressed her respectfully. It was a great thing, he thought, to be kin to Penny Baxter.

He said, "I got somethin' purty for you, home."

"Have? 'Twouldn't be red and shiny, would it?"

"You found it!"

"I got to clean house now and agin."

"You like it?"

"Purty as kin be. I'd of wore it, but I figgered you'd want to give it to me. You want to know what I got hid for you, or no?"

"Tell me."

"I got a sack o' pep'mint candy. And your Pa made you a deer-leg scabbard for the knife Oliver give you. And he made a buckskin collar for your fawn."

"How'd he do it without me knowin'?"

"When you're oncet asleep, he could put a new roof over you, and you'd not know it."

He sighed with repletion of soul and body. He looked at the remnants of cake in his hands. He thrust them at his mother.

"I don't like it," he said.

"About time."

He looked about at the company and was again stabbed with shyness. Eulalie Boyles was doing a hop-skip-and-jump in a corner with the wordless boy who sometimes ran the ferry. Jody stared from a distance. He would scarcely have known her. She had on a white dress with blue ruffles and blue bows of ribbon swung at the ends of her pig-tails. He was swept with resentment, not of her, but of the ferry-boy. Eulalie in a remote fashion belonged to him, Jody, to do with as he pleased, if only to throw potatoes at her.

The Forresters had formed a group of their own at the end of the church near the door. The bolder of the women had taken them plates of food. To look twice at a Forrester was to invite scandal. The more roistering of the men were with them, and the bottles were going around again. The Forrester voices boomed above the hum of the festivities. The fiddlers went outside and brought in their instruments and began to tune and scrape. A square dance was formed and called. Buck and Mill-wheel and Gabby induced giggling girls to be their partners. Lem frowned from the outskirts.

The Yearling

The Forresters made a violent and noisy affair of the dance. Grandma Hutto retired to a far bench. Her black eyes snapped.

"You'd never of got me here, did I know them black devils was comin'."

"Nor me," Ma Baxter said.

They sat stonily side by side, for once in agreement and harmony. Jody was half-drunk himself with the noise and music, the cake and the excitement. The outside world was cold, but the inside of the church was hot and stuffy with the roaring wood-stove and the heat of the packed and sweating bodies.

A man, a newcomer, entered the door. A cold gust of air followed him, so that every one looked up to see what had brought it. A few noticed that Lem Forrester spoke to him, and the man answered, and Lem said something to his brothers. In a moment the Forresters went out together. The group around Penny had been filled and satisfied with his story of the hunt and was now supplementing it with tales of their own. The square dance continued with a reduced number. Some of the women went to the group of hunters, protesting their absorption. The newcomer was brought to the still-loaded tables for food. He was a traveller who had disembarked from a steamer that had stopped for wood at the river landing.

He said, "I was tellin' the men, ladies, there was other passengers got off here. I reckon you know 'em. Mr. Oliver Hutto and a young lady."

Grandma Hutto stood up.

"You sure o' that name?"

"Why, yes, Ma'am. He said his home was here."

Penny was pushing his way toward her. He took her aside.

He said, "I see you've done had the news. I'm feered the Forresters has gone to your house. I'm fixin' to go there to try to ward off trouble. You want to go? Could be, they'd behave theirselves better was you there to shame 'em."

341

She bustled about for her shawl and bonnet.

Ma Baxter said, "Now I'll jest go with you. I'd as soon give them varmints a piece o' my own mind."

Jody trailed behind them. They piled in the Baxter wagon and turned back toward the river. The sky was strangely bright.

Penny said, "Must be a woods fire some'eres. Oh, my God."

The position of the fire was unmistakable. Around the bend of the road, down the lane of oleanders, flames were shooting high into the air. Grandma Hutto's house was burning. They turned into the yard. The house was a bonfire. The flames showed details of the rooms within. Fluff ran to them, his tail between his legs. They jumped down from the wagon.

Grandma called, "Oliver! Oliver!"

It was impossible to approach within yards. Grandma ran toward the blaze. Penny pulled her back.

He shouted above the roaring and crackling, "You want to git burnt to death?"

"Oliver's there! Oliver! Oliver!"

"He cain't be. He'd of got out."

"They've shot him! He's in there! Oliver!"

He struggled with her. In the bright light the earth was plain. It was cut and trampled with the hooves of horses. But the Forresters and their mounts were gone.

Ma Baxter said, "There's jest nothin' them black buzzards won't do."

Grandma Hutto fought to break free.

Penny said, "Jody, for the Lord's sake, drive back to Boyles' store and see kin you find somebody seed where Oliver headed when he left the boat. If there's nobody there, go on to the doin's and find out from the stranger."

Jody clambered to the wagon seat and turned Cæsar back up the lane. His hands seemed wooden and he fumbled with the reins. He was panicked and could not remember whether his father had told him to go first to the doings or first to the store. If Oliver was alive, he would never be unfaithful to him, even in his mind, again. He turned into the road. The winter night was bright with stars. Cæsar snorted. A man and woman were walking down the road toward the river. He heard the man laugh.

He cried, "Oliver!" and jumped from the moving wagon.

Oliver called, "Now look who's drivin' around by hisself. Hey, Jody."

The woman was Twink Weatherby.

Jody said, "Git in the wagon, quick, Oliver."

"What's the hurry? Where's your manners? Speak to the lady."

"Oliver, Grandma's house is a-fire. The Forresters done it."

Oliver tossed his bags into the wagon. He lifted Twink and swung her to the seat, then vaulted the wheel and took the reins. Jody scrambled up beside him. Oliver groped with one hand inside his shirt and laid his revolver on the seat.

"The Forresters is gone," Jody said.

Oliver whipped the horse to a trot and turned down the lane. The frame of the house stood revealed around the flames, as though a box enclosed them. Oliver caught his breath.

"Ma wasn't in it?"

"She's yonder."

Oliver stopped the wagon and they climbed down.

He called, "Ma!"

Grandma threw her arms in the air and ran to her son.

He said, "Easy, there, old lady. Quit tremblin' now. Easy."

Penny joined them.

He said, "No man's voice was never more welcome, Oliver."

Oliver pushed Grandma aside and stared at the house. The roof crashed and a fresh blaze leaped to the moss in the live oaks.

He said, "Which-a-way has the Forresters gone?"

Jody heard Grandma murmur, "Oh God."

The Yearling

She braced herself.

She said loudly, "Now what in tarnation you want o' the Forresters?"

Oliver wheeled.

"Jody said they done it."

"Jody, you fool young un. The idees a boy'll git. I left a lamp burnin' by a open window. The curtain must of blowed and ketched. Hit worried me all through the evenin' at the doin's. Jody, you must want a ruckus mighty bad."

Jody gaped at her. His mother's mouth was open.

Ma Baxter said, "Why, you know——"

Jody saw his father grip her arm.

Penny said, "Yes, son, you got no business thinkin' sich things of innocent men is miles away."

Oliver let out his breath slowly.

He said, "I'm shore proud 'twasn't their doin'. I'd not of left one alive." He turned and drew Twink close to him. "Folks, meet my wife."

Grandma Hutto wavered, then walked to the girl and kissed her cheek.

"Now I'm glad you got it settled," she said. "Mebbe Oliver'll take time to visit with me now and again."

Oliver took Twink by the hand and went to circle the house. Grandma turned fiercely on the Baxters.

"If you dast to let it out— You think I aim to have two counties strowed with Forrester blood and my boy's bones, for a burnt-up house?"

Penny laid his hands on her shoulders.

"Ol' lady," he said. "Ol' lady— Did I have the sense you got——"

She was quivering. Penny held her and she quieted. Oliver and Twink returned.

Oliver said, "Don't take it too hard, Ma. We'll build you the best house on the river."

She gathered her strength.

"I don't want it. I'm too old. I want to live in Boston."

344

The Yearling

Jody looked at his father. Penny's face was drawn.
She said defiantly, "I want to go in the mornin'."
Oliver said, "Why, Ma— Leave here?"
His face lightened.
He said slowly, "I always ship out of Boston. Ma, I'd love
it. But do I turn you loose amongst them Yankees, I'm feered
you'll start another war between the states."

Chapter XXVII

THE Baxters stood at the river landing in the cold dawn, saying good-by to Grandma and Oliver and Twink and Fluff. Around the bend to the south, the north-bound steamboat whistled for the landing. Grandma and Ma Baxter embraced. Grandma caught Jody to her and held him tight.

"You learn to write, so you kin write to Grandma in Boston."

Oliver shook hands with Penny.

Penny said, "Jody and me'll miss you fearful."

Oliver put out his hand to Jody.

"I thank you for stickin' by me," he said. "I'll not forget you. Not even in the China Sea."

Grandma's chin was a flint arrowhead. Her mouth was tight.

Penny said, "If you folks ever change your minds and want to come back, there's a welcome at the Island day or night."

The steamboat rounded the bend and warped in to the landing. It carried a few lights, for the river between its banks was still dark.

Twink said, "We 'bout to fergit what we got for Jody."

Oliver fished in his pocket and handed her a round parcel.

She said, "This is for you, Jody, 'cause you he'ped fight for Oliver."

He was numb with the happenings of the day. He took it and stared stupidly. She leaned forward and kissed him on the forehead. Her touch was strangely agreeable. Her lips were soft and her yellow hair was fragrant.

The gang-plank was thrown down. A bundle of freight was tossed to the dock. Grandma stooped and gathered Fluff in her arms. Penny took her soft wrinkled face between his hands and laid his cheek against hers.

He said, "I got a real love for you. I—" His voice broke.

The Huttos filed up the gang-plank. The paddle-wheels thrashed the water, the current sucked at the boat. It swung out into mid-stream. Grandma and Oliver stood at the rail and waved to them. The boat whistle blew again and the steamer moved down the river. Jody stirred in his numbness and waved violently.

"Good-by, Grandma! Good-by, Oliver! Good-by, Twink!"

"Good-by, Jody——"

Their voices trailed away. It seemed to Jody that they were moving away from him into another world. It was as though he saw them die. There were rosy streaks across the east but the daylight seemed even colder than the night had been. The ashes of the Hutto house glowed faintly.

The Baxters drove home toward the scrub. Penny was wracked with sorrow for his friends. His face was strained. Jody was swept with so contradictory a tumult of thoughts that he gave up trying to sort them and snuggled down on the wagon-seat between the warmth of his mother and father. He opened the package Twink had given him. It was a small pewter canister for his gunpowder. He hugged it to him. He remembered that Easy Ozell was on the east coast, and wondered if he would follow Grandma Hutto to Boston when he found her gone. The wagon jogged on to the clearing. The day would be cold but brilliant.

Ma Baxter said, "Now if 'twas me, I'd not of left without havin' the law on them baboons."

Penny said, "Nobody couldn't prove a thing. Them horse tracks? Why, the Forresters'd only say they seed the fire and come to watch it. They could say the county was full o' horses and 'twasn't even them had been there."

"Then I'd of let Oliver know the truth."

"Yes, and what'd he of done then? Lit in and killed two-three of 'em. Oliver's hot-headed and why wouldn't he be?

Most ary man'd take out after fellers did sich as that to him.
All right. Kill him a few Forresters and mebbe hang for it.
Or else have the rest of 'em pitch in and kill the bunch of
'em, him and his Ma and his purty leetle wife."

"Purty leetle wife!" she snorted. "Chipperdale!"

Jody felt a new loyalty surge up in him.

"She do be mighty purty, Ma," he said.

"Men is all alike," she said conclusively.

Baxter's Island was at hand. A sense of safety, of well-
being, came over Jody. Other people had catastrophe, but
the clearing was beyond it. The cabin waited for him, and
the smoke-house full of good meat, with old Slewfoot's carcass added to it, and Flag. Above all, Flag. He could scarcely
contain himself until he reached the shed. He had a tale to
tell him.

Chapter XXVIII

THE January weather was mild. Now and then the sun would set in a cold red stillness, quilts would be inadequate through the night, and morning would show a thin film of ice on the water buckets. Then in a day or two it would be so warm that Ma Baxter could sit on the porch in the sun in the afternoon and work at her mending and patching, and Jody could run through the woods without his wool jacket.

The Baxter life had quieted along with the weather. The river folk were no doubt in a swivet, Penny said, over the burning of the Hutto house and the migration of the sharp-tongued mother, never understood, the sailor son, almost like a foreigner, and their own golden-headed Twink. Belief must be general that the drunken Forresters had set fire to the place on receipt of the word that Oliver had returned with the girl. But the river was a long way off, and news filtered slowly to Baxter's Island. Penny and Ma and Jody sat by the hearth-fire evening after evening, reliving the night through which they had stood with the Huttos and watched the house char into embers; had waited with them, warmed by its heat, for the morning boat that nothing could dissuade Grandma from taking.

"To my notion," Penny said, "if that stranger that come in to the doin's had knowed it was Oliver's wife, and not jest said it were a gal with him, not even Lem'd of bothered 'em. They'd of figgered 'twas time to call quits, oncet she was married."

"Wife or no wife, hit's low-down varmints'll burn a house down, figgerin' somebody's in it."

Penny sighed and was forced to agree. The Forresters must

349

be doing their trading at Fort Gates. They never passed. They had not picked up their share of the bear meat on their return. Their avoidance of Penny made their guilt incontrovertible. It saddened him. His hard-won peace lay shattered about him. A stone thrown at some distance, and meant for some one else, had struck him. He was bruised and troubled.

Jody was concerned, but it was the anxiety he felt for characters in a tale. Grandma and Oliver and Fluff and Twink had steamed away down the river as people in a book might steam. Oliver became one with the stories he had told of distant places. Now, in the stories, there were Grandma and Twink and Fluff. Oliver had said, "I'll not forget you, not even in the China Sea." And it was in the China Sea, for the most part, that he pictured him, infinitely remote and abused by people as fictitious as he.

The end of January brought continued warmth. There would be frost, even, perhaps, a freeze again, before spring truly came. But the balmy days were a harbinger. Penny plowed the fields that would have early crops. He turned the new ground that Buck had cleared for him during his illness from the rattler's striking. He had decided to try a little cotton for a money crop. The low ground near the north hammock would go into tobacco. He prepared his seed-beds between the house and the grape-arbor. With the stock reduced to old Cæsar and Trixie, he decided to plant cow-peas more sparingly and to put the extra land in corn. There seemed never to be enough. The chickens went short of feed, the hogs were not properly fattened, the Baxters themselves gave out of meal at the end of summer, all for lack of enough corn. Nothing on the clearing was more important. Jody helped him carry the winter's compost from the lot and scatter it over the sandy acres. He planned to have the ground in good condition, bedded up and ready to plant in early March, by the time the first whip-poor-will should call.

Ma Baxter complained bitterly that she had always

wanted a ginger bed. Every one else had one. The store-keeper's wife at the river had promised her roots any time she was ready for them. Penny and Jody prepared the bed. They dug down four feet deep at the side of the house and laid down cypress slats. They hauled clay from the southwest and filled it in. The first time he went trading to the river, Penny promised to bring back the roots, knobby and peaked, like antlers.

The hunting was poor. The bears were feeding over a wide range, preparing themselves to go in February into hibernation. Their dens were under up-turned hurricane stumps, or where two large logs lay crossed, affording protection. Sometimes they dragged in oak and palmetto limbs and piled them in a hollow tree to make a rough nest. Wherever the bed, it was hollowed out in a trench, over the edge of which the bear would rest his forequarters. Jody thought that it was strange that they did not go into their winter beds in December, when the first really cold weather came, and then come out earlier, in March instead of April.

"I reckon they know their own business," Penny said.

The deer were distressingly scarce, both because of the plague and the increased voracity of the remaining killers. The bucks were in poor condition, the meat lean, their coats moss-gray and shabby. They wandered usually alone. The does traveled alone or in pairs. An old doe traveled with a maiden doe, or with her male yearling. Many of the does were already heavy with fawn.

The principal work once the land was turned was hauling in wood and chopping and splitting it for both fire-places. Wood at least was more easily gotten than ever before, for the storm had brought down large numbers of trees, and the weakening of their roots from the long days of rain and steady wind had toppled still more. Timber had died by the acre in the low places. The effect was as though fire, not flood, had passed through such sections, for the dead trees stood gray and naked.

Penny said, "Now I'm proud I live in a high place. Hit'd fret me, havin' to look at all that bleakness."

Jody loved the morning jaunts for wood as well as a hunt. They were leisurely. Penny would hitch old Cæsar to the wagon on a cool sparkling morning after breakfast, and they would jog one way or another along the road as their fancy took them. The dogs would trot under the wagon and Flag would gallop ahead or to the side. He looked peculiarly wise in his buckskin collar. They would turn off into a clear place in the woods and prowl on foot for a suitable fallen tree, water oak or yellow pine by preference. There was abundant fat pine. This made the hottest and brightest hearth-fire and made fine kindling, but it smoked and smuttied the pots and kettles. They would take turns chopping, or use the cross-cut saw together, Jody liked the rhythmic swing of the saw, the singing hum as it ate into the wood, the sweet smell of the sawdust sifting to the ground.

The dogs nosed nearby in the bushes or ran rabbits. Flag nibbled at the leaf-buds or found a succulent sprig of grass that had escaped the frost. Penny always carried his shotgun. Sometimes Julia ran a rabbit within range, or a fox squirrel whisked injudiciously up a nearby pine, and there was pilau for supper. One day a pure white fox squirrel peered boldly at them and Penny would not shoot. It was a curiosity, he said, like the albino 'coon. The meat of old Slewfoot had been coarse and stringy with age and it took long cooking to tender it. The Baxters had been glad when the last of it was gone. Most of it had been smoked for the dogs, and while it would have been edible in necessity, no one was ever tempted to ask for it. His fat, however, tried out, filled a large wooden bucket. It was as clear and golden as early honey and was fine for all cooking. The cracklings were as flavory as those from a prime hog. There was a double satisfaction whenever any of the Baxters snapped them between their teeth.

Ma Baxter spent long hours at her quilting. Penny held Jody to his lessons. The evenings were spent by the hearth-fire, blazing brightly to supply light as well as heat. The wind howled cozily around the house. On still nights of moonlight, the foxes could be heard barking in the hammock. Then the lesson stopped and Penny nodded to Jody and they listened together. The foxes seldom came to raid the Baxter hen-roost.

"They know ever' hair o' Julia's head," Penny chuckled. "They ain't temptin' Providence."

One cold bright night at the end of January, Penny and Ma Baxter had gone to bed while Jody lingered with Flag by the fire. He heard a sound outside in the yard, as though the dogs were scuffling. The commotion was livelier than the pair usually made. He went to the front window and pressed his face to the cold pane. A strange dog was romping with Rip in play. Julia watched tolerantly. He caught his breath. It was not a dog. It was a gray wolf, lean and lame. He turned to run and call his father, then, irresistibly drawn, went back to watch again. Wolf and dog had plainly played together before. They were not strangers. They played silently, as though the dogs kept the secret. Jody went to the door of the bedroom and called softly. Penny came.

"What's the matter, son?"

Jody tiptoed to the window, beckoning. Penny followed on bare feet and looked out where Jody pointed. He whistled under his breath. He made no move for his gun. They watched silently. In the bright moonlight the motions of the animals were plain. The visitor was crippled in one hip. Its movements were clumsy.

Penny whispered, "Someway piteeful, ain't it?"

"Reckon it's one o' them we rounded up that day at the ponds?"

Penny nodded.

"Hit's almost certain the last one. Pore thing, hurt and lonesome— Come visitin' its nighest kin to pick a play."

Perhaps the sibilance of their whispers reached beyond the closed window or their scent drifted to the wolf's nose. Soundlessly, it turned and left the dogs and clambered with difficulty over the fence and was gone into the night.

Jody asked, "Will it do harm here?"

Penny stretched out his feet to the embers on the hearth.

"I mis-doubt it's in shape to ketch itself a square meal. I'd not dream o' botherin' it. A bear'll finish it, or a panther. Leave it live out the rest of its life."

They squatted together by the hearth, caught up in the sadness and the strangeness. It was a harsh thing, even for a wolf, to be so alone that it must turn to the yard of its enemy for companionship. Jody laid an arm across Flag. He wished Flag could understand that he had been spared desolation in the forest. As for himself, Flag had eased a loneliness that had harassed him in the very heart of his family.

He saw the lone wolf once again on the waning moon. It never came again. By tacit consent, its visits were not revealed to Ma Baxter. She would have demanded its death, whether or no. Penny believed that the dogs had made its acquaintance on one of their hunts, or perhaps when they were cutting wood, and the dogs had wandered away on their own business.

Chapter XXIX

IN FEBRUARY, Penny became badly crippled for a time with his rheumatism. It had bothered him for several years in cold or wet weather. He was careless always about exposure, doing whatever he wished to do, or what seemed necessary, regardless of the weather and unsparing of himself. It was as good a time as any, Ma Baxter said, for him to be laid up, but he was uneasy for fear he would not be ready for his spring planting.

"Then let Jody do it," she said impatiently.

"He's never done nothin' but foller me at it. There's so many things a boy kin do wrong at sich work as that."

"Yes, and whose fault is it he don't know more about it? You've spared him too long. When you was nearly thirteen, wasn't you plowin' like a man?"

"Yes, and that's jest why I don't crave for him to do it 'til he's got his growth and his strength."

"Old butter-hearted," she muttered. "Plowin' never hurt nobody."

She pounded poke-root and boiled it and made poultices for him, and made him a tonic of prickly ash and poke-root and potassium. He accepted her ministrations gratefully, but was no better. He went back to his panther oil, and rubbed his knees patiently with it, an hour at a time, and said it helped him more than the other remedies.

While his father was idle, Jody did the light chores and kept up with the wood. He had an incentive to hurry at his work, for when it was done, he was free to wander away with Flag. Penny even permitted him to take the shotgun with him. He missed his father's company, yet he liked to hunt alone. He and Flag were free together. They liked best going

355

to the sink-hole. They had stumbled on a game there one day when Flag had gone with him when he went to fetch drinking water. The game was a mad one of tag, up and down the steep slopes of the great green bowl. Flag was unbeatable at it, for he was up and down one side half a dozen times while Jody was making one climb to the top. Finding that he could not be caught, he alternated between a teasing business of wearing Jody out, and a more satisfying and ingratiating trick of deliberately allowing himself to be captured.

On a warm sunny day in mid-February, Jody looked up from the bottom of the sink-hole. Flag stood in silhouette at the top. For a startled moment, it seemed to him that it was another deer. Flag was so big— He had not seen how fast he was growing. Many a young yearling shot for food was no bigger than he. He went home to Penny in excitement. Penny sat by the kitchen hearth, wrapped in quilts, though the day was mild.

Jody burst out, "Pa, you reckon Flag's near about a yearlin'?"

Penny looked at him quizzically.

"I been thinkin' that myself lately. Give him a month more, I'd say he was a yearlin'."

"How'll he be different?"

"Well, he'll stay off in the woods longer. He'll grow a good bit bigger. He'll be betwixt and between. He'll be like a person standin' on the state line. He'll be leavin' one and turnin' into t'other. Behind him's the fawn. Before him's the buck."

Jody stared into vacancy.

"Will he have horns?"

"He'll likely not show no horns before July. The bucks is sheddin' their horns right now. They'll be butt-headed all through the spring. Then along in the summer the spikes'll show and by ruttin' season they'll have full sets agin."

Jody examined Flag's head carefully. He felt the hard edge of his forehead. Ma Baxter passed by with a pan in her hand.

The Yearling

"Hey, Ma, Flag'll soon be a yearlin'. Won't he be purty, Ma, with leetle ol' horns? Won't his horns be purty?"

"He'd not look purty to me did he have a crown on. And angel's wings."

He followed her to cajole her. She sat down to look over the dried cow-peas in the pan. He rubbed his nose over the down of her cheek. He liked the furry feel of it.

"Ma, you smell like a roastin' ear. A roastin' ear in the sun."

"Oh git along. I been mixin' cornbread."

" 'Tain't that. Listen, Ma, you don't keer do Flag have horns or no. Do you?"

"Hit'll be that much more to butt and bother."

He did not press the point. Flag was in increasing disgrace, at best. He had learned to slip free from the halter about his neck. When it was tightened so that he could not get out of it, he used the same tactics that a calf used against restraint. He strained against it until his eyes bulged and his breathing choked, and to save his perverse life, it was necessary to release him. Then when he was free, he raised havoc. There was no holding him in the shed. He would have razed it to the ground. He was wild and impudent. He was allowed in the house only when Jody was on hand to keep up with him. But the closed door seemed to make him possessed to enter. If it was not barred, he butted it open. He watched his chance and slipped in to cause some minor damage whenever Ma Baxter's back was turned.

She set the dish of shelled dried peas on the table and went to the hearth. Jody went to his room to look for a piece of rawhide. There was a clatter and commotion and then Ma Baxter's storm of fury. Flag had leaped onto the table, seized a mouthful of the peas and sent the pan sprawling, the peas scattered from one end of the kitchen to the other. Jody came running. His mother threw the door open and drove Flag out with the broom. He seemed to enjoy the fracas. He kicked up his heels, flicked his white flag of a tail, shook his head as though threatening to attack with imaginary antlers, sailed over the fence and galloped away to the woods.

Jody said, "That were my fault, Ma. I shouldn't of left him. He were hongry, Ma. The pore feller didn't git enough for breakfast. You should of beat me, Ma, not him."

"I'll tear down all two of you. Now git down and pick up ever' one o' them peas and wash 'em off."

He was only too glad to do so. He crawled under the table and reached behind the kitchen safe and under the inside water-shelf and in every corner, to retrieve them. He washed them carefully and went to the sink-hole for extra water, to replace what he had used, and more. He felt entirely righteous.

"Now see, Ma," he said, "they's no harm done. Ary leetle harm Flag do, you kin depend on me to take keer of it."

Flag did not return until sunset. Jody fed him outside and waited to smuggle him into his bedroom after Penny and Ma were in bed. Flag had lost his fawn's willingness to sleep long hours and had been increasingly restless at night. Ma Baxter had complained that she had heard him tripping about in Jody's room or the front room several times. Jody had invented a plausible tale of rats on the roof, but his mother was sceptical. Perhaps Flag had had a sleep that afternoon in the woods, for this night he left his moss pallet and pushed open the rickety door of Jody's bedroom and wandered about the house. Jody was aroused by a piercing shriek from his mother. Flag had awakened her from a sound sleep by pushing his wet muzzle against her face. Jody slipped the fawn out by the front door before she should do a more thorough job of it.

"Now that ends it," she raged. "The creetur gives me no peace day or night. Now he cain't come in this house, no time, never no more."

Penny had kept apart from the controversy. Now he spoke from his bed.

The Yearling

"Your Ma's right, boy. He's got too big and restless to be in the house."

Jody went back to bed and lay wakeful, wondering if Flag were cold. He thought it was unreasonable of his mother to object to the clean soft nose against her own. He could never get enough of fondling the delicate muzzle, himself. She was a mean, hard woman and did not care if he was lonely. His resentment eased him and he went to sleep, clutching his pillow and pretending that it was Flag. The fawn snorted and stamped around the house most of the night.

In the morning Penny felt well enough to dress and hobble around the clearing, leaning on a stick. He made the rounds. He returned to the rear of the house. His face was grave. He called Jody to him. Flag had trampled back and forth across the tobacco seed-bed. The young plants were almost ready to set out. He had destroyed nearly half of them. There would be enough for the usual patch for Penny's own use. There would be no money crop, as he had planned, for storekeeper Boyles at Volusia.

"I don't figger Flag done it malicious," he said. "He were jest racin' back and forth and it were somethin' to jump on, was all. Now you go set up stakes all through the bed amongst the plants and all around the bed, to keep him offen the rest of 'em. I should of done it before, I reckon, but I never studied on him rompin' in that pertickler place."

Penny's reasonableness and kindness depressed Jody as his mother's rage had not done. He turned away disconsolately to do the job.

Penny said, "Now it jest bein' accidental-like, we'll not say nothin' to your Ma. Hit'd be a pore time for her to know it."

As Jody worked, he tried to think of a way to keep Flag out of mischief. Most of his tricks he considered only clever, but the destruction of the seed-bed was serious. He was sure that such a thing would never happen again.

Chapter XXX

ARCH came in with a cool and sunny splendor. The yellow jessamine bloomed late and covered the fences and filled the clearing with its sweetness. The peach trees blossomed, and the wild plums. The red birds sang all day, and when they had done with their song in the evening, the mocking-birds continued. The ground doves nested and cooed one to another and walked about the sand of the clearing like shadows bobbing.

Penny said, "If I was dead, I'd set up and take notice, a day like this un."

There had been a light shower during the night and the hazy substance of the sunrise indicated there would be another before night. But the morning itself was luminous.

"Jest right for corn," Penny said. "Jest right for cotton. Jest right for 'baccy."

"I take it you're pleased with the day," Ma Baxter said.

He grinned and finished his breakfast.

"Now jest 'cause you feel better," she warned him, "don't git in the field and kill yourself."

"I feel so good," he said, "I'll kill ary thing keeps me from plantin'. All day. I'm fixin' to plant all day. Today. Tomorrer. The next day. Plantin'. Corn. Cotton. 'Baccy."

"I heered you," she said.

He stood up and thumped her on the back.

"Cow-peas! 'Taters! Greens!"

She had to laugh at him, and Jody laughed too.

"Hear you tell it," she said, "you're fixin' to plant the world."

"I'd purely love it." He threw out his arms. "A day like this un, I'd love to plant rows from here to Boston and back agin to Texas. Then when I come to Texas, I'd turn around and go back to Boston to see had the seeds come up yit."

"I see where Jody gits his fairy-tales," she said.

He pounded Jody on the back.

"You got a sweet job, boy. You kin set out the 'baccy plants. If my back didn't near about kill me when I stoop, I'd take it from you, for I love settin' plants. Leetle ol' young green things— Givin' 'em a chancet to grow."

He went whistling to his work. Jody gulped his breakfast and followed him. Penny was at the tobacco seed-bed, lifting out the tender plants.

"You belong to handle 'em like they was new-borned babies," he said.

He set out a dozen plants by way of lesson, then watched and corrected Jody while he went on with the row. He brought old Cæsar and the scooter plow and turned in to the field, laid off and bedded up ready for the corn, to open the furrows for the planting. Jody hunched along on his heels, or dropped to his knees when his legs grew tired. He worked leisurely, for Penny said there was no hurry, and that the job must be done well. The March sun grew strong in mid-morning, but a fresh breeze blew. The tobacco plants wilted behind him, but the night's dark coolness would bring them upright again. He watered them as he went and had to go twice to the sink-hole for water. Flag had disappeared after breakfast and was not in sight. Jody missed him, but he was relieved that the fawn had chosen the particular morning to stay away. If he joined him, and gamboled about as usual, he would destroy the plants faster than Jody could set them out. He finished the task by dinner time. The tobacco patch filled only a portion of the ground that Penny had prepared for it according to the original size of the seed-bed. When Penny went with him after dinner to look it over, his father's exuberance ebbed.

"You ain't left no plants in the bed, boy? You got 'em all?"

"Ever' one. I even set them leetle ol' spindly ones."

The Yearling

"Well— I'll put in somethin' else to fill out."

Jody offered eagerly, "I kin he'p you with t'other plantin' now. Or tote water for you."

"No need to water. Hit looks more prosperous for a shower ever' minute. You kin he'p plant."

Penny had the furrows open for the corn. Now he went ahead, drilling his holes with a pointed stick down the long rows. Jody followed, dropping two kernels to the hole. He was anxious to please, to have his father forget the shrunken tobacco patch.

He called, "Goes fast, two workin', don't it, Pa?"

Penny did not answer. Yet as the early spring day clouded and the light wind shifted into the southeast and it was plain that a shower would come on the planting, insuring the quick sprouting of the corn, his spirits lifted again. The rain caught them in the late afternoon, but they continued to work and finished the field. It rolled gently, well-tilled and tawny, its soft bosom receptive to the rain. Leaving it, Penny rested on the split-rail fence and looked back over it with satisfaction. There was a wistful look in his eyes as well, as though he were obliged now to leave his handiwork to forces he could only trust blindly not to betray him.

Flag came bounding out of the rain from the south. He came to Jody to be scratched behind the ears. He leaped back and forth in a zig-zag across the fence, then stopped under a mulberry tree and reached up to catch the tip of a bough. Jody sat on the fence beside his father. He turned to call Penny's attention to the slim neck of the fawn stretched up to the new green leaves of the mulberry. His father was studying the young deer with an unfathomable expression. His eyes were narrowed and speculative. He seemed, as when he had set out after old Slewfoot, a stranger. A chill passed over the boy that was not of the dampness of the rain.

He said, "Pa——"

Penny turned to him, startled from his thoughts. He looked down, as though to hide a thing in his eyes.

362

The Yearling

He said carelessly, "That fawn o' yourn shore growed up in a hurry. He ain't the baby you toted home in your arms all the way that black night— He's a yearlin' now, for shore."

The words gave Jody little pleasure. Somehow, he sensed they were not quite what his father had been thinking. Penny laid his hand an instant on his son's knee.

"You're a pair o' yearlin's," he said. "Hit grieves me."

They slid from the fence and went to the lot to do the chores, then to the house to dry out by the fire. The rain beat lightly on the shingled roof. Flag bleated outside to be allowed to come in. Jody looked appealingly at his mother but she was deaf and blind. Penny felt stiff and sat with his back close to the heat, rubbing his knees. Jody begged some stale cornbread and went outside. He made a fresh bed in the shed and enticed Flag inside with the bread. He sat down and the deer finally doubled his long legs under him and lay down beside him. Jody took hold of the two pointed ears and rubbed his nose against the wet muzzle.

"You a yearlin' now," he said. "You hear me? You growed up. Now you listen to me. You got to be good, now you're growed. You cain't go gallivantin' acrost no t'baccy. Don't you git Pa down on you. You listenin'?"

Flag chewed ruminatively.

"All right, then. Now soon as we git done with the plantin', I kin go off with you agin. You wait for me. You was gone too long today. Don't you go wild, jest 'cause I told you you was a yearlin'."

He left Flag and had the satisfaction of seeing him remain contentedly in the shed. Ma Baxter and Penny had begun supper when he went into the kitchen. They made no comment on his lateness. They ate in silence. Penny went to bed at once. Jody was suddenly tired out and dropped into bed without washing his dusty feet. When his mother came to his door to remind him of it, he was asleep with one arm thrown back over the pillow. She stood looking at him, then turned away without arousing him.

The Yearling

In the morning, Penny was blithe again.

"Today's cotton day," he said.

The soft rain had stopped in the night. The morning was dewy. The fields were rosy, dipping into lavender at the far misty edges. The mocking-birds made a musical din along the fence-rows.

"They tryin' to hurry the mulberries," Penny said.

The cotton was sowed free in drills. Later it would be chopped out to a stand, a foot apart, with the hoe. Jody followed his father as before, dropping the small shining seeds. He was curious about the new Baxter crop and asked endless questions. Flag had disappeared shortly after breakfast, but came trotting to the planters in mid-morning. Again Penny watched him. His sharp hooves cut deeply into the soft moist earth, but the seeds were planted deeply enough so that no harm was possible.

"He do take out after you when he misses you," Penny said.

"He's like a dog that-a-way, ain't he, Pa? He wants to tag me jest like Julia tags you."

"You think a heap of him, don't you, boy?"

"Why, shore."

He stared at his father.

Penny said, "Well, we'll wait and see."

The remark made no particular sense and Jody ignored it.

The planting continued all week. Cow-peas followed the corn and cotton. Sweet potatoes followed the cow-peas. The vegetable garden back of the house was planted to onions and turnips, for the moon was dark, and root crops must be planted then. Penny had been forced by his rheumatism to let pass the fourteenth of February, the date on which collards should be planted, so as not to go to seed. He was tempted to put them in now, but since the leafy crops did best when planted on an increasing moon, he decided to wait a week or so.

He was up early each day and finished late. He drove himself mercilessly. The planting itself was done, but he was not content. He was in a fever over the spring work, for weather conditions were favorable and the year's living depended on the immediate results. He carried the two heavy buckets full of water from the sink-hole again and again to water the tobacco plants and the garden.

A stump that Buck Forrester had left to rot out in the new ground where the cotton was planted, annoyed him. He dug and chopped around it, then hooked trace chains to it and put old Cæsar at pulling on it. The old horse tugged and strained, his sides heaving. Penny lashed a rope about the stump, said "Gee-up!" to Cæsar and pulled with him. Jody saw his father's face turn white. Penny clutched at his groin and sank to his knees. Jody ran to him.

"Hit's all right. I'll be all right in a minute— Reckon I strained myself——"

He dropped to the ground and stirred in agony.

He murmured, "I'll be all right— Go put Cæsar up— Wait— Take a-holt o' my hand— I'll ride him in."

He was bent double and could not straighten, for pain. Jody helped him to the stump. From there he managed to clamber on Cæsar's back. He leaned forward, resting his head on Cæsar's neck, gripping the mane. Jody unhitched the trace chains and led the horse out of the field and through the gate into the yard. Penny made no move to get down. Jody brought a chair for him to stand on, to break the descent. Penny slid to it and to the ground and crept into the house. Ma Baxter turned from her work at the kitchen table. She dropped a pan with a clatter.

"I knowed it! You've hurted yourself. You don't never know to quit."

He shuffled to his bed and threw himself face down on it. She followed and turned him over and put a pillow under his head. She pulled off his shoes and laid a light quilt over him. He stretched out his legs with relief. He closed his eyes.

"That's good— Oh Ory, that's good— I'll be all right in a minute. Must o' strained myself——"

365

Chapter XXXI

PENNY did not recover. He lay suffering without complaint. Ma Baxter wanted Jody to ride for Doc Wilson, but Penny would not allow it.

"I owe him a'ready," he said. "I'll git easement direckly."

"You're likely ruptured."

"Even so— Hit'll clare up."

Ma Baxter lamented, "If you had a mite o' sense— But you'll try to do like as if you was big as a Forrester."

"My uncle Miles were a big man and he were ruptured. He got around all right. Please to hush, Ory."

"I'll not hush. I want you should learn your lesson and learn it good."

"I've done learned it. Please hush."

Jody was disturbed. Yet Penny was always having minor accidents, trying, with his small stout physique, to do the work of ten. Jody could remember dimly when a tree that Penny was felling had caught him, crushing one shoulder. His father had carried his arm in a sling for long months, but he had recovered and been as strong as ever. Nothing could harm Penny for long. Not even a rattlesnake, he thought comfortingly, could kill him. Penny was inviolable, as the earth was inviolable. Only Ma Baxter fretted and fumed, but she would have done so if it were only a little finger that had been strained.

Shortly after Penny was laid up, Jody came in to report that the corn was up. The stand was perfect.

"Now ain't that fine!"

The pale face on the pillow was bright.

"Now if it so happen I ain't outen the bed, you're jest the

366

feller to plow it out." He frowned. "Boy, you know as good as I do, you got to keep that yearlin' outen the fields."

"I'll keep him out. He ain't bothered nary thing."

"That's fine. That's jest fine. But you keep him out, religious."

Jody spent most of the next day on a hunt with Flag. They went nearly to Juniper Spring and returned with four squirrels.

Penny said, "Now that's what I call a son. Come in with rations for his old man."

Ma Baxter made a pilau of the squirrels for supper.

"They do eat good," she said.

"Why, the meat's so tender," Penny said, "you could kiss it off the bones."

Jody, and Flag with him, was in high favor.

A light rain fell in the night. In the morning he went to the cornfield at Penny's request to see whether the rain had pushed the corn and whether there was any sign of cutworms. He leaped the split-rail fence and set out across the field. He had gone some yards when it occurred to him that he should be seeing the pale green shoots of the corn. There were none. He was bewildered. He went farther. There was no corn visible. It was not until he reached the far end of the field that the delicate sprouts appeared. He walked back along the rows. Flag's sharp tracks were plain. He had pulled up the corn in the early morning as neatly as though it had been pulled by hand.

Jody was frightened. He dawdled about the field, hoping to have a miracle happen and the corn appear again when his back was turned. Perhaps he was having a nightmare in which Flag had eaten the corn crop, and when he awakened he would go out and find it growing, green and tender. He pushed a stick into one arm to make sure. The dull misery he felt was that of a bad dream, but the pain in his arm was as real as the destruction of the corn. He dragged back to the house with slow and heavy feet. He sat down in the kitchen

and did not go to his father. Penny called him. He went to
the bedroom.

"Well, boy? How's the crops?"

"The cotton's up. Hit looks like okry, don't it?" His enthusiasm was spurious. "The cow-peas is breakin' the ground."

He spread the toes of his bare feet and wriggled them. He
was absorbed in them, as though they had developed an
interesting new function.

"And the corn, Jody?"

His heart beat as fast as a humming-bird's wings. He swallowed and took the plunge.

"Somethin's et off most of it."

Penny lay silent. His silence was a nightmare, too. At last
he spoke.

"Couldn't you tell what 'twas, done it?"

He looked at his father. His eyes were desperate and be-
seeching.

Penny said, "Ne' mind. I'll git your Ma to go look. She
kin tell."

"Don't send Ma!"

"She's obliged to know."

"Don't send her!"

"Hit were Flag done it, wa'n't it?"

Jody's lips trembled.

"I reckon— Yes, sir."

Penny looked at him pityingly.

"I'm sorry, boy. I more'n half looked for him to do it. You
go play a while. Tell your Ma to come here."

"Don't tell her, Pa. Please don't tell her."

"She's got to know, Jody. Now go on. I aim to do the best
I kin for you."

He stumbled to the kitchen.

"Pa wants you, Ma."

He went out of the house. He called Flag, quaveringly.
The deer came to him from the black-jack. Jody walked
down the road with his arm across his back. He loved him

more than ever, in his sin. Flag kicked up his heels and invited him to romp. He had no heart for play. He walked slowly as far as the sink-hole. It was lovely as a spring flower garden. The dog-wood had not finished blooming. The last blossoms were white against the pale green of the sweet gums and the hickories. He was not even tempted to walk around it. He turned back to the house and went inside. His mother and father were still talking. Penny called to him to come in beside the bed. Ma Baxter's face was flushed. She was hot with defeat. Her mouth was a tight line.

Penny said quietly, "We've come to a agreement, Jody. What's happened is powerful bad, but we'll have a try at a remedy. I take it you're willin' to work extry hard to fix things."

"I'll jest do ary thing, Pa. I'll keep Flag shut up 'til the crops is made——"

"We got no earthly place to shut up a wild thing like that. Now listen to me. You go now and git corn from the crib. Pick the best ears. Your Ma'll he'p you shell it. You go then and plant it jest like we done before, right where the first lot was put. Drill your holes like I done, and go back over and drop the seed and kiver it."

"I know jest how."

"Then time you git that done, likely along tomorrer mornin', you hitch Cæsar to the wagon and go yonder to the old clearin' on the way to the Forresters, where the road turns off. You tear down that old rail fence there and load the rails on the wagon. Not too heavy a load, for Cæsar cain't pull too much on that piece of up-grade. You make as many trips as you need to. Pile the rails here and yon along our fence. Dump your first loads along the south side o' the cornfield and along the east side, borderin' the house yard. Then you build up that fence—workin' first on them two sides—jest as high as you got the rails to do it. I been noticin' your yearlin' allus takes the fence on this end. If you kin keep him out up here, he'll mebbe stay out 'til you kin build up the rest."

The Yearling

It seemed to Jody that he had been shut up in a small black box and now the lid was off, and the sun and light and air came in across him, and he was free.

Penny said, "Now when you git your fence higher'n you kin reach, if I ain't on my feet by then, your Ma'll he'p you with the riders."

Jody turned joyously to embrace his mother. She was patting one foot ominously on the floor. She stared straight ahead and did not speak. He decided that it was probably best not to touch her. Nothing could alter his relief. He ran outside. Flag was feeding along the road near the gate. Jody threw his arms around him.

"Pa's fixed it," he told him. "Ma's pattin' her foot, but Pa's fixed it."

Flag's mind was on the tender sprigs of grass and he shook free. Jody went whistling to the crib and sorted over the corn for the ears with the largest kernels. It would take a good many ears of the remaining corn for seed for the second planting. He carried it in a sack to the back door and sat down on the stoop and began the shelling. His mother came and sat beside him. Her face was a frigid mask. She picked up an ear and went to work.

"Huh!" she snorted.

Penny had forbidden her outright to scold Jody. He had not forbidden her to talk to herself.

" 'Spare his feelin's!' Huh! And who's to spare our bellies this winter? Huh!"

Jody swung around so that his back was partly turned on her. He hummed under his breath, ignoring her.

"Hush that racket."

He left off his humming. It was no moment to be impudent or to argue. His fingers flew. The corn popped from the cobs. He wanted to be away from her and at his planting as quickly as possible. He gathered up the sack of seed and slung it over his shoulder and went to the field. It was nearly dinner time, but he could get in an hour's work. In the open field he

370

was free to sing and whistle. A mocking-bird in the hammock sang, whether in competition or harmony, he could not tell. The March day was blue and gold. The feel of the corn in his fingers, the feel of the earth that reached out to enclose the corn, was good. Flag discovered him and joined him.

He said, "You do your rompin' right now, ol' feller. You goin' to git barred out."

He bolted his dinner at noon and hurried back to the planting. He worked so fast that a couple of hours would finish it the next morning. He sat at Penny's bedside after supper, chattering like a squirrel. Penny listened gravely, as always, but his responses were sometimes detached and vacant, and his thoughts were elsewhere. Ma Baxter kept stonily to herself. Dinner and supper had both been meager and indifferently cooked, as though she took her revenge from behind her own citadel, the cook-pot. Jody paused for breath. In the hammock, a whip-poor-will called. Penny's face brightened.

" 'When the first whip-poor-will calls, the corn had ought to be in the ground.' We still not too late, boy."

"Ever' last bit'll be in tomorrer mornin'."

"That's good."

He closed his eyes. Relief from acute agony had come, as long as he lay quiet. When he moved, the pain was excruciating. He was wracked constantly with his rheumatism.

He said, "You go on to bed now and git your rest."

Jody left him and washed his feet without being told. He went to bed, peaceful of mind and tired of body, and was asleep in an instant. He awakened before dawn with a feeling of responsibility. He got out of bed and dressed immediately.

Ma Baxter said, "Pity hit take a thing like this to make you put out."

In standing between her and Flag during the past months, he had learned the value of his father's trick of an unarguing silence. It annoyed his mother more for the moment, but she stopped scolding sooner. He ate heartily but hurriedly, slipped a handful of biscuits inside his shirt for Flag, and went at once to his work. He could scarcely see, at first, to plant. He watched the sun rise beyond the grape arbor. In the thin golden light the young leaves and tendrils of the Scuppernong were like Twink Weatherby's hair. He decided that sunrise and sunset both gave him a pleasantly sad feeling. The sunrise brought a wild, free sadness; the sunset, a lonely yet a comforting one. He indulged his agreeable melancholy until the earth under him turned from gray to lavender and then to the color of dried corn husks. He went at his work vigorously. Flag came to him from the woods where he had evidently spent the night. He fed him the biscuits and let him nose inside his shirt bosom for the crumbs. He tingled with the sensation of the soft wet nose against his bare flesh.

When the planting of the corn was finished in the early morning, he bounded back to the lot. Old Cæsar was pasturing south of it. He lifted his grizzled head from the grass with a mild astonishment. Jody had seldom had the harnessing of him. He behaved meekly for the hitching and stepped backward politely between the shafts of the wagon. It gave Jody an agreeable sense of authority. He made his voice as deep as possible and gave unnecessary orders. Cæsar obeyed humbly. Jody took his seat alone, slapped the reins and set off to the abandoned clearing to the west. Flag was pleased with the business and trotted ahead. Now and then he stopped dead in the middle of the road, for mischievousness, and Jody had to stop the horse and cajole the deer into moving.

"You mighty biggety now you're a yearlin'," he called to him.

He flicked the reins and made Cæsar jog-trot, then remembered that he would have many trips to make, and allowed the old animal to slow down to his usual walk. At the clearing, it was no job at all to pull the old split-rail fence apart. The stakes and riders collapsed conveniently. The loading seemed easy for a time, then his back and arms began to ache and he had to stop and rest. There was no danger of over-loading, because it was too difficult to pile the rails past a certain height. He tried to coax Flag to jump up on the seat beside him. The yearling eyed the narrow space and turned away and could not be induced. Jody tried to lift him in, but he was astonishingly heavy and he could no more than get his front legs over the wagon wheel. He gave it up and turned around and drove home. Flag went into a sprint and was waiting ahead of him when he reached there. He decided to begin dumping his piles at the fence corner near the house and working in both directions, alternately. In that way, when the rails gave out, he would have built up the fence highest across Flag's favorite crossing places.

The hauling and unloading took longer than he dreamed of. Midway, it seemed an endless and a hopeless task. The corn would be up before he had begun the fencing. The weather was dry and the corn was slow in germinating. Each morning he looked fearfully for the pale shoots. Each morning he found with relief that they were not yet showing. He was up each day in the dark before dawn and either ate a cold breakfast without disturbing his mother, or hauled a load before he came to the table. He worked at night until the sun had set, and the red and orange faded through the pines, and the split rails merged with the color of the earth. He had dark circles under his eyes for lack of enough sleep. Penny had not had time to cut his hair, and it hung shaggily in his eyes. He made no complaint when, his eyelids drooping after supper, his mother asked him to fetch in wood that she could easily have brought in herself during the day. Penny watched him with a pain keener than the rupture in his groin. He called him to the bed one night.

"I'm proud to see you workin' so hard, boy, but even the yearlin', much as you think of him, ain't wuth killin' yourself over."

Jody said doggedly, "I ain't killin' myself. Feel my muscle. I'm gittin' powerful strong."

The Yearling

Penny felt of the thin hard arm. It was true. The regular and heavy lifting and heaving of the rails were developing his arms and back and shoulders.

Penny said, "I'd give a year o' my life to be to where I could he'p you with this."

"I'll git it done."

On the fourth morning he decided to begin building up the fence at the end Flag had been using. Then if the corn was up before he had finished, Flag would not take him unaware. He would even tie him by the legs to a tree, day and night, and let him kick and flounder, if necessary, until the fence was done. He found to his relief that the work went rapidly. In two days, he had raised the south and east fence lines to a height of five feet. Ma Baxter, seeing the impossible materialize, softened. On the morning of the sixth day, she said, "I got nothin' to do today. I'll he'p you git another foot on that fence."

"Oh, Ma. You good ol' Ma——"

"Now ne' mind squeezin' the life outen me. I never figgered you had it in you to work this-a-way."

She gave out of breath easily, but the work itself, while arduous, was not heavy with a pair of hands at each end of the light rails. The swing of it was rhythmic, like the swing of the cross-cut saw. She grew red in the face and panted and sweat, but she laughed and stayed with him most of the day and part of the next. There were enough rails piled at the corner to go even higher, and they built it well over the six feet that Penny had said would be high enough to keep out the yearling.

"If 'twas a full-growed buck now," he said, "he could clear eight feet easy."

That night Jody discovered the corn breaking the ground. In the morning he tried to put a hobble on Flag. He tied a rope from one hind shin to the other, with a foot of play between. Flag bucked and kicked and threw himself on the ground in a frenzy. He stumbled to his knees and fought so

374

wildly that it was plain he would break a leg if he were not released. Jody cut the rope and let him go. He galloped away to the woods and was gone all day. Jody worked furiously at the west fence line, for that would be the yearling's most logical line of attack on the field when the south and east ends turned him. Ma Baxter gave him two or three hours of help in the afternoon. He used up all the rails he had dumped to the west and north.

Two showers of rain pushed the corn. It was more than an inch high. On the morning that Jody was ready to return to the old clearing for more rails, he went to the new high fence and climbed to the top to look over the field. His eye caught sight of Flag, feeding on the corn near the north hammock. He jumped down and called his mother.

"Ma, will you go he'p me haul rails? I got to hurry. Flag's done come in the north end."

She hurried outside with him and climbed part-way up the fence until she could peer over.

"North end nothin'," she said. "He takened the fence right here at the highest corner."

He looked down where she pointed. The sharp tracks led to the fence and appeared again on the other side, inside the cornfield.

"And he's got this crop, too," she said.

Jody stared. Again, the shoots had been pulled up by the roots. The rows were bare. The yearling's tracks led regularly up and down between them.

"He ain't gone fur, Ma. Look, the corn's still there, yonder. He ain't et but a leetle ways."

"Yes, and what's to keep him from finishin' it?"

She dropped back to the ground and walked stolidly back into the house.

"This settles it," she said. "I was a fool to give in before."

Jody clung to the fence. He was numb. He could neither feel nor think. Flag scented him, lifted his head and came bounding to him. Jody climbed down into the yard. He did not want to see him. As he stood, Flag cleared, as lightly as a mocking-bird in flight, the high fence on which he had labored. Jody turned his back on him and went into the house. He went to his room and threw himself on his bed and buried his face in his pillow.

He was prepared for his father to call him. The talk between Penny and Ma Baxter this time had not taken long. He was prepared for trouble. He was prepared for something ominous that had dogged him for days. He was not prepared for the impossible. He was not prepared for his father's words.

Penny said, "Jody, all's been done was possible. I'm sorry. I cain't never tell you, how sorry. But we cain't have our year's crops destroyed. We cain't all go hongry. Take the yearlin' out in the woods and tie him and shoot him."

Chapter XXXII

ODY wandered west with Flag beside him. He carried Penny's shotgun over his shoulder. His heart beat and stopped and beat again.

He said under his breath, "I'll not do it. I'll jest not."

He stopped in the road.

He said out loud, "They cain't make me do it."

Flag looked at him with big eyes, then bent his head to a wisp of grass by the roadside. Jody walked on again slowly.

"I'll not. I'll not. I'll jest not. They kin beat me. They kin kill me. I'll not."

He held imaginary conversations with his mother and father. He told them both that he hated them. His mother stormed and Penny was quiet. His mother whipped him with a hickory switch until he felt the blood run down his legs. He bit her hand and she whipped him again. He kicked her in the ankles and she whipped him once more and threw him in a corner.

He lifted his head from the floor and said, "You cain't make me. I'll not do it."

He fought them in his mind until he was exhausted. He stopped at the abandoned clearing. A short length of fence was left that he had not yet torn down. He threw himself in the grass under an old chinaberry tree and sobbed until he could sob no more. Flag nuzzled him and he clutched him. He lay panting.

He said, "I'll not. I'll jest not."

He was dizzy when he stood up. He leaned against the rough trunk of the chinaberry. It was in bloom. The bees buzzed in it and the fragrance was sweet across the spring air. He was ashamed of himself for having taken time to cry. It was no time to cry. He would have to think. He would have to study his way out of it, as Penny did out of things that threatened him. At first he conjectured wildly. He would build a pen for Flag. A pen ten feet tall. He would gather acorns and grass and berries and feed him there. But it would take all his time to gather feed for a penned animal— Penny was on his back in the bed— The crops would have to be worked— There was no one but himself to do it.

He thought of Oliver Hutto. Oliver would have come and helped him work the crops until Penny was better. But Oliver had gone to Boston and the China Sea, away from the treachery that had swooped down on him. He thought of the Forresters. He regretted bitterly that they were now the Baxters' enemies. Buck would have helped him. Even now— But what could Buck do? A thought struck him sharply. It seemed to him that he could endure to be parted from Flag if he knew that somewhere in the world the yearling was alive. He could think of him, alive and mischievous, carrying his flag-like tail high and merry. He would go to Buck and throw himself on his mercy. He would remind Buck of Fodder-wing, talk of Fodder-wing until Buck's throat choked. Then he would ask him to take Flag in the wagon, as he had taken the bear cubs, to Jacksonville. Flag would be taken to a broad park where people came to look at the animals. He would bound about and be given plenty of feed, and a doe, and every one would admire him. He, Jody, would raise money crops of his own, and once a year he would go and visit Flag. He would save his money and he would get a place of his own, and he would buy Flag back, and they would live together.

He was flooded with excitement. He turned from the clearing up the road to the Forresters', trotting. His throat was dry and his eyes were swollen and smarting. His hope refreshed him and in a little while, when he swung up the Forresters' trail under the live oaks, he felt all right again.

The Yearling

He ran to the house and up the steps. He rapped at the open door and stepped inside. There was no one in the room but Pa and Ma Forrester. They sat immobile in their chairs.

He said breathlessly, "Howdy. Where's Buck?"

Pa Forrester turned his head slowly on his withered neck, like a turtle.

"Been a long time since you was here," he said.

"Where's Buck, please, sir?"

"Buck? Why, Buck and the hull passel of 'em has rode off to Kentucky, hoss-tradin'."

"In plantin' time?"

"Plantin' time be tradin' time. They'd ruther trade than plow. They figgered they'd make enough, tradin', to buy our rations." The old man spat. "And likely, they will."

"They're all gone?"

"Ever' one of 'em. Pack and Gabby'll be back in April."

Ma Forrester said, "Heap o' good it do a woman to birth a mess o' young uns and raise 'em and then have 'em all go off to oncet. I will say, they left rations and stacked wood. We won't need nothin' 'til some of 'em's back in April."

"April——"

He turned dully from the door.

"Come set with us, boy. I'd be proud to cook dinner for you. Raisin puddin', eh? You and Fodder-wing allus loved my raisin puddin'."

"I got to go," he said. "I thank you."

He turned back.

He burst out desperately, "What would you do, did you have a yearlin' et up the corn and you couldn't keep it out no-way and your Pa told you to go shoot it?"

They blinked at him. Ma Forrester cackled.

Pa Forrester said, "Why, I'd go shoot it."

He realized that he had not made the matter clear.

He said, "Supposin' it was a yearlin' you loved like you-all loved Fodder-wing?"

Pa Forrester said, "Why, love's got nothin' to do with corn.

379

You cain't have a thing eatin' the crops. Lessen you got boys like mine, has got other ways o' makin' a livin'.''

Ma Forrester asked, "Hit that fawn you carried here last summer for Fodder-wing to put a name to?"

"That's him. Flag," he said. "Cain't you-all take him? Fodder-wing would of takened him."

"Why, we got no better way'n you o' keepin' him. He'd not stay here, no-how. What's four mile to a yearlin' deer?"

They too were a stone wall.

He said, "Well, good-by," and went away.

The Forrester clearing was desolate without the big men and their horses. They had taken most of the dogs with them. Only a mangy pair remained, chained at the side of the house, scratching themselves mournfully. He was glad to get away again.

He would walk to Jacksonville with Flag himself. He looked about for something to make a halter by which to lead him, so that he would not turn and run home, as he had done on the Christmas hunt. He hacked laboriously at a grapevine with his pocket knife. He looped a length of it around Flag's neck and set off to the northeast. The trail came out somewhere near Hopkins Prairie, he knew, on the Fort Gates road on which he and Penny had intercepted the Forresters. Flag was docile for a time under the leash, then grew impatient of the restraint and tugged against it.

Jody said, "How come you to grow up so unlawful?"

It wore him out, trying to coax the yearling into going willingly. At last he gave it up and took off the grapevine halter. Flag was then perversely content to keep in sight. In the afternoon, Jody found himself tired with a fatigue born of hunger. He had left the house without breakfast. He had wanted only to get away. He looked along the road for berries to eat, but it was too early and there were none. The blackberries had not yet finished blooming. He chewed some leaves, as Flag was doing, but they made him feel emptier than before. His feet dragged. He lay down by the road in the sun for a rest and induced Flag to lie beside him. He was drugged with hunger and misery and the strong March sun on his head. He fell asleep. When he awakened, Flag had gone. He followed his tracks. They led in and out of the scrub, then turned back to the road and continued evenly toward home.

There was nothing to do but follow. He was too weary to think further. He reached Baxter's Island after dark. A candle burned in the kitchen. The dogs came to him. He patted them to quiet them. He crept close silently and peered in. Supper was over. His mother sat in the candle-light, sewing her endless patchwork pieces. He was trying to make up his mind whether to go in or not, when Flag galloped across the yard. He saw his mother lift her head and listen.

He slipped hurriedly beyond the smoke-house and called Flag in a low voice. The yearling came to him. He crouched at the corner. His mother came to the kitchen door and threw it open. A bar of light lay across the sand. The door closed. He waited a long time until the light went out in the kitchen. He allowed time for her to go to bed and to sleep. He prowled inside the smoke-house and found the remainder of the smoked bear-meat. He hacked off a strip. It was hard and dry, but he chewed on it. He supposed Flag had fed on buds in the woods, but he could not bear to think of him hungry. He went to the corn-crib and took two ears of corn and shelled them and fed the kernels to him. He chewed some kernels himself. He thought longingly of the cold cooked food that must be in the kitchen safe but he dared not go in after it. He felt like a stranger and a thief. This was the way the wolves felt, he thought, and the wild-cats and the panthers and all the varmints, looking in at the clearing with big eyes and empty bellies. He made a bed in a stall at the lot with an armful of the scant remaining marsh-grass hay. He slept there with Flag beside him, not quite warm enough through the chill March night.

He awakened after sunrise, stiff and miserable. Flag was

gone. He went reluctantly but compelled to the house. At the gate he heard his mother's voice raised in a storm of anger. She had discovered the shotgun where he had leaned it against the smoke-house wall. She had discovered Flag. She had discovered, too, that the yearling had made the most of the early hours and had fed, not only across the sprouting corn, but across a wide section of the cow-peas. He went helplessly to her to meet her wrath. He stood with his head down while she flailed him with her tongue.

She said finally, "Git to your Pa. For oncet, he's with me."

He went into the bedroom. His father's face was drawn.

Penny said gently, "How come you not to do what I told you?"

"Pa, I jest couldn't. I cain't do it."

Penny leaned his head back against the pillow.

"Come here clost to me, boy. Jody, you know I've done all I could to keep your leetle deer for you."

"Yes, sir."

"You know we depend on our crops to live."

"Yes, sir."

"You know they ain't a way in the world to keep that wild yearlin' from destroyin' 'em."

"Yes, sir."

"Then why don't you do what's got to be done?"

"I cain't."

Penny lay silent.

"Tell you Ma to come here. Go to your room and shut the door."

"Yes, sir."

There was a relief in following simple orders.

"Pa says to go to him."

He went to his room and closed the door. He sat on the side of the bed, twisting his hands. He heard low voices. He heard steps. He heard a shot. He ran from the room to the open kitchen door. His mother stood on the stoop with the shotgun smoking in her hands. Flag lay floundering beside the fence.

She said, "I didn't want to hurt the creetur. I cain't shoot straight. You know I cain't."

Jody ran to Flag. The yearling heaved to his three good legs and stumbled away, as though the boy himself were his enemy. He was bleeding from a torn left forequarter. Penny dragged himself from his bed. He sank on one knee in the doorway, clutching it for support.

He called, "I'd do it if I could. I jest cain't stand up— Go finish him, Jody. You got to put him outen his torment."

Jody ran back and snatched the gun from his mother.

He screamed, "You done it o' purpose. You allus hated him."

He turned on his father.

"You went back on me. You told her to do it."

He screeched so that his throat felt torn.

"I hate you. I hope you die. I hope I never see you agin."

He ran after Flag, whimpering as he ran.

Penny called, "He'p me, Ory. I cain't git up——"

Flag ran on three legs in pain and terror. Twice he fell and Jody caught up to him.

He shrieked, "Hit's me! Hit's me! Flag!"

Flag thrashed to his feet and was off again. Blood flowed in a steady stream. The yearling made the edge of the sink-hole. He wavered an instant and toppled. He rolled down the side. Jody ran after him. Flag lay beside the pool. He opened great liquid eyes and turned them on the boy with a glazed look of wonder. Jody pressed the muzzle of the gun barrel at the back of the smooth neck and pulled the trigger. Flag quivered a moment and then lay still.

Jody threw the gun aside and dropped flat on his stomach. He retched and vomited and retched again. He clawed into the earth with his finger-nails. He beat it with his fists. The sink-hole rocked around him. A far roaring became a thin humming. He sank into blackness as into a dark pool.

Chapter XXXIII

ODY walked north up the Fort Gates road. His gait was wooden, as though nothing of him were alive except his legs. He had left the dead yearling without daring to look at him. Nothing mattered but getting away. There was no place to go. That did not matter, either. Above Fort Gates he would cross the river on the ferry. His plans became clear. He was headed for Jacksonville. He was going to Boston. He would find Oliver Hutto in Boston and go to sea with him, leaving his betrayal behind him, as Oliver had done.

The best way to get to Jacksonville and Boston was by boat. He had better get on the river itself at once. He needed a boat. He remembered Nellie Ginright's discarded dug-out, in which he and Penny had crossed Salt Springs Run on the hunt for old Slewfoot. At thought of his father, a sharp knife struck his cold numbness, then the wound froze over again. He would tear his shirt in strips and stuff the cracks of the dug-out and pole down the creek to Lake George, then north down the big river. Somewhere along it he would hail a passing steamer and go to Boston. Oliver would pay his fare when he got there. If he could not find him, they would put him in jail. That did not matter, either.

He turned in at Salt Springs. He was thirsty and waded out in the shallow water and bent and drank from the bubbling spring. Mullet jumped nearby and blue crabs scuttled sideways. Below the spring a fisherman was setting out. Jody walked along the bank and called to him.

"Kin I go down with you a piece to my boat?"

"I reckon."

The fisherman swung in to shore and he stepped in.

The Yearling

The man asked, "You live around here?"

He shook his head.

"Where's your boat at?"

"Down past Mis' Nellie Ginright's."

"You kin to her?"

He shook his head. Questions from a stranger were probes in his wounds. The man looked at him curiously, then gave himself to his rowing. The rough boat moved smoothly down the swift current. The run was broad at its upper reaches. The water was blue and the March sky over it was blue. A light wind stirred the white clouds. It was the kind of day he had always liked particularly. The banks were of a rosy red, for the swamp maple and the red-bud were in full spring color. Swamp laurel was in bloom and its sweetness filled the creek. An ache choked him, so that he wanted to put his hand to his throat and tear it out. The beauty of the late March day held only pain to hurt him. He did not want to look at the new-needled cypresses. He watched the water and the garfish and the turtles and did not lift his eyes again.

The fisherman said, "Here's Mis' Nellie's place. You want to stop?"

He shook his head.

"My boat's on yonder."

As they passed the bluff, he saw Mis' Nellie standing in front of her house. The fisherman lifted his hand to her and she waved. Jody did not stir. He remembered the night in her house and the morning when she had cooked breakfast and had joked with Penny, and sent them on their way feeling warm and strong and friendly. He pushed the memory aside. The run narrowed. The banks came close and there were swamp and cat-tails.

He said, "Yonder's my boat."

"Why, boy, hit's half-sunk."

"I aim to fix it."

"You got ary one comin' to he'p you? You got oars?"

The Yearling

He shook his head.

"Here's a piece of a paddle. Shore don't look like much of a boat to me. Well, so long."

The man pushed out into the current and waved to the boy. He took a biscuit and a piece of meat from a box under the board seat and began cramming them in his mouth as he moved away. The odor of the food came to Jody. It reminded him that he had had nothing to eat in two days except the few mouthfuls of smoked bear meat and the few kernels of dried corn. That did not matter. He was not hungry.

He pulled the dug-out on land and bailed it. Long immersion had swelled it, and the bottom was tight. There were cracks in the bow that let in water. He tore the sleeves from his shirt and ripped them in strips and caulked the cracks. He went to a pine and scraped resin with his pocket knife and worked it in on the outside.

He pushed the dug-out into the stream and picked up the broken paddle and began to paddle downstream. He was clumsy at it and the current took him from one bank to the other. He landed in sawgrass and cut his hands trying to push through it. The dug-out swung sideways and stuck in the soft muck along the south bank. He pushed free. The trick of it began to come to him, but he felt weak and faint. He wished that he had asked the fisherman to wait for him. There was nothing living in sight except a buzzard, wheeling in the blue sky. The buzzards would find Flag by the pool in the sink-hole. He began to be sick again and let the boat drift among the cat-tails. He rested his head on his knees until the nausea passed.

He stiffened and began paddling. He was on his way to Boston. His mouth was tight. His eyes were narrowed. The sun was well down in the sky when he came to the end of the run. The creek emptied at once into a broad bay of big Lake George. A spit of dry land extended a little distance to the south. On the opposite side there was only swamp. He

turned the dug-out and swung up to the land, stepped out
and pulled the boat high. He sat down under a live oak and
leaned against the trunk and stared out to the open waters.
He had hoped that he might encounter a river boat at the
end of the run. He saw one passing south, but it was far out
in the lake. He realized that the end of the creek must
join only an arm or bay.

It was no more than an hour or two until sunset. He was
afraid to let dark find him on the open lake waters in the
unsteady canoe. He decided to wait on the point of land for
a passing boat. If none came, he would sleep under the live
oak and paddle farther in the morning. Numbness had held
off his thoughts all day. Now they poured in on him, as
the wolves had poured in to the calf-pen. They tore him,
so that it seemed to him that he must, invisibly, be bleeding,
as Flag had bled. Flag was dead. He would never run to
him again. He tortured himself with saying the words.

"Flag's dead."

They were as bitter as alum-root tea.

He had not yet probed the deepest pain.

He said aloud, "Pa went back on me."

It was a sharper horror than if Penny had died of the
snake-bite. He rubbed his knuckles over his forehead. Death
could be borne. Fodder-wing had died and he was able to
bear it. Betrayal was intolerable. If Flag had died, if bear
or wolf or panther had slipped in on him, he would have
grieved with a great grief, but he could have endured it.
He would have turned to his father, and his father would
have comforted him. Without Penny, there was no comfort
anywhere. The solid earth had dissolved under him. His
bitterness absorbed his sorrow, and they were one.

The sun dropped below the tree-tops. He gave up hope
of hailing any vessel before night. He gathered moss and
made a bed for himself at the base of the oak tree. A bittern
cried rustily in the swamp across the run, and as the sun set,
the frogs began to croak and sing. He had always liked the

sound of their music, coming from the sink-hole at home. The cry they were making now was mournful. He hated it. They seemed to be grieving. Thousands of them were crying out in an endless and unappeasable sorrow. A wood-duck called, and its cry, too, was sad.

The lake was rosy, but shadows had taken over the land. It would be supper-time at home. In spite of his nausea, he thought now of food. His stomach began to ache as though there was too much in it, instead of nothing. He remembered the smell of the fisherman's meat and biscuit. His mouth watered. He ate some stalks of grass. He ripped the joints with his teeth, as animals ripped flesh. Instantly he saw creatures creeping in to Flag's carcass. He vomited the grass.

Darkness filled both land and water. A hoot owl cried in the thicket near him. He shivered. The night wind stirred and was chill. He heard a rustling that might be leaves moving ahead of the wind, or small creatures passing. He was not afraid. It seemed to him that if a bear came, or a panther, he might touch it and stroke it and it would understand his grief. Yet the night sounds about him made his flesh creep. It would be good to have a camp-fire. Penny could start a fire even without his tinder-horn, in the way the Indians did, but he had never been able to do it. If Penny were here, there would be a blazing fire, and warmth and food and comfort. He was not afraid. He was only desolate. He pulled the moss over him and cried himself to sleep.

The sun awakened him, and the red-winged blackbirds chattering in the reeds. He stood up and pulled the long strands of moss from his hair and clothing. He was weak and dizzy. Now that he was rested, he knew that he was hungry. The thought of food was torture. Cramps struck like small hot knives across his stomach. He thought of paddling back up the run to Mis' Nellie Ginright and asking her to feed him. But she would ask him questions. She would ask him why he was here alone, and there was no answer, except that his father had betrayed him, and in the betrayal, Flag was dead. It would be better to go on, as he had planned.

A fresh wave of loneliness swept over him. He had lost Flag and he had lost his father, too. The gaunt little man he had last seen crouched in pain in the kitchen doorway, calling for help to stand, was a stranger. He pushed out his dug-out and took up his paddle and headed for the open waters. He was out in the world, and it seemed to him that he was alien here, and alone, and that he was being carried away into a void. He paddled for the location where he had seen the steamer pass. Living was no longer the grief behind him, but the anxiety ahead. Leaving the mouth of the creek behind him, he found the wind freshening. Out from the shelter of the land a brisk breeze was blowing. He ignored the gnawing in his belly and paddled desperately. The wind caught the dug-out and slewed it around. He could not keep it headed. The waves were mounting. Their soft lapping changed to a hissing. They began to break over the bow of the canoe. When it swung sideways, they washed in and it tipped and rolled. There was an inch of water across the bottom. There was no vessel of any sort in sight.

He looked back. The shore had receded alarmingly. Ahead of him, the open water seemed to stretch without an end. He turned about in a panic and paddled madly for the shore. It would be best, after all, to go back up the creek and get help from Mis' Nellie Ginright. It might be better even to walk to Fort Gates and make his way from there. The wind behind him helped him, and it seemed to him that he could feel the north-bound current of the great river. He headed for an opening that must be the end of the Salt Springs run. When he reached it, it was a blind opening in the shore that led only into swamp. The mouth of the run was nowhere to be found.

He was trembling from his exertion and from his fear. He told himself that he was not lost, for the river ran north out

of Lake George and came at the end to Jacksonville, and he
had only to follow it. But it was so wide, and the shore line
was so confusing— He rested a long time, then began to
paddle slowly north, close to the thick-cypressed land, following the endless curves and bays and indentations. The
gnawing in his stomach was an acute pain. He began to have
a feverish vision of the usual Baxter table. He saw slices of
ham steaming, brown and dripping in their own juice. He
smelled the sweet savor. He saw tawny biscuits and dark-
crusted cornbread and swimming bowls of cow-peas, with
squares of white bacon floating among them. He smelled
fried squirrel so definitely that the saliva ran in his mouth.
He tasted the warm foam of Trixie's milk. He could have
fought with the dogs for their pan of cold grits and gravy.

This, then, was hunger. This was what his mother had
meant when she had said, "We'll all go hongry." He had
laughed, for he had thought he had known hunger, and it
was faintly pleasant. He knew now that it had been only
appetite. This was another thing. The thing was terrifying.
It had a great maw to envelop him and claws that raked
across his vitals. He fought off a new panic. He would soon
reach a cabin or a fisherman's camp, he told himself. He
would beg food shamelessly before continuing. No man
refused another rations.

He worked his way north along the shore line all day. In
the late afternoon he was sick at his stomach from the heat
of the sun, but there was nothing to vomit but the river
water he had drunk. A cabin showed ahead among trees
and he pulled in to it hopefully. It was deserted. He prowled
inside, like a hungry 'coon or 'possum. There were cans on
a dusty shelf, but all were empty. In a jar he found a cupful
of musty flour. He mixed it with water and ate the paste.
It was flavorless, even in his hunger, but it stopped the pain
in his stomach. There were birds and squirrels in the trees
and he tried to hit them with stones, but he only drove them
all away. He was feverish and exhausted and the flour in his

JODY LOST

belly made him sleepy. The cabin offered shelter, and he made a pallet of some rags, from which the roaches scurried. He slept a drugged, nightmare-ridden sleep.

In the morning he was again conscious of acute hunger, and the cramps were sharp-nailed fingers that twisted his entrails. He found some last year's acorns that the squirrels had buried and ate them so ravenously that the hard, un-chewed pieces were fresh knives in his contracting stomach. A lethargy settled on him, and he could scarcely force him-self to take up his paddle. If the current had not been with him, he decided he could have gone no farther. He covered only a short distance during the morning. In the afternoon, three boats passed in mid-stream. He stood up and waved his arms and shouted. They paid no attention to his cries. When they had passed from sight, he was torn unwillingly with sobbing. He decided to cut out away from the shore to intercept the next vessel. The wind had died. The water was calm. The glare from it burned his face and neck and bare arms. The sun was scalding. His head throbbed. Black spots alternated before his eyes with bobbing golden balls. A thin humming whined in his ears. The humming snapped.

All that he knew when he opened his eyes was that it was dark and he was being lifted up.

A man's voice said, "He ain't drunk. It's a boy."

Another said, "Lay him in the bunk there. He's sick. Tie his dug-out on behind."

Jody looked up. He lay in a bunk on what must be the mail-boat. A lamp flickered on the wall. A man leaned over him.

"What's the matter, young un? We near about run you down in the dark."

He tried to answer but his lips were swollen.

A voice called from above, "Try him on somethin' to eat."

"You hungry, boy?"

He nodded. The boat was now in motion. The man in the cabin clattered at the galley-stove. Jody saw a thick cup thrust in front of him. He lifted his head and clutched at it. The cup held cold soup, thick and greasy. For a mouthful or two it had no taste at all. Then the saliva ran in his mouth and his whole being reached out for it, and he bolted it so ravenously that he choked on bits of meat and potato.

The man said curiously, "How long since you et?"

"I don't know."

"Hey, Cap, the young un don't even know when he et last."

"Give him plenty but feed him slow. Don't give him too much or he'll puke in my bunk."

The cup came back again, and biscuits with it. He tried to control himself, but he trembled when the man waited too long between feedings. The third cupful tasted infinitely better than the first, then further food was refused him.

The man said, "Where'd you come from?"

A languor crept over him. He breathed deeply. The swinging lamp drew his eyes back and forth. He closed them. He dropped into a sleep as deep as the river.

He was awakened by the stopping of the small steamer. He thought for a moment that he was in the dug-out, drifting with the current. He got to his feet and rubbed his eyes. He looked at the galley-stove and remembered the soup and biscuits. The ache in his stomach was gone. He climbed the few steps to the open deck. Day was breaking. The mail sack was being lowered to a landing. He recognized Volusia. The captain turned to him.

"You had a close call, young feller. Now what did you say your name was, and where do you think you're goin'?"

"I was headin' for Boston," he said.

"You know where Boston lies? So far north it'd take you the rest of your life to get there, the way you was travelin'."

Jody stared.

"Hurry up, now. This is a gov'ment boat. I can't wait on you all day. Where you live?"

"Baxter's Island."

"Never heard of no Baxter's Island in this river."

The mate spoke up.

" 'Tain't a real island, Cap. It's a place off in the scrub. 'Bout fifteen miles up the road from here."

"Then you want to get off here, boy. Boston? Hell. You got folks?"

Jody nodded.

"They know where you was goin'?"

He shook his head.

"Runnin' away, eh? Well, if I was a scrawny little big-eyed booger like you, I'd stay home. Nobody but your folks'll bother with a little ol' shirt-tail boy like you. Swing him down to the dock, Joe."

Brawny arms lifted him down.

"Turn his dug-out a-loose. Catch it, boy. Let's go."

The whistle blew. The side-wheels churned. The mail-boat chugged up-stream. The wake boiled after her. A stranger lifted the mail sack and slung it over his shoulder. Jody crouched on his heels, holding the bow of the dug-out. The stranger glanced at him and walked away toward Volusia with the mail. The first rays of the sun lay on the river. Alligator lilies on the far bank caught them like white cups. The current tugged at the dug-out. His arm was tired, holding it. The stranger's footsteps faded up the road. There was no place left to go, but Baxter's Island.

He dropped into the canoe and took up his paddle. He paddled across to the west shore. He tethered the dug-out to a stake. He looked back across the river. The rising sun lay on the charred ruins of the Hutto house. His throat tightened. The world had discarded him. He turned and walked slowly up the road. He was weak, and conscious again of hunger, but the night's food had renewed him. The nausea was gone, and the pain.

He walked west without plan. There was no other direction in which to go. Baxter's Island drew him like a magnet. There was no reality but the clearing. He trudged on. He wondered if he dared go home. Probably they would not want him. He had caused them a great deal of trouble. Perhaps if he walked into the kitchen, his mother would drive him out as she had driven Flag. He was no good to anybody. He had prowled and played and eaten recklessly. They had put up with his impudence and his appetite. And Flag had destroyed the better part of the year's living. Almost certainly, they would feel they were better off without him, and he would not be welcome.

He loitered along the road. The sun was strong. The winter was over. He thought hazily that it must now be April. Spring had taken over the scrub, and the brids were mating and singing in the bushes. Only he, in all the world, was homeless. He had been out in the world, and the world was a troubled dream, fluid and desolate, flanked by swamps and cypresses. He stopped to rest in mid-morning at the intersection of the main road and the north road. The low vegetation here was open to the heat of the sun. His head began to ache and he got to his feet and headed north toward Silver Glen. He told himself that he did not mean to go home. He would only go to the spring, and go down between the cool dark banks, and lie a little while in the running water. The north road dipped and rose and dipped again. The sand was scalding under his bare feet. The sweat ran down the grime of his face. At the top of a rise, he could look down and see Lake George far below him to the east. It was pitilessly blue. Thin white lines were the implacable choppy waves that had turned him back to the unfriendly shore. He trudged on.

To the east, the vegetation became luxuriant. There was water near. He turned down the trail to Silver Glen. The steep bank dropped to the ribbon of creek that ran south of the great spring itself, and had a kindred source. He ached in all his bones. He was so thirsty that his tongue seemed glued to the roof of his mouth. He stumbled down the bank and fell flat beside the cool shallow water and drank. The water bubbled over his lips and nose. He drank until his belly was swollen. He felt sickened and rolled over on his back and closed his eyes. The nausea passed and he was drowsy. He lay in a stupor of weariness. He hung suspended in a timeless space. He could go neither forward nor back. Something was ended. Nothing was begun.

In the late afternoon, he roused. He sat up. An early magnolia blossom was wax-white over him.

He thought, " 'Tis April."

A memory stirred him. He had come here a year ago, on a bland and tender day. He had splashed in the creek water and lain, as now, among the ferns and grasses. Something had been fine and lovely. He had built himself a flutter-mill. He rose and moved with a quickening of his pulse to the location. It seemed to him that if he found it, he would discover with it all the other things that had vanished. The flutter-mill was gone. The flood had washed it away, and all its merry turning.

He thought stubbornly, "I'll build me another."

He cut twigs for the supports, and the roller to turn across them, from the wild cherry tree. He whittled feverishly. He cut strips from a palmetto frond and made his paddles. He sunk the uprights in the stream bed and set the paddles turning. Up, over, down. Up, over, down. The flutter-mill was turning. The silver water dripped. But it was only palmetto strips brushing the water. There was no magic in the motion. The flutter-mill had lost its comfort.

He said, "Play-dolly——"

He kicked it apart with one foot. The broken bits floated down the creek. He threw himself on the ground and sobbed bitterly. There was no comfort anywhere.

There was Penny. A wave of homesickness washed over him so that it was suddenly intolerable not to see him. The sound of his father's voice was a necessity. He longed for the sight of his stooped shoulders as he had never, in the sharpest of his hunger, longed for food. He clambered to his feet and up the bank and began to run down the road to

395

the clearing, crying as he ran. His father might not be there. He might be dead. With the crops ruined, and his son gone, he might have packed up in despair and moved away and he would never find him.

He sobbed, "Pa— Wait for me."

The sun was setting. He was in a panic that he would not reach the clearing before dark. He exhausted himself, and was obliged to slow down to a walk. His flesh quivered. His heart pounded. He had to stop entirely and rest. Darkness overtook him half a mile from home. Even in the dusk, landmarks were familiar. The tall pines of the clearing were recognizable, blacker than the creeping night. He came to the slat fence. He felt his way along it. He opened the gate and went into the yard. He passed around the side of the house to the kitchen stoop and stepped up on it. He crept to the window on bare silent feet and peered in.

A fire burned low on the hearth. Penny sat hunched beside it, wrapped in quilts. One hand covered his eyes. Jody went to the door and unlatched it and stepped inside. Penny lifted his head.

"Ory?"

"Hit's me."

He thought his father had not heard him.

"Hit's Jody."

Penny turned his head and looked at him wonderingly, as though the gaunt ragged boy with sweat and tear-streaks down the grime, with hollow eyes under matted hair, were some stranger of whom he expected that he state his business.

He said, "Jody."

Jody dropped his eyes.

"Come clost."

He went to his father and stood beside him. Penny reached out for his hand and took it and turned it over and rubbed it slowly between his own. Jody felt drops on his hand like a warm rain.

The Yearling

"Boy— I near about give you out."

Penny felt along his arm. He looked up at him.

"You all right?"

He nodded.

"You all right— You ain't dead nor gone. You all right."
A light filled his face. "Glory be."

It was unbelievable, Jody thought. He was wanted.

He said, "I had to come home."

"Why, shore you did."

"I ain't meant what I said. Hatin' you——"

The light broke into the familiar smile.

"Why, shore you ain't. 'When I was a child, I spake as a child.'"

Penny stirred in his chair.

"They's rations in the safe. In the kittle there. You hongry?"

"I ain't et but oncet. Last night."

"Not but oncet? Then now you know. Ol' Starvation—"
His eyes shone in the firelight as Jody had pictured them.
"Ol' Starvation—he's got a face meaner'n ol' Slewfoot, ain't he?"

"Hit's fearful."

"There's biscuits there. Open the honey. There's due to be milk in the gourd."

Jody fumbled among the dishes. He ate standing, wolfing down the food. He dipped into a dish of cooked cow-peas with his fingers, scooping them into his mouth. Penny stared at him.

He said, "I'm sorry you had to learn it that-a-way."

"Where's Ma?"

"She's drove the wagon to the Forresters to trade for seed-corn. She figgered she'd try to plant a part of a crop agin. She carried the chickens, to trade. It hurted her pride turrible, but she was obliged to go."

Jody closed the door of the cabinet.

He said, "I should of washed. I'm awful dirty."

397

"There's warm water on the hearth."

Jody poured water in the basin and scrubbed his face and arms and hands. The water was too dark even for his feet. He threw it out of the door and poured more, and sat on the floor and washed his feet.

Penny said, "I'd be proud to know where you been."

"I been on the river. I aimed to go to Boston."

"I see."

He looked small and shrunken inside the quilts.

Jody said, "How you makin' it, Pa? You better?"

Penny looked a long time into the embers on the hearth.

He said, "You jest as good to know the truth. I ain't scarcely wuth shootin'."

Jody said, "When I git the work done, you got to leave me go fetch ol' Doc to you."

Penny studied him.

He said, "You've done come back different. You've takened a punishment. You ain't a yearlin' no longer. Jody——"

"Yes, sir."

"I'm goin' to talk to you, man to man. You figgered I went back on you. Now there's a thing ever' man has got to know. Mebbe you know it a'ready. 'Twa'n't only me. 'Twa'n't only your yearlin' deer havin' to be destroyed. Boy, life goes back on you."

Jody looked at his father. He nodded.

Penny said, "You've seed how things goes in the world o' men. You've knowed men to be low-down and mean. You've seed ol' Death at his tricks. You've messed around with ol' Starvation. Ever' man wants life to be a fine thing, and a easy. 'Tis fine, boy, powerful fine, but 'tain't easy. Life knocks a man down and he gits up and it knocks him down agin. I've been uneasy all my life."

His hands worked at the folds of the quilt.

"I've wanted life to be easy for you. Easier'n 'twas for me. A man's heart aches, seein' his young uns face the world.

Knowin' they got to git their guts tore out, the way his was tore. I wanted to spare you, long as I could. I wanted you to frolic with your yearlin'. I knowed the lonesomeness he eased for you. But ever' man's lonesome. What's he to do then? What's he to do when he gits knocked down? Why, take it for his share and go on."

Jody said, "I'm 'shamed I runned off."

Penny sat upright.

He said, "You're near enough growed to do your choosin'. Could be you'd crave to go to sea, like Oliver. There's men seems made for the land, and men seems made for the sea. But I'd be proud did you choose to live here and farm the clearin'. I'd be proud to see the day when you got a well dug, so's no woman here'd be obliged to do her washin' on a seepage hillside. You willin'?"

"I'm willin'."

"Shake hands."

He closed his eyes. The fire on the hearth had burned to embers. Jody banked them with the ashes, to assure live coals in the morning.

Penny said, "Now I'll need some he'p, gittin' to the bed. Looks like your Ma's spendin' the night."

Jody put his shoulder under him and Penny leaned heavily on it. He hobbled to his bed. Jody drew the quilt over him.

"Hit's food and drink to have you home, boy. Git to bed and git your rest. 'Night."

The words warmed him through.

" 'Night, Pa."

He went to his room and closed the door. He took off his tattered shirt and breeches and climbed in under the warm quilts. His bed was soft and yielding. He lay luxuriously, stretching his legs. He must be up early in the morning, to milk the cow and bring in wood and work the crops. When he worked them, Flag would not be there to play about with him. His father would no longer take the heavy part of the burden. It did not matter. He could manage alone.

He found himself listening for something. It was the sound of the yearling for which he listened, running around the house or stirring on his moss pallet in the corner of the bedroom. He would never hear him again. He wondered if his mother had thrown dirt over Flag's carcass, or if the buzzards had cleaned it. Flag— He did not believe he should ever again love anything, man or woman or his own child, as he had loved the yearling. He would be lonely all his life. But a man took it for his share and went on.

In the beginning of his sleep, he cried out, "Flag!"

It was not his own voice that called. It was a boy's voice. Somewhere beyond the sink-hole, past the magnolia, under the live oaks, a boy and a yearling ran side by side, and were gone forever.

DATE DUE

DEMCO 38-297